S0-AHZ-907

FEB 2020

A MARVELOUS LIFE

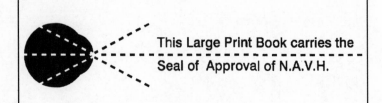

This Large Print Book carries the
Seal of Approval of N.A.V.H.

A MARVELOUS LIFE

THE AMAZING STORY OF STAN LEE

DANNY FINGEROTH

THORNDIKE PRESS
A part of Gale, a Cengage Company

Copyright © 2019 by Daniel Fingeroth.
Thorndike Press, a part of Gale, a Cengage Company.

ALL RIGHTS RESERVED
Thorndike Press® Large Print Biography and Memoir.
The text of this Large Print edition is unabridged.
Other aspects of the book may vary from the original edition.
Set in 16 pt. Plantin.

LIBRARY OF CONGRESS CIP DATA ON FILE.
CATALOGUING IN PUBLICATION FOR THIS BOOK
IS AVAILABLE FROM THE LIBRARY OF CONGRESS

ISBN-13: 978-1-4328-7387-5 (hardcover alk. paper)

Published in 2020 by arrangement with Macmillan Publishing Group,
LLC/St. Martin's Publishing Group

Printed in Mexico
Print Number: 01   Print Year: 2020

For Varda.
Thanks for the marvelous life.

CONTENTS

PREFACE

If you ask most culturally aware people to name their top three comic book creators, they will likely respond: "Stan Lee."

And then they will stop. That's the only comic book creator most people know.

Those same people could probably name *ten* film directors or novelists. Maybe even ten painters. But comic book creators? One: Stan Lee.

Which is strange, for any number of reasons.

For starters, Lee was a comic book (or, as he preferred to spell it, *comicbook*) writer, editor, art director, publisher, and executive. However, despite the very visual nature of comics, Lee did not draw professionally (although he was a more-than-decent doodler). He was *not* a comic book artist.

Also, while the characters he was involved with have become some of the most popular and lucrative entertainment franchises of all time — Spider-Man, the Avengers, the

9

X-Men, to name just a few — Lee did not design the characters or draw their adventures. He needed artists to do that, and he collaborated with incredibly gifted ones to create Marvel's most famous superheroes.

Lee's two most significant collaborators were Jack Kirby and Steve Ditko. You would think that, as the men who partnered with Lee to breathe life into the characters and their adventures, they would be as world-famous as Lee, wouldn't you? But they aren't.

Beyond that, logic would seem to dictate that, since Lee was associated with Marvel (which had previously been known as Timely and Atlas) for more than seventy-five years, he must have been one of the company's owners; that every time a ticket for a Marvel movie was sold, some fraction of it must have gone to him.

That, however, is not true. Lee was always an *employee* of the company — a well-paid one, to be sure — but one who owned no percentage of any of the characters he worked on there.

And yet Lee became the voice and face not just of Marvel Comics but eventually, whether he intended to or not, of COMICS in general.

This fame was based, originally, on the long stream of success that Marvel's comics had from 1961 to 1970, when its most famous characters were created, when Marvel was part of the cultural conversation — along

10

with James Bond, Kurt Vonnegut, Betty Friedan, Mickey Mantle, Muhammad Ali, and the Beatles. That's ten years in a life that lasted more than ninety-five and a career that went for almost eighty.

So the questions arise: What in his early life and in the first twenty years of his career enabled this popular culture explosion? And after you've exploded the culture — how do you follow that up?

Lee's was a classic American success story. A Greatest Generation child of impoverished Jewish immigrants, Lee, born in 1922, made his way through the Great Depression, served in the army in World War II, and found his way into comics, a universally derided medium where con men and gangsters battled for literal nickels and dimes.

Gifted with an engaging, charismatic personality, high intelligence, and a wide creative streak, Lee rose to become the editorial director of Timely/Atlas/Marvel, which, in the '40s and '50s, was one of the highest-volume producers of comic books in the country. He was making a respectable, middle-class living, and had a wife and daughter and a home in the suburbs.

But being the top editorial dog in a business that was ignored at best — and reviled at worst — by anyone over fourteen was a mixed blessing.

11

He didn't receive the respect of, say, a lawyer or possess the glamour of an advertising or movie executive. He had vague notions of wanting to write a novel or do something that would be noticed — like his cousin, movie director Mel Stuart (*Willy Wonka*), or his high school classmate, playwright and screenwriter Paddy Chayefsky (*Marty*) — but he was stuck in the comfortable rut of a fairly interesting job that paid well.

Then, in 1961, as he was approaching forty, already a twenty-year veteran in the comics business, Stan Lee's life became a classic American midlife crisis story.

Bored but comfortable, glad to have survived a recent downturn in the comics business, Lee (and cocreators Kirby and Ditko) came up with a new, relatively more "realistic" approach to superhero comics that caught on with readers. These new heroes would behave more like you or I would if we had superpowers. They might try to do the right thing, but their all-too-human frailties would regularly get in the way.

Lee used the name *Marvel* to brand the comics. Of course, he had no idea if the popularity of what Marvel was doing would be lasting or be just another short-lived pop culture fad like the Hula-Hoop.

That's where I came in.

I was a boomer kid who fell under the spell

12

of '60s Marvel. I had been reading comics and had heard about *Fantastic Four,* the first "modern" Marvel comic. I found the fourth issue, which featured the return of some character called the Sub-Mariner, who I'd never heard of but who Lee, in the issue, convinced me was urgently important.

I was immediately hooked, not just on the comics and the characters but on the people writing and drawing them, as well. After all, Stan Lee made a point of telling us just how special they (including he) were — and how special *we* were for just reading the comics! I was totally immersed in the inside news, gossip, and wisecracks found in the comics' letters page responses and Bullpen Bulletins that Lee wrote.

And I loved visiting with — or was it being visited *by?* — the literary creation, found in those pages, known as "Stan Lee." Sure, I worshipped Jack Kirby and Steve Ditko, but it was clear that Stan Lee was the one whose supervision held it all together. Some combination of the Lee-overseen comics' words and pictures and colors — and even the *ads* — made up an imaginary world that I loved.

It was a world that, after abandoning it for a while, I returned to, getting a job shortly after graduating college as an assistant editor in an obscure Marvel department. I figured I'd be there just a few months, but the business proved a good fit, and comics — this

13

hobby I'd had, starting when I was six years old — became my career. I wrote many stories for the company and came to be the editorial director of its Spider-Man division. (Spider-Man had grown to be a company within a company, with some twenty titles related to the character coming out each month.)

I worked at Marvel for eighteen years as a writer and editor. (Sometimes I was Stan Lee's editor. That was weird.) So I have some understanding of what it was like to walk in his shoes. In addition, in the course of those years and in the decades since, I've had many conversations, both formal — numerous interviews with him, including new ones for this book — and informal — chatting over a meal — with Lee. I've tried to bring whatever unique observations I can, from that insider's point of view, to this book.

Needless to say, while Marvel's comics and their media adaptations have gone through numerous ups and downs over the decades, Marvel has proven to be much more than a short-lived fad and has come to dominate popular culture, making Lee more well known than ever.

To most people, Stan Lee was that spry, wisecracking old man of a thousand cameos in Marvel's movies and TV shows. They're not sure exactly what he does or did, but they

14

know he somehow was involved with Marvel in its earliest days, and that he's adorable, like a charming, mischievous, elderly relative you see at weddings and funerals. You're not really sure how he's related to you, but he's always fun to schmooze with for a couple of minutes, and you walk away with a smile on your face.

To those who know something of comics history, Lee was the cocreator of the Marvel Universe and the main — for a long time, the *only* — promoter of the comics and the people who made them, who at a certain point had his name above the title as the "presenter" of the comics, and who spent recent decades doing unspecified show-business business in Hollywood.

To many of those who worked for and with him, Stan Lee was a great boss who provided them with regular assignments, was concerned about them and their families, and inspired them to do their best work. To others, he was a flawed but decent guy, who they wished had perhaps been better than he was.

And to a small group of comics fans and professionals, he was the most dastardly of villains, exploiting victimized artists who did all the real creative work, while he was just a lucky, slimy manipulator who was in the right place at the right time. (That's a pretty good lucky streak, one that lasted for more than seventy-five years!)

15

Whatever you may think you know about Stan Lee — or even if you don't know much about him at all — I'm hoping this biography will give a bit of depth and dimension to the man and his achievements and show you that, no matter what you thought, there was more to the story than you realized.

What Stan Lee set into motion — and how it grew beyond anyone's wildest expectations — is a fascinating story, every bit as strange and unlikely as any of the adventures of superhuman mutants and spider-men that Marvel's comics told.

If you want to understand America's popular culture — the stories we tell ourselves to explain ourselves — Stan Lee's life story is a pretty good place to start.

Danny Fingeroth
May 2019

16

1
JFK, THE BEATLES . . . AND STAN LEE

Stan Lee . . . helped revolutionize and update the American comic book industry in the 1960s in the way that Elvis and the Beatles revolutionized the music industry and transformed an entire culture.
— "Stan Lee: An Appreciation,"
The Boston Herald, November 13, 2018[1]

We can *never* allow this nation to be dictated to by . . . *Doctor Doom!* . . . We must move forward and proceed with great vigor! And now, gentlemen, if you'll excuse me, it's Caroline's bedtime!
— President John F. Kennedy, as channeled by Stan Lee, in
Fantastic Four #17, dated August 1963

In May 1963, Stan Lee proclaimed to the world that it was "the Marvel Age of Comics."

Indeed, the covers of most of the Marvel comics that came out that month announced that fact in big, bold blurbs:

17

MARVEL COMICS GROUP USHERS IN "THE MARVEL AGE OF COMICS!"

It turned out to be more than clever hype. Lee and his creative collaborators were in the midst of creating that very "Marvel Age" — or, as you may know it, the sixties.

Nineteen sixty-three was perhaps the most innovative year of Lee's life. With creative partners Jack Kirby, Steve Ditko, Larry Lieber (Lee's brother), Don Heck, and a few others, Lee was reinventing comics, coming up with characters who would change pop culture. That year alone saw the flowering of Spider-Man, Dr. Strange, the Avengers, and the X-Men, as well as the ongoing excitement from the Fantastic Four, whom Lee and Kirby had unleashed in '61.

Youthful and energetic at forty, despite his receding hairline, Lee did whatever it took to come up with comics like no one had ever seen. At its giddiest, this included jumping on desks and striking poses to impress on his artists the kind of extreme action and power he wanted the stories to possess. Besides simply demonstrating poses, though, the jumping and shouting and gesturing was his way of conveying excitement to the artists — and (ideally) sparking that same excitement in them!

But for all his enthusiasm, even Lee couldn't know that Spider-Man would be-

18

come the poster child for every kid who ever felt like he didn't belong — just as the X-Men would make every alienated adolescent feel like there was a family of freaks he or she could fit into. He didn't know that pot-smoking hipsters would look at Ditko's weird Dr. Strange stories and immediately assume that the people making these stories were likewise high on something. (And this when R. Crumb was still drawing birthday cards for a living!)

All Stan Lee thought he was doing was running — and writing much of — a line of superhero comic books that seemed to be catching on with kids, teens, and — this was something new — college students. He'd been trying to catch a somewhat older audience — he'd even put out a comic called *Amazing Adult Fantasy,* whose slogan was "The magazine that respects your intelligence" — and indications were that he might actually be succeeding.

Lee was famous as a high-energy smart aleck who liked to have fun with his staff. Problem was, though, that severe cutbacks in 1957 had left him without much of a staff to have fun with. So, with little other outlet, that playfulness — in what he felt was his last-ditch attempt to stay in comics altogether — had started coming out in his whole approach to how he told stories and spoke to his readers, including proclaiming an "age"

19

for his line of titles.

That zany approach, combined with his own serious storytelling skills and those of the artists he worked with, was touching a nerve. Kids who loved the irreverent, if sometimes over-their-heads, humor of Steve Allen and Jonathan Winters and Ernie Kovacs seemed to find Lee's approach to comics novel and appealing. Sales were up — and so was attention being paid by kids to the comics. Lee could tell that from the letters that were pouring onto his desk and from the steady stream of preadolescents trying to sneak into Marvel's offices to meet him and the imaginary "bullpen" of artists he had convinced them were just waiting there to shake their hands.

Even so, it would still be a couple of years before people like directors Federico Fellini and Alain Resnais would show up at Marvel to meet Lee; before San Francisco rock stars in town on tour would drop by to say hello; before *Esquire* magazine would devote significant space to Marvel's comics and their fans; and certainly before a Princeton English major would anoint Marvel Comics as "the Twentieth Century mythology and you [Lee] as this generation's Homer." It would even be a good year before colleges would start inviting him as a guest speaker.

Lee knew he was impacting the kid-conversation in drugstores and school cafete-

20

rias. But a pair of momentous events led him to realize that what he was doing was not merely responding to the times but was starting to have an impact on them, as well, taking a place in the cultural conversation.

Lee had been through enough booms and busts in comics to not put all his eggs in one basket. Always looking for side-gigs — or even a total exit from the low-rent world of comic books — whether doing freelance advertising work or pitching syndicated newspaper strips, he also did writing and editing when he could for Martin Goodman's non-comics magazines. These were published by Goodman's Magazine Management Company, of which Marvel was a part. (Besides being his boss, Goodman was also Lee's cousin by marriage, which would prove, over the years, to be a mixed blessing.)

And so, for Magazine Management, Lee was producing a humor publication called *You Don't Say*. The magazine consisted of photos of celebrities of the day, including politicians, for which he would write funny dialogue balloons. It was easy and enjoyable work that generated extra income. Beyond that, Lee believed that the level of humor he put into the magazine might even allow it to compete with the revered *New Yorker* magazine! And even more: he felt *You Don't Say* had the potential to become an important

21

magazine that would enable him to ditch comics for a more stable field, one appropriate for an adult.[2]

The first two issues sold well. For the third issue's cover, Lee used a photo of then-president John F. Kennedy (who had actually done unbilled cameos in a few Marvel comics). The universally recognized figure was behind a podium with huge versions of the presidential seal both on the podium and on the wall behind him. Lee's gag for this redundant image was to have JFK saying, "Allow me to introduce myself."

Lee recalled:

While the magazine was at the press, John F. Kennedy was assassinated.

There was no way we could allow that issue to go on sale. Every copy was destroyed. I was so sick at heart that I couldn't even consider continuing with *You Don't Say.*[3]

(It seems that at least a few copies were shipped from the printer, since there are, from time to time, copies for sale online.)

Lee's recently hired "gal Friday," Flo Steinberg, noted the bonding effect the national tragedy had. As she recalled:

The people over at Magazine Management would make fun of us [the comic book

22

people] . . . The only time the different departments ever really came together was when we heard that President Kennedy had been killed. Everybody sort of dropped everything and came together to listen to the radio reports.[4]

The entire nation was stunned by the November 22 Kennedy assassination. Marvel comics had embodied much of the same playful, optimistic sensibility that people associated with the youthful Kennedy administration. (Like JFK, Lee and Kirby were part of the World War II generation. Kirby was born the same year — 1917 — as Kennedy.)

Would anyone have been offended had the issue of *You Don't Say* been widely distributed? In the wake of the assassination, there were so many magazines with Kennedy on the cover, it's hard to imagine this one would have generated much negative attention.

More important was Lee's sense of himself and his work as being important enough that the magazine *needed* to be held back from the public. Even if the world outside of a hip, in-the-know audience — and numerous ten-year-olds — didn't yet realize that what he was doing was significant — well, *he* did. (And in the '40s and '50s, material he worked on *did* draw media attention. Why would it not *now*?) Before too long, the world would, indeed, come to agree with him about how

23

important Marvel's comics were.

As the country struggled to process and understand the murder of its president, Lee, like entertainers everywhere, kept going, making his deadlines, putting out comics, building momentum for Marvel.

During that same period, there was another significant middle-aged cultural figure who, on a larger playing field, had to deal with the same challenges: Ed Sullivan. Sullivan was the influential host of a popular TV variety show that bore his name. Like Lee, he had to figure out how to entertain the American public in the wake of a national trauma.

Sullivan had recently been to England, where he had witnessed firsthand the phenomenon called "Beatlemania." The Beatles weren't just an extremely popular rock band; they inspired a level of seeming hysteria, especially in their female teen fans, that was unprecedented. Seeing that the Liverpool-spawned musicians were also starting to become popular in the United States, Sullivan booked them for three consecutive early '64 episodes of his New York–based Sunday night show. While experts like pop music guru Dick Clark thought the band wasn't very significant, Sullivan's instincts told him something else.

By the time of their February 9 live debut on Sullivan, the Beatles had become hugely

24

popular in the United States, as well as in Britain, and by the time the show was over, they were even bigger. Watching the group on their first Sullivan performance became a cultural touchstone. As with the JFK assassination, baby boomers would ask when meeting each other, "Where were you?" when the group first stepped onto Sullivan's stage.

Stan Lee's solution to the challenge of how to respond in print to the Kennedy assassination had been to just keep on making comic books. No direct mention was made in the comics of the murder. Perhaps he felt there was nothing appropriate he could say. (In a few years, his attitude toward publicly commenting on current events would change dramatically.) But he was certainly noticing what was going on in the culture as a whole — including the Beatles phenomenon. In the letters page of *Fantastic Four* #31, which was on the stands in July '64, David Grace, a reader from Liverpool, wrote:

By the way, did you know that America had two Fantastic Fours for thirteen days? . . . [the second was] the Beatles! They dominate the [music] scene as your comics dominate the comic scene.

To which Lee replied:

Thanks, Dave! Although we're not quite sure

25

whether your letter should have been sent to us — or the Beatles!

And in *Strange Tales* #130, on sale later in '64, Lee, with artists Bob Powell and Chic Stone, presented a story with the same title as the Beatles' first American album, "Meet the Beatles." The story — starring the FF's Thing and Human Torch — involved a subplot where the heroes and their girlfriends had tickets for a Beatles concert, but, due to hero duties, the teammates had to miss the show. The mop-tops did make a couple of cameo appearances in the story, so at least the *readers* got to "meet" the Beatles.

Like Ed Sullivan, Stan Lee knew that the Beatles were important to the cultural moment, even if he didn't fully understand why — and even as he was busy producing comics that were themselves important to the moment. Unlike the Beatles, Lee didn't have (not yet, anyway) a live audience that would show up in concert halls to cheer his work. In a manner similar to that of the Beatles, though, with their fans and fan clubs, Lee succeeded in making Marvel's readers feel, simultaneously, part of a mass movement *and* of a secret community of like-minded aficionados. This was no mean feat.

Like Sullivan, Lee was doing what we'd now call *curating* the culture, giving his audience what they didn't know they wanted until

26

his comics gave it to them. As comics writer Dennis O'Neil has said of Lee in the '60s, "There were about seven years where Stan didn't make a single mistake. He just really was on an incredible roll, and everything worked for him."[5] Given the eventual phenomenal success of the characters and the company he was so instrumental in creating, it's fair to say that Lee was ahead of his time, even if he didn't fully realize it back in the early '60s.

It would be a number of years before Stan Lee would meet — and talk business with — a couple of Beatles (although they were reportedly Marvel fans).[6] But he would. And, in time, he would even hobnob with presidents. In the meantime, he was helping shape the culture, one superhero adventure at a time, one letter column response at a time, one hyperbolic cover blurb at a time.

With his artist-collaborators, he was creating Marvel's *stories.* On his *own,* he was using those stories — and the personas he grafted onto himself and the artists — to create the Marvel Age. (To a reader who complained that calling the era the Marvel Age was presumptuous, since there were other companies in the business, Lee replied, "Okay, so let them make up their own age! It's a free country!")[7]

In retrospect, it was plain that, among those

27

figures shaping the times, Stan Lee and Marvel Comics — which from almost their beginnings were synonymous — were on the road to becoming important cultural players. While Kennedy and the Beatles played out their lives and careers on much larger platforms than Lee was then doing, the influence the comics he was producing would end up having on the cultural conversation then, and to the present day, is undeniable.

So, was Stan Lee at the right place at the right time — or did he make his time and place the right ones?

Well, if you've read this far, then you're no doubt curious about how Lee came to be the pivotal figure that he was. To figure that out, then — in the finest tradition of superhero comics and movies — it's time for us to go into flashbacks and uncover . . .

. . . the secret origin of Stan Lee!

2
THE DRESS CUTTER'S SON

[My father] was . . . was not lucky. . . . He couldn't find a job. He would be sitting home reading the want ads. I felt so sorry for him.
— Stan Lee[1]

Nine-year-old Stanley Martin Lieber sat transfixed in his seat in the opulent upper Manhattan movie palace, the only light coming from the silvery screen upon which a dreamworld was projected.

Bigger than life, charismatic movie star Warren William, playing a powerful prosecutor in the 1932 Warner Bros. melodrama *The Mouthpiece,* seemed to be staring right at young Stanley — staring *through* him, perhaps — as he summed up his case against an accused killer:

The eminent attorney for the defense has made the point that this case is based upon a chain of circumstantial evidence. That is true.

But the evidence is a *strong* chain, one

29

that *cannot* be broken — a chain that has wrapped itself around this murderer like an *avenging python* — and delivered him into the hands of the *law*!

Entranced by this bravura performance, Stanley decided that, when he grew up, he would become a lawyer. Or an actor. Or *both*.[2]

One way or another, he wanted to, like Warren William, reach out to people, to make them think — and feel!

It made no sense that Stan Lee's family lived at 777 West End Avenue when he was born.

But they did.

The building, at the corner of West Ninety-eighth Street, was built in 1910, as West End Avenue was becoming a coveted address among the rising Jewish middle class in New York. High-rise luxury buildings like 777 were appearing, replacing the smaller tenements that had lined the avenue.

Jack Lieber was born in 1885 (any siblings he might have had are unknown), and his wife, Celia Solomon Lieber, the third of six siblings, was born in 1890. Both were Romanian-Jewish immigrants who had arrived in New York in the early years of the twentieth century and met in the city. By most accounts, the couple didn't have much money, although Jack seemed to have somewhat regular work as a dress cutter until the middle of the decade.[3]

When Lee was born — as Stanley Martin Lieber — on December 28, 1922, his parents, Jack and Celia, shouldn't have been able to afford to live at 777. The neighborhood, off the IRT subway line, was ideally located for Jack Lieber's work in the garment center, which encompassed much of Manhattan's West Thirties around Seventh Avenue. However, Jack didn't make much money as a garment worker and was chronically unemployed starting around 1926.[4] The apartment was small and certainly not glamorous. Lee slept in the living room and found it in general depressing that his family always lived in rear-facing apartments, his only view a brick wall.[5]

But even a tiny, dark apartment in a luxurious building would have been difficult for a factory worker like Jack to afford. Lee didn't remember the West End Avenue apartment at all, saying, "I think my parents [and I] lived there for a very short time before they moved. . . . I lived there when I was, like, six months old, so my memories of it aren't too clear."[6]

Perhaps the Liebers had a sympathetic landlord or a generous relative — some of Celia's relatives had some money[7] — which enabled the family to be living in a posh building when their first child was born.

However they did it, they couldn't do it

31

long, and soon moved to the more affordable regions of upper Manhattan — in this case, Washington Heights — in the decade before the George Washington Bridge was built. The family would spend the next twenty years bouncing between apartments in the Heights and in similar working-class, immigrant neighborhoods in the Bronx.

Born the same year as Kurt Vonnegut and Jack Kerouac, Lee entered the world in the middle of the Jazz Age and Prohibition (and the ensuing speak-easy culture) and the beginning of an economic recovery that followed a post–World War I economic dip. But it doesn't seem as if his family was involved with the glamour of the flapper era. They were simply poor people trying to survive. Both Lee and his brother, writer and artist Larry Lieber (born October 26, 1931), remember their parents as not getting along well, frequently anxious and arguing about money.[8]

If the Liebers had financial issues in the relatively prosperous years of 1922 and '23, then it's unlikely that the stock market crash of October 29, 1929 — when Lee was six years old — made things any better for them. Lee recalled going to elementary school at PS 173, which he remembered as being on University Avenue in the Bronx.[9] But PS 173 was actually in Washington Heights. It seems most likely that he was living in the Heights when he was in elementary school, moving to the Bronx for high school, and then moving back to the Heights sometime after he graduated.

According to Jordan Raphael and Tom Spurgeon in *Stan Lee and the Rise and Fall of the American Comic Book,* "Money was scarce in the Lieber home, and the family often accepted financial help from Celia's sisters, who were better off. . . . Jack was intelligent, but difficult and demanding, recalls Jean Goodman, a close relative. 'He was exacting with his boys. . . .' Celia, on the other hand, was warm and nurturing to the point of self-sacrifice. 'The demanding father and the persecuted mother, that made the atmosphere difficult,' Goodman says."[10]

As Lee recalled of his father:

[My father] was not a good businessman, and he was not lucky. Most of the time I knew him, he just wasn't working. He couldn't find a job. He would be sitting home reading the want ads. I felt so sorry for him.[11]

While his brother, Larry, was nine years younger than Stan, and so couldn't have witnessed their parents' treatment of his brother before he was born, Larry did remember his mother regularly urging him to

33

be more like his brother, whom she likened to President Roosevelt.[12] So it seems safe to say there was no lack of support from Celia Lieber toward Stanley.

Money or no money, kids will make do with what they have. Lee recalled, in 2002, for the now-defunct website Yesterdayland.com, some of the diversions he enjoyed as a kid:

> One thing I remember . . . was, as if it was an official thing, there were seasons. For example: it would be handball season. All of a sudden, all the kids in the neighborhood would be playing handball. . . . Then it was hockey season . . . and we'd all be playing hockey [on roller skates] in the gutter, risking our lives because the traffic kept coming around us.[13]

There was one toy that proved to be the most exciting — and liberating — thing in Stanley's young life:

> I was about 10 years old, I don't know where my parents got the money, but they finally bought me a big red two-wheeled bicycle. . . . I could go wherever I wanted.[14]

Unknown to Lee, it was Ida Davis — Jean Goodman's mother — who paid for the bicycle, as well as for some minor sinus surgery Stanley would have in 1934.[15] The

34

George Washington Bridge was first opened to the public on October 25, 1931 (a day before Larry was born). So to ride a bike across the new, man-made wonder must have been especially awe-inspiring.

Lee described himself as an "average student" who "couldn't wait to get out of school. . . . I didn't hate being in school, but I just kept wishing it was over and I could get into the real world, because I wasn't studying anything I was particularly interested in."[16]

Asked if he were a sports fan, Lee replied, "Yeah, but just a casual sports fan. I wasn't the kind of guy that would run through the neighborhood breaking store windows if my team lost. Or won."[17] Nonetheless, living close to both Yankee Stadium and the Polo Grounds, home of the New York Giants baseball team, Lee recalled of being so close to both stadiums, "It was wonderful" and that he was a fan of "both of them."[18]

What he was particularly interested in was reading (anything and everything) and popular culture in general, especially the movies and the radio.

Lee recalled reading popular kids' book series, including the Hardy Boys, the Boy Allies, and Tom Swift. Two of his favorite series, Jerry Todd and Poppy Ott, were written by Leo Edwards (the pen name of Edward Edson Lee — no relation). He especially loved those because they had more humor than the

35

others. And, he noted:

best of all was the end of the [Jerry Todd] book[s] . . . there were letters from readers with answers by the author. I thought that was so wonderful. It made me feel I was part of this thing and I knew him.[19]

Some of the other authors he loved to read included H. G. Wells, Sir Arthur Conan Doyle, Mark Twain, and Edgar Rice Burroughs. As he grew older, he discovered Edgar Allan Poe, Charles Dickens, Edmond Rostand, Omar Khayyam, Émile Zola, "and, of course, Shakespeare . . . [and] the Bible."[20] "I think my biggest influence was Shakespeare, who was my god. . . . I loved Shakespeare. . . . To me, he was the complete writer . . ."[21]

Lee also loved the radio, which was a bonding experience with his family. "Sunday night in our house was family night. We'd have delicatessen. We'd have hot dogs, beans, sauerkraut, if times were good."[22] He also recalled:

Sunday night we listened to the comedians. . . . There was Fred Allen and Jack Benny, Edgar Bergen and Charlie McCarthy and there was W.C. Fields. . . . [T]he funny thing to me [was] . . . when it was time for the family to gather 'round and listen to the

36

radio, all the chairs were turned facing the radio. Everybody sat looking at the radio just as if it was television.[23]

Unsurprisingly, young Lee liked comic strips, both in the newspapers and in the collected editions that made up the first comic books. His favorites were, "the ones by Milton Caniff . . . *Terry and the Pirates.* That was the big one. And then there was *Li'l Abner.* I liked the humor stuff. I liked the adventure stuff."[24] His likes also included *The Katzenjammer Kids, Skippy, Dick Tracy, Smitty,* and *The Gumps.*[25] But as he said in the 2000 documentary, *With Great Power,* "Creating comic books was never part of my childhood dream. I never thought of that at all."

Perhaps more than any other entertainment, Lee loved the movies. There were five movie theaters in his Washington Heights neighborhood.[26]

He was especially moved by the 1932 movie *The Mouthpiece,* starring Warren William, whose performance in it "hypnotized" young Stanley.[27]

William was indeed outstanding in the film, playing an aggressive prosecutor, Vincent Day, who unwittingly sends an innocent man to the electric chair. This so traumatizes Day that he becomes a defense attorney who then ends up becoming corrupted, getting wealthy criminals, who are very much guilty, off the

37

hook. As you might imagine, his life becomes complicated and tragic, not unlike the melodramas that would, years later, be found in Lee's comics.

While Lee mentioned in his 2002 memoir, *Excelsior!,* a number of movie stars — notably Errol Flynn — of whom he was a fan, *The Mouthpiece* was the only specific movie he singled out in the book as making a big impression on him. After seeing the film, Lee daydreamed of becoming a lawyer and would become the president of the Future Lawyers Club in high school.[28]

Of note about the film, as well, although apparently not consciously noted by Lee, was that the female lead is named Celia — the same as Lee's mother. In addition, Celia was played by Sidney Fox, an eastern European Jewish immigrant who came to America as a young child and who, before her move to Hollywood, lived in Washington Heights at the same time and in the same area as the Lieber family.

It's not the wildest speculation to imagine that seeing a familiar neighborhood face twelve feet tall on a movie screen, attached to a character with the same name as his mother, might have made as big an impression on Lee as the bravura performance by Warren William, and made the film significant in his memory.

■ ■ ■ ■

Lee didn't recall his family being especially religious. His parents didn't keep a kosher home, but Jack Lieber, according to Larry Lieber,[29] was a semi-regular attendee at synagogue services. While Lee didn't have any substantive Jewish education, he did have a bar mitzvah. As he recalled in 2006, "My father insisted I be bar mitzvahed, and I took a crash course in learning to read Hebrew, all of which I'm sorry to say I've forgotten by now. My parents didn't have much money at that time, and I remember during the [bar mitzvah] ceremony at the temple, there was my father and me, and maybe two other people had wandered in. That was the whole thing."[30]

Lee developed an interest in acting — and in a girl — which led him to regularly show up at a Washington Heights synagogue (whether or not the same one where he had his bar mitzvah is unknown) around the same time as his bar mitzvah. As he recalled:

There was a time I wanted to be an actor, and there was place called . . . the Hebrew [Tabernacle] of Washington Heights [on West 161 Street]. . . . And they had a theatrical group, so I joined that outfit in order to be part of the theatrical group and

39

be in their plays. . . . See, the big thing, there was a girl that I liked who was part of the group. I still remember her first name was Martha, and she was a blond Spanish girl, very pretty, so I enjoyed being there because of Martha.[31]

It's also unknown whether Lee's interest in Martha was reciprocated and, if so, to what extent.

As was common in the era, Lee skipped a couple of grades over the years. That enabled him to eventually go into the working world sooner. But it also regularly made him the youngest kid in his class, so it was hard for him to relate to his schoolmates, and vice versa.[32]

When time for high school came, the Liebers were likely living at 1720 University Avenue in the Bronx's University Heights. (Decades later, comics writer and editor Len Wein would live, as a child, in the same building.) The avenue and the area were named for the "uptown" branch of New York University (today, Bronx Community College), which was on the thoroughfare. Once again, the family lived in a rear-facing apartment. Lee attended DeWitt Clinton High School, an enormous institution on a sprawling campus on the borough's Mosholu Parkway. The all-boys school was fed by a large part of

40

the Bronx's population and, at its peak, hosted twelve thousand students.[33]

Clinton, with its mix of Jewish, Italian, and Irish children of immigrants, along with a number of African American students, has one of the most impressive alumni rosters of any school in the country, with graduates who went on to achievement and fame in numerous fields. Other notable alumni from Lee's era include author James Baldwin, playwright Paddy Chayefsky, and photographer Richard Avedon. Clinton boys besides Lee who ended up in the comics industry included Bob Kane and Bill Finger (creators of Batman), Will Eisner (creator of the Spirit and pioneer of the modern graphic novel), and Irwin Hasen (*Wonder Woman* and *Dondi* artist).

According to his yearbook entry, Lee was a member of numerous organizations, including the Future Lawyers Club.[34] While he was not an editor of the school literary magazine, *The Magpie* (Chayefsky took that role), he *was* listed on its staff pages as the magazine's publicist.[35]

It was while working in the *Magpie* office that he pulled a prank that he frequently described with pride (and a bit of shame, too). As he recalled:

I must have been a little bit crazy, even then, because I remember they had a school magazine called *The Magpie* . . . and

41

it was published in a room called The Tower, which had a very high ceiling, and there was no way anybody could ever reach that ceiling. . . . One day, it was being painted, and one of the painters had left the ladder when he went down for lunch, so I climbed up and wrote "Stan Lee is God," on the ceiling, which was one of the earliest evidences of my overpowering inferiority complex.[36]

Interestingly, when speaking about the prank to this author in 2017, Lee noted, "I'm so ashamed of that, but, as far as I know, it's still up there."[37]

When asked, "So you were calling yourself 'Stan Lee' even back in high school?" Lee realized, "No, I wasn't calling myself Stan Lee then, I don't believe. I guess I told it that way because I now think of myself as Stan Lee. But I must have written Stan *Lieber.*"[38]

When he was fifteen, Lee won a small, seventh-place prize and a couple of honorable mentions in three different weeks of a regular "Biggest News of the Week" contest run in the *New York Herald Tribune.* This was certainly nothing to be ashamed of, but, for whatever reason, Lee would, years later, always say that he had won first prize in the contest three weeks in a row. No evidence of such triumphs, however, has been found.[39]

At some point during his high school years,

42

Lee was "initiated into the mysteries and pleasures of sex . . . one of my great regrets is that that I cannot remember the name of the daughter of the neighborhood candy store proprietor with whom I lost my virginity."[40]

While eager to get out into the world, Lee still found time to participate in extracurricular life at Clinton, even while holding down a number of part-time jobs. He sold subscriptions to the *New York Herald Tribune* to fellow students, modeling himself on a student named John J. McKenna, who impressed him doing a similar job for *The New York Times.* He also delivered sandwiches for Manhattan's Jack May's Pharmacy, near Rockefeller Center, where he prided himself on his efficiency, which thereby enabled him to collect more tips than the other delivery boys.[41]

Lee often spoke of being employed by the Works Progress Administration's Federal Theatre Project at the same time that Orson Welles was (freely admitting that they didn't work together or know each other). Welles left the WPA in 1937, so Lee's time there must have been while he was still in high school. However, in *Excelsior!,* coauthor George Mair wrote that Lee was with the project "sometime after graduating high school." In any case, Lee joined the project to meet a girl who was involved with it. They did indeed date for a time. And after appearing in a few shows, he got to love acting, but the pay was so low, he was forced to quit. The romance with the girl had ended, anyway, making leaving the WPA easier.[42]

After graduating DeWitt Clinton in June 1939, at age sixteen, Lee worked as an usher at the Rivoli Theatre in midtown Manhattan, where, he recalled, he had a memorable encounter with First Lady Eleanor Roosevelt:

One day . . . Mrs. Roosevelt came into the theater . . . and we all hoped she'd come down our aisle, and I got her. Well, I was so proud. I walked down the aisle with my flashlight shining for her feet, my head high and my shoulders back, and I said, "This way, Mrs. President." Which, of course, was the wrong thing to say. ["Mrs. Roosevelt" would have been the correct form of address.] I tripped and fell over the foot of some son of a bitch who had his foot stuck in the aisle, and the next thing I know, "Mrs. President" was helping me to my feet with her arms around my shoulders. "Are you all right, young man?" You can imagine how embarrassed I was.[43]

Lee then had a stint writing celebrity obituaries for a wire service (although he sometimes recalled having this job while in high school), which he found depressing,

44

since he was assigned to write death notices for people who were still alive, and so left the job.[44]

Lee's cousin on his mother's side, Jean Goodman, was married to Martin Goodman, a publisher who had hit it big putting out a wide variety of pulp magazines. Martin would go on to be one of the most important people in Lee's life, but at this point, they didn't know each other well. The Goodmans connected their cousin with Jewish communal organization B'nai B'rith's recently founded Vocational Service Program.[45] Through the program, Lee got a job writing publicity materials for National Jewish Health, a tuberculosis hospital in Denver, although he did the work in New York. (Lee recalled that there was also someone named "Charlie Plotkin," who "wore a sweater all the time," involved in getting him this and possibly other writing jobs.)[46]

Lee claimed that "I could never understand what I was trying to do [with that job] — get people to get tuberculosis so they go to the hospital? But anyway, the idea was that if anybody had tuberculosis, we had to convince them to go to that hospital."[47]

Lee's connection with the Vocational Service Program didn't last long, and he ended up getting a job as an office boy for H. Lissner Co., a Manhattan trouser manufacturer, where he felt exploited and unappreciated by

45

supervisors who never even bothered to learn his name. He was fired from that job because he had less seniority than another office boy, even though he felt he worked much harder than the other guy.

Angry about this unjust dismissal, on his way out the door, Lee impulsively upended a few large batches of cutting tickets — sheets that listed data about different types of trousers.[48] Luckily, he never had to ask H. Lissner Co. for a reference.

But as awful as that job was, Lee couldn't afford to be without one. He urgently needed to find new employment.

While Lee was a teenager, making his way through school, various jobs, and a romance or two, America was pulling out of the Depression, even as the world seemed to be erupting. Germany's invasion of Poland on September 1, 1939 — a couple of months after Lee's graduation from Clinton — triggered the start of World War II. The United States wasn't in that conflict when it began, but it seemed like just a matter of time before it would be.

In the world of popular culture, while 1939 was famous for the classic movies released that year, including *The Wizard of Oz, Gone with the Wind,* and *Stagecoach,* in the less high-profile world of comic books, major events were also transpiring. In 1938, Super-

46

man had debuted in *Action Comics* #1, and in early 1939, Batman had his first appearance in *Detective Comics* #27. Both characters were enormous hits out of the gate, and publishers — especially pulp publishers, whose magazines were experiencing severe sales slumps — rushed to jump on the new superhero comic book fad.

Among those pulp publishers was Martin Goodman, Lee's cousin by marriage, who in the summer of '39 had launched a comic book line under the Timely imprint, starting with *Marvel Comics* #1, which was hugely successful, selling close to a million copies, with very few returns from news dealers. The comic introduced, among other characters, the Sub-Mariner and the Human Torch.

Marvel Comics #1 and subsequent Timely titles had been produced for Goodman by an outside packager, Funnies Inc. But the publisher soon wanted his own in-house comic book line that would be produced by staffers and freelancers working directly for him. To accomplish this, he had, in early 1940, hired two young men — both of whom were skilled writers and artists — who were making a name for themselves in the still-young comic book business: editor Joe Simon and art director Jack Kirby.

Out of Timely's offices in the McGraw-Hill Building on West Forty-second Street, the two were producing comics for Goodman,

47

done by themselves as well as by others. In late 1940, Simon (then twenty-seven) and Kirby (then twenty-three) came up with what would be Timely's biggest hit: *Captain America Comics* #1. The magazine went on sale in most areas in the United States around December 20.

And it was shortly before that landmark comic book debuted that seventeen-year-old Stanley Martin Lieber appeared at Timely's door, looking for a job.[49]

48

3
THE PIED PIPER OF WEST FORTY-SECOND STREET

I thought [Stan Lee] was the Orson Welles of the comic book business. He had energy and was young, tall, and good-looking.
— Timely artist David Gantz[1]

Stanley Martin Lieber wasn't just Jean Goodman's cousin. In a stranger-than-fiction twist, his mother's brother — Robbie Solomon — was married to Martin Goodman's sister.[2]

So Stanley was doubly related to the owner of Timely Comics. In addition, several of Martin's brothers also worked for his overall publishing operation. This sort of arrangement was not uncommon in businesses run by immigrants or first-generation American-born children of immigrants. That way, you had people you trusted working for you, plus you didn't have to worry about your relatives finding jobs.

By most accounts, Uncle Robbie's role, whatever his official title, was to be Martin's eyes and ears around the company. He made it his business to know what was going on in every department — hence his reputation as an annoying busybody. What some people didn't seem to get was that that *was* his unofficial job description.[3]

As Joe Simon recalled, Solomon brought Lee to him in December 1940 in Timely's McGraw-Hill Building office on far West Forty-second Street and said, "Martin wants you to just keep him out of the way. Put him to work."[4] But according to Lee, on his first day at work, Goodman seemed surprised to see him and asked, "What are you doing here?" Lee never figured out if Martin was kidding or serious.[5]

Lee became Simon and Kirby's all-around assistant and "gopher." He went for coffee and sandwiches, cleaned up pages, did proofreading — whatever was needed to make the comics office run smoothly. As Simon recalled:

Mostly, we had Stan erasing the pencils off of the inked artwork, and going out for coffee. He followed us around, we took him to lunch, and he tried to be friends with us. When he didn't have anything to do, he would sit in a corner of the art department and play his little flute or piccolo, driving Kirby nuts. . . . I thought he was a cute kid.[6]

Since Stanley aspired to become a writer, the comic books he was assisting on provided just the venue he needed. In order to be shipped to readers and distributors at a lower rate via US Mail, a periodical had to have at least two pages of text. Every comic book, therefore, had a two-page prose feature. It was generally assumed that most readers didn't bother with them, that they skipped over them the way they would over an ad that didn't grab their attention.

So Simon assigned Stanley to write the text feature in *Captain America Comics* #3. The teenager wrote a story called "Captain America Foils the Traitor's Revenge." But the story ran not under the byline of Stanley Martin Lieber but under that of someone named "Stan Lee."[7] Lee had always claimed he was saving his real name for the great American novel he was destined to write. "I felt, well, if someday I'm going to become a writer or a great actor, I want to use that name for the really important things I do."[8] The story contained two new illustrations by Jack Kirby, making it Lee and Kirby's first collaboration.

Soon, besides continuing to grind out text pieces, the newly self-christened Stan Lee — although he wouldn't change his name legally until decades later — also got to write comic book scripts, starting with a story (drawn by Charles Wojtkoski) starring a new character named Jack Frost in *USA Comics* #1, which was on sale early in May 1941. That was fol-

51

lowed by a story featuring the Black Marvel, drawn by Al Avison and Al Gabriele, in *All Winners Comics* #1, published later in the month. That, in turn, was followed, at the end of the month, by the debut of the Lee-written "Headline Hunter, Foreign Correspondent," drawn by Charles Nicholas (possibly a pen name for Wojtkoski), in *Captain America* #5. The same team also did a story featuring Hurricane, Master of Speed, in that issue.[9]

As Lee was establishing a writing career, thereby also earning, in addition to his eight-dollars-per-week salary, a fifty-cents-per-page writing fee, Simon and Kirby were producing — along with packagers Funnies Inc. — an expanding line of comics for Goodman. They added Syd Shores as an in-house artist, and the comics line expanded to more than a half dozen sixty-four-page titles.

In the midst of the booming business at Timely and other companies, comic books were gaining more and more attention — and not all of it was welcome. Sterling North, the literary editor of *The Chicago Daily News,* had written in the May 8, 1940, issue — half a year before Stanley Lieber was hired at Timely — that comic books were "a poisonous mushroom growth" and that their publishers were guilty of a "cultural slaughter of

52

the innocents." His diatribe was published in *The News* and picked up by dozens of other papers. This was the beginning of an anti-comics movement that would ebb and flow over the decades and would complicate Stan Lee's life time and again.

But for now, things were flying high at Timely, with *Captain America,* their biggest hit, selling close to a million copies per issue. The comic was so well known that members of the Nazi organization, the German American Bund, regularly hounded the creators. As Simon recalled, "The pro-Nazi supporters were vocal, and there were a lot of them. They were constantly threatening us, to the point that we had police stationed outside our offices, and the FBI got involved." New York mayor Fiorello La Guardia called Simon to assure him that the city would protect them.[10]

Simon and Kirby had a handshake agreement with Goodman, whereby they were entitled to 25 percent of *Captain America*'s profits. They should have been raking in large royalties. But Goodman claimed the comic wasn't making much money. Goodman's accountant, Maurice Coyne — who was also a partner in MLJ, the company that would become Archie Comics — informed Simon and Kirby that the reason for the lack of profits was that Goodman was deducting the expenses for his whole comics line from *Cap-*

53

tain America's revenues. Perhaps Coyne was hoping that an angry Simon and Kirby would leave Timely and come do comics for MLJ.[11]

When he received Coyne's information, Simon contacted Jack Liebowitz, president of National (a.k.a. DC Comics, publishers of *Superman* and *Batman*), and made a deal for Simon and Kirby to do work for that company while still employed at Timely.[12] Simon might have figured that the only way to get any kind of royalty was to keep showing up at the office. Alternatively, he might have thought that they could have continued working for both companies; this was not an unusual kind of arrangement in the comics business at the time. In any case, it would only be a matter of time before their recognizable work — along with a major promotional push — would appear in DC's titles and they would be forced into some kind of confrontation with Goodman.

Lee found out what his bosses were doing and swore he would keep their secret safe. Still, one way or another, Goodman, as was inevitable, found out. A couple of his brothers, as well as Rob Solomon, confronted Simon and Kirby and fired them — but insisted they finish the issue of *Captain America* they were working on — #10 — before they left. Lee forever insisted he didn't rat them out, but according to Simon, Kirby always believed that Stanley *did* tell Goodman and held it against Lee. Simon himself believed that Lee kept their moonlighting a secret and that in the gossip-driven world of comics, it could have been any number of people who revealed what they were doing.[13] Needless to say, once their DC work hit the stands — complete with cover blurbs proclaiming their presence — the whole world would have known, anyway.

Goodman put his brother Abe in place as temporary comics editor for a few months and then assigned Stanley to do the job until Martin found "a real grown-up."[14] Lee's running joke until the end of his life was that Martin must still be looking for that adult, because he never — with one intentionally temporary exception — placed anyone in the editor's role besides Lee.[15] Lee's first official credit as editor appeared in *Captain America* #12, which was published in early January 1942.

So in late 1941 — less than a year after he'd first been hired by Simon — Stan Lee, eighteen years old, now became the editor of a line of comics that was poised for explosive growth. With a good deal of the line's material still being provided by Funnies Inc., much of Lee's job would be administrative, not creative. (This would change over time, as the ratio of packaged material to work commissioned directly to creators would shift to favor the latter.) Still, it was a hell of a lot

55

of responsibility for a kid.[16]

Not only did Lee not crumble from the pressure, though, the young man actually seemed to *thrive* under it. Perhaps in a business so young, not knowing what he couldn't do was an asset. As writer and artist Al Jaffee, who started freelancing for Lee that year (and who would go on to become one of *Mad* magazine's legendary "Usual Gang of Idiots"), recalled, "The fact of the matter is, Stan was, all the time I ever knew him, which started at the beginning of his career — he was juggling ten balls in the air all the time."[17] Jaffee also said of Lee that "the one thing that impressed me greatly about Stan was his 'can do' attitude."[18]

While increasing Timely's superhero titles, Goodman and Lee were also adding funny animal comics in the style of the Disney and other cartoons that were then popular. Lee was writing many of these stories as well as numerous superhero tales, in addition to editing the titles. At that point, the energetic young man didn't seem to have much if any editorial assistance.

When Jaffee arrived at Lee's door, showing him work he'd ghosted for Chad Grothkopf, an artist Lee was already using, Lee quickly offered him a chance to do a funny-cops feature called "Squat Car Squad." Jaffee took the script Lee gave him and improvised on it as he drew the story. He broke the fourth

56

and every other wall there was to break, drawing himself and Lee literally barging into the tale. As Mary-Lou Weisman wrote in the biography *Al Jaffee's Mad Life:*

Al inserted a caricature of himself into the story . . . pratfalling SPLAT on the sidewalk. Then he pushed further . . . he let his characters blame him for not following Stan Lee's direction. "It's as if we were all alive — the cops, the artist, the editor — all of us. We could wander in and out of the panels at will. Stan loved it, and I had a wonderful time. Stan never edited me. He never told me what to write."[19]

Lee was so impressed, he gave Jaffee the "Squat Car Squad" feature to write and draw regularly. A bit later, when Lee wanted a new humor comic character, Jaffee recalled:

I created Silly Seal, and, after a while, Stan said to me, "Why don't we give Silly a partner — how about a pig called Ziggy?" I said, "Great." And we put the two together and he gave me a free hand writing [and drawing] those things . . . we never discussed stories. There really isn't a hell of a lot to discuss when you're doing "Ziggy Pig and Silly Seal."[20]

Indeed, this was the key to how Lee was

57

able to juggle so many titles over the years. While he didn't hesitate to edit or tweak, he generally preferred to work with people he trusted and who he could just let loose. In that era before the need for tight continuity between stories, oversight — especially on humor stories — could be looser in general.

Artist David Gantz, a high school classmate of Jaffee's, at Jaffee's suggestion, showed his samples to Lee. The editor gave him regular art assignments on such humor comics as *Patsy Walker* and *Super Rabbit*. Many years later, Gantz would, in a memoir/essay comic, "Jews and the Graphic Novel," recall meeting Lee.[21] In it, the artist described Lee as "a lanky young guy wearing cowboy boots [who] was trying to play the pennywhistle, with little success," and depicted Lee leading him from his office into the artists' bullpen while still playing the instrument. Gantz drew himself with a thought balloon that read, "I felt like a kid following a tone-deaf pied piper."

In the story, Gantz then drew Lee literally flying around the office. ("Should we shut the window?" "Yeah. We don't want to be responsible for losing him.") Gantz also depicted Lee acting out story scenes in extreme poses ("What I want is action, AC-TION, *ACTION!*") — something many other artists would recall him doing over the years.

Early Timely artist Allen Bellman remem-

58

bered the company's adventure/superhero staff artists in late 1942 as including himself and other artists who would become prominent in comics, such as Mike Sekowsky, Frank Giacoia, George Klein, Frank Carino, and Chris Rule. Bellman recalled that "Stan was wonderful to work for. He was good-natured but strict with his editing. He wanted perfection. If you drew a cup on a table in one panel, do not leave that cup out in the next panel."[22]

Jim Mooney, who would go on to be a mainstay for decades at Marvel and DC, remembered Lee from that era, as well, when the two worked on a humor strip called *The Ginch and Claude Pennygrabber.* He recalled working on it with Lee in what years later came to be called the "Marvel Method," where he and Lee would talk out the story.[23]

Mooney said of his first meeting with Lee:

I came in, being somewhat young and cocky at the time, and Stan asked me what I did. I said I penciled; he said "What else?" I said I inked. He said, "What else?" I said color. "Do anything else?" I said, "Yeah, I letter, too." He said, "Do you print the damn books, too?"

In the same interview, Mooney observed:

At Marvel, I had a feeling of being involved,

59

and being a part of it, particularly when I was penciling and worked with the outline script Stan provided . . . . because you did contribute something. You broke it down the way you wanted to.[24]

While doing a lot of superhero writing, Lee also created — with Chad Grothkopf (with Jaffee doing much of the penciling) — *The Imp,* in *Captain America. The Imp* was a humor feature starring a mischievous creature who spoke solely in rhyme (as did his stories' narrator). The strip had a playful, anything-goes air to it that gave the feeling that everyone involved was having fun.

The world changed in an instant when Japanese forces attacked Pearl Harbor on December 7, 1941, bringing the United States into World War II. Lee enlisted, entering the army on November 9, 1942.

Perhaps anticipating that he'd soon be doing military service one way or another, and thereby losing access to writing work — and extra income for his parents and brother, as well as himself — Lee stepped up his freelance writing for Timely, doing adventure and humor comics, including a couple of issues of *Young Allies,* in which he wrote forty-five-page stories, quite lengthy for the era.

In addition to comics, he was also doing work on some of Goodman's non-comics magazines, writing short humor features for *Joker, Stag,* and *Comedy* magazines. And he had two prose fiction stories in Goodman's *Male Home Companion* magazine, edited by Solomon, cover dated October 1942. One was credited to Stan Lee, the other to "Stanley Martin."

Asked about his decision to enlist, as opposed to seeking a deferment or waiting to be drafted, Lee recalled:

I think I could have gotten a deferment, but . . . it was the kind of war you were a son of a bitch if you didn't get into it. It was too important not to fight. . . .

I was going to go overseas, and they taught me to do electrical wiring [for radio communications] . . . and [the idea was] I'd be going ahead of the troops, installing this wiring so they could communicate with each other. . . . I felt . . . that would be terrific. I'm doing something important.

But I was waiting on the pier for the boat to take me to Europe . . . and somebody tapped me on the shoulder and said . . . "We need you back here. Your plans have been changed." So they never sent me overseas. They brought me to Long Island, where they had their training film division, because they found out I had done writing.[25]

61

Lee had arranged for his friend, animator Vince Fago, to run Timely's editorial department in his absence, which proved to be a good move. Besides superheroes, the trend was growing for comics that resembled or were based on bigfoot-style animated characters, human and animal. With his background in just such types of characters, Fago was the perfect person for the job. As or more important, Fago's ambitions didn't seem to lie in staying in the job for life. As Michael Vassallo put it:

Fago's forte was humor features, especially funny-animal antics necessitating frenetic panel-to-panel progressions, a talent that perfectly coincided with Timely's recent expansion into humor comic books with the launching of *Comedy Comics, Krazy Komics, Joker Comics* and *Terrytoons,* the latter featuring characters licensed from the Paul Terry studio.[26]

Lee was constantly busy with assignments (his army classification — shared with only eight others, including legendary novelist William Saroyan — was "playwright"); he was also able to, after a seven-month gap, continue freelancing for Timely and even carry on a social life. After basic training in New Jersey, Lee was assigned to work on training and informational material in Queens and

62

then was assigned to similar posts at Duke University in Durham, North Carolina, and in Indianapolis, Indiana. While at the latter, he recalled dating several women. One of them, he said:

lived in Indianapolis, and her parents were very wealthy. . . . I was so in awe of the house she lived in. It took up a whole city block. I think her father had been one of the people — or the person — who built Boulder Dam or something. She was such a nice girl, and I liked her so much. But it didn't turn out to be a love affair.

And there was [another] gal I really had a crush on. She worked in the army laundry, of all things. She was the one who took the clothes from the soldiers and gave them to whoever she gave them to. She was blond and beautiful. But she had one horrible habit I couldn't stand. Anytime anything displeased her, which was quite often, she'd go, "Oh, rats! Oh, rats!" I just couldn't see myself spending my life with a girl who kept saying, "Oh, rats!"

And then I had another girl that I was really serious with, and I thought I could marry her when I got out of the army. I was about to get out — I was twenty-something years old — and I found out she was only sixteen. I felt that wouldn't be fair to her, so I walked away from it. But she was the clos-

63

est I came to getting married before I met Joan.[27]

When he wasn't dating, Lee wrote scripts for training films and did other informational/educational work, including for an anti-venereal disease campaign ("VD? Not me!"), and helped devise methods for army payroll staffs to be more efficient. He even wrote a humorous marching song for the payroll workers. While in the service, after a brief hiatus, he also continued doing freelance writing for Timely, once risking brig time for "stealing" his own mail when the base post office was closed.[28]

In retrospect, Lee didn't think the service had changed him any more than anything else he might have done in his early twenties. "I was just three years older," he said. "So when you're in your early twenties and you age three years, it changes you whether you're in the army or not. . . . I served, I did what I had to do, I came home, and I looked for a girl to marry."[29] Still, in later years, he would look back proudly on his years in the army and be pleased accept honors from veterans' associations.

While in the service, Lee bought his first car, a used 1936 Plymouth, and eventually traded that in for a secondhand, jet-black Buick convertible with red leather seats and whitewall tires. He credited the glamorous

64

car for his having a steady dating life.[30]

Jim Mooney recalled an experience he and Lee shared when Lee was in the army:

We worked together when he was stationed in Duke University, North Carolina. I came down there to work with him on a Terrytoons [comic book] project. We were on a tight deadline, so Stan found a place for me to work in a pathology lab. I was surrounded by jars of pickled eyeballs and various body parts. The incentive was for getting out of there fast. That speeded me up tremendously.[31]

Discharged on September 29, 1945, Lee returned to work at Timely, which had grown — and had moved to offices on the fourteenth floor of the Empire State Building. The operation now included two artists' rooms, one for superhero and other adventure material ("illustrators"), and the other for humor and teen comics ("animators").[32] As well as pencilers and inkers, Lee also amassed a staff of editors working under him, including Al Jaffee and Leon Lazarus.

Meanwhile, he was writing numerous stories, largely humorous ones. Inspired by the success of the movie *My Friend Irma,* about a quirky young woman, the comics Lee was writing included *Millie the Model, Tessie the Typist,* and, eventually, a licensed, ongoing

65

adaptation of *My Friend Irma* itself. (He and artist Dan DeCarlo would eventually take over the *Irma* newspaper strip in its last days.) Aiming many of its comics at a female audience, Timely experimented with superheroines, including Venus and the Blonde Phantom. But the superhero era was drawing to a close, and neither lasted long.

It was in 1946 that Lee first met and became close friends with artist Ken Bald, who would go on to significant careers in comic strips and advertising. As Bald recalled:

I met Stan Lee. He and I hit it off right away and we became friends. . . . He was referred to as "the boy wonder" when I met him. He was a nice-looking, tall, thin man. Stan was impressed by my having been a marine. We double-dated almost immediately. He gave me all the work I wanted, and we've been friends ever since. . . . Stan was always a workaholic. We always had fun together.[33]

Bald recalled an especially amusing incident:

We'd get together at Longchamps [a Manhattan restaurant] for lunch once a week. One time, coming back from lunch, a bird flew overhead and *pfft!* right on Stan's shoulder. Stan shook his fist in the air and

66

yelled at the bird, "For the Gentiles, you sing!" I couldn't stop laughing. That was Stan: always finding humor in things.[34]

While his family was living on West 170th Street in Washington Heights, Lee, twenty-two years old, soon moved into a room at the Alamac Hotel on Broadway and Seventy-first Street in Manhattan. He seemed to be living a carefree, bachelor life, although one dating experience turned out somewhat differently than he'd expected. An extremely attractive woman surprisingly asked him up to her room in the hotel after he'd just met her.

We hit it off great together and became good friends. The reason I know we hit it off so well is because she didn't ask me for any payment. It turned out she was a very high-priced lady who was, to put it as gallantly as possible, in business for herself.[35]

According to Lee, they remained together "for many months." Hopefully, the VD-prevention lessons he taught in the army stuck with him.

Dating regularly, Lee nonetheless felt ready to settle down. In December 1946, he went to a holiday party thrown by his cousin Morton Feldman at Feldman's hat company. Cousin Morty invited him to come to the

67

soirée to meet a "gorgeous redhead" model named Betty.[36]

It was hat model Joan Clayton Boocock, though, who answered the door. Lee was smitten on the spot and decided she was the woman he'd been looking for all his life. They started dating, and she soon eagerly agreed to marry him. There was only one problem: Joan was already married. She was a war bride, having married an American serviceman, Sanford Dorf Weiss, who had been stationed in England.[37]

But as *People* magazine reported in 1979:

"I had only known him [my first husband] 24 hours when we decided to get married," [Joan] said. "In many aspects it was a great marriage, but after living with him a year, I was finding him sort of boring."[38]

However, she found Lee thrilling. "He wore a marvelous floppy hat and scarf and spouted Omar Khayyam when he took me for a hamburger at Prexy's," she said. "He reminded me of that beautiful man, [British actor] Leslie Howard."[39]

Joan headed to Reno, as she had already been planning, where she needed to spend six weeks to have a quickie divorce take effect. But Lee received a letter from her while she was away that began, "Dear Jack," and figured he'd better get there as soon as pos-

68

sible to make sure nothing went wrong, which he did.

Luckily, whoever Jack was, Joan's relationship with him wasn't serious. As soon as the divorce was finalized, Lee insisted the same judge who granted it immediately marry the two of them. The judge did just that, and on December 5, 1947, Stan and Joan were married.[40]

(Surrealistically, a 1952 Goodman-published comic called *My Own Romance,* issue #24, would feature a story called "Two Men Love Joan." The art was by Al Hartley. Comics historian Michael Vassallo believes the script was written either by Stan or Joan. The story satirized their courtship and marriage and was certainly an odd mash-up of life and art.)[41]

Soon after the Reno marriage, Stan and Joan, according to Larry Lieber, were also married (possibly by a rabbi) in the Lieber living room.[42] The couple moved into a top-floor apartment with a skylight window in a quaint brownstone at 15 East Ninety-fourth Street in Manhattan.

But Stan and Larry's mother, Celia, had been battling stomach cancer and passed away less than two weeks later, on December 16, 1947.

Lee recalled of the period:

When my mother died . . . we found it

69

necessary to move to a house. The reason was Larry, my then fifteen-year-old brother, who had been living with my mother, but now had to move in with us.[43]

Larry didn't ascribe Stan and Joan's moving to 1048 Broadway in Woodmere as having anything to do with him, simply that the trend for young couples of the day was to move to the suburbs, and that's what his brother and sister-in-law did.[44] Larry, who would have actually been sixteen at the time, not fifteen, and who'd been sent to live with Rob Solomon and his wife — Martin Goodman's sister, Sylvia — so as to be spared having to witness his mother's progressive decline, recalled:

I didn't like school, particularly, so I wanted to get out. So during the summer, I took some [courses] at home [and] I graduated [George Washington] high school at sixteen-and-a-half [in June 1948]. I lived with my Aunt Mitzi and Uncle Arthur Jeffries in the Bronx [until I graduated]. . . . After I graduated, I went out to stay with Stan and Joan. . . . I lived there . . . a year-and-a-half.[45]

It's unknown exactly why, after Celia's death, Larry didn't live with his father. Larry has guessed: "He did not ask me to live with

70

him because I think he knew we wouldn't get along so easily. . . . He did not ask me to live with him, and nobody else in the family even suggested that I should."[46]

Always spoken of as a difficult person, it's likely that Jack Lieber was not up to the challenge of being a single parent. He would never remarry. While Stan rarely spoke in any detail of their mother's death, for Larry, then still a teenager, losing her was deeply traumatic.[47]

Larry's relationship with Stan was always complicated and only became more so once his brother had married Joan. While praising Stan as being, in general, a good boss when they worked together on comics projects, certainly as they got older, Larry carries the memory of numerous psychological and emotional hurts inflicted on him over the decades by the Goodmans as well as by his brother and sister-in-law. Whether these were intentional or accidental, Larry's treatment by his family can at the least be seen as at times insensitive, especially knowing how deeply he tended to experience things.

For one example, Larry recalled how, in the period after he graduated high school, he was doing inking for Stan on humor titles at Timely, making good money, especially for a teenager. He recalled that "evidently, it [the inking] was okay. He used it. He never

71

complained about the quality of it." Lieber continued:

I was happy. I made actually $110 or $120 a week, so it took some of the misery out of my mother's death. . . . Now, after a while . . . Stan said, "I'm taking the inking away from you. . . . If you become an inker, you'll never be a penciler."[48]

Lee's intentions might have been good, wanting his brother to realize his ambition of becoming a comics penciler. But he didn't substitute penciling work, or anything else, for the inking he had taken away. Larry was left to scramble for work, ending up, for a time, doing pasteups in Magazine Management's production department. He recalled Stan's removal of the work as the reason he moved out of Stan and Joan's Woodmere house and moved into a room in the Manhattan Towers hotel on Broadway and Seventh-sixth Street.[49]

By the same token, some years later, after Larry had returned after serving four years in the air force during and after the Korean War, including significant time in Okinawa, Stan, believing that his brother had the potential to write professionally ("I've read your letters when you were in the service"), taught Larry to write comics and even went typewriter shopping with him. And in the '70s, when

72

Larry was writing and penciling *The Hulk* syndicated strip, Stan read some of it and complimented his brother. "Well, this is good," Larry recalled him saying. "Alas, I think it's more dramatic than *Spider-Man* [the syndicated strip Lee was writing]."[50]

According to Michael Vassallo's research, Lee did no substantial writing of comics stories between 1945 and 1947. He was, in this period, of course, running a line of comics, as well as supervising subeditors, including Al Jaffee and Al Sulman.

In addition, Lee was stretching his professional muscles, dipping his toe into the world of self-publishing. Under the name Famous Enterprises Inc., he released a hundred-page book called *Secrets Behind the Comics*. In it, he described himself as "the Managing Editor and Art Director of Timely Comics," and, speaking of himself in the third person, added, "He has been in complete charge of more comic magazines than any other living editor." After listing some of his editing credits, the book went on to say, "So, you see, Stan Lee knows what he's writing about, and you know that what Stan Lee writes is TRUE!"

The book did indeed give useful tips on how to write, draw, and submit comics and showed a not inaccurate — though simplified — look at life behind the scenes at a large

73

comics publisher. It was illustrated by Lee's colleagues, mostly Ken Bald, but also Dave Berg (later a *Mad* magazine regular) and Morris Weiss. The book also contained the offer that, for one dollar, Lee would critique your comic book drawing. There was no expiration date on the offer, and so for decades after, fans would occasionally send him their samples and a buck. An artist named Russ Maheras sent him, in 1972, *two* dollars, to account for inflation. Lee, by then busy with innumerable executive duties, nonetheless sent him back a critique.[51]

A troubling aspect of *Secrets,* though, was its comics-format retelling of how Captain America came to be. This version sourced the idea for the character back to patriotic Timely publisher Martin Goodman, who then took it to some unnamed creators to execute, the names Joe Simon and Jack Kirby nowhere to be found. Although *Secrets* was self-published by Lee, it clearly seems that he was, in it, involved in either rewriting history at Goodman's request and/or just plain sucking up to his boss. Of course, with Simon and Kirby long gone from Timely, it would have been surprising if they *had* been included in the book. But bringing up Captain America's origin seems to have been a strange editorial choice to have made in the first place.

74

■ ■ ■ ■

Between his new marriage and his numerous projects in and out of the office, Lee certainly seemed to be enjoying himself. As Raphael and Spurgeon noted, when Lee resumed writing comics stories:

For a brief period, Stan had three secretaries seated in plain view of the entire office, to whom he dictated stories simultaneously. "I was kind of cocky, and I think I enjoyed doing it," Lee recalls. "But then I said to myself, 'What the hell are you doing? You're a show-off. If I was someone else, I'd hate a guy like you.' So I stopped."[52]

The same year that he published *Secrets,* 1947, Lee was seen looking very much the successful young writer and editor posing with prop-pipe for the cover of *Writer's Digest*'s November issue. The issue contained his article, "There's Money in Comics," which would capture the attention of media critic and philosopher Marshall McLuhan, who would write about it in somewhat condescending tones in his 1951 book, *The Mechanical Bride.*

By mid-1948, Lee was again writing a full slate of comics, mostly in the crime, romance, Western, and humor genres. Also that year, Lee crossed over a fair amount into Good-

75

man's magazine line, becoming editorial director of the quarterly *Film Album* magazine, which featured stills from popular movies. He would also edit, in the '50s, Goodman's *Focus* magazine, which featured such articles as "Murder at a Nudist Camp!" and "The Nazis Still Run Germany."

In that era, as newlyweds without any children, Stan and Joan spent time with good friends, including the Balds and the Mooneys, and apparently also spent much time socializing with the Goodman family. As Raphael and Spurgeon noted:

Martin Goodman's eldest son, Iden, who recalls the Lees' time on Long Island in idyllic fashion, was a constant visitor from the Goodman home two miles away. "I remember it as a very warm, happy place," he says, and the Lees were "very generous, welcoming." Iden learned to drive a car in the Lees' driveway.[53]

Larry Lieber recalled that the Lees spent a lot of time socializing with the Goodmans, Stan and Joan very concerned about Jean and Martin's opinions of them.[54]

As far as nonrelatives the Lees were friendly with, Lee and Ken Bald would remain close friends for the remainder of Stan's life, their families often getting together. As Lee said:

76

Ken Bald was actually my best friend. He and his wife used to double-date with Joan and me, and we were all over the city. We went to the clubs whenever we had time. They were a wonderful couple. His wife had been an actress. I hated Ken because he was so handsome. I didn't need to be out with anybody that handsome. Do you remember Tyrone Power? He looked like Tyrone Power. . . .

[Ken] was great. He could draw anything. He was a marine captain or sergeant during World War II, [fought at] Iwo Jima. I mean, he was a real guy, and his wife was wonderful, and Joan and I just enjoyed being with him.[55]

Bald's daughter Victoria Dollon recalled about Stan and Joan:

Stan was the most charming man I have ever met in my life. No one could dislike him. He and his wife, who was equally as charming, were so entertaining, always telling stories about their real-life events and putting an incredibly comic twist on them. Stan was also rather physical in his humor, often acting out all the pieces of the tale for greater effect. . . . they were both incredibly glamorous and loving people. Joan was particularly captivating. . . .

My parents were also extremely glamor-

77

ous people, so it was quite the show when the four of them got together. They were so beautiful and enchanting. I just remember lots of laughter. . . . Stan adored kids and loved entertaining us. Of course, we adored him back.

I believe I was ten or eleven at the time, a very awkward age. Stan and Joan rolled into our driveway in the most gorgeous Silver Cloud Rolls-Royce. It was unforgettably beautiful. . . . Joan then had a brilliant idea; let's all ride around town in it. So my mom, dad, younger sister, and I all crammed in.

Our town was a very run-of-the-mill suburban town, so a Rolls-Royce cruising the streets was a very big deal. We had a blast, waving out the windows with Stan tooting the horn. My favorite part was when Joan devilishly suggested that we drive by the homes of stuck-up kids in our classes and stick out our tongues! It was so much fun showing off!

With Stan, what you saw was what you got. Stan was the same man in public and private — fun-loving, charming, energetic, entertaining, and special. He was very genuine.

Stan always claimed that he was very clumsy, which my father loved to attest to. I remember a particularly funny story Stan told about tripping while walking on the

78

sidewalks of New York. He did a complete somersault, but ended up landing on his feet. According to Stan, bystanders began to clap, so he responded with bows and thanks, claiming, "I meant to do that!" Of course, he acted this out for us, so it was doubly funny![56]

Another close friend, Jim Mooney, recalled of the Lees:

We'd go out to lunch together [when we were single] . . . later on, [in] the early '70s, my wife [Carol] had an antiques business, and I worked in the business, and Stan's wife, Joan, had the same thing in Long Island, so we used to get together and exchange views on what to buy, and what not to buy — this was a bore to Stan.[57]

And Lee said of Mooney and his wife:

Jim was one of my best friends. He was just a wonderful guy . . . and Jim had this gorgeous wife, Carol, and . . . he loved antiques. He and my wife would go antiquing. . . . I'm not the least interested in an old, antique doorknob. But they would go to these antique shows up by Woodstock after it had rained, and everything was wet and damp, and you walked in puddles, and it was horrible. And he and Joan would be, "Look at this, look at that! I found a hinge

79

from an old house!" And I'm standing there, soaking wet, thinking that I'll kill the son of a bitch if he doesn't come home.[58]

Artist Gene Colan, later known for *Daredevil* and other major series, started working with Lee in the late '40s. Colan recalled of Lee that

the very first time I ever met him . . . he had on his head a beanie cap with a propeller on the top, and the window was open. That thing would spin around. I couldn't believe it. I always got along well with him. . . . Stan was wonderful to work with. He did a lot of kidding around. . . . Very funny. He always reminded me of Jack Lemmon. . . .
He's one of the nicest people I've ever known in the business. He was not a complainer, and he wouldn't put you down. Other editors I could not say that about.[59]

Another notable figure who worked for Lee in the late '40s was Harvey Kurtzman, who would go on to create *Mad* magazine in the 1950s. Kurtzman did short humor pieces for Lee — especially, eventually, 150 "Hey Look!" one-pagers that showed off his quirky comic sensibility. Lee's secretary, Adele Hasan — who was dating and, in 1946, would marry Kurtzman — rigged a Timely reader popularity write-in poll that year for

80

favorite humor feature so that "Hey Look!" won, getting Lee to give Kurtzman more work.[60]

Apparently, this gaming of the vote by Adele didn't generate ill feelings in Lee, assuming he eventually found out about it, since he and Kurtzman remained friends until Kurtzman's 1993 death. Kurtzman actually did a savage parody of Goodman and his magazine company in a story called "The Organization Man in the Grey Flannel Executive Suite" in his 1959 *Jungle Book*, but Lee wasn't targeted in the satire.

By 1949, things seemed to be going about as well as could be imagined for Stan Lee. He was earning a good combined staff and freelance income. He was working with interesting, creative people on a booming line of comics and was even doing some work on Goodman's magazines. And he was engaged in side projects like *Secrets Behind the Comics*. In addition, he and Joan had moved to suburban Woodmere, a place perfect for a young couple that might be contemplating doing their part to contribute to the ongoing baby boom.

Sure, anti-comics fanatics, in particular psychiatrist Fredric Wertham, weren't pleased with how well Timely and other comics publishers were doing. But they didn't pose any kind of real threat. Besides, the publish-

81

ers had formed the Association of Comics Magazine Publishers (ACMP) in July 1948 to protect the industry from just such misguided do-gooders. Timely even had its own advisor-psychiatrist to counter whatever the Werthams of the world might come up with.

The bottom line was the bottom line: Timely's sales were high, largely thanks to Stan Lee and his talented writers, artists, and editors. Their positions seemed to be the very definition of secure.

Which is why it was so shocking when Martin Goodman told Stan Lee to fire everybody.

4
THE PSYCHOPATHOLOGY OF COMIC BOOKS

We're businessmen who can't be expected to protect maladjusted children who might be affected by cops-and-robbers stories.
— Stanley Lieber,
The New York Herald Tribune, May 9, 1948

Like Stanley Lieber, Judith Klein was born in 1922, she in the Bronx.

In that same year, Friedrich Ignatz Wertheimer came to the United States from Austria to complete his training in psychiatry at Johns Hopkins University.

By 1948 — as Stan Lee, Judith Crist, and Fredric Wertham — their lives would for a time be fatefully intertwined by circumstances related to Goodman's startling directive.

Why would Martin Goodman order Stan Lee to fire his staff of artists when business was booming?

One explanation that has come down through history is largely economic.

83

To make sure the company had enough material for so many comics — in the neighborhood of seventy titles per month — and because he didn't like to say no to anybody in need of work — Lee had amassed an enormous quantity of inventoried stories, stories that could be slotted in when and where needed. Supposedly, when Goodman one day discovered all these pages in a closet — one would think he would have noticed the buildup before that — he was so infuriated he decided to fire everybody and burn off the excess.

On examination, this makes little sense. Cutting back on staff, perhaps, or ramping up the number of titles temporarily to use the accumulated art would have made more sense if excess inventory were such a problem. (After all, much of the excess had been generated by artists in the course of their day jobs, not just by freelance work executed by moonlighting staffers and others.) But what if a new fad that they needed to jump on came along, which seemed inevitable to happen sooner rather than later? Then they'd be stuck.

Another, more plausible explanation was that someone in Goodman's company — possibly comptroller Monroe Froehlich Jr. — discovered that new tax regulations made it a better business move to convert the artists to freelance status (as most of the writers

84

already were) and have them work from home. At the very least, it would save on renting space for staff artists, not to mention on whatever benefits they might have been getting. It would also make the company, in some ways, able to respond more nimbly to changing market conditions, using only those artists appropriate to a given trend.

Raphael and Spurgeon noted, "Most of the staffers were let go in a series of fits and starts beginning around Christmas of 1949," and that "Lee was able to offer a sizeable amount of freelance work to former members of the bullpen by the end of 1950 and into 1951."[1]

It was concern over those changing market conditions that led Goodman to leave his distributor, Kable News, and start his own distribution company for his comic books and magazines.[2] As Raphael and Spurgeon observed, "By starting Atlas News Company [distributors], which was anchored in part by the eighty-two monthly titles that Stan Lee and the boys were producing in the comic-book division, Goodman could increase profits by eliminating the middleman. He could also respond much more rapidly to evolving trends and sales figures."[3]

There was a major factor in the "evolving trends" above and beyond the usual issue of readers' tastes. It was the ongoing attack on comics, which had continued from the 1940 Sterling North editorial (and before him was

85

conducted by others attacking comics, starting with the earliest syndicated comic strips) and carried on, starting in the late '40s, by psychiatrist Fredric Wertham, who was the most vocal and visible of a growing number of comic book critics.

Goodman, Froehlich, and Stan Lee realized that the movement against comics had impacted public perception of their industry, and they needed to be nimble and adaptable to survive whatever impact that movement would have on them. Anti-comics legislation had been introduced in dozens of localities, and there were even comic book burnings around the country, including in Binghamton, New York, just a few hours' drive from the Manhattan offices of the majority of comic book publishers.

Numerous comics companies had gone out of business or soon would. Goodman's structural adjustments meant that he wasn't just surviving. With fewer companies producing comics for the still sizeable audience, his comics line was *thriving.* People were still buying millions of comics of all kinds — although, notably, they weren't buying nearly as many superhero comics as they used to.

A few years earlier, with the end of World War II, the superhero fad had waned, but comic books were as popular as ever, if not more so. The medium was growing in diversity, with all manner of genres represented. Of course, there would always be more and less popular genres over time, and in the late 1940s and early 1950s, there were four genres that were more popular than others.

There was the romance genre, newly invented by Simon and Kirby for Crestwood Publications but soon adopted by the rest of the industry. There was crime, exemplified by titles like *Justice Traps the GUILTY!* and *CRIME Does Not Pay.* There was the horror genre, intent on giving intentionally shocking thrills to readers. War comics were quite popular, too, especially during the Korean War.

Publisher William M. Gaines's EC Comics line was known for its publications' high quality of scripts and art. Lee studied EC's comics, especially when Goodman encouraged him to imitate what was working for that company. And, as Raphael and Spurgeon noted, Lee was fascinated by the way EC "was able to create an identity for the entire line despite the fact that EC, like Atlas, always worked in multiple genres."[4]

However, what EC, as well as some other publishers, did was push the boundaries of acceptable content with their crime and horror stories. One extreme, now classic, example was the EC story "Foul Play" in *Haunt of Fear* #19 (dated June 1953), which depicted a baseball game that employed a hated charac-

87

ter's body parts — his head as the ball and his intestines as base lines. Many crime comics emphasized brutal violence and often featured highly sexualized femmes fatales. Stories like these were noticed and seized on by comics critics and became the subject of much negative media scrutiny.

Goodman's Timely/Atlas (the company has come to be known by both names, although Atlas was technically only the name of the distribution arm) was the most prolific — and highest quality — of the EC imitators. This was in part due to the ongoing closing of comics companies that made more top artists available to Goodman and Lee. While their crime and horror comics were rarely as extreme as those of EC and some others, they played in the same general arena.

In municipalities all over the country, attempts were being made to ban or regulate comics, especially crime and horror comics. While Lee made sure his comics weren't as intense in their depictions of violence and gore as some of the other publishers', they could still get fairly extreme, at least in the eyes of comics' critics. Most prominent among the critics was psychiatrist Fredric Wertham.

Wertham was active in a variety of causes, and in 1954, his research was used as evidence of the negative effects of segregation and in favor of school integration in the

88

landmark *Brown v. Board of Education* case. He also ran a low-cost psychiatric clinic in Harlem.

Working largely with poor, African American children in the Harlem clinic, Wertham had become convinced that the problems many of them faced were, if not caused, then exacerbated by violence and misogyny as portrayed in popular culture, especially in comic books.

As opposed to some other opponents of comics who came at them from a religious and/or socially conservative point of view, Wertham was a liberal progressive who believed that comics, as a "secret" subculture that kids could access for dimes, could do damage to impressionable young people that parents wouldn't even be aware of. While Wertham seemed sincere in his concerns, he needed publicity to get his word out, and he did not shy from seeking it. He became a very public intellectual, publishing articles about his concerns regarding comics in many mainstream magazines. His ideas found an eager reception among adults concerned about a perceived rise — in numbers as well as the level of brutality — in youth crime, also known as "juvenile delinquency."

(In recent years, comics historian Carol Tilley has discovered what many suspected: that Wertham often faked and fudged his data to conform to his desired results.)[5]

■ ■ ■ ■

Interestingly, Wertham would, time and again, have his anti-comics activities covered by a young reporter, a woman who, at least once, had interviewed Stan Lee.

Judith Klein, daughter of a once-prosperous New York fur trader who'd lost everything when his business tanked in the Depression, had attended Morris High School in the Bronx and Hunter College in Manhattan. She then earned a master's degree from Columbia University's journalism school. In 1945, she went to work for *The New York Herald Tribune* as a general assignment reporter. In 1947, she married public relations man William Crist and took his surname. As Judith Crist, she would, of course, go on to be one of the most well-known film critics of all time. But in 1947, as a young reporter, she was assigned to cover Fredric Wertham. As she recalled in 2008:

I was a reporter [on the *Herald Tribune*'s] Social Significance Page . . . and the editor of that page was Dorothy Dunbar Bromley, who was a prominent woman columnist in her day . . . and she apparently read or heard something about Wertham. So she sent me down to interview him at his apartment. . . . I remember his making a great case [against comics] . . . and so I wrote an

90

interview. . . .

He did some work that I admired. . . . I had one of his books. The most memorable of his pieces is something called "Medea in Long Island" or something like that . . . about a woman who had killed her children on Long Island somewhere. He paralleled it with the Medea complex, and so on. It was a fascinating and truly unforgettable piece about a modern Medea.[6] [The piece was called "The People vs. Medea," and it originally appeared in *Harper's Bazaar*'s January 1948 issue.][7]

Another fan of Wertham's writings about insane murderers was Stan Lee. As he recalled:

When I was a kid, about thirteen years old, I had read a book [*Dark Legend*] written by a psychiatrist . . . and I thought it was a wonderfully written book. Really, it touched on some important issues. . . . Years later, I found out it was the same Dr. Wertham [as the one attacking comics] who had written that book. I don't know what made him go crazy years later.[8]

Dark Legend was published in 1941, so Lee was already eighteen and working at Timely when it came out, but the fact remains that he recalled the book more than seven decades

91

after it was published.
Judith Crist went on to recall:

[Wertham] was a very impressive man. He was also very charming. . . . We kind of kept in touch vaguely. . . . I believe he sent me a copy of his collected essays or something. . . . I think that he was a thorough-going egotist. He didn't see very far beyond his own principles. Not a man that I worshipped in any way, but he did stick in my memory.[9]

Apparently, Crist was indeed impressed and charmed by him, even if she didn't worship him. In any case, for whatever reasons — perhaps just being a young reporter whose instincts told her to stick with a story — she wrote numerous stories for the *Herald Tribune* about Wertham and his anti-comics activities.

For the December 28, 1947 (Lee's twenty-fifth birthday), *Herald Tribune,* Crist wrote a Wertham-centric article with the headline comic books are called obscene by n.y. psychiatrist at hearing. The subhead read: "Dr. Wertham Says They Present 'a Glorification of Sadistic-Masochistic Sexual Attitudes'; He Defends Nudist Society's Magazine."

In the article, Wertham, testifying on behalf of the publishers of nudist magazine *Natural Herald* at a Washington, D.C. Post Office

92

Department obscenity hearing, declared that the magazine was far from obscene. The article continued with a tortured leap of logic:

But if obscenity, the psychiatrist declared, is to be gauged by its lewdness or its effect in stimulating the average person sexually, then, he suggested, it was time for official cognizance be given to comic books. These he termed "definitely harmful — guilty of instilling the wrong attitudes about sex and violence."

Crist also covered, for the *Herald Tribune,* the Psychopathology of Comic Books symposium conducted by Wertham at New York University on March 19, 1948. At it, speakers besides Wertham included cultural critics Gershon Legman and Wertham's research partner, Hilde Mosse. In the audience — but not given a chance to speak — were members of the comics industry, including cartoonist Harvey Kurtzman, who was at the time doing short humor pieces for Lee at Timely. Wertham likened their presence there to "distillers attending a symposium on alcoholism."[10]

Perhaps Crist's best-known article about comics — and Wertham — was published in the March 27, 1948, issue of *Collier's* magazine. The piece was titled "Horror in the

93

Nursery." ("I was a little surprised at the headline," she reflected in 2008, indicating that it was more lurid than she had wanted.)[11] In it, she gave Wertham a forum in a popular national magazine, even as the photos depicted child actors "torturing" each other based on actions allegedly seen in comic books. In the piece, Wertham — through Crist — made a number of points. For just a few examples, he said:

> The comic books, in intent and effect, are demoralizing the morals of youth. They make violence alluring and cruelly heroic. . . . If those responsible refuse to clean up the comic-book market . . . the time has come to legislate these books off the newsstands and out of the candystores.[12]

While Wertham generally did not advocate censorship of comics for adults, he certainly wished they didn't exist and that their sale to children under age fifteen be regulated. Of psychiatrists who defended comics, he said:

> The fact that child psychiatrists endorse comic books does not prove the healthy state of the comic books. It only proves the unhealthy state of child psychiatry.[13]

In a May 9, 1948, *Herald Tribune* article

94

entitled controversy over "crime" comic books grows, Crist covered local government attempts to regulate comics in Detroit, Indianapolis, and other cities. In the piece, she noted that:

> Most of the editors [I spoke to] emphasized their personal integrity, as did Stanley Lieber, editor of five of the banned [crime comic] books.

Stan Lee, apparently going by his real (and still legal) name for his interview with Crist, told her:

> We're not selling books on the basis of bosoms and blood. We're businessmen who can't be expected to protect maladjusted children who might be affected by cops-and-robbers stories. We feel we use stringent self-censorship.

This didn't sound like the affable, propeller-beanie-wearing Stan Lee that his colleagues had come to know. Perhaps Lee/Lieber hadn't yet learned how to charm reporters. Or perhaps his most venal-sounding statement made for the most attention-grabbing quote for an article about the pernicious influence of comic books.

By October 1948, fifty cities had enacted

measures to ban or censor comic books.[14] Like other companies, Timely hired an expert to counter the onslaught of negative attention. In this case, it was Dr. Jean Thompson, "a psychiatrist in the Child Guidance Bureau of the New York City Board of Education," as the editorial in the November and December 1948 cover-dated issues of Timely's comics declared. (This piece, and three subsequent editorials, referred to the company as Marvel Comic Group, a name it sometimes used over the years before making it permanent in the '60s.)

The editorials were all signed, "The Editors, Marvel Comic Group." Historian Michael Vassallo believes that they were written by editor Stan Lee "most certainly under the direction of publisher Martin Goodman."[15] It does seem likely that such important communication with readers would be produced by the company's editorial boss.

The first editorial, written in a friendly but serious manner, stated that:

We want to help you protect your right to buy and read your favorite magazines, as long as they contain nothing that might be hurtful to you.

It went on to say that Dr. Thompson "will insure the fact that our comics contain nothing that might meet with objections from

96

your parents, teachers or friends."

The second editorial, in the January through March 1949 cover-dated comics, is less casual and more specific. Referencing an article by Wertham in *The Saturday Review of Literature,* the editorial declared that

a Dr. Wertham discussed the problem of juvenile delinquency in America today, and pinned the blame for some of the cases on comic magazines. . . .

Now the enemies of comics were distilled into one person: Dr. Wertham.

After quoting an eloquent response to Wertham in a later issue of *Saturday Review* by fourteen-year-old David Pace Wigransky ("In none of these cases was it proved that reading comic books was the cause of the delinquency"), Lee went on to ask

why not give the comics credit for the good influence that they have been on these millions of healthy, normal kids, instead of just blaming them for our handful of delinquents?

By the third editorial, in his comics cover-dated April and May 1949, Lee tried another tack entirely — doing his best to establish comics as a natural step in the evolution of great literature:

97

Let these critics of today look to their history. Let them decide if they want to be remembered as the 20th Century counterpart of the people who called *Robinson Crusoe* "slop."

The anger beneath the editorial's words is palpable. Lee was asking Wertham, Legman, and other comics-negative academics and intellectuals to consider how history would judge them. This was pretty audacious for a twenty-six-year-old whose most advanced credential was a diploma from a New York public high school.

The fourth, and final, editorial, in the Marvel/Timely comics cover-dated June and July 1949, framed the company's argument in a passionate, yet wistful, manner, with the writer seeming to almost sigh as he lamented:

The grown-ups of this world owe you young people an apology, because we haven't made the world a very secure and peaceful place in which to live. . . .

He then went on to reflect that, at least in the comics, the good guys always win. He then pointed out that:

Just as there are good and bad people, good and bad radio programs, good and bad movies, so there is good and bad literature . . . comics, with their many pictures, are just one type of literature.

Comics, the editorial continued, are "a stepping-stone to your appreciation of books that have stood the test of time."

Here, Lee has tossed in the proverbial kitchen sink, telling readers that the world might be an ugly place, but at least in comics, as opposed to real life, the good guys always win; that some comics are "good" — although he conflates "good" as meaning enjoyable with good as meaning "beneficial" — and that comics are just part of "our vast literary heritage" and not the only thing you should read.

You can't accuse the guy of not trying.

While it's hard to know the actual effect of the editorials, they were at least, it could be argued, one factor in the company's staying in business over the next eight years, while numerous competitors would shutter their doors.

Interestingly, the voice in the editorials is familiar as the editorial voice that Lee had been developing since his first published work — the prose story in *Captain America Comics* #3 — and that would fully blossom as the voice of Marvel and of Stan Lee in the '60s in Marvel's letters pages and Bullpen Bulletins.

99

■ ■ ■ ■

As Wertham's fight against comics was gaining momentum, life went on for Stan Lee, his family, and his company.

Lee was still overseeing dozens of comics a month and writing several comics stories each week. Even, or especially, after the layoffs of 1949, there was still much work to be done. Now, though, with a few exceptions, Lee dealt with the artists as freelancers. New names that would become familiar to comics readers in the coming years started showing up in the comics. While there were some veterans of the '30s and '40s doing work — notably Carl Burgos and Bill Everett — there were also numerous artists working for the company who were too young to have been involved in the first years of the superhero craze, who were kids or teens reading those stories, and who were eager to get into the field. To even the most enthusiastic, though, comics were still a way to earn some quick money, an avenue to be used as a stepping-stone to careers in illustration or advertising.

Nonetheless, this was the era when the work of such artists as John Romita, Joe Maneely, Gene Colan, Dick Ayers, and Joe Sinnott started appearing in the books. Even Jerry Robinson — famous for his work on Batman in the '40s — came to work for

100

Timely from 1950 to 1960. Of working for Lee, he recalled:

> I guess he must have known my work from Batman or elsewhere, because he said, "Gee, I'd love to work with you". . . . . He enticed me back to comic books, since I wasn't interested in doing them at the time. . . . We had a very nice relationship for those [ten] years. And he was a very easy editor. I guess he had confidence in what I would do, so I didn't have to check anything with him.[16]

Somewhere in the period when Robinson worked for Lee, he would introduce the editor to a student of his at the Cartoonists and Illustrators School (soon to be called the School of Visual Arts), Steve Ditko.

Over that period of about six months, from 1949 into 1950, Stan Lee went about letting his staff artists go, although he would soon start rehiring them, but on a freelance basis. Even dependable creators who doubled as editors were let go. Lee regarded many of them as friends, people whose families he knew and cared about. He recalled the layoff period as "black days for me."[17] For instance, Al Jaffee went from editing teen comics to writing and drawing them.

But Timely, in fact, was actually thriving —

101

although always in the shadow of impending doom. Smaller companies were going out of business, but Goodman's self-distribution enabled him to pick up the pieces from the other publishers who were leaving the field or severely downsizing. (Goodman also cut freelancer rates as part of a strategy for survival.) Stan Lee was overseeing more than seventy comic book titles.[18]

The list of artists who worked for Lee in the period between 1950 and 1957 is an incredible who's who of people who were or would become legendary comic book creators, including John Romita, Gene Colan, Stan Goldberg, Joe Sinnott, Jerry Robinson, Bernard Krigstein, Al Feldstein, Al Jaffee, and so many more. Some of their memories give insight into the times and Lee's role in them.

Goldberg, the head staff colorist, socialized with the Lees. But even then, Lee was looking to expand his horizons. According to Goldberg:

Even when we would go visit his and Joan's house . . . he would say, "Come on upstairs!" That's where he worked. "Let's go over some ideas that I have." These were ideas that we would try to submit for syndication. . . . One was a single-panel gag strip . . . we called it "Doc." It was about a friendly little doctor. . . . [It didn't sell to a syndicate, but] We were able to get rid of about 75% of the Doc material to medical journals.[19]

Goldberg's wife, Pauline, recalled:

I can always remember SG saying he usually went to lunch with SL. SL would drag him all around town to pick up out of town papers to check the comics. . . . SG said that when he got back to the office, he was exhausted and his shins killed him [from the long walks Lee was famous for]. . . . SL was always very good to SG. He would always raise his salary without SG asking. Also, he would always critique his work, which SG really appreciated, and as a result, he felt his work really improved. SG was always very thankful for that. He always mentioned it. SG always felt he owed his career to SL.

I also remember going to their house for dinner in Hewlett Harbor on a snowy winter evening, and there was SL standing at a bar in their home wearing a blue blazer and white pants, looking dashing, I might add. He looked like he was on a ship [docked] on a Caribbean island. . . . [Stan and Joan] were very charismatic. They were a perfect pair.[20]

Artist Joe Sinnott, who started working for Lee in 1950, recalled:

103

Stan always liked to see things exaggerated. He would actually get up on his desk and show you a certain pose that he wanted. . . . He took his job seriously. . . . And I don't think you could find a better editor than Stan. [And] he wrote stories that were interesting . . . and they were easy to draw as far as [visually] telling the story.[21]

Artist Bernard Krigstein would go on to legendary status for his work at EC, notably on a story called "Master Race," written by Al Feldstein. Krigstein actually did more than seventy stories for Lee at Timely/Atlas between 1950 and 1957 — many more than he ever did for EC or any other publisher — and with generally more creative freedom than he'd gotten anywhere else.[22] Nonetheless, he was not among those who came away with good feelings about Lee. They parted over what could politely be called "creative differences."

An artist who enjoyed working with Lee and with whom Lee equally loved working, as well as enjoyed a personal rapport with, was Joe Maneely. Maneely could draw beautifully in just about any genre, including humor. He penciled and inked his own stories and was extraordinarily fast. He and Lee would even do a moderately successful syndicated strip together, *Mrs. Lyons' Cubs.*

John Romita joined Atlas in 1949 and,

104

between then and 1957, would draw over two hundred stories for Lee. Gene Colan would do a similar quantity over that period. Both men would go on to become mainstays of Marvel in the 1960s.

Carl Burgos, who had created the Human Torch in 1939, was on staff in the office, drawing plenty of stories but serving also as de facto cover editor. Many of Atlas's covers of the 1950s had a consistent look because, in that period, he touched up a large percentage of them — a process Vassallo, whose research shed light on Burgos's role in the office — calls "Burgosizing."

In April 1950, Joan Lee gave birth to a daughter, Joan Celia Lee, who would come to be nicknamed "JC" to differentiate her from her mother. Asked if becoming a father changed his outlook on life, Lee recalled, in 2017:

No, it didn't change anything as far as my outlook. The only thing it did, it gave me less time to write because I had to spend more time with my daughter.[23]

And Joan Lee said of her husband's adjustment to parenting:

When my daughter was born, [Stan] would always make time to take her to the carni-

105

vals and merry-go-rounds. No matter how hard he worked, he always had time for her and for me. He always found the time to spend with her [JC]. In fact, the three of us sometimes worry that we are too close. When we go off to the Great Unknown, she'll really miss us because she's insane about her father . . . and her mother.[24]

Later that year, in Goodman's *Focus* magazine's October 1950 issue, edited by Lee, an article appeared — credited to "Stanley Martin" — entitled "Don't Legalize Prostitution." The piece is interesting not just for the fact that it's a rare nonfiction piece written by Lee for a Magazine Management publication — and *Focus* was also one of the relatively few Goodman magazines he edited over the years — but also because it seems to make use of data on venereal disease that Lee most likely became familiar with when he was conducting his anti-VD campaign while in the army.

Whether the opinion voiced in the article was indeed Lee's at the time — that legalizing prostitution tended to increase, not decrease, incidence of venereal disease, so prostitution should stay illegal — he certainly made a data-strong case (along with a few unsubstantiated assertions) for the argument. While Lee had written fiction and humor material for Goodman's magazines over the

106

years, this was one of the few — perhaps only — nonfiction, research-based pieces he would ever write for them.

Larry Lieber, who'd been doing production work for Magazine Management, came back to the comics to do some work, first inking humor and teen titles, then penciling and inking at least one story — "Cop on the Beat" — in *All True Crime* #44, cover-dated May 1951. Lieber would soon join the U.S. Air Force, where he would serve, partly in Okinawa, until 1955.

It was in 1952 that Martin Goodman started doing his own distribution of his comics and magazines, under the name Atlas. (Timely's comics from this period are generally referred to as *Atlas Comics,* since the Atlas logo was the only consistent branding that appeared on the covers.) Perhaps he and company comptroller Froehlich were concerned that, with all the negative publicity comics were getting, distributors would not give them the attention they needed, and so he'd be better off distributing them himself (although this wouldn't explain why doing his own distribution on the non-comics magazines seemed preferable). In theory, Goodman would also now have been able to keep a larger percentage of the profits of the comics (as well as of the magazines), which would have been

107

especially important, as retailers — in light of the negative publicity comics were getting — were carrying fewer comics, or even none at all. In any case, the switch seemed to work, and Goodman's comics and magazines continued to thrive.

That same year, the Lees moved to a new home, "a remodeled carriage house on Richards Lane in Long Island's Hewlett Harbor . . . incorporated from a private club in the 1920s and home to what local historians describe as the island's most 'socially prominent and very wealthy families.' "[25] Stan and Joan's philosophy was to buy the oldest, most affordable home in an area's high-end neighborhood.[26] Like their previous home, this one was also not far from Martin Goodman's opulent estate.

In 1953, Joan Lee gave birth to another daughter, whom she and her husband named Jan. The infant died, however, when she was less than a week old. Joan reflected:

Our one big tragedy was when we lost a daughter. She only lived a few days after birth and we couldn't have any more children. Perhaps that is why Stan, our daughter and I have always been such a close-knit family. Aside from that one tragic event, I've been terribly, terribly blessed.[27]

Told by their doctor that Joan couldn't have

108

any more children, the couple tried to adopt, but Joan's fragile emotional state after losing baby Jan made agencies wary of letting them. The fact that Stan was Jewish and Joan Episcopalian also presented an issue to the agencies they applied to. For better or worse, they gave up trying to expand their family.[28]

In 1953, despite the general lack of interest in superheroes on the newsstands (of the major heroes, only Superman, Batman, and Wonder Woman were still appearing regularly), the *Superman* TV series was a big hit, which led Goodman and Lee to revive Timely's three top superheroes in several titles. John Romita — already, in his early twenties, establishing the style that would make him a superstar comics artist in the 1960s — drew Captain America stories for the revival. Carl Burgos, who had created the Human Torch, and newcomer Dick Ayers, worked on that character. Bill Everett returned to his creation, the Sub-Mariner. The revival would last less than a year, except in the case of the Sub-Mariner, who held on for another year, into 1955, with the prospect of a TV series adaptation of the character keeping the print version alive. The TV series would never happen, though.

While writing some superhero stories that year, Lee mostly confined his writing to humor and Westerns, as well as doing some

109

mystery, horror, and war stories.

In issue #29 of *Suspense,* dated April 1953, Lee and Maneely — in a thinly veiled attack on Wertham — did a story called "The Raving Maniac." In it, an overexcited, disheveled man barges into the office of the comic's editor to tell him off for printing scary stories. The editor is a dead ringer for Stan Lee. He angrily refutes the frantic complainer by showing him the day's newspaper, filled with terrifying headlines (NEW H BOMB MAY DESTROY THE EARTH) and tells him, "At least our readers know that our stories aren't true!! They can put our magazine down and forget about it! But you can scare yourself to death by reading a newspaper nowadays!" Further, he tells the agitated office-crasher that if he doesn't like the stories:

Don't read 'em! Nobody's shoving 'em down your throat!! That's one of the wonderful things about this great nation of ours . . . everybody is free to do what he wants to do, as long as it doesn't injure anybody else!

A moment later, attendants from an unspecified institution come to haul the "raving maniac" back there. The editor heads home at the end of his workday, where he is happy to see his wife (who looks exactly like Joan Lee) and young daughter. The story ends with the editor telling the child a bedtime

110

story that begins:

Once upon a time an excited little man, with nothing more important on his mind, ran into an editor's office to complain about some magazines . . .

Lee would edit, and write the stories for, the first eight issues of a new horror and fantasy series called *Menace,* which debuted with cover date March 1953. Perhaps wanting to show that he — and Atlas — could give EC a run for its money, the title seemed to have become a pet project for him. In the series, Lee's editorial voice came through, informally speaking to the readers at the beginning and end of many stories. The series would, as Lee's pet project, use his favorite artists, including Joe Maneely, Bill Everett, Russ Heath, Joe Sinnott, John Romita, Gene Colan, and George Tuska.

Menace #7 included another anti-anti-comics story, "The Witch in the Woods," by Lee and Joe Sinnott. It involves a concerned father who takes away his son's comic books and reads the kid a fairy tale instead. But the gruesome fairy tale proves too upsetting for the well-meaning father, who is unable to finish reading the story. The kid demands, "C'mon, Dad . . . tell me! What happened next?"

The terrified, sweating father replies, "I

111

can't! It's too awful! It's making me ill!"

And the son supplies the story's kicker:

Golly, Dad . . . you oughtta take up reading comics for a while . . . those fairy tales are *really* gruesome!

Also in 1953 and '54, Lee and Goodman, imitating EC's successful *Mad* — which was at first a color comic that largely spoofed other comic books and comic strips — put out three short-lived imitators: *Crazy, Wild,* and *Riot* comics. Comics historians are unable to determine if Lee wrote any of the stories in the comics, but he certainly, as editor, used some of his favorite artists, including John Severin, Joe Maneely, Russ Heath, Dan DeCarlo, and Al Hartley. The three humor series, however, all ended by mid-1954.

Around the same time, Fredric Wertham's crusade was gaining momentum, especially with the publication of his bestselling anticomics tome, *Seduction of the Innocent,* released in April 1954. Meanwhile, Senator Estes Kefauver took up the cudgel against juvenile delinquency and the possible comics connection to it. Hearings were held in Washington, D.C., even as *Seduction* was making big waves.

While comics publishers sent representatives to the hearings, at which Wertham

112

himself testified, the only publisher to personally testify was EC's William M. Gaines, whose April 21, 1954, testimony history has generally come to be regarded as a fiasco for himself, his company, and the industry. Gaines ended up having to defend an EC cover featuring a woman's severed head as being "in good taste."

As Joe Simon recalled it, he and Kirby and their families were watching the televised proceedings together. Seeing Gaines's testimony, Simon recalled, "We knew we were in trouble."[29]

Froehlich, not Goodman, testified before the committee on behalf of Timely. Whereas Gaines had hoped to somehow convince the senators that EC's horror comics were all in good fun — even while displaying a condescending attitude toward his interrogators — Froehlich's testimony was literally businesslike, downplaying Timely's crime and horror comics, saying they only published the ones they did to stay competitive with other publishers. He noted that they had published Bible comics ("Our editor went up to Yale Divinity School for guidance") but that they had tanked.

Having reeled off facts and figures, Froehlich then switched gears and waxed poetic:

If violence per se had been outlawed from

113

all literature, the weird and savage and taboo, would Mary Shelley have written *Frankenstein*? Would Shakespeare have written *Macbeth*?[30]

While Froehlich might have charmed the committee, Timely/Atlas was nonetheless pilloried along with everyone else. Invoking Shelley and Shakespeare was no defense when a committee member displayed a copy of Goodman's *Strange Tales* #28, noting that it contained "five stories in which thirteen people die violently."[31]

In response to the government attention, publishers formed the Comics Magazine Association of America (CMAA) — replacing the Association of Comic Magazine Publishers — and instituted the Comics Code, a set of internal censorship guidelines for the comics industry. Unwilling to join the CMAA, and unable to gain marketplace traction with a line of "New Direction" comics — especially because so many distributors and retailers were wary of the EC brand — Gaines ended up transforming his successful Kurtzman-edited *Mad* comic book into a large black-and-white magazine, free — in that format — from the code. *Mad* magazine became an enormous hit, saving Gaines's company. Lee, always a lover of humor, put out Timely's answer to it: *Snafu*.

114

A mildly naughty, military-originated acronym (Situation Normal All Fucked Up — or Fouled Up, for more delicate sensibilities), *Snafu* was entirely written by Lee, except for a few features that were written by their artists. The credits for the first issue read: "The entire project was, for the most part, lovingly WRITTEN and EDITED by STAN LEE."

Among the other humorous credits are "Founded by Irving Forbush" and "Losted by Marvin Forbush," Lee here using funny-sounding names that could have been taken from a Jewish vaudeville comedy routine. This is possibly the first mention in print of Irving Forbush, a name Lee would use over the years to evoke humor with a mildly Yiddish flavor. As far as can be told, the name Marvin Forbush hasn't been used since.

For the second issue, Lee again went Yiddish, with his credit reading: "The whole mashuguna affair is WRITTEN and EDITED by smiling STAN LEE."

Not only was Stan "smiling," but all the people listed in the credits in the issue were also given endearing nicknames, as Lee would be famous for granting to his co-creators in the Marvel Age. The others used in *Snafu* #2 included: "fun-loving" Martin Goodman; "merry" Monroe Froelich Jr. (of whom it's noted that "Irving Forbush would be proud of him" — perhaps for having an equally funny Jewishy-sounding name?);

115

"jolly" Joe Maneely; and "jovial" Johnny Severin. Interestingly, Severin's sister was named on the credits page: "In charge of PRODUCTION is madcap MARIE SEVERIN." Marie had recently joined Timely, in the wake of the severe reduction of the line at EC, where she had been head colorist. She would go on to become one of Marvel's top artists in the 1960s.

A humor magazine like *Snafu* — competing with his friend and former artist Harvey Kurtzman's *Mad* — was smack-dab in the middle of Lee's wheelhouse. While humor is subjective, some items of note in a couple of the issues stand out:

Issue #1 (dated November 1955) has a feature called "Cheesecake." It contains seven fairly tame photos of female models in swimsuits or the equivalent. At the bottom of the page, a caption inside an arrow says, "Turn this page for the world's biggest cheesecake picture!" The next page consists solely of a photo of — maybe you've already guessed — a large *cheesecake.*

Issue #3 (dated March 1956) contains a photo feature called "You Don't Say!" This was a title Lee would use numerous times, including for the *fumetti* (photo funnies) magazine he'd put out in the '60s. In this case, it's a two-page spread with eight photos of a young woman with short dark hair who is addressing, to unknown listeners, "some

116

typical remarks that a typical girl might utter." Underneath each remark, however, is "the true thought that our *Snafu* girl is thinking."

For instance, one caption reads, "Oh, Nancy, MUST you leave so soon?" Underneath that is what the woman in the photo is thinking: *"(One more minute with this insufferable bore and I'll SCRRREAM!)"* The "girl" in the photos (all of which have imaginative doodled backgrounds) is none other than an uncredited Joan Boocock Lee. She also appears as a model wearing a chaste, one-piece swimsuit in the same issue's "Let 'Em Have Cheesecake!" section, where she is identified only as one of "eight delicious dishes." There are no baked goods in this version, but each photo has a humorous caption.

The third issue has a letters column, with letters that seem mostly faked for humorous effect. A short one of note reads:

Dear Stan:
Potrzebie!
Karvey Hurtzman
(address withheld for fear of retaliation)

How many readers got these inside jokes is hard to determine. (Besides the play on Kurtzman's name, *potrzebie* was a nonsense word frequently used in *Mad.*) In any event, issue #3 was the last issue of *Snafu*.

117

The magazine was immediately followed on newsstands by three more issues (#4–6), in a traditional color comic book format, of *Riot,* all with writing credits attributed to Lee. These issues spoofed comic strips, comic books, movies, and more. Two standout features were Lee and Maneely's "The Seventeen-Year Itch" and their dead-on *Dennis the Menace* satire, "Pascal the Rascal."

By 1956, Larry Lieber, who had returned from the air force the year before, was drawing — and possibly writing — romance comics for Timely/Atlas. He was living with the Goodmans and was also taking classes at the Art Students League in Manhattan.[32]

That same year, Jack Kirby, having split with Joe Simon, was doing freelance work for DC. But in need of more income, he returned to Timely/Atlas for the first time since his and Simon's falling-out with Goodman in 1941. There, he did some short science-fiction stories, as well as three issues of the Fu Manchu–inspired *Yellow Claw* comic. It's likely this was all material he wrote, as well as penciled. But Kirby's — and everybody else's — work at Timely would soon come to a sudden, crashing halt.

While Atlas's sales were reasonably good, the entire anti-comics mood in the country had inevitably affected even that company's revenues. Freelancer rates were regularly reduced. According to Raphael and Spurgeon: "Frightened by the decline in comic book titles and the potential effects of the Senate hearings and the Comics Code, Goodman closed Atlas News [distribution] in November 1956 to sign a deal with the largest comic-book [and magazine] distributor of the mid-1950s, American News."[33]

But American News, it turned out, was itself in disastrous financial condition. "Fun-loving" Martin Goodman — advised by "merry" Monroe Froehlich (who had perhaps seen the writing on the wall when he addressed the Senate committee in 1954) — had made what Raphael and Spurgeon termed, "the worst business decision of his career . . . American News left the market in early 1957, forcing Goodman to scramble for another distributor."[34]

History is vague as to why Goodman didn't simply take hat in hand, apologize to the wholesalers and retailers he'd abandoned, and reestablish his own distribution company.

Whatever the reasons, Goodman shifted his distribution to the giant Independent News (IND), which was actually a subsidiary of National Periodical Publications / DC Comics. But wary of Goodman's habit of flooding markets, IND limited him to eight comics per month (which he fulfilled as sixteen bimonthlies). In effect, Goodman was suddenly publishing 80 percent fewer comics per

119

month.[35]

Lee stopped giving out freelance assignments as he scrambled to use up the material he'd accumulated. He had to, once again, tell artists that there was no work for them. By one account, he went to the men's room after each firing and threw up.[36]

Among the many freelancers Lee ordered to stop working, in this case, through a phone call from a secretary — perhaps afraid to directly confront a man he held in high regard — was John Romita. As Romita recalled:

> I thought I would never be in comics again . . . When Stan pulled a Western book out from under me in the middle of a story, I figured, "That's it." I never got paid for it, and I told [my wife] Virginia, "If Stan Lee calls, tell him to go to hell."[37]

She didn't have to bother.
He was already there.

120

5
BREAKING OUT
AND STAYING IN

Probably one of the most unnecessary lines ever penned is: "I sincerely hope you like the strip." — But I sure do!
— Stan Lee, in an October 3, 1957, letter to Robert Cooper of the *Chicago Sun-Times* syndicate, accompanying samples of the *Mrs. Lyons' Cubs* comic strip

Nineteen fifty-seven was the beginning of the end. Again.

With the ringing alarms of anti-comics crusaders and the competition for time and attention that television represented, Stan Lee had already started looking for a way out of comics — or at least a way to supplement his comics-related income — at least a year or more earlier. Now, with four-fifths of the comics he'd been working on suddenly canceled, the idea of generating income outside his comic book work had suddenly become a lot more urgent.

Even without those menaces to his position at Atlas, it could be argued that Lee had started looking to expand, if not change, his horizons with the publication of his 1947 book, *Secrets Behind the Comics,* as well as with a couple of forays into syndicated comics.

The first was a short syndication stint: a month writing the *Howdy Doody* newspaper strip (the strips appeared in early 1951) — with art by Chad Grothkopf — based on the popular children's TV show. That was followed by a short 1952 venture into the syndicated world via the *My Friend Irma* strip — a radio and TV series spin-off. Lee was a natural for it, since he (with Dan DeCarlo as artist) was already writing the comic book version of the character. But neither of those were long-term assignments.

But the "Timely Implosion," as it has come to be known, was a wake-up call for Lee. This cushy staff gig that he'd been taking for granted might not be so secure after all. He needed to make other plans, and he had to make them quickly.

Lee referred to this period when he was working virtually alone in the office as his "human pilot light" phase, waiting around to see if and when circumstances would allow the comics line to expand.[1] Some, including former Goodman editor Bruce Jay Friedman (who would go on to become a legendary novelist and screenwriter), whose Magazine

122

Management office was next to Lee's, have speculated that Goodman felt he couldn't fire a relative and so was trying to humiliate him into quitting — if only Stan would take the hint and go.[2]

While Lee had dabbled in doing some writing and editing for Goodman's magazines, doing a lot more of it didn't seem to be an option for him at this point. Asked about it in 2017, Lee said, "I think I might have liked to [edit for the magazines], but they never asked me to do it. And I never asked him if I could do it. I think he wanted to keep me on the comics. He didn't want me to do anything else."[3]

So Lee stuck around, and Martin seemed willing to let him do so. But Stan was also busy making plans should Goodman decide there wasn't a reason compelling enough to keep him around any longer. Starting in earnest in this period, Lee would spend the rest of his life — even after his and Marvel's success were indisputably established — working on outside projects, perhaps in some way always waiting for a call telling him that the worst had occurred. In truth, Lee would never fully recover from the uncertainty brought on by this latest shake-up in the company.

It was during this period that Lee was hired to write promotional comics for the Bob's Big Boy hamburger chain. Originally packaged by Timely Illustrated Features, Goodman's small licensed comics (comics done for hire for other companies) division, the comic would then go on to be independently produced by freelance writer and artist — and future Marvel staffer and executive — Sol Brodsky, with Lee writing many of the stories, and art chores handled by such Timely veterans as Bill Everett and Dan DeCarlo. Well after Marvel's comics had solidly taken off, Lee would continue this assignment for his friend and colleague Brodsky.

Lee also wrote "fun books" specialty comics through Timely Illustrated Features for Birds Eye foods (done with Maneely) that, in 1958, won the Best Tie-In Sales Premium Plan award of the Premium Industry Club and the Key of Achievement award, presented by the Student Marketing Institute, for "an outstanding activity designed to reach, influence and sell the youth of the nation," according to an April 30, 1958, letter from Edward Tabibian, Birds Eye's sales promotion manager.[4] Not exactly an Academy Award, but better than *not* getting an award.

But the holy grail for many comics creators was getting a syndicated strip. The potential earnings — as well as some measure of mainstream respect — was much higher for those who succeeded in that arena. Syndicated cartoonists like Al Capp and Milton Caniff were treated like — and *were* —

124

celebrities who earned like movie stars. Like many comic book people, Lee was always eager to enter this world. The near shuttering of his company was now an added impetus for him to try his hand at syndicated success.

Lee worked with various artists on proposals for syndicated newspaper comic strips. Through his agent, Toni Mendez, Lee, teamed up with various artists, pitched numerous strip ideas, some successfully. Riffing on popular strip genres of the era, he would put his own spin on them. A small-town vignette strip, done with DeCarlo, *Willie Lumpkin* focused on letter carrier Lumpkin and the kooky characters with whom he interacted. (Willie Lumpkin was a name Lee would use as a recurring *Fantastic Four* supporting character years later, even playing Willie in the 2005 *Fantastic Four* movie.) The strip was mildly successful. So was his suburban kid-comedy, *Mrs. Lyons' Cubs,* done with Timely mainstay Maneely, one of Lee's favorite artists. Unsurprisingly, Mrs. Lyons herself was a dead ringer for Joan Boocock Lee. (As she was in *Snafu,* Joan was often Lee's go-to model, sometimes for glamour photo shoots, sometimes as a representative of an "everyday gal," be she married or single.)

The December 1957 issue of *Editor & Publisher* magazine featured an article promoting

125

the February 10, 1958 debuting *Mrs. Lyons* and its creators. About Lee, it said: "Stan, editorial and art director of a New York publishing company, has authored more than 1,000 comic magazines, written and produced specialized magazines for the government and industry, and put in time as a freelance writer, publicist, and promotion writer." The piece described him as "tall, Madison-Avenue-ish in appearance, with a smile that reaches across the room."

Discussing the strip, Lee said in the article that, although he'd done much Cub Scout–related research, "there will be nothing pedantic about the strip — nothing dry, nothing self-laudatory."

The article continued with this frank confession:

"I suppose we shouldn't admit this," Joe said. "But this is not our first attempt. Stan and I have worked out other strip ideas that didn't get anywhere."

"Yeah," Stan agreed. "I remember one especially, that we thought was pretty good, but we never got it out of the shop. I pasted it up in my daughter's room and forgot about it."

And dramatically, the piece reflected that "They are young. This is the moment, the opportunity. You do it now or else. You

126

understood how Stan Lee, writer, and Joe Maneely, artist, felt."[5]

While a successful syndicated strip could make its creators literally rich and famous, à la Al Capp's *Li'l Abner* or Milton Caniff's *Terry and the Pirates,* less successful strips like *Cubs* might provide their creators a decent income, although by no means an extravagant one. So Lee continued to pitch other projects, while holding on to his comic book writing and editing gigs. Throughout his career, Lee would always hold on to the security of a staff position and title.

In early 1958, while doing his comic book writing and editing and also writing *Cubs,* Lee — with Vince Colletta, and through Mendez — shopped around *For the Love of Linda,* a soap opera strip about a young Manhattan woman who inherits a small-town newspaper. Despite Lee's snappy prose and Colletta's attractive artwork, the strip didn't sell.

Interestingly, while one of Lee's business stationery letterheads from the '50s proclaims him to be the "managing editor, director of art, Timely Comics," a contemporaneous letterhead he used merely listed his name and Timely's office address, but without a company name or a title for Lee. And in various letters from Mendez accompanying Lee's strip pitches, she refers to him as "the Editor

127

and Art Director of Magazine Management Co." Clearly, being the chief editor and art director of a comic book company was a credential to be used only in certain situations. This jibes with Lee's tales of trying to avoid telling people at cocktail parties what kind of writing he did, because they would invariably walk away once hearing the "children's magazines" he was associated with were comic books.[6]

While we'll never know how many of Lee's strip ideas went no further than a few scrawled words on random scraps of paper, Toni Mendez's files contain many fascinating documents that tell us a good deal about the ones that succeeded, as well as a number of the misses.

Mendez, a native New Yorker, was the go-to agent for accomplished cartoonists and was highly regarded in the field. Starting her career as a Radio City Music Hall Rockette dancer, Mendez represented cartoonists and strip writers (as well as prose authors) continually from 1946 to her death in 2003 at ninety-four. She also helped found the National Cartoonists Society and was the aunt of Cynthia Weil, who cowrote — with Weil's husband, Barry Mann — classic pop tunes, including "We Gotta Get Out of This Place" and "On Broadway." Mendez's voluminous files are housed at the Billy Ireland Cartoon Library and Museum at Ohio State University. Her many clients over the years included Milton Caniff, Rube Goldberg, Ernie Bushmiller — and Stan Lee.

With his membership in numerous cartoonist and media organizations (including the National Cartoonists Society, the Newspaper Council, and the Academy of Television Arts and Sciences) and his not-insignificant record in publishing, Lee was able to enlist Mendez to represent him and the artists who would draw his strips. Among the first properties Mendez pitched for Lee was an advertising-industry-based strip called *Clay Murdock, V.P,* done with Colletta. Mendez was apparently quite enthusiastic about Lee. In a letter to Philip Steitz, editorial research director of Chicago's Publishers Syndicate, she wrote, "Lee is an unusual type of individual and I'm sure you will enjoy working with him."

From 1956 to at least 1961, Mendez regularly sent out packages of samples on Lee's behalf, even when she and Lee (with *Willie Lumpkin* artist DeCarlo) were involved in a lawsuit over royalties against each other. Fore-shadowing Lee's 2002 "friendly lawsuit" against Marvel, he and Mendez maintained cordial relations even when they were, technically, adversaries. In one 1960 letter to her, Lee detailed specific language for a contract designed to not impede his right to sue her and closed with, "If lawyers got paid by the word, mine would be the highest paid in the business!" Cordial correspondence between them exists at least as far as the '70s and '80s.

Lee's two successful strips — *Mrs. Lyons' Cubs* and *Willie Lumpkin* — were both the beneficiaries of ad campaigns by the respective syndicates that were distributing them.

For instance, in an elaborate brochure for *Mrs. Lyons' Cubs,* prepared by the *Chicago Sun-Times* syndicate — with Joan Lee–ringer Mrs. Lyons smiling knowingly at the strip's logo, while the eponymous Cubs giggle below — we're told that the feature is "a brand new daily strip and Sunday page, packed with appeal; ideas for Cubs and den mothers; chuckles for everyone!" We're likewise informed that the strip is "approved by the National Council, Boy Scouts of America."

Inside the brochure, where it's further added that it's "the *only* comic approved by the National Council of the Boy Scouts of America," we see a reproduction of the October 30, 1957, letter that grants that very approval, signed by Rebel Robertson, the BSA's director of public relations. (Correspondence in Mendez's archives indicates that Lee and Maneely certainly earned that approval by, as indicated in the *Editor & Publisher* article, doing a great deal of research to get all the details about scouting right — but only after initially missing the mark.)

And just as Joan Lee would be instrumental

in the legend of how, several years later, Marvel Comics came to be, she was also active in the promotional push for *Mrs. Lyons' Cubs*. Doing telephone outreach the Cub Scouts offices couldn't do (for, they claimed, ethical reasons) and the syndicate didn't seem willing or able to do, Joan called numerous Cub Scout troop leaders around the country to inform them of the existence of *Mrs. Lyons' Cubs* and inspired several of them, according to their letters, to buy the local newspapers in which it was appearing or, where it wasn't appearing, to urge their papers to carry the strip.[7]

Whatever success Lee might have had in syndication, it was limited, so his staff job, along with his self-assigned freelance writing income, was not something to casually walk away from. Though he would have liked it if Martin had offered him a steady position on one or more of his non-comics magazines, such an offer was never forthcoming.[8] Of course, Lee didn't fit the profile of Goodman's cadre of magazine staffers — Ivy League graduates and postgraduates that Goodman liked to hire and lord over, bragging about the high-class origins of his staff, hastening to point out that, despite their coveted educations, they were here, working for him, a man who had not even graduated high school, in his schlock magazine mill.

131

(It also seems possible that Lee, though highly intelligent, creative, and hardworking, might have had some form of ADD or ADHD, making him most suited to working on an endless stream of short-form pieces, as opposed to projects that would require much sustained attention.)

By the same token, perhaps Goodman figured that, indeed, his comics line would eventually be allowed to grow and that Lee, if he didn't leave in shame, would be the right man for that return — and, also, that keeping him there would spare Martin family aggravation. By this point, Lee and his family were living near Goodman in Hewlett Harbor and saw the Goodmans socially. Lee often shared rides from and to the office with Martin.

Also possible was that Goodman might have simply felt that his familial duty began and ended with finding his relatives steady work. That the work might be fulfilling or prestigious was something that was, literally, not his problem. For his part, Lee had contemplated looking for work at publications outside Goodman's sphere, but always felt as if his comics background would mark him as unqualified out of the gate. He imagined himself going up to a publisher like Simon & Schuster and saying, "I used to edit comics. Got anything for me?" It left him with "a nagging feeling of insecurity."[9]

Lee has said that he also worked on numer-

132

ous other types of material besides comic books and strips, but the record is vague about it. He recalled:

I used to write radio shows. . . . I can't mention the titles, because I ghosted them under other people's names. . . . I ghosted a number of television shows. I ghosted newspaper comic strips. I wrote the *Howdy Doody* newspaper strip. . . . I did some advertising work.[10]

Apparently, whatever extracurricular writing work Lee did, it didn't earn enough to make him feel he could leave the security, however fragile, at Timely. So, convinced he had no choice, Lee stuck around, but he would keep on pitching ideas for syndicated strips and other projects.

When the backlog of Timely/Atlas comic book material was on its way to being used up and the company's distribution issues were resolved by going with Independent, Lee would soon find himself with more to do at the office, finally allowed to commission new stories. Filling eight to ten comics a month — producing approximately two hundred pages of new material every thirty days — was a respectable workload for any comic book editor, especially when he was also writing many of the stories. Indeed, it was almost the perfect number if the editor were ever inclined to do more than just give a cursory look to the material that crossed his desk — but would, instead, give it some thought and consideration. Why, under those circumstances, a smart writer-editor might even start to think about themes and characterization, might even figure out some kind of strategy for marketing and advertising.

And, with a staff of artists to call on that included such talents as Jack Kirby, Steve Ditko, Don Heck, and especially the exquisitely talented and quick-drawing Maneely, maybe Timely or Atlas or whatever the hell the company was called (a lot of artists just called it "Stan Lee's company") could come up with some stories that might have a bit of substance, maybe even some meaning.

Of course, that was the kind of thing that dreamers like the legendary Will Eisner used to talk about — and Eisner himself had, by 1952, gotten out of producing regular genre comics, even his revered syndicated comic, *The Spirit.* Eisner was spending his time producing educational and instructional comics for the military, corporations, and government agencies, which provided him a nice lifestyle. His career path gave him the opportunity to spend quality time with his young children and the financial means to give them a pleasant suburban life, far from the turmoil of the New York streets he, like

134

Lee, had grown up on. If that was good enough for a genius like Eisner, who was Stan Lee to aspire to more?

So Lee hung in, and by mid-1958, things at Timely/Atlas were on something of an upswing. The company had survived, and he was finally able to offer new work to freelancers. Meanwhile, *Mrs. Lyons' Cubs* was moderately successful.

But on June 7, 1958, things would once again, suddenly and dramatically, change for Stan Lee.

On that day, Joe Maneely was killed while riding a commuter train from Manhattan back to his New Jersey home. Not wearing his glasses, which had recently broken, he took a fatal misstep and fell between cars while the train was moving.

Lee was devastated both professionally and personally. In terms of the former, between *Mrs. Lyons' Cubs* and the numerous comic book assignments Maneely was handling, there was a sudden, gaping chasm in Lee's world.

As if on cue, it was that same week that Jack Kirby chose to visit Lee's office.

135

6
GATHERING FORCES

I was about to quit. I was really bored with what I was doing. This was about 1960.
— Stan Lee to journalist Leonard Pitts Jr., 1981[1]

Unsurprisingly, history is unclear as to whether Stan Lee called Jack Kirby in to discuss new assignments or Kirby dropped into the Timely offices to explore what possibilities might have opened up with Joe Maneely's passing.

After artist Frank Giacoia had facilitated his return to the company in 1956 and '57, Kirby had been doing some writing and drawing for Timely before the American News distribution debacle. The ensuing moratorium on new assignments had sent him to Archie and DC Comics and to syndication with a space race–inspired strip called *Sky Masters of the Space Force*. But those doors had been or were in the process of being closed to him. He needed work. Lee had already given some of Maneely's assignments

136

to at least Steve Ditko, so the apportioning of the newly available work was under way.[2]

In later years, Kirby would claim the company was on the verge of disappearing, Lee sitting there weeping, unsure what to do, movers repossessing furniture, and that he came in and turned the entire situation around.[3] Lee, for his part, has denied both that he was crying and that the company was on the verge of dissolution. Perhaps Kirby mistook tears Lee was shedding over losing his friend Maneely as having some other cause.

In any case, out of a mix of his need for a new high-volume producer and his genuine admiration for Kirby's talents, Lee immediately put him to work. Together, they would create science-fiction stories inspired by the monster movies of the era, such at *Them!* and *The Blob,* as well as Western and other genre work. These were usually the cover features and lead stories of comics including *Tales to Astonish* and *Strange Tales* and had titles like "I Discovered the Secret of the Flying Saucers" and "The Thing Called . . . It!"

Out of these formulaic potboilers — as well as out of the humor and romance comics the company was producing — would eventually emerge the idiosyncratic amalgam of ideas and personalities that would come to change the pop culture landscape. But for the time

137

being, survival, as individuals and as a company, was the main thing on everyone's mind.

While Lee would rarely bring in outside writers post-Implosion, he made an exception for his brother, Larry. Since leaving the service in 1955, Larry had been working a series of jobs for *The New York Times* as well as for Magazine Management, mostly in their pasteup departments. Having ambitions to follow in the footsteps of his artistic idol, Kirby — who would regularly give Larry drawing advice, including to not worry so much about correct anatomy — Larry had taken courses at the Art Students League and Pratt Institute.[4] At some point, Stan and Larry had even briefly collaborated on a pitch for a syndicated strip about a suburban couple — titled *Jack and Jill* — that Stan wrote and Larry drew. But Larry's slowness with the art put that project to rest.[5]

Now, Lee, having found no one he felt could write the books the way he wanted them to be written, turned to his younger sibling. While Larry hadn't thought of himself as a writer, Stan told him that his letters home from the air force were very well written and that he could teach Larry to write comics.[6] Though Larry started out writing romance scripts, eventually Lee would delegate the scripting of many of the Kirby-

138

drawn monster stories to his brother to write.

Larry would take Lee's brief plot outlines, and, an artist by nature, he would break them down into small-size thumbnail drawings. He would add dialogue and then translate those drawings into typed, panel-by-panel "full scripts" for Kirby to draw.[7] Larry would continue to write stories for Kirby up through the early Marvel-era adventures of characters including Thor, Ant-Man, Iron Man, and the Human Torch. Whether the initial plot ideas given to Larry by Stan were solely created by Stan or whether they were the product of story conferences between Lee and Kirby is, typically, unclear, although Larry had always assumed they were created by Stan alone.[8]

One fact is indisputable: starting in 1958, Jack Kirby did many stories, in a variety of genres, with and for Stan Lee. More than other artists of the era, Kirby set the look and feel of Goodman's action and adventure comics. Lacking a company name, it was Kirby's art that gave those comics an identifiable flavor. The pairing of Lee and Kirby (and sometimes Lieber) produced a stream of dependably exciting — if sometimes silly — sci-fi and Western stories. It would take some time before those stories would evolve into something else. Stan Lee and Jack Kirby were not yet STAN LEE & JACK KIRBY. But they were getting there.

139

■ ■ ■

In this period, as assignments were opening up, Lee gathered around himself, to do most of the drawing, a tight coterie of artists who could be counted on to do competent, on-time work on a regular basis. Besides Kirby, these included Don Heck, Dick Ayers, Paul Reinman, Joe Sinnott, and Steve Ditko, along with Larry Lieber, who was also doing regular script work. Heck would say of this group, "That's one of the things I think that Marvel did there, which is nice. Stan got a whole bunch of caring people, doing all this stuff, and they're all different. Ditko and Kirby and myself and Dick Ayers, at that time, is primarily what they had."[9]

Heck seems to have understood one of the key things that made Lee, and in effect Timely/Atlas, attractive to artists. While the idea that the overall effect was "nice" doesn't seem like effusive praise, it was a significant difference from the competition. The other main market for action-adventure artists, National Comics, was structured and run in an efficient, corporate fashion. Editorial offices were set up as competitors. If an artist worked for one DC editor, then he was de facto forbidden from seeking or accepting work from another.

In such an atmosphere, in a time of scarcity,

140

some of National's editors would exercise their power through demeaning, condescending behavior toward their freelance staffs — not "nice" at all. One editor was famous for rejecting as "toilet paper" the work a writer would give him, only to then pass the rejected idea off as his own and order a second writer to use the same plot. There were rumors of "pay-to-play" editorial kickbacks there and elsewhere. Impressive work was produced there, certainly work that fulfilled the need of entertaining children, and often far beyond that. But the atmosphere at the company was not designed to foster innovation and excitement. It was designed to keep sales steady and to keep a tight-knit group of veteran creators employed and loyal. While National had an editorial director, Irwin Donenfeld, he was focused on what he saw as bigger-picture concerns — what made a given cover sell more than another, for instance — and generally let the editorial fiefdoms run on their own.

At Timely/Atlas in the post-Implosion era, there was only Stan Lee to deal with, with Martin Goodman chiming in now and then, but generally leaving Lee to deal with freelancers. While not incapable of a snappy wisecrack or subtle put-down, Lee was generally an enthusiastic cheerleader for, and fan of, his artists. In addition, he was known to not hold grudges. If he was angry over something,

141

it was generally over one specific thing for one specific moment. Heck recalled Lee as an "easy" guy to work with. "I never had any problem with him."[10]

Of course, DC did offer significantly higher rates than Timely/Atlas. And a DC editor was unlikely to — as Stan often did — try to get a freelancer who was in to drop off work to sit down for a few minutes and do some desperately needed art corrections — gratis — on a job by another artist that was about to go to the printer.

So Lee's natural inclination to be friendly and welcoming served him well. Of necessity, but also by nature, he would deploy the force of his big personality to make artists feel that they were special and that they were welcome by him — and by extension by the company. There seemed to have been something exciting and energizing to many about being in Stan's presence. If, as Heck says, Lee got a bunch of "caring people" to work with him on his books, it was in large part because he was able to *get* them to care. Throughout his career, he seemed to have frequently inspired people to do their best work, usually *for* him, sometimes in *spite* of him. In addition, Lee was known for not making artists wait for a next assignment. He rewarded loyalty with loyalty. At a company paying lower rates than many, having a next assignment ready was smart business.

142

∎ ∎ ∎

Although he never gave up his day job, Lee continued to spend much of his time and energy on ambitious side projects, including several more syndicated newspaper strip pitches. After all, while Goodman's anonymous comics line was creeping back to health, its future was by no means assured. It was now operating out of two small rooms at Magazine Management's 655 Madison Avenue offices. The glory of the Empire State Building was a thing of the past. So Lee kept on working on other projects.

He recruited Timely humor artist Al Hartley to take Maneely's place on *Mrs. Lyons' Cubs,* but the strip didn't survive much longer, and it last saw print on December 27, 1958.

Toni Mendez tried to sell Lee's premise for a book called *Art Script,* which would add funny captions to classic (and public domain) works of art. While others would later have success with a similar concept, this one wasn't destined to fly.[11]

In 1959, again through Mendez, Lee made a deal with the Bettmann Archive to produce a book of nineteenth-century etchings from their collection, likely for a book entitled *Look Back in Laughter,* that would pair Lee-written funny captions with the Bettmann images.

143

This was rejected by publishers, including the World Publishing Company and Scribner's. Mendez would also pitch something called "Stag Line" for Lee. This seems to have been a "male Dear Abby" type of project, although little else is known about it.[12]

In April of 1959, Mendez pitched a project called "L'il Repute" by Lee and artist Russ Heath, apparently a risqué adult comic strip. Mendez tried to sell it to McGraw-Hill and Simon & Schuster, among others. "The gorgeous art would have made for a very pretty and funny package, I believe," wrote comics historian Ger Apeldoorn (who has created a logical and credible timeline for the Lee material in Mendez's archives) in *Alter Ego* #150. "But," Apeldoorn continued, "maybe [it was] a bit too racy for its time. Not as a subject (plenty of books around the time had a prostitute as the main character), but there was no one doing art as sexy as Russ Heath's."

There was also a never-published *Cartoonists Cookbook* coloring book that Lee tried to do with multiple artists who were affiliated with the National Cartoonists Society that never got off the ground.

And then there was *Willie Lumpkin.*

Starting out as a proposal by Lee and Dan DeCarlo for *Barney's Beat,* a humor strip about a neighborhood police patrolman, the

144

strip evolved (against Lee's instincts) into a single panel, and then a multipanel, strip about a small-town *letter carrier* who would comment on local events and personalities. Publishers Syndicate gave it an enthusiastic push, creating brochures and other promotional material.[13]

"You'll laugh! You'll love! And you'll like the folks you meet . . . in the Wonderful World of Willie Lumpkin," declares the cover of one sales brochure. Also supplied by the syndicate was a series of ads for the strip that could be inserted anywhere a given paper had some extra space. And at least one paper — *The Oklahoma City Oklahoman and Times* — held a tie-in promotional contest, "Who's the Friendliest Postman?" (Spoiler alert: There were *two* winners! One letter carrier received a one-hundred-dollar U.S. savings bond, the other was awarded two pairs of shoes.) The strip debuted on December 7, 1959.[14]

The syndicate's "Men Behind Willie Lumpkin" promotional profile article was designed to portray Lee and DeCarlo as themselves archetypal suburbanites, the ultimate upwardly striving '50s "regular guys." It quoted Lee as saying, "If people like *Willie Lumpkin,* I suppose it's because we try to pick out funny things that the reader can readily recognize — because he or she experiences many of the same situations in day to day living." A bit later, the piece gave us this reflection: " 'As a

145

child, I wanted to be the usual fireman, policeman, circus performer and baseball star,' Lee confides, 'so naturally I became a writer!' " The profile concludes: "Though now a confirmed suburbanite, Stan still adds with some pride that he belongs to a select group of 'nearly extinct native New Yorkers.' "[15]

Despite being carried at one point by more than fifty papers, many in large markets, *Willie Lumpkin* ended on May 28, 1961, after an eighteen-month run. Due at least in part to a national recession, leading papers to cut back on strips, *Willie,* like *Mrs. Lyons' Cubs,* was not destined for a long haul.

Although he put on a public front of enjoying doing *Mrs. Lyons' Cubs* and *Willie Lumpkin,* Lee admitted, years later, that they weren't what he'd wanted them to be:

> *Willie* was . . . about a [city] cop. . . . I brought it to this newspaper syndicate . . . [they] wanted me to change it to a mailman . . . in a small town. . . . I thought they knew best . . . it [only] lasted about a year. [Then] one day I said . . . "I'll bet if I did something about Boy Scouts they'd take it. . . ." [T]hey took it . . . so I was stuck with a strip I didn't particularly want.[16]

After the cancellations of the two strips,

146

Lee seems to have shifted his non-Timely/ Atlas attention to self-publishing short humor books, a throwback to his publishing of *Secrets Behind the Comics* in 1947.

Golfers Anonymous and *Blushing Blurbs,* both published in 1961, were produced under Lee's Madison Publishing banner. *Golfers Anonymous* — subtitled "A Hilarious Look at Life on the Links" — consisted of drawings (probably, according to Apeldoorn, by Stan Goldberg) and photos, all adorned with humorous captions. *Blushing Blurbs* ("A Ribald Reader for the Bon Vivant") consisted of mildly racy photos — including a cover photo of Joan Lee posing as a streetwalker — also accompanied by funny captions written by her husband. These books came out and, according to Lee's memoir, they sold well — ten thousand copies of each — but he never bothered to go back to press with them for additional printings.[17]

In addition, artifacts in Lee's University of Wyoming archives indicate that he had in the works another item called *My Own Executive Doodle Book* (or possibly *A First Reader for the Thoughtful Executive*), that he would both write and draw. "Doodle books" of various kinds — with blank pages for readers to draw on — were popular then, and this seems to have been an attempt to capitalize on that trend. The book might indeed have even been

147

published sometime in 1962, according to Apeldoorn, but as of this writing, a printed copy has not been located.

From this time onward, for the next ten years or so, it seems — at least from available evidence — that anything outside of comics that Lee did was within the confines of Goodman's publishing company, such as the 1963 photo-funny magazine, *You Don't Say*. Still, it wouldn't be shocking to discover at some point that Lee's forays into syndication and self-publishing continued, although the paper trail in the Mendez archives does seem to pause during this period, not picking up again until the mid-1970s.

Back on the comic book front, 1957–1961 would, in retrospect, be known as the prelude to the Marvel Age of Comics, although at the time, of course, none of the principals involved — nor the readers, largely the first few waves of the baby boom generation — would have any idea of what was coming until its unheralded arrival (later made up for with much heralding). While they didn't realize it, Lee and his collaborators were waiting for boomers to grow sophisticated enough in their comics reading tastes to appreciate the phenomenon Timely was unknowingly building toward. The baby boom began roughly in 1945, as GIs returning from World War II started families, and lasted until roughly

1964, peaking in 1957, with more births in that year than any previous year in American history.

While Timely was struggling to survive, National was moving along steadily. If only because so many companies had gone out of business, they and a handful of others had survived. DC had gambled on launching updated versions of its superheroes, starting, tentatively, with the Flash, in 1956, and the gamble was slowly but surely paying off. Editor Julius Schwartz successfully launched revamped versions of Flash, Green Lantern, the Atom, and Hawkman. By 1959, Flash and Green Lantern — along with Superman, Batman, and Wonder Woman, all of whose comics had never stopped being produced, as well as the 1955-debuting Manhunter from Mars — were teamed up as the Justice League of America. The team would go on to have great sales success.

Nineteen fifty-seven saw the beginning of the space race, with the USSR's Sputnik satellite shockingly beating the USA's launch of Explorer 1 the following year. Nuclear fear was in the air as the arms race with the Soviet Union progressed. It was also the beginning of a recession (which exacerbated Goodman's distribution issues). The Eisenhower era's air of optimism was shot through with fear that the great ride everyone was on might end — violently and irrevocably — at any moment.

Nineteen fifty-nine introduced Rod Serling's *The Twilight Zone* TV series to the world. It debuted on October 2. The show's O. Henry–style short dramas would inspire Lee, who intuited that those types of stories would lend themselves to the art style of Pennsylvania-born Steve Ditko. While much of Timely's fantasy/sci-fi output was already in the twist-ending tradition — owing a debt to everything from Poe to EC horror comics to the radio serials of the 1930s — *The Twilight Zone,* as well as drama anthologies such as *Alfred Hitchcock Presents,* set the tone for Atlas's irony-drenched tales. Lee and Ditko, especially, became masters of the eerie, five-page vignette stories that echoed modern anxieties, told in a style that looked of its time and yet, simultaneously, thanks to Ditko's distinctive artwork, also of decades previous. Many of the stories were created in what would come to be called the "Marvel Method" of short plot discussion, followed by pencil art, followed by dialogue, and then inks and colors.[18] That method would come to be the source of much controversy in Lee's life.

Even by 1960, though, with the last major distribution crisis three years in the past, Lee could still not provide enough work to keep his core of artists constantly busy. Kirby, essentially blackballed at National after a legal

150

dispute with editor Jack Schiff, had found work with Joe Simon over at Archie Comics, where he cocreated the Fly and Private Strong with and for his former partner. But Simon's bosses, looking for the supposedly more elegant style that DC's artists were producing, were so critical of Kirby's rough-hewn drawings that, out of frustration, he walked.[19] His newspaper strip, *Sky Masters,* the source of Kirby's grief with Schiff, who had brokered its sale, was finally canceled. He needed more work to support his growing family, and Lee did what he could to supply it. Ditko, for his part, while working for Lee, was also still producing work — at even lower rates than Timely's — for Connecticut's Charlton Comics.

Timely/Atlas Comics kept following the trends. With Westerns on TV and in movies popular, and especially with the breakout success of the Clint Eastwood–starring *Rawhide* TV series, which had debuted in the fall of 1959, Lee teamed up with Kirby to introduce a new version of an old Timely Western character, the Rawhide Kid, in *Rawhide Kid* #17 (despite the numbering, a first issue), dated August 1960. Although Kirby had at this point been back at Timely for a while and had done numerous stories with Lee, this was their first collaboration on a new *continuing* character.

Nearly a year later, in *Amazing Adventures*

151

#1, dated June 1961, the Lee-Kirby team would try their hand at a new superhero — inked by Ditko — the magic-themed Dr. Droom. Whether, for Droom, Lee did entire scripts or simply provided short plot outlines for Larry to script is unclear, but there's no doubt Kirby penciled the first four issues. Lost in the various narratives of Marvel's 1960s superhero revolution, Dr. Droom was really the company's first toe in the superhero waters of the era. Besides just not capturing the necessary lightning in a bottle, perhaps Droom's early abandonment (and later erasure from history) was related to his origin as a Caucasian doctor who is transformed into an Asian sorcerer for no discernible reason, awkward even in 1961. Perhaps Droom's short-lived status was as simple as his never being granted the magazine's cover — although that alone would have indicated a lack of faith in the character from the get-go. In any case, Kirby would do the first four episodes of Droom's adventures, with a fifth — in *Amazing Adventures* #6 — drawn by Paul Reinman.

By issue #7, the magazine's title was changed to *Amazing Adult Fantasy* and became a comic whose sole contents were Lee-Ditko *Twilight Zone*–style short stories. Lee had decided that the magazine, still an anthology, would be where he and one of his favorite collaborators would have the entire

152

title as their playground, creating stories that were allegedly more sophisticated (i.e., "adult") than those seen in other comics. (The comic's slogan was "The magazine that respects your intelligence.") Playing with readers' perceptions, bantering versions of Lee and Ditko appear in issue #12's story "Something Fantastic?" Lee would do this meta kind of thing across genres, frequently having himself and the artist of a story appear in the story as themselves — more than once in *Millie the Model* — often at a fictionalized version of the company's offices, imagined as the workplace where the creative team spent its days making comics and dealing with crackpots, fans, and the stars of the comic books.

Amazing Adult Fantasy, unlike most other comics, had a table of contents, as well as messages from the editor/writer, messages whose tone addressed the reader directly and also assumed that reader had a certain level of sophistication — that they were perhaps fifteen years old instead of ten.

Meanwhile, the 1960s were dawning, the world shifting in ways both large and small.

John F. Kennedy became president in January of 1961. The Bay of Pigs incident, in April of that year, was his first test of command, and it turned into a fiasco. Meanwhile, Kennedy was slowly but steadily escalating the

153

United States' involvement in Vietnam. And while no one was looking, the USSR launched the first manned space flight, shooting cosmonaut Yuri Gagarin into space on April 12, 1961, and returning him safely. The race to the stars was well under way — and the United States was losing! And as if to demonstrate that World War II was nowhere near being truly over — and it would never really end in the comics — high-ranking Nazi war criminal Adolf Eichmann, captured the year before by Mossad agents in Buenos Aires, stood trial in Israel in 1961 for his savage Holocaust crimes, for which he was executed in 1962.

In popular culture, 1961 was the year of the home run competition between New York Yankee sluggers Mickey Mantle and Roger Maris. Maris would go on to break Babe Ruth's record that fall but be forever haunted by the asterisk that marred his feat. Several miles south of Yankee Stadium, a young folk singer named Bob Dylan had started gaining attention in Greenwich Village. Movies as diverse as *West Side Story, The Parent Trap,* and *Last Year at Marienbad* (directed by Alain Resnais, later to become a close friend of Lee's) were in theaters. Besides Westerns like *Rawhide* and *Have Gun–Will Travel,* TV shows like *The Dick Van Dyke Show, The Many Loves of Dobie Gillis,* and *77 Sunset Strip* were hits. The baby boom was flexing its cultural and purchasing muscle.

In the world of comics, publishers were realizing there was an interest in comics that had some measure of depth and introspection. Superman's comics, for instance, were developing a sense of history, as the Man of Steel explored the tragic nature of actually *being* the last survivor of the planet Krypton, something he'd rarely bothered to notice before. (At around the same time, he would discover that he wasn't really the last or only survivor, but the point was made — superhero sagas could have some degree of depth.)

Interestingly, comics such as DC's *Our Army at War,* featuring Sgt. Rock, focused on tales of World War II, which made perfect sense. Children of the veterans of that conflagration wanted to read adventures whose heroes were idealized versions of their parents. The DC superheroes' adventures of the early '60s also acknowledged the presence of history, having the characters meet their war-era counterparts — who lived on a parallel world, "Earth 2" — and who had started to go gray but were still formidable enemies of evil. "Flash of Two Worlds," a groundbreaking 1961 story from DC, established a link between the current Flash character and the one from the 1940s, which led to revivals of a number of other DC heroes, who had been the readers' parents' heroes. Ten-year-olds were becoming nostalgic for comics published

155

before they were even born. Something was changing. Something at DC was leading some of its writers to deepen the stories a bit. Maybe it was just a more mature perspective brought on by the company's creators and editors entering middle age, as well as by the sense of history that older fans like Jerry Bails and Roy Thomas brought to the table.

Over at Timely/Atlas, like many on the DC editorial and creative staffs, Stan Lee (thirty-eight years old) and Jack Kirby (forty-three years old) were also World War II veterans, Lee having served stateside working on propaganda material, Kirby having seen brutal combat. They, too, had matured and gained perspective. They, too, had powerful stories to tell and complex emotions to unleash. They, too, would find they had life lessons they wanted to pass on to a next generation.

But they weren't working at DC Comics. They were working for Martin Goodman's nameless and risk-averse comics line — a line that had recently almost disappeared, a line committed to avoiding risk in order to survive. From any reasonable point of view, therefore, Lee and Kirby seemed to be doing the sensible thing: producing simple stories based on genres popular in the movies and on TV.

Kirby was doing all the drawing work he could get, almost all of it assigned by the one editor who would give him as much as he could handle: Stan Lee. Lee, for his part, was constructing a career with enough variety to keep his interest up, while also taking steps to ensure that he would not have to depend on any single revenue stream. He had a day job — albeit with the mixed blessing of working for a relative — where he had the luxury of being able to assign himself all the freelance writing work he could handle. But recent history had taught him that his employment situation was by no means guaranteed.

But Lee also had a reasonably, though by no means spectacularly, successful track record in syndicated strips and an agent who had faith in him so that he could pitch new strip ideas should he so choose. In addition, he had gained some experience in self-publishing, experience that could be deployed again if the desire or need arose.

Was it a brilliant career? No. But for someone who'd nearly become unemployed a few short years ago, it wasn't bad at all. He had a solid base from which he could plan his next moves, and he also had options and contacts that could come in handy once he decided exactly what he was going to do. That was all good — because, one way or another, he was determined to get the hell out of comic books.[20]

157

■ ■ ■ ■

Then one day in early 1961, Martin Goodman suggested to Stan Lee that it might be a good idea for the company to try doing some superheroes again.

7
FROM THE ASHES

In the '60s, the ideas for the new characters originated with me because that was my responsibility. . . . I dreamed up the *Fantastic Four,* and I wrote a brief outline. I gave that to Jack Kirby, who did a wonderful job on it.

— Stan Lee videotaped deposition on May 13, 2010, for *Marvel Worldwide Inc., v. Kirby et al.*

I came up with *The Fantastic Four.* I came up with *Thor.* Whatever it took to sell a book, I came up with. Stan Lee has never been editorial minded. It wasn't possible for a man like Stan Lee to come up with new things — or old things for that matter.

— Jack Kirby *The Comics Journal* #134, February 1990

According to Lee's many-times-told story, in early 1961, he had been about to quit his job when he was called into publisher Martin Goodman's office. According to a 1998

159

conversation Roy Thomas had with him, Lee was about to resign literally the day that Goodman told him they should do superheroes, piquing Lee's interest enough for him to postpone quitting.[1] Goodman had found out that superhero-team comic *Justice League of America* was a hit for DC Comics. Debunked legend has Martin finding it out from a bragging DC executive during a golf game. However he found out, a publisher as obsessed with circulation as Goodman would have made it his business to know, one way or another, what and how his competition was doing.

With the slow but steady superhero revival with the newly reimagined *Flash* and *Green Lantern,* as well as *Justice League* (as well as continued publication of the never-canceled titles featuring Superman, Batman, and Wonder Woman), Goodman knew that there was a trend in the marketplace for such characters, and especially for superhero *teams.* True, Timely's experiment with new superhero Dr. Droom earlier that year seemed to be going nowhere. But maybe a team book would do better.

And so, he directed Lee to produce a superhero team book, no doubt assuming Stan would dredge up Timely's old heroes, maybe add one or two new ones, and rush out a team comic something like his *All Win-*

160

ners comics of the 1940s. Kids were kids. If they liked superhero teams, give them a superhero team.

Lee, however, didn't want to just revive the old Timely heroes, at the very least because the last time they tried that, in 1954, the books had tanked. Telling Joan about his newest assignment, Lee recalled how she told him (as she seems to have told him numerous times in an ongoing conversation) that he might as well try to do something different — quit complaining about being forced to churn out formulaic pap — and see what would develop. The worst that could happen is that Martin would fire him (unlikely, since Lee was a relative and the new book would just be one of a number of titles), and he'd been claiming to want to quit, anyway. Lee has said that he came up with the characters, wrote a story outline, and gave it to his "most talented and dependable artist," Jack Kirby.[2]

In various versions of Lee's telling of this story, sometimes Martin is excited and enthusiastic about reviving superheroes; other times, he's detached and neutral, just making another in a long series of business decisions. In some, Martin calls Lee into his office; in others, Martin comes to Lee's office. While the differences are subtle, they seemed to reflect Lee's feelings about Martin and about comics in general when the various versions

161

were told. Interestingly, though, in *all* the versions, Martin is the active participant, giving Lee the order to revive superheroes. Significant variations regard whether Lee was literally about to quit that same day or whether he was just going about his regular work duties, with no specific plan for leaving the company. For instance, as Lee said in 2010:

Martin Goodman asked me to create a group of heroes because he found out that National Comics had a group that was selling well. So I went home, and I thought about it, and I wanted to make these different than the average comic book heroes. I didn't want them to have a double — a secret — identity.

And I wanted to make it as realistic as possible. Instead of them living in Gotham City or Metropolis, I felt I will have them live in New York City. . . .

I wanted everything real, and I wanted their relationship to be real. Instead of a girl who didn't know that the hero was really a superhero, not only did she know who he was, but they were engaged to be married, and she also had a superpower.

So, you know, things like that. And I thought I would try that. So I wrote up a very brief synopsis about that, and naturally I called Jack, because he was our best artist, and I asked him if he would do it. He

162

seemed to like the idea.

He took the synopsis, and he drew the story and put in his own touches, which were brilliant.[3]

On being shown a copy of the original synopsis, Lee commented:

We discussed it, and we embellished it, and we made little changes. But this was the beginning of it.[4]

As Lee recalled, either before or after — or perhaps both before and after — writing up the story synopsis, he discussed the characters with Kirby. Kirby drew the first issue, which was then scripted by Lee and inked by, probably, George Klein, who was a regular DC and sometime Timely inker. And the rest, as they say, was history. Or a version of history.

Kirby's version of the team's creation was significantly different (as well as inconsistent across various tellings). The two men's opposing visions and versions are, of course, the source of much conflict to this very day.

In a nutshell, Kirby is on record as saying, at various times, that he brought the new team and the first issue full-blown to Lee, who, desperate to keep his job, was thrilled to be able to publish it. Kirby has said that he'd been urging Goodman to start publishing superheroes again, realizing that they

163

were having a resurgence in popularity. "I had a lot of faith in the superhero character, that [superheroes] could be brought back very, very vigorously," Kirby told comics pioneer Will Eisner. "I had to fight for the superheroes. . . . I had to regenerate the entire [Timely] line. I felt there was nobody there who was qualified to do it. Stan Lee was my vehicle to do it. He was my bridge to Martin.

"Stan Lee was not writing," he told Eisner. "I was doing the writing."[5]

Whoever came up with them, the team consisted of Reed Richards ("Mr. Fantastic," who had super-stretching powers); Ben Grimm (the superhumanly strong "Thing"); Susan Storm (the "Invisible Girl" who, well, could turn invisible at will); and Johnny Storm (the "Human Torch" who had control over fire). These were the four characters who formed the core of what would become known as the Marvel Universe, the future icons who debuted in *Fantastic Four* #1.

Before he'd burned his bridges at DC and returned to Timely, Kirby had drawn and been involved with creating and writing for that company, the *Challengers of the Unknown* series, which featured a quartet of adventurers who, like the FF, were formed after a fateful aircraft crash-landing. Some have pointed to the similarity in origins as proof that Kirby's version of the creation of the FF is closer to the truth.

164

And yet . . . while *Fantastic Four* does indeed bear some resemblance to Kirby's *Challengers* (cocreated by Kirby with Joe Simon), it also resembles other teams, in and out of comics, including the Justice League and Timely's own All-Winners Squad. The Human Torch (albeit another version) had been a Timely character. Mr. Fantastic was similar to classic superheroes Plastic Man and the Elongated Man, who were both reminiscent of sideshow "rubber men." The Invisible Girl was one of many invisible characters in fiction. The Thing was, on the surface, not unlike the monsters that Lee and Kirby had been churning out for several years. The space race story elements were torn from the headlines of the day. (And there is even a theory that the second part of the first issue — the battle with the Mole Man — was a reworked Timely/Atlas monster story that was in the drawer, although Lee has denied that.)

Strangely, as if to show that the comic was not foremost in either man's agenda, the art in *Fantastic Four* #1 is arguably weaker than work Kirby was doing that same month in *Rawhide Kid* and on the story of the monster called Orrgo in *Strange Tales*. And yet editor / writer / art director Lee — not to mention Goodman himself — let *FF* go to the printers. It almost seems as if this comic was executed as what the cocreators likely saw it

165

as: an extra assignment given to them by a publisher who had nothing better to do than hand down an edict based on an informed hunch, while they were busting their humps to put out the already-existing titles. It's as if Lee and Kirby were saying: *Here's your superhero team comic, Martin — in case you didn't notice, we* don't *own Superman or Batman. But you're the boss, so here's your superhero team book — from a company that hasn't produced a viable superhero for years. You can put them in the hall of fame next to Dr. Droom.*

And so, here, with the start of *Fantastic Four,* is the beginning of the most historically significant part of Lee's and Marvel's stories — and it is also the part most shrouded in ambiguity. This is the period that everyone would love to have a detailed chronology of, an unambiguous ringside seat to what "really happened." Because, while lightning would be caught by the Lee and Kirby team in multiple bottles multiple times, this was the first time they had captured it — even though they had worked together on numerous stories before.

Over the course of two years, the major heroes of the Marvel Universe were created or, in some cases, reinvented. The questions that beg to be answered are: How did it happen? How did this small team of solid,

166

dependable professionals, with Lee and Kirby and Ditko at its core, whose members had been plugging away at comics for anywhere from seven years to more than two decades, suddenly come up with a pantheon of pop-culture icons who, today, nearly six decades since their creation, are generating more interest and income than anyone would ever have dreamed? Show us the magic, describe who did what, dissect each and every word and image in each story, so we can see exactly who created which parts of Marvel's pantheon — and, while you're at it, acknowledge and reward each of them fairly and appropriately.

Of course, there are no clear answers to those questions. Comics writers and artists, even if they discuss their collaborations in advance, work largely in isolation, at desks and typewriters (later, computers) and drawing boards. Much of their work is done in their heads, in their supposed "off hours," and is then brought to life on paper. Or it is spontaneously generated with little or no conscious forethought. Rarely is the creative process documented. Why would it be?

The resulting comics can be scrutinized and analyzed, even the remaining evidence of typed and drawn material can be looked at and dissected, but in the end, it remains a mystery, despite the number — and passion — of people convinced they know the definitive answers.

As Kirby biographer Mark Evanier has written:

> Among those who worked around them at the time, there was a unanimous view: that *Fantastic Four* was created by Stan and Jack. No further division of credit seemed appropriate. Not on that, not on all the wonderment yet to come.[6]

And as Raphael and Spurgeon wrote:

> When . . . the new Marvel comics became successful, who created which character, to what extent, and when became important questions, both legally and ethically. But . . . as the new formula books spilled out of Marvel's offices . . . the way to ensure the best possible new superhero line, created on the run, was for everyone involved to contribute whatever ideas they had when they had them.[7]

When *Fantastic Four* debuted, it seemed indeed a half-hearted follow-up to the ambivalently presented first "modern" Timely/Atlas superhero, Dr. Droom. Who knows? Perhaps Goodman had suggested superheroes in that case, too, and Droom was a passive-aggressive attempt to just do one and be done with this whim of Martin's so that they could

168

get on with the work they had already committed to getting done.

Indeed, the same month that *FF* made its debut, the company also released five fantasy comics, two Westerns, three romance titles, and one humor comic. (This was a total of twelve comics, demonstrating that the eight-titles-a-month restriction originally imposed by distributor Independent News was being relaxed.) Looking closely, it does seem that most of the other titles the company put out that month were crafted with more effort and enthusiasm than *Fantastic Four.* But clearly, there was a buried spark of some kind in the team's debut.

The relatively lackluster feel of the premiere *FF* issue, as well as its potential, were noticed by at least one fan, one who had an informed sense of the history of the medium and of the company. Writing in the *ComiCollector* fanzine, twenty-four-year-old Missouri high school English teacher Roy Thomas wrote:

Despite its faults — and this first issue has some glaring ones — THE FANTASTIC FOUR holds promise of becoming one of the better comics now on the stands, in this reviewer's opinion.[8]

Thomas heaped praise on the Thing, calling him "a frightening champion of justice,"

169

continuing, "Something is needed in a period of all-too-handsome supermen to remind us that goodness of heart and an attractive physical appearance are not necessarily synonymous."

Indeed, Thomas (who would, of course, go on to write and edit for Marvel for many years) sensed here perhaps the most innovative and passionate element in the debut *FF* issue: the Thing. While Reed Richards — physically resembling Hugh Beaumont's Ward Cleaver from the 1950s *Leave It to Beaver* TV series — spoke like a scientist from a '50s science-fiction movie, and Johnny and Sue Storm adhered to fairly stereotypical comic book speech patterns, Ben Grimm's Thing character actually *evolved* in the course of the story, almost as if Lee were developing Grimm's personality as the story progressed. Early on in the issue, the Thing spoke in a formal manner, declaring, after a panicked cop's failed shot at him: "His first shot missed . . . but he'll not get another chance."

But by the team's origin's end, on page 13 (of the 25 that the story will occupy), Ben declares, in a much more colloquial manner: "I ain't Ben anymore — I'm what Susan called me — THE THING." Later in the story, when the team is in action against the issue's villain — the Mole Man — the Thing defeats a monstrous stone warrior. Seeing

170

this, Sue declares, "You've done it, Ben! You've beaten him!" To this, Ben replies, "What did you expect? I'm the Thing, ain't I?"

So, in the space of one issue, the Thing/ Grimm character has quickly evolved from someone who speaks in a formal, somber manner, into a character who utilizes the William Bendix / Broderick Crawford way of speaking that has come to be associated with him. A close view of the word balloon with the sentence "I'm the Thing, ain't I?" shows an extra space between *ain't* and *I.* One can speculate that Lee might have originally written *aren't I?,* or even, *am I not?,* then realized that the character's persona as it was developing demanded that he speak more informally.

Kirby, too, lavished what seemed to be more attention — as did inker George Klein — on the Thing than on the other characters in the book. Drawn with more power, personality, and mood than others in the issue, it's clear that Kirby, as much as Lee, somehow seemed to identify with and personalize his handling of the character, even in this earliest appearance. In later years, Kirby would come to increasingly identify with the Thing, to the point where Jack would make himself the character's alter ego in a 1978 story (in which Kirby also presented Lee in the Mr. Fantastic team leader role).

A bit later in his *ComiCollector* review,

171

Thomas opined: "With a little added imagination in both stories and artwork — plus, perhaps the addition of a fifth character, such as the Sub-Mariner . . . I think this comic could be worthy of a large circulation."[9]

Of course, the series — starting with issue #2 and certainly by #3 — did indeed come to incorporate that "added imagination." It also came to understand what it actually was and what it could be. But in issue #1, what was there was largely potential. As if in rebellion against the tightly plotted stories being done by DC Comics at the time, *Fantastic Four* #1 is a chaotic mess. Assuming that Lee's plot outline (one of the few that exists for the Lee-Kirby team's working history) for a thirteen-page origin was the template Kirby used to draw the artwork, the story is nonetheless all over the map. (The synopsis can be found in numerous places, including *Fantastic Four* #358.) Lee's opening instructions in the outline/synopsis were:

Story might open with a meeting of Fantastic Four. As meeting starts, caption tells reader that we go back a few weeks to see how it all began . . .

From there, the synopsis goes into a flashback of the team's origin. But as drawn by Kirby in the published story, the first eight pages take place in the *present*. Reed Rich-

172

ards shoots off a flare signal, summoning the rest of the team to their headquarters (in Central City in an unnamed building). Without any mention in Lee's synopsis, we now get an introductory scene for each of the three other members of the team.

We see Susan Storm bolting from a society tea, startling bystanders knocked over by this invisible being. We see the Thing — disguised in overcoat, hat, and shades — as he tries to buy some clothes for his massive frame, who then smashes his way through streets and sewers as he heads for the meeting. Finally, we see Johnny Storm, working on a hot rod in a local garage, burst into flame and zoom through the sky toward the source of the signal, chased by air force planes whose pilots don't know who or what he is — in a route that, according to the narrative captions, takes him "less than an hour" for some reason. The planes fire *nuclear missiles* at him, from which, at the last minute, he is saved by a stretching Mr. Fantastic.

The exciting, albeit illogical, character introductions take seven pages. Finally, on page 9, we at last go into the flashback Lee had asked for and learn the origin of the team, of their ill-fated spaceflight "to the stars" to beat the "commies" to it. Bombarded by cosmic rays — as more than one wonk has noted, genius Reed "forgot" to adequately shield the spacecraft — they are

173

transformed into the Fantastic Four and vow to use their powers to help mankind. The vow takes place on page 13.

On page 14, back in the present, Reed tells them about the mysterious disappearance of atomic plants all over the world, and then we cut away, on page 15, to "French Africa," where another such plant is sucked into a hole in the earth, from which then emerges a monster — the giant green one seen on the issue's cover — that terrorizes a group of soldiers. Then, commanded by its master — the Mole Man (or Moleman as he's called in this, his first appearance) — the monster returns to "the Earth's core."

The story then cuts back to FF headquarters, where the team learns of this latest A-plant theft. Reed improbably figures out that the source of all the trouble is on Monster Isle. The team then flies in its private jet to the island, its name no doubt a deterrent to curious tourists, where they battle a pair of — what else? — monsters. Johnny and Reed are captured by the Mole Man. Mole Man then flashes back to his own origin — and his discovery of the island and its eponymous inhabitants.

In a climactic final scene that takes two pages, consisting of fifteen very cramped panels, the team escapes the monsters. The Torch then uses his flame to "cause a rockslide, sealing us off from those creatures,"

174

although the art sure makes it look like he's roasting them alive underground. Told that Reed let the Mole Man go — "I left him behind — he'll never trouble anyone again!" says Reed — the team flies off, looking to the future in one of the least exciting panels ever drawn by Jack Kirby.

To say the issue was feeling its way is an understatement. The story is choppy, internally inconsistent, lackadaisically drawn, and indifferently plotted, whether by Lee or Kirby or a combination of the two. The other stories the team did that were on sale that same month, such as those in *Rawhide Kid* and *Strange Tales,* were, as far as craft and readability, far superior, far more polished. As reader Bill Sarill wrote of the story in a letter published in issue #3's letter column:

Just finished reading *Fantastic Four* [#1] and must admit to being disappointed. I expect better things from the team of Lee-Kirby. Jack is capable of better art work [*sic*]. . . . The story also suffers from "Creeping Monsterism" to paraphrase Jean Shepard [*sic*], that has dominated most, if not all, of your comics for some time.

Sarill was obviously a serious fan, as opposed to a casual reader, as evidenced by his knowledge of Lee and Kirby's names and careers. That the title's premier letter column

175

would print a negative letter like his was fairly remarkable. Though Lee would often say that he knew *FF* was a hit because of the sudden deluge of mail, the fact is that the first few letter columns contained numerous letters from staff members and comics freelancers, including Sol Brodsky, Stan Goldberg, and Jim Mooney, whose knowing winks accompanying their missives would have been apparent to the few aware of who they were. Other letters were from serious capital-*F* Fans, such as Thomas himself and Ronn Foss. Yet here, interestingly, with Sarill's letter, Lee allowed use of the precious letter page real estate (essentially, a promotional page in disguise) to print a note that doesn't merely point out a misspelling or coloring error but that takes him and Kirby to task for not doing their best work.

Equally as interesting, Lee's response was not to defend himself and Kirby, but to literally say, "See how fair we are? We print the knocks as well as the boosts."

Of course, printing Sarill's letter also enabled Stan to get hip writer and radio personality Jean Shepherd's name into a superhero comic, a subliminal way to tell readers that this comic — this company — this *editor* — was something different from what they had encountered before. Dropping the name of a campus icon like Shepherd in a response to a brutally critical letter was an

176

indication that, while it might not be *The Paris Review,* there was something going on in these comics worth sticking around for, no matter what Bill Sarill thought. (Shepherd, incidentally, popularized the catchphrase "Excelsior!" before Lee took it up as his own.)

As was true even in some of Lee and Kirby's later, more polished work, significant scenes of action in *Fantastic Four #*1 are not shown, but are, bewilderingly, described in captions, indicating that Lee was determined to tell a story that was different in some ways from the one Kirby had drawn. Kirby, pacing the story at his own discretion — which much more often than not would yield works of astonishing power and expressivity — had left a lot of story for the last couple of pages, which are composed of numerous small panels, where a reader might reasonably expect to have been given *more* pages with *larger* panels to show the explosive action going on.

While it's unlikely children of 1961 were reading the story so closely that they'd consciously notice this, in retrospect, the issue reads like the comics equivalent of two captains fighting for control of a ship's wheel. Lee and Kirby's struggle for story control would continue throughout the next ten years but, almost miraculously, would lead to comics that were usually all the better for the conflict.

Still, as Thomas — and others — sensed, despite the chaotic and almost tossed-off nature of the story — maybe even *because* of it — there was a sense that there was something going on here. As Raphael and Spurgeon noted:

Twenty years of benign neglect and creative contempt for the superhero now worked in Kirby and Lee's favor. Even their smallest changes seemed radical and daring.[10]

What came through was both Lee's and Kirby's instincts to go with their gut, to care less about the logic and consistency of the stories and more about the *emotional* impact of what they were writing and drawing. For Kirby, the dominant imperative would be to portray, through his art, his characters' raw feelings and the steamroller intensity of the narrative. For Lee, *how* his characters said what they said — how poignantly they expressed their thoughts, feelings, and personalities — was as or more important than the stories themselves — and was what ultimately made the stories work. Academics might call this a dialectic, an ongoing arm-wrestling match for dominance between the two creators. Comics readers of the era, including

178

many college students, called it *cool.*

With all his interest and enthusiasm, Thomas was a relatively rare kind of reader. He and *ComiCollector* editor Jerry Bails, as well as other adult aficionados of comics, some of whom wrote and read fanzines, were hardly numerous enough to create and sustain an interest in a particular comic book or publishing company. These were dedicated hobbyists, equally, if not *more,* interested in revisiting the comics-reading joys of their childhoods with adult eyes than with seeing what new superhero fare was being published. Their attention, understandably, was largely with the more numerous and established DC heroes — and DC editor Julius Schwartz did give the capital-*F* Fans attention and inside information, as did Lee. But at this point in history, such mavens didn't have the ability to move the needle in sales. What they *did* have was the ability to influence the editors of the comics as far as content — as seen by Thomas's suggestion of returning Golden Age Timely antihero the Sub-Mariner to the comics pages — though they would not have had any influence with the average comic book reader to sway them into trying *Fantastic Four.*

But as Goodman had realized, if DC's *Justice League* was popular, then maybe a kid,

179

seeing *Fantastic Four* on a newsstand, would be willing to gamble a dime on a *new* team of superheroes. At the same time, the cover copy implied that these new characters might actually be *familiar* heroes, declaring that they were "together for the first time in one mighty magazine." And besides superhero-lovers, maybe the audience that liked Timely's other comics — especially the fantasy, sci-fi, and monster titles — would likewise be willing to invest one-tenth of a dollar on something new like *FF* to while away the August days as the end of summer vacation neared.

Fantastic Four #1 went on sale, depending on region, on or around August 8, 1961. The Cold War and the space race were in full swing. Russian Yuri Gagarin had been the first man shot into space on April 17. Alan Shepard became the first *American* in space on May 5, followed on July 21 by Gus Grissom. Less than a week after *FF* #1 went on sale, ongoing tensions between the Soviets and the West would be embodied in the commencement of the construction of the Berlin Wall in the eastern, Soviet-controlled, half of that city. Aware of the headlines as well as the zeitgeist, a kid perusing the contents of *FF* at a candy store might well be tempted to actually buy the comic, featuring Americans bravely rocketing into outer space.

But after getting kids to try a new comic, getting them to *come back* for the next issue *and* to tell their friends about the new publication were the other important steps to creating a hit. If other kids could be induced, by word of mouth, to add one more title to what they would pick up — that was what a publisher needed. Hey, it's only a dime. One less Hershey bar that week? One less Spaldeen? Sure, why not?

Indeed, what Thomas and other older fans saw in the comic must have also been apparent to a significant number of less rabid comic book readers. In a letter dated August 29, 1961, Lee wrote to Bails, "Judging by early sales reports, I think we have a winner on our hands!"

He went on to write:

As for the future of the F.F., we WILL have:
COSTUMES
A DIFFERENT TREATMENT (art-wise) OF THE TORCH
ADDITIONAL NEW CHARACTERS IN MONTHS TO COME
(Don't be too surprised to meet Sub-Mariner again, or Captain America . . . so stay with us, pal!)

Lee concluded by saying that

we have purposely refrained from . . . giving TOO MUCH [*sic*] super powers to our characters, as we feel that effects like those

181

are chiefly of appeal to the YOUNGER readers, and we are trying (perhaps vainly?) to
reach a slightly older, more sophisticated
group.[11]

Lee and Bails also corresponded about
Amazing Adult Fantasy #7 — the retitled and
reimagined *Amazing Adventures* — which
came out the same month *Fantastic Four*
debuted. Each issue of *AAF* would contain
multiple short, surprise-ending fantasy stories
written by Lee and drawn by Ditko. The
stories weren't much different from the other
fantasy and science-fiction shorts that were
appearing in numerous comics in the line,
but having Ditko's distinctive art style in
every story in the magazine gave *AAF* a
unique look and feel. Marketing the package
as somehow being for more intelligent readers — and the use of the word "adult" when
it meant *mature,* not pornographic — was an
important step in developing a sense in the
readership of being special. That sense of being exceptional simply because you were
reading the comic, as well as of being in on
something important, would become key elements in Lee's approach to creating and
promoting the entire Marvel brand.

Bails wrote to Lee that *AAF* "is excellent,
and will probably sell well." He also noted
that "fans are complaining that they can't
find your mags at local stands." How many

182

fans? Well, later in the same letter, he says that there are "some 500 active fans," which most likely means that there were around 500 people who subscribed to his *ComiCollector* and/or *Alter Ego* magazines. He added that, referring to the changes Lee promised: "Most of my correspondents clamored for these changes even before seeing Roy's review."

So somewhere between Lee's desire to do a comic "the way he wanted," as well as his awareness of the possibility of a larger, more sophisticated audience, he somehow intuited that success would be dependent not just on children, and not just on nostalgic, longtime comic book fans, but on a somewhat older, casual reader (or an intelligent younger one) looking for something with more heft than what they'd been reading. *Fantastic Four* and *Amazing Adult Fantasy* were the beginnings of his explorations of the possibilities and potential that might be out there somewhere.

Whether he knew it or not, Stan Lee was developing a publishing strategy that was also a *personal* strategy, a way to at least survive in a marginal company in a marginal industry. Here he was, age thirty-eight, enmeshed in a classic midlife crisis. He wanted more of a challenge and also *needed* to broaden his résumé in case he felt it necessary to leave or was somehow forced to. His self-publishing and syndicated ventures were successful to a

183

point, but not to the point where he could leave his staff position. But even if he didn't end up leaving Timely, he needed to enhance his position there. Goodman would give him occasional editing and writing work for the non-comics magazines, but not enough that Stan could switch entirely to that side of the company. And the comics, though stable for now, very recently were not. How long would they continue to be?

Lee had become accustomed to the middle-class, suburban lifestyle that his day job and freelance work afforded him and his family. He wanted out of comics, but he needed to stay put. To be able to do both — to have his cake and eat it, too — would indeed be an "Amazing Adult Fantasy." As he told historian David Hajdu, of his situation pre–*Fantastic Four*:

I hated it [working in comics in that era]. I always felt I was going to quit. "I'll stay here another few months, or I'll stay another year, get some money together, and then I'll quit." But I never got enough money together, and every time I thought of quitting, I'd get a raise, or we'd add a few new books, and they'd get a little bit interesting. And I did enjoy working with the artists. I made a lot of friends.

So I always, in the back of my mind, [thought] "Well, maybe I'll quit next year,"

184

because I never felt that it was the kind of work for an adult, for a guy who wanted to get somewhere. I was writing these stories — Martin Goodman always felt they were either for young kids or moronic older people.[12]

So with *Fantastic Four* and *Amazing Adult Fantasy,* Lee was beginning a transformation while staying in place. He would, as always, give his boss what he wanted — in this case, a share of the current superhero fad in the comics market — but he would also cultivate an older, more sophisticated audience. He would make comics for people who were culturally aware enough to know who Jean Shepherd was. He would somehow try to make his comics not just kids' adventures but would also, somehow, engage the magazines in the cultural conversation of the day.

Maybe he wasn't one of the Ivy League elite that Goodman employed to work on his schlocky magazines. Maybe he hadn't gone beyond DeWitt Clinton High School. But why couldn't he, like his high school classmate Paddy Chayefsky, aspire to bigger and better things? Maybe if he associated himself with more sophisticated work, someone at a "real" publishing house would take a chance on him. And if that strategy didn't work, what did it matter, really? He had nothing to lose.

It wasn't a plan, exactly — for his career or

185

for his comics line — but it was the beginning of *something*. Maybe it could lead somewhere.

8
WEBS TANGLED AND OTHERWISE

One of the luckiest days of my life was when Steve was available — and willing — to tackle Spider-Man with me.
— Stan Lee, in his introduction to 2013's
The Art of Ditko

As *Fantastic Four* was finding its audience — and Lee and Kirby were finding their combined voice — Timely/Atlas/Marvel was still putting out its Western and humor and horror stories, while still trying to capitalize on the resurgent superhero trend in comics. This led to the creation of Lee and Kirby's Incredible Hulk, who first appeared in an eponymous comic dated May 1962, which would have put it on sale sometime in February. *Incredible Hulk* replaced *Teen-Age Romance* in the limited Goodman lineup. The series — the saga of timid scientist Bruce Banner, transformed by gamma radiation into a raging engine of destruction — lasted a mere six bimonthly issues, with the treatment of the character changing from issue to issue. It

187

would be a couple of years before the Hulk would catch on.

(Although Lee wouldn't start calling the modern incarnation of the company Marvel Comics until the May 1962–dated comics, a small box with the letters *MC* started appearing on the company's covers on a couple of comics dated June 1961, and then on all the rest of the line starting with comics dated July. But no one has ever been able to confirm whether those innocuous letters did indeed stand for Marvel Comics or had some other obscure meaning, perhaps something of note to distributors or retailers.)

A more successful character — although it took some time to realize his success — would be the amazing Spider-Man. Debuting in the final issue of *Amazing Fantasy* (losing the *Adult* for its swan song), dated August 1962, the character would disappear for seven months before reappearing in his own magazine when Lee and Goodman realized how popular that one appearance had been. The creation of Spider-Man, perhaps the most iconic character in the company's history, had much in common with that of the other '60s Marvel superheroes, including existing in the same shared universe. The other Marvel characters were mainly created by Lee and Kirby. Spider-Man, while sharing its writer and editor with the rest of the heroes, had as Lee's cocreator and visualizer Steve

Ditko, whose presence made Spider-Man, as was noted on the first page of his origin story, "just a bit . . . different!"

Spider-Man's origin, as recounted in the character's *Amazing Fantasy* #15 debut, has been related countless times in many media. It goes like this:

Peter Parker, an unpopular but brilliant teenager, is bitten by a radiation-saturated spider. The bite grants Peter spiderlike powers, which he decides to use to make a lot of money for his doting aunt and uncle, who raised the orphaned boy from an early age. But selfishly deciding to not stop a criminal he easily could have, Peter is devastated to find that the same thief has later murdered his beloved Uncle Ben. Capturing the criminal, Peter realizes that "with great power, there must also come great responsibility" and vows to dedicate his life to fighting crime and to making sure, as much as he is able, that no one else ever has to suffer a loss like his.

With Spider-Man's origin, Lee's and Ditko's combined skills produced a pop culture milestone. To many, this is the perfect superhero origin, surpassing even the simple elegance of Superman's and Batman's traumatic beginnings, the former the lone survivor of a doomed planet, the latter the lone survivor of a doomed family.

From his first appearance in *AF* #15,

Spider-Man's milieu was *high school,* as both a metaphor for modern American life, and as a literal and figurative backdrop and battleground during adolescence. As Kurt Vonnegut observed: "High school is closer to the core of the American experience than anything else I can think of."[1] And for his first few years, Spider-Man demonstrated just that.

While Lee and Kirby possessed different temperaments, they both came from a background common to many comic book creators of their era, both being children of poor New York Jewish families. Their common experiences and origins were as much a factor in their work as their contrasting personalities. As historian Mark Alexander observed, "Lee and Kirby both had proletarian Jewish backgrounds. They were both fast, indefatigable workers who could produce stories of remarkable quality and quantity without ever missing a deadline. Other than that, they were diametrically opposite in every possible way."[2]

Steve Ditko, though also possessed of a very different temperament than Lee's, was from a very different background than either Lee or Kirby. As critic Greg Rowland has observed:

While Stan Lee and Jack Kirby reflected aspects of the New York Jewish psyche,

190

Ditko hailed from a small (Johnstown, PA) Czech-American community. In fact, Ditko's work is suffused with the paranoia of a small Middle European nation forever bullied by Empires on all sides (J. Jonah Jameson's toothbrush moustache is no coincidence.)[3]

Kirby's worldview also seemed to be very much shaped by his experiences in combat and conflict, whether on the streets of the Lower East Side or in the battlefields of World War II Europe. Neither Lee nor Ditko seem to have had childhoods filled with street fights, and while they both served in the military, their experiences there, unlike Kirby's, didn't involve combat.

Indeed, it seems that, for all their differences, the common, formative experience that Lee and Ditko brought to the teenage superhero called Spider-Man was that of the American high school. Before exploring Spider-Man's success, some information about his creators' high school years, would seem to be in order.

Stanley M. Lieber's 1939 DeWitt Clinton High School yearbook entry, accompanied by an affable, smiling photo of young Stanley, lists a dozen different clubs and committees he belonged to at the Bronx school, more than any other guy — it was an all-boys school — on the page. (At graduation, Lee

191

was sixteen years old, having skipped a grade or two.)

Always energetic, it seems possible that Stanley might indeed have belonged to all those organizations, but perhaps some were wishful thinking. That he was the president of the Public Speakers Club seems plausible. Membership in the Chess Club would make sense. But was he really the editor of the De-Witt Clinton *Law Journal*? Did he really belong to the French Club? While he had spoken of having a fantasy of being a lawyer, Lee was not known for dropping Gallic phrases into casual conversation. By the same, token, he did recall: "I formed a lot of clubs [in high school]. I formed the Law Society . . . and I think I formed a debating society. But I never stayed with anything much."[4] So he does seem to have been socially active, if only in short bursts.

In many ways, what clubs Lee truly belonged to is beside the point. That he wanted people to *believe* he was active in these dozen organizations is as, or more, significant than if he actually was a member — or if all of them even existed! (Interestingly, though, in a school noted for its accomplished sports teams, Lee lists no athletic activities.) His stated goal, printed next to his picture is: "Reach the Top — And STAY There!" (Classmate Daniel Licker, by contrast, lists his goal as "Aeronautical Engineer.") Each grad was

192

apparently asked for a quote. Lee's was "Join the navy, so the world can see *me!*" — a riff on the navy recruiting slogan, "Join the navy and see the world!" Stan Lieber's nickname was, unsurprisingly, listed as "Gabby."

Most of the other boys on the page list a college in their entry. It's unclear if that's where they hoped to go or where they were actually admitted. Stanley Lieber's entry, though, does not list a college — a bit strange, perhaps, for the editor of the *Law Journal* and president of the Law Society?

The text accompanying seventeen-year-old Stephen J. Ditko's 1945 Johnstown, Pennsylvania, high school yearbook photo — a pleasant, half-smiling shot — lists no clubs or witty sayings, although those of his classmates do. His nickname is given as: "Steve." His plans for his future: "Undecided."

In high school, Ditko "joined a club of teenagers who carved balsa wood into model planes to train airplane spotters in identifying enemy aircraft." This certainly seems like something nerdy Peter Parker might have done. In addition, "the high school Ditko illustrated [in *Spider-Man*] was his from Johnstown, with the same little crenellated battlements at the top. The character of Flash Thompson existed in Ditko's shop class — the bully, beating up other kids for their lunch money."[5]

193

Clearly, high school made a big impression on Steve Ditko, too.

Ditko would go on to serve in the U.S. Army in postwar Germany, return home to pursue an art career, and eventually end up studying at New York's Cartoonists and Illustrators School (today the School of Visual Arts) with Jerry Robinson — renowned for his work on early Batman comics, who would go on to an even more illustrious career in syndicated comic strips and much more. Robinson said of Ditko that he was "very dedicated, and always quiet and reserved. . . . He was in my class for two years, four or five days a week, five hours a night. It was very intense." It was Robinson who introduced Ditko to Stan Lee, who was visiting the class in search of new artistic talent.[6]

His comics career interrupted by a bout of tuberculosis, which sent him back to Johnstown to recuperate, Ditko would return to New York to resume his career in 1955, continuing, like Lee, working until the end of his life. Ditko did his first work for Lee in '56, drawing seventeen stories for him over a six-month period. These were mostly fantasy and science fiction stories, but he also drew a story in *2-Gun Western* #4, dated May 1956, featuring his first collaboration with Lee as his writer, or at least the first one signed by both men.

194

■ ■ ■

While one shouldn't read too much into a literal and figurative snapshot of someone from a formative period in his or her life such as high school, it does seem that there were certain signposts of personality at play in those respective yearbook entries of each man.

With Stanley Lieber — eager to let everyone know his accomplishments, not that concerned if there was an element of exaggeration in his entry — the essence of the adult is already there: a smart, witty, socially adept character, eager to please, probably a lot of fun, if sometimes a bit annoying, to be around. Conversely, Stephen Ditko's photo tells you he's someone who knows something you don't and who doesn't feel he needs to impress you with a list of his accomplishments. That *he* knows them is enough.

While Lee has always spoken proudly of DeWitt Clinton and its illustrious alumni, he has said, "I didn't hate being in school, but I just kept wishing it was over and I could get into the real world, because I wasn't studying anything that I was particularly interested in."[7] This is a not uncommon feeling, although he has also said that if he could have afforded to go to college, he would have, maybe studying "literature, journalism, writ-

195

ing — something like that."[8] He did briefly attend City College of New York because a girl he liked was a student there. But when they broke up, he dropped out.

For Lee, as for many other comics professionals whose formal education was relatively limited and whose need to enter the work world was urgent, high school served the role that college or art school might for future generations of comics makers. It's where identities were discovered, explored, and discarded, where future selves were molded.

For those of Lee's generation in the comic book business, there were the Harvard, Princeton, and Yale of comics — the Bronx's DeWitt Clinton, Manhattan's High School of Music & Art, and Cleveland's Glenville High School — whose ghosts, good and bad, would haunt them forever. For these working-class kids, the fantasy world that for some — those with more means or perhaps a burning desire to pursue academics — was college would end up being their high school years. Not having really attended college, for Lee, the touchstones of his high school years loomed large as turning points, inspiration, story fodder, and more. Notable teachers, such as Leon B. Ginsberg (who taught him that humor often makes it easier to get points across), and memorable schoolmates, like John J. McKenna (a natural public speaker and salesman), regularly turned up in his

196

recollections.[9] Similarly, throughout much of twentieth-century American pop culture, the metaphor of high school — Andy Hardy, Archie Andrews, Ferris Bueller — looms large.

Most comic book superhero fantasies involve, at least in part, enabling a child or teen reading them to imagine being not merely an adult but an adult with astonishing powers and abilities, and possessing the wisdom to use those powers and abilities wisely. Perhaps the ultimate realization of that was the original 1940 Captain Marvel character (published by Fawcett), who literally transformed from being a kid named Billy Batson into an adult superhero.

Kid or teen superheroes like Batman's Robin, the Boy Wonder, and Captain America's Bucky Barnes were usually *sidekicks.* They catered to a fantasy of having a heroic big brother or father or cool adult friend that you could pal around with, who would mentor you in your imagined costumed adventurer career — and who you'd even get to save once in a while.

Stan Lee hated sidekicks.

As he said about Spider-Man: "I hated teenagers in comics because they were always sidekicks. And I always felt if I were a superhero, there's no way I'd pal around with some teenager."[10]

197

There were, over the years, solo kid super-heroes — Superboy, Captain Marvel Jr., Kid Flash — who were child or teen versions of an adult hero, their identities dependent on those of their mentors. But in most cases, a superhero was understood to be a full-grown adult in both civilian and superhero identities, the idea being that no kid wants, deep down, to be a kid, subject to adult whims and orders. The superhero fantasy is about vicariously being an adult with the agency to make important decisions and powerfully affect situations. In addition, many superheroes were really *dual* fantasies for readers to latch onto. While the hero aspect was, of course, imbued with extraordinary powers and/or possessed incredible technology, the characters' civilian identities were usually *also* accomplished and, if not wealthy, then well-to-do, respected professionals — doctors, lawyers, scientists, police officers, billionaire playboys, and so on. There were no prominent heroes who were unemployed or worked as janitors or busboys. Even timid, bumbling Clark Kent was a star reporter for a major metropolitan newspaper.

Which brings us to Spider-Man.

As Lee recalled about Spider-Man: "I thought it might be interesting to make the teenager the actual hero. What would happen if a teenage kid got a power? And then I thought it'd be even more interesting to make him a kid with the normal problems that so many teenagers have."[11]

First assigned to Kirby to draw, a complicated path led to Ditko being assigned by Lee as Spider-Man's artist. Spider-Man did not conform to any of the templates for adult or kid superheroes. Peter Parker did not have money or status.

Readers got this. One, Dan Fleming, said of Spider-Man, in a letter printed in *Amazing Spider-Man* #5:

It's nice that you have a "poor" boy with powers, unlike all those crazy millionaires that have been floating around for years.

Peter Parker was a kid with a lot in common with the teenage Stan Lieber. Peter was on his way to *becoming.* His loving Aunt May and Uncle Ben had no extra money but doted on him, buying him a microscope he'd coveted even though they couldn't afford it — reminiscent of Lee's parents getting him a new bicycle when they couldn't afford one without help from a relative. While Lee was an extrovert (which Peter would become after not too long), he was also, like Peter, a bookworm.

Peter Parker was the regular guy — typical teenager — who, like all "typical" people wasn't — or hoped he wasn't. Peter was an

199

orphan, raised by loving relatives, but ones who *weren't,* at the end of the day, his parents. There was a tragic element to his life before readers even met him. He was bright — brilliant, even — but self-conscious and unsure of himself. Often misunderstood, he alienated the peers he most wanted acceptance from.

It took a radioactive spider bite — and the loss of a third beloved parental figure, Uncle Ben — to give Peter the chance to change all that. But becoming Spider-Man created as many or more problems as it solved for Peter. In some ways, it magnified the adversity he felt life had thrown at him. Watching Peter deal with the changes in his life, his successes and failures as teenager, nephew, classmate, and superhero, became irresistible to readers. So did Peter's sense of humor, unleashed when he put on the webbed mask, but which was also showing more and more when he wasn't in costume. Becoming superpowered — though it regularly nearly cost him his life — gave him a confidence, or perhaps unleashed a confidence that might have been there all along. Suddenly, he developed a romantic life and a social life. Would it all have blossomed had he not gained superpowers? Do the powers make the man, or does the man make the powers?

Whatever the answers, Lee and Ditko together created — and kept creating as they went along — this character who was constantly *becoming* in both his costumed and civilian identities. Peter Parker behaved in, and reacted to, situations the way many young people thought they themselves would — or *wished* they would. He was far from perfect, but *he never stopped trying.* He complained and fretted but always ended up doing the right thing. His creators had discovered a unique combination that would become the template for a whole new style of superhero. He was the best "you," but without losing your problems or deficiencies. He — and you — *overcame* (with much struggle) your problems and deficiencies. And, like you, he had to do it over and over.

In a 1975 interview with Steve Chapman for *The Harvard Crimson,* Lee spoke about his days with the WPA Federal Theatre Project. At one point, he mentioned why he'd left that very-low-paying organization. It would have been easy for him to say something about it being the Depression and him needing to kick in to the family pot. Rising from rags to riches is a perennial favorite narrative successful people tell, especially successful people who grew up impoverished during the Great Depression.

But Lee gave it a special, personal twist. What he said (in a casual, matter-of-fact manner, as he so often would embed revelatory insights) was:

You couldn't make any money in those days . . . and I had a family to support, so I got all kinds of little writing jobs.[12]

Not to help his family. Not to assist his family. To *support* his family.

Lee was never hesitant to speak of his father's regular state of unemployment, the older man spending angst-filled hours at the kitchen table reading help-wanted ads, going out to seek jobs he would never get, returning home depressed and defeated. And yet somehow, the idea of the family being *beyond* poor, *beyond* struggling, to the point where the eldest son's duty was to go out and bring home money so that the family could *survive,* was a stunning statement.

"I had a family to support."

And while he was supporting them (along with whatever help — seemingly unknown to him — other relatives may have been contributing), his mother died. Along with the emotional repercussions for himself, now, through his kid brother, Larry's eyes, Stan would understand the effect of the traumatic death of a parent on a teenager. Perhaps their mother's death was not as theatrically dramatic as the murder of Peter Parker's Uncle Ben, but, certainly for Larry — who has spoken of the trauma of their mother's death

202

— it was life-changing.[13]

Stan Lee knew all too early, if not about great power, then certainly about great responsibility.

The look and feel of Peter Parker's Ditkonian world, despite being set in the present of the early 1960s, is something out of our collective mind's-eye image of the Great Depression. With clothing styles that are more evocative of the '30s than the '60s, with New York streetscapes that might as well have been extrapolated from Edward Hopper's *Nighthawks* painting — as well as from the ecstatically oppressive urban landscapes of Ditko's artistic idols Will Eisner and Jerry Robinson — Ditko's pages exuded a sense of angst and despair. Perhaps he hadn't witnessed the ongoing, daily emotional torment that Lee did, but his life was not untouched by adversity. Spending much of 1955 fighting tuberculosis (with his mother taking care of him — shades of doting Aunt May), just as his career was beginning to take off — when TB was still a dreaded disease that crippled and killed — could not have been easy for Ditko.

Together, Lee and Ditko managed to, through Spider-Man, unleash the dirty little secret of adolescence: it is not all — or even *nearly* all — fun. There are, of course, moments of joy and triumph, but much of it is

203

the confusing struggle of figuring out who one is (or might be) and then trying to devise some kind of strategy for becoming that person. Lee and Ditko together somehow told the truth about being a teenager, a truth enfolded into a tale of a gifted Depression-era kid, even if that kid was ostensibly living in the atomic age.

Spider-Man's villains were also cast from the same Ditkonian metal, even if they were cocreated by Lee. Oddballs and kooks significantly more damaged than the merely neurotic Peter Parker, the Vulture, Dr. Octopus, the Sandman, and the Lizard are all physical freaks who could have been incubated in the pages of Chester Gould's *Dick Tracy,* with added twists of horror stories from *Frankenstein* to *The Twilight Zone.*

There are, unsurprisingly, multiple stories surrounding the creation of Spider-Man. The closest to a truth we have, combining accounts from Lee, Ditko, Kirby, and even Joe Simon, seems to be that either before or after Lee had decided to come up with an insect-derived, teenage superhero, Kirby tried to sell Lee a Spider-Man that was actually a revamped version of the Fly, a character he and Simon had created for Archie Comics' adventure line in 1959. Ditko saw the pages in the office and told Stan that they were very similar to the origin of the Fly, which Lee

204

claimed to never have read. Lee then rejected the pages, still wanting to come up with a new take on his concept.[14]

But this creation tale has numerous versions. Lee wrote in *Origins of Marvel Comics:*

> For quite a while I'd been toying with the idea of doing a strip that would . . . actually feature a teenager as the star, instead of making him an (ugh!) adult hero's sidekick! . . . A strip in which nothing would progress according to formula — the situations, the cast of characters, and their relationship to each other would all be unusual and unexpected![15]

Lee went on, noting that he gave Kirby a plot for a new Spider-Man origin.

> But . . . when I saw the first few pages that Jack had drawn, I realized we had a problem. . . . Try as he might, he had apparently been unable to deglamorize Spidey enough.[16]

An alternative view to the change in artists could be that Kirby figured, if he couldn't sell the pitch he came in with, he'd just drop it. After all, Jack had drawn plenty of scrawny characters in his time, such as the pre-heroic Captain America, Steve Rogers. In either scenario, Kirby was still the workhorse and

205

main artist of the Goodman comics line. Next week, there'd be another character to develop, as well as working on the ones he'd already committed to.

But Lee didn't want to let go of the idea of a spider-powered, teen superhero. He gave it to Ditko, who — in addition to the fantasy stories he was drawing for Lee — was also drawing a superhero that he'd cocreated, Captain Atom, for Charlton Comics. Ditko could do superheroes, he could do weird, and he could portray prosaic, everyday life in a highly charged, dramatic way. And that was what Lee somehow knew he needed. As Raphael and Spurgeon noted: "Ditko's strength was the emotional authenticity he invested in the character, the tortured quality he gave to Spider-Man's existence." The title, they observed, became "an emotionally brutal and funny examination of the frustrations of being a teenager that was as far from Archie Andrews and the gang at Riverdale High as Dustin Hoffman's star turn in *The Graduate* was from Mickey Rooney's Andy Hardy."[17]

Ditko recalled things differently, though his and Lee's recollections seemed to start off converging. Ditko wrote that Lee described to him the five-page "Spider-Man" story done by Kirby, and he told Lee that it seemed exactly like Simon and Kirby's Archie Comics character, the Fly. At that point, he recounts, Lee took Kirby off the new series

206

and assigned it to Ditko.[18]

Over the years, many journalists have, if only for the sake of brevity, credited Lee as sole creator of Spider-Man. About this, in the installment of his ongoing "Tsk! Tsk!" feature in July 1999's *The Comics!,* Ditko wrote:

On what *factual grounds* do some people *talk, write* and *claim* that Spider-Man is a *one-man* creation?

Beneath that, under the heading "Stan Lee's Spider-Man 'Creation,' " there is a vertical rectangle with the words:

SPIDER-MAN

A 1 OR 2 PAGE SYNOPSIS
FOR THE ARTIST WHO MUST
DRAW 21-24 PAGES OF
STORY/ART PANELS.

(DIALOGUE MUST THEN BE
ADDED WORKING FROM
THE ARTIST'S ROUGH PANEL SCRIPT.)

Next to this is an equal-sized rectangle under the words "Steve Ditko's Spider-Man 'Creation.' " Inside this second rectangle is a wordless drawing of Spider-Man as we know him, shooting webs, shining his spider-signal,

207

his head surrounded by squiggly "spider-sense" lines, his face divided into half Parker, half Spider-Man, a look Ditko had invented. Underneath the artwork, Ditko wrote:

IS MARVEL'S SPIDER-MAN COMIC BOOK CHARACTER A **ONE-MAN** CREATION? OR A **COCREATION**?[19]

Are we to infer from this that Ditko felt, that, while he and Stan might have cocreated the character, that Steve deserved the lion's share of the credit? That seems to be a likely reading but doesn't specifically say it.

In another article, Ditko wrote:

Stan wanted me to take Peter Parker/ Spider-man off the wire, ceiling, etc., to change the *spider-like* poses, action.

Why? Stan was afraid The Comics Code "judges" *might* or *would* reject Spider-Man because Peter Parker . . . would be seen by young buyers as something non-human . . . causing all kinds of mental health and behavioral problems. . . .

I said . . . that we should wait until The Code complains. . . .

The Code didn't complain.

Ditko concluded the article (one in a series), saying:

208

No one mind and hand created the Marvel-published S-m "creation."[20]

In his own attempt to set the record straight, Lee regularly and publicly credited Ditko as cocreator. In 1999, in response to Ditko's seeming anger, Lee wrote an open letter, saying in it that

I have always considered Steve Ditko to be Spider-Man's cocreator.

Far from grateful, Ditko was irritated with what he saw as the qualified endorsement implied by the phrase *I have always considered.* He felt that it diluted the fact of co-creation.[21]

In an attempt to be conciliatory, Lee has several times expanded on his statement in the 1999 letter, but not in ways that would seem likely to satisfy Ditko's ire. For instance, in 2004, Lee told Tom DeFalco:

I'm willing to say he's the co-creator. . . . Even though Spider-Man was my idea, Steve believes that an idea is just that, an idea. It's nothing until it becomes fully fleshed out. Spider-Man needed Steve to transform him from an idea into artwork on paper. . . . I actually have no problem with saying that he and I co-created Spider-Man together. . . . Although in my heart of hearts,

209

I still feel that the guy who comes up with the original idea for something is the guy who created it, especially if he's the guy who develops the name and the personality and the gimmicks behind the character.[22]

And in Jonathan Ross's 2007 documentary, *In Search of Steve Ditko,* Lee and Ross had the following exchange:

ROSS: Do you yourself believe that he co-created it [Spider-Man]?

LEE: I'm willing to say so.

ROSS: That's not what I'm asking you, Stan.

LEE: No, and that's the best answer I can give you.

ROSS: So it's a "no" then, really?

LEE: I really think the guy who dreams the thing up created it. You dream it up and then you give it to anybody to draw it.

ROSS: But if it had been drawn differently, then it might not have been successful or a hit.

LEE: Then I would have created something that didn't succeed.

So, although Lee was willing to cede cocreator status to Ditko, it seemed that he really *did* consider himself the creator of Spider-Man, by his own personal definition, because

210

he's "the guy who came up with the idea." This concept seemed to hold true for, say, George Lucas being considered the creator of *Star Wars* and its characters or Gene Roddenberry the creator of the characters in *Star Trek*. It didn't seem unreasonable for Lee to feel that, according to the rules that, at least, Hollywood plays by, he was indeed the creator of Spider-Man.

Kirby biographer Mark Evanier, who worked, at different times, for and with Kirby and Lee, and is himself a Hollywood veteran, has said of that argument:

> Stan used to say, and I think he was dead wrong about this, "If I were to say, 'Let's do a TV show called *The A-Team,*' then I created it, no matter what else anybody can say." And I'd say, "No, Stan, that's not how it works. You don't get a creator credit on television unless you wrote the pilot." And he says, "Is that so?" And then he goes on and says the same thing again. It's like he didn't hear me.[23]

Ditko wrote, in a 2008 essay entitled "Roislecxe" (*Excelsior* spelled backward):

> Lee created and executed his idea [for Spider-Man] in a synopsis. That synopsis is Lee's creation. His S-M creation ends there, a creation of words. . . . Lee can make the

211

valid claim to be the creator of the S-M synopsis. That is his creation. . . . A synopsis of a writer's ideas is not like an architect's blueprint with all the necessary details . . . needed to fully erect the properly desired structure.[24]

Interestingly, and mostly unnoticed by the general public, in his introduction to 2013's *The Art of Ditko* (edited by Craig Yoe), Lee wrote:

So, what makes me qualified to write this intro . . . ? It's because Steve Ditko and I co-created one of the world's most popular superheroes. . . . One of the luckiest days of my life was when Steve was available — and willing — to tackle Spider-Man with me.

No hesitation. No qualifying phraseology. "Steve Ditko and I co-created."

Ditko's response to these words of Stan's, if any, is unknown.

Reading Ditko's writings in his 2008 anthology, *The Avenging Mind,* it becomes clear that the disagreement between the two men was as much philosophical as it was about interpretations or recollections of history. Ditko seemed to simply believe that Lee was not credible, apparently because he did not share Ditko's philosophical principles. The belief was so powerful that, while acknowl-

212

edging Lee as Spider-Man's cocreator, he seemed to feel Stan's role in the birth of the character was minimal. A contempt for Lee comes through clearly, and Ditko gave little, if any, weight to Stan's contributions as scripter, editor, art director, and, yes, coplotter for many of the Spider-Man stories they did together, before Lee agreed to give Ditko full plotting credit.[25]

In many ways, Lee and Ditko's disagreement can be boiled down to what Lee said he "feels" and what Ditko claimed he "proves" in his essays. As with Kirby and Lee and their cocreations, the life experience, talents, interests, and obsessions of the cocreators of Spider-Man combined to come up with a unique pop culture phenomenon. As with Kirby and Lee, outside observers will forever argue, as the creators themselves did, over who did what. And, of course, apart from those disagreements, corporate officials and courts of law will determine who receives what official credit and what financial reward.

Regarding the latter, Lee has been well compensated far beyond the initial writing and editing fees he received. Ditko's actual part of the Spider-Man financial jackpot has never been revealed and is the subject of rumor and speculation.

While the later issues of Ditko's *Spider-Man* run (and probably the entire run from at least

213

issue #18 on) were fully plotted by Ditko — and still scripted, and hence "interpreted" by Lee — the early issues were most likely true collaborations, perhaps with some of the same push-pull interaction that informed the early *Fantastic Four*. But it's pretty much impossible to not see Lee's sensibilities echoed in Peter Parker and his alter ego, no matter what parts of the Lee-Ditko/Ditko-Lee run is considered.

As Raphael and Spurgeon have noted, Spider-Man's early adventures became a way "to explore the nature of growing up, the need to become more reliable, and the spectacular ways in which a young person might be expected to fail." Further, they observed that Lee and Ditko's Spider-Man "largely lived in his own world, an unpleasant place full of rotten people with personal grudges and ungrateful peers who couldn't see past Peter Parker's glasses."[26]

Peter Parker had to navigate an adult world, a world that, in many ways, life had not prepared him for. Like Stanley M. Lieber, Peter Parker became the de facto head of his household. No wonder this teen character chose not to call himself Spider-*Kid* or Spider-*Boy* but Spider-*Man* — and chose to keep his entire face covered to maintain the illusion that he was an adult. (Ditko credited himself with inventing this visual aspect, which seems reasonable.) Even if he looked

214

and sounded much like an adolescent, the world he was inhabiting — a world full of forces trying to destroy him — had to be made to believe that he was not a boy. If he was burdened with an adult's responsibilities, then he would be as much of an adult hero as he could pretend.

But all this angst was not unleavened. Despite the gloominess of the art and writing, there was a sense of it somehow being *fun* to be Spider-Man. In that regard, it was a lot like the reality of being a teenager. True, Spider-Man's victories were laced with drama and tragedy, but they were indeed victories — and sometimes they were even *enjoyable!* And while the origin story does make Peter out to be a friendless outcast, by the first issue of his eponymous comic (published seven months after his debut in *Amazing Fantasy* #15, but by all evidence originally planned to appear shortly after the origin), Peter seems to be the oddball in a group of classmates, but definitely *part* of the group — which is different from having *no* friends. He's regularly ridiculed and belittled by his cohorts, but they do seem to feel that he is, somehow, *connected* to them.

And while Peter's pretty and popular classmate, Liz Allen, generally seems to prefer überjock Flash Thompson to Peter, she does agree to go on a date with Parker (which he then breaks because of his superhero obliga-

215

tions). And J. Jonah Jameson's secretary Betty Brant (who is Peter's age — she dropped out of school for, yes, financial reasons and went to work for Jameson) also seems to have a thing for Peter. She is essentially his peer, and it is with Betty — who knows Peter not as a weirdo nerd but as a daredevil freelance photographer, always taking risks to get "impossible" shots of Spider-Man and his deadly foes — that Peter blossoms into his own, as a pseudo-adult who carries his own weight in an *adult* workplace dominated by the mean-spirited Jameson. And it is with Jameson that Peter asserts his own place in the world, making Jonah pay for his mean-spiritedness — and having his ongoing joke on Jonah — by making the Spider-Man-loathing publisher have to pay Spider-Man for pictures of Spider-Man.

It's here that Lee's life story really assumes a key part in the Spider-Man mythos, despite Ditko's part-to-full role in plotting. Perhaps this is because the two creators were not as dissimilar as they might each have thought.

While it's unclear which dull, menial jobs Lee had while he was still in school and which he had in the period between graduation and his start at Timely, he did seem to repeatedly find himself (aside from a few freelance writing gigs) in jobs where he was treated like a kid or an idiot. These jobs, working for people, especially at the garment

216

center job, who were capricious and abusive, sound exactly like the relationship Parker has with Jameson — with the exception of the wish-fulfillment parts when Parker outsmarts Jameson, even plays pranks like webbing Jonah to the ceiling. (Although Lee's story about overturning the container of cutting tickets does come close.) It's every wage slave's revenge fantasy — which may slightly adjust the power equation, but, in the end, it's Jameson who has the money and the power and the influence. Even then, though — more wish-fulfillment vengeance — Lee gets to show just how shallow Jameson is by having him admit, in a classic soliloquy in *Amazing Spider-Man* #11, why he is so obsessed with Spider-Man. Even if it was Ditko who invented the scene, it was Lee who put the words in Jameson's mouth: "Spider-Man represents everything I'm *not*! He's brave, powerful, and unselfish! The *truth* is, I envy him! . . . But I can *never* climb to his level! So all that remains is for me is to tear him down, because, heaven help me — I'm *jealous* of him!"

(And, of course, giving Peter a nemesis who is a periodical publisher, one who is egotistical and manipulative and changes his mind on a dime, was perfect fodder for Lee to satirize publishing in general, Martin Goodman in particular, and even himself as a boss.)

217

One way or another, the adolescent at the core of Peter Parker — and of Stan Lee — wasn't ever forgotten. The saga of Spider-Man is the story of a young man living in a bubble of love that is shattered suddenly and traumatically, who must then deal with the simultaneous multiple repercussions of such an all-too-real event. Peter must deal with his uncle's death (for which he blames himself — the way the child of an unemployable father might blame himself for the family's woes) and the financial needs of his elderly aunt, as well as her ongoing medical crises, echoing, arguably, Lee's mother's battle with the cancer that ultimately took her life. Peter Parker's life is trauma upon trauma, an echo of Stan's (and Larry's) own difficult journey.

But paradoxically, preserved through strength of character — albeit character shrouded in neuroses — is the Peter Parker who loves life, who devises the way to make best use of the unexpected gift of his super-human powers. The trauma of Uncle Ben's murder shifts Peter away from a showbiz career — which Lee himself had always coveted — into a career as a costumed superhero, albeit one who is, nonetheless, more than a bit of a showboat. Peter becomes a costumed vigilante who flamboyantly fights crime, making sure everyone knows he was there — up to and including inventing a glowing spider-signal that emits from his belt.

How much different is that from climbing on a ladder and painting "Stan Lieber is God" on a ceiling?

And yet, like Peter Parker, Stan Lee was also prone to occasionally making morose observations about his life. "I think I should have gotten out of this business twenty years ago," he told reporter Ira Wolfman in 1978. "I would have liked to make movies, to be a director or a screenwriter."[27]

Similarly, Peter Parker, at the end of many of his Lee-scripted adventures, wonders whether the personal losses he suffers as a result of being Spider-Man are worth it. As early as 1963's *Amazing Spider-Man* #4, he asked himself:

Am I really some sort of a crack-pot, wasting my time seeking fame and glory?? Am I more interested in the adventure of being Spider-Man than I am in helping people?? Why do I do it? Why don't I give up the whole thing?

Spider-Man, at the character's best, experiences great highs and lows *that the reader experiences along with him.* And more, despite his serious intent, "Spidey" often *does* engage in actions and behaviors that have nothing to do with his famous power-and-responsibility equation. He's Spider-Man for all sorts of other reasons. He does need to make money

219

for his aunt. But he also enjoys being Spider-Man because it's fun to web-swing around the city and clobber bad guys. Further, he enjoys selling pictures of himself to the unsuspecting Jameson. Longtime Spider-Man writer and editor Tom DeFalco has observed that, like a real person, Peter Parker has numerous motivations and rationalizations for why he does what he does.[28] Indeed, as described by the narrator (Lee!) in the final panel of issue #9, Spider-Man is "the superhero who could be *you!*"

Ditko's writings, as confusing as they can be, do make clear that, as much as Lee or Kirby, the Spider-Man artist and cocreator had a need to think about and get inside the minds of the characters he was working on. Somehow, the mix of the needs, obsessions, neuroses, and creative talent of Lee and Ditko invested Spider-Man with a sensibility that was simultaneously "theirs," and yet also identifiably *Marvel* — though radically different from the larger section of the shared Marvel Universe that was built upon the Lee-Kirby collaborations.

While in his later, more Randian writings, Ditko would rage against what he saw as weak-willed or ethically compromised thinking (especially when he perceived such thinking coming from Stan Lee, which was frequently), the images (if not always the ideas)

220

he provided in their collaborations gave Lee the foundation he needed to imbue Spider-Man with greater capacity for nuanced, even self-contradictory, behavior — for *doubt* — than the artist had probably ever intended he possess. Peter Parker, as published, was a character of contradictions. Proud and ashamed. Powerful and weak. Focused and scattered.

It is hard, though, to not, at least in part, read Ditko's angry writings about Lee as having their source in some kind of personal disappointment in Stan as a friend and colleague, somehow a feeling of personal betrayal or disappointment, as much as in creative or philosophical or even financial disagreements the two might have had. Similarly, as with his feelings about Kirby, Lee's confusion and disappointment about the difficulties in his relationship with Ditko seem to be related to regret and anger over losing a friend as much as any conflict in their attitudes or opinions about the work they did together.

While Spider-Man can be said to have been an idiosyncratic, combined autobiographical work of his creators, the character also — perhaps *because* of that combining — resonated powerfully with readers. In some fans, Spider-Man's persona seemed to bring out Peter Parker–like contradictions. A letter in

Amazing Spider-Man #8 from Doug Storer of Butte, Montana, started out in a highly complimentary manner:

Your latest and greatest creation, AMAZING SPIDER-MAN, has surpassed anything I've ever seen hit the stands. . . . Everything about Spider-Man can and must be discussed in the superlative.

But the letter then took a different path:

However, there is one thing that bothers me about Spider-Man. He may, in due season, become "just another hero." You may call me a pessimist, but I've seen it happen before and it can happen again. . . . You see, I'm very worried about what will happen to my now favorite mag.

Storer didn't just like or even empathize with Spider-Man. Like Aunt May, he *worried* about the guy. Lee and Ditko had come up with something — *someone* — who really touched people.

For another example, in issue #12's letters page, Jodene Green Acciavatti of Brookline, Massachusetts, pleaded:

Please don't change Spider-Man. He seems so human right now. I know that people can be as aggravating as his schoolmates are

222

to him. . . . He is too busy to conform to their personal code, so as he is different, they scorn him. Don't they have anything better to do? I have the same problem, so I feel akin to Spider-Man. . . . What makes Spider-Man different is that he must battle alone through life.

The passive-aggressive tug-of-war between Lee and Ditko over the content of the stories they collaborated on continued over time, with readers none the wiser, until, for many months before Ditko's 1966 departure from Marvel, he and Lee had stopped speaking to each other (Sol Brodsky usually acted as intermediary), each, in later years, blaming the other for that turn of events.

Whether Spider-Man's lone battle was as a Randian avatar or as, perhaps, a superpowered, traumatized version of flaky '60s TV teenager Dobie Gillis, all depended on your point of view. But because he was the one who got to put the words in the captions and balloons, it ultimately depended on *Stan Lee's* point of view.

Meanwhile, Marvel's popularity kept growing, and readers — and Martin Goodman — were demanding more superheroes in the style of the FF and Spider-Man. There was still plenty of room in this nascent fictional universe for other types of heroes, other audi-

223

ences — and other aspects of the existing audience — to be tapped into and cultivated. Stan Lee was determined to do exactly that.

Things were just beginning to get interesting.

9
CREATING CHARACTERS

Disney bought Marvel Comics not because Marvel Comics is the place that basically gave us the metaphor for homosexual struggles in America, and for the struggles of the immigrant and struggles of minorities, which is really the basis of Marvel's whole message. It was because of the kid-friendly face, and that was provided by Stan.
— longtime Marvel writer and editor
Gerry Conway[1]

The origin stories of Marvel's superheroes have a kind of comfortable sameness. Most, if not all the line's 1960s characters were somehow or other radiation-derived — in an era when elementary schools regularly held nuclear-attack preparedness drills — such as those transformations experienced by the Fantastic Four, the Hulk, and Spider-Man. Radiation was an easy plot device to use.

A more charitable reading of the heroes' beginning would say they were, intentionally or not, tied together thematically. This view

225

would not be incorrect. All were hatched by a small group of men, over a short span of time, in a specific era — one obsessed with the perils of nuclear power.

The other thing the characters' origins have in common is that, though they were created mostly by Lee and Kirby — with Ditko, of course, heavily involved on a couple of significant heroes (Spider-Man and Dr. Strange) — there is little agreement on who exactly did what *conceptually* on these now-classic characters' creation. The pencilers, obviously, did the visual storytelling. Beyond that, there are the stories of who came up with what, told by the principals, which seem to vary from telling to telling, and there are logical assumptions made by people who came on the scene relatively shortly after the characters were created. There is also endless detective work done by fans and historians to try to piece together the "authentic" credits for the early adventures and stories.

But there were, as far as we know, no tape recorders operating when the characters were spawned. (Artists Gene Colan and Dick Ayers have both drawn comics — Colan's with Lee as writer — that depict themselves recording their plot conferences with Lee, and John Romita Sr. has also mentioned recording plotting sessions, but these were all done long after the characters were first created.) Indeed, many of the characters were not even thought of at the time of their debuts as being especially novel. They were riffs on characters that had appeared in mythology or in classic fiction or the works of Shakespeare or that were seen that week on TV, or heard on the radio decades earlier, or viewed in a movie theater sometime, or were even echoes of characters published in a competitor's (or Goodman's own) comics.

In his 2017 acceptance speech for his Nobel Prize, singer-songwriter Bob Dylan cited works of music that informed his sensibilities. He then went on to note:

I had principles and sensibilities and an informed view of the world. And I had had that for a while. Learned it all in grammar school. *Don Quixote, Ivanhoe, Robinson Crusoe, Gulliver's Travels, Tale of Two Cities,* all the rest — typical grammar school reading that gave you a way of looking at life, an understanding of human nature, and a standard to measure things by. . . . And the themes from those books worked their way into many of my songs, either knowingly or unintentionally.[2]

"Typical grammar school reading," but of course, filtered through Dylan's unique sensibility — that thing we call *talent,* and sometimes even *genius.* Everyone in a society is routinely and regularly exposed to certain

227

works of fiction and history. But only some can take that material and look at it in ways that no one has before.

Similarly, Lee and Kirby took that common, familiar material and made it into something new. So did Lee and Ditko and Lee and his other collaborators. They transmogrified familiar cultural elements into something else. Through the mundane need to make a deadline and earn a living, they created a modern mythology that — as much as it is commercial "product" — also means a tremendous amount to so many. In a 2001 interview with *Tripwire Magazine,* Will Eisner referred to Lee as "kind of a magician" who got the best out of his artists.[3] But it's equally true that the artists simultaneously brought out the best in Stan Lee. They were, indeed, the right people at the right place at the right time.

Following *Fantastic Four* #1 (dated November 1961), in an astonishingly short period of time, the original Marvel pantheon came into existence, and with few exceptions, the new characters were enthusiastically received by the comics-reading public. With each success, Lee and Goodman decided that Lee and Kirby needed to come up with more superheroes — and they did.

In the order in which their debuts were published, the new — or newly spotlighted

228

— characters following the Fantastic Four showed up thus:

The Incredible Hulk, debuting in his own magazine (dated January 1962), was a hybrid of Jekyll and Hyde and the Frankenstein monster. Scientist Bruce Banner is caught in a gamma-bomb explosion and becomes the green-skinned engine of destruction. *The Incredible Hulk* series wasn't a big hit, lasting only six issues, but Lee had faith in the character, guest-starring him after his own series' cancellation in issues of *Fantastic Four* and *Spider-Man,* and eventually, he caught on, returning to costar with Ant-Man in *Tales to Astonish,* starting with issue #60, dated October 1964.

Thor, first appearing in *Journey into Mystery* #83, cover-dated August 1962 (the same month as Spider-Man's debut in *Amazing Fantasy* #15), was birthed by Lee (plot), Lieber (script), and Kirby (pencils and probably plot input). Crippled, frail American doctor Donald Blake, on a Scandinavian vacation, finds an enchanted, gnarled wooden stick that transforms him into the Norse god of thunder. Worth noting is that Lieber's stories were usually done "full script," from Lee's short plots, so the artist — usually Kirby — would be working from a much more structured blueprint than when working directly with Lee.

229

In *Tales to Astonish* #27, appearing the same month the Hulk debuted (dated January 1962), Henry Pym invented a chemical formula that could shrink him to ant size. But he didn't put on a superhero costume and call himself Ant-Man until issue #35, dated September. He would later gain the power to also make himself giant-sized. Before too long, Ant-Man/Giant-Man is joined by socialite Janet Van Dyne, whom he transforms into the Wasp (a tongue-in-cheek comment from Jewish creators Lee, Lieber, and Kirby?).

The cosmic ray–spawned Human Torch, while remaining part of the Fantastic Four, would spin off into a solo series in the pages of *Strange Tales,* starting in issue #101, dated October 1962. Some of his early stories would be scripted by Superman cocreator Jerry Siegel, who had (again) been black-balled at DC. But most were written by Lee and Lieber, with Kirby and Ayers, or just Ayers, doing the art.

In *Tales of Suspense* #39 (dated March 1963), industrialist Tony Stark is the victim of a Vietnam battlefield booby trap that damages his heart. Held captive by the Viet Cong, Stark creates the first Iron Man armor. The origin story was by Lee, Lieber, and Don Heck. Iron Man's costume was designed by Kirby, and, a year later, modified by Ditko. In this same month of Iron Man's debut,

Spider-Man's own comic premiered, seven months after his *Amazing Fantasy* #15 appearance.

Dr. Strange was first seen in *Strange Tales* #110 (cover-dated July 1963). Superstar surgeon Stephen Strange's toxic hubris leads to a car crash and nerve damage that ends his medical career and starts him on his path to becoming the Master of the Mystic Arts. Strange's is a lifelong struggle — like Spider-Man's — to atone for his selfish behavior. Created by Ditko, Strange is a riff on the recently terminated Dr. Droom, also drawing (as did Droom — and for that matter, as did FF villain Dr. *Doom*) on elements of '30s radio series like Lee's childhood favorite, *Chandu the Magician,* and on *Lost Horizon* — the book and the movie based on it. Lee's ambivalence toward Dr. Strange was exhibited in a January 9, 1963, letter to Jerry Bails:

Well, we have a new character in the works for STRANGE TALES (just a 5-page filler named DR. STRANGE —). Steve Ditko is gonna draw him. Sort of a black magic theme. The first story is nothing great, but perhaps we can make something of him —'twas Steve's idea, and I figgered we'd give it a chance although, again, we had to rush the first one too much.[4]

The words *'twas Steve's idea* leave unclear

231

if Lee was referring to the character, the character's origin, the series' mystical motif, the plot to the first story, or some combination of those elements. Clearly, it's not something Lee — at least early on — was very enthusiastic about, nor did he seem especially concerned about expressing reservations regarding the new strip to a member of the fan press. Although Ditko was one of his favorite artists to work with, the strain in their relationship seems to have been developing even this early in their collaborations for Marvel's superhero era. This was borne out in Ditko's later writings, where he expressed deep resentment regarding what he felt was Lee's attitude toward the character and toward Ditko himself. As he wrote:

"Nothing great" so undercutting, dismissing my total contribution, my original idea's worth, value.

The "perhaps we . . ." is only an apparent Lee giving, because the implication is that Lee has to do all of the work in making "something out of it." . . . We have Lee's apparent giving, undercutting and taking away and ending up with Lee as the only real, creative mind.[5]

But the new heroes did not end with Dr. Strange. According to Lee, to prove that the Marvel "formula" could work in any genre, he and Kirby came up with the World War II–set battle comic *Sgt. Fury and His Howling Commandos,* whose eponymous first issue was dated May 1963.[6] (A couple of years after that, Fury — now sporting an eye patch — would become the new leader of the covert spy group called S.H.I.E.L.D., a Lee-Kirby creation, which would debut in *Strange Tales* #135, dated August 1965.)

In *X-Men* #1, dated September 1963, Charles Xavier gathers together a team of young people whose mutant powers (generally ascribed to some type of exposure to radiation, before the heroes' births, of their parents) make them hated and feared by the world around them, despite their dedication to protecting that world. The X-Men were created by Lee and Kirby.

The Avengers #1, also cover-dated September 1963, gathers together Thor, Iron Man, Ant-Man, the Wasp, and (for a short time) the Hulk into a team. Lee and Kirby have now given Goodman the superhero group — comprised, like the Justice League, of established characters — that he had wanted.

Young Matt Murdock gains enhanced senses from a fateful encounter with — no surprise — radioactive material. As an adult, after avenging his father's murder, Matt, moonlighting as a lawyer, embarks on a career as Daredevil, in *Daredevil* #1. That comic was dated April '64 but had originally

233

been scheduled as September '63. When returning artist Bill Everett (creator of the Sub-Mariner, and a Timely/Atlas mainstay through the '50s) had deadline problems due to a demanding day job as an ad agency art director, the series was postponed, replaced in the schedule by *The Avengers.*

Captain America would be revived in *Avengers* #4 (dated March 1964) and soon get his own feature in *Tales of Suspense* (issue #59, dated November 1964). The Sub-Mariner would costar in *Tales to Astonish,* starting in issue #70, dated August 1965. New and established superheroes would eventually take over most of Goodman's science-fiction and fantasy lines.

But the ball was now rolling, zooming under its own momentum, as the pieces were firmly in place for the fictional universe that thrives to this day in multiple media. Of course, in 1964, there was no way to know that. With the exception of *Daredevil* — which had been scheduled to debut seven months earlier than it finally did — the new characters were all introduced to the Marvel Universe less than two years from the debut of *Fantastic Four.* And with the exception of Dr. Strange and Spider-Man, all the characters emerged from some combination of the talents of Stan Lee and Jack Kirby, with Larry Lieber contributing, although Larry has never claimed to have conceived or

234

designed any of the characters. (He did, however, name Anthony Stark, Henry Pym, and Donald Blake.)

And all this was produced while Marvel was still churning out Westerns, romance, humor, and other non-superhero genre fare. For instance, the same month in 1963 that *Avengers* and *X-Men* debuted, Marvel also put out titles including *Kid Colt Outlaw* #112, *Millie the Model* #116, *Modeling with Millie* #25, *Patsy Walker* #109, *Sgt. Fury* #3, and *Two-Gun Kid* #65. In addition, the anthology titles that were now featuring superheroes still had, and would have for some time to come, fantasy and science-fiction stories filling out their pages.

While Lee has claimed to not have read many of the comics that other companies were putting out, except to perhaps scan them to see who was drawing them (and he's certainly said in a 1990s video interview that he "loved" EC's comics), the fact remains that there was a lot of competition around. Perhaps there weren't as many comics being published in the early '60s as there were in the heyday of the 1940s and 1950s, but there were plenty of them; comics of one kind or another were ubiquitous, published by at least a dozen companies. And Goodman wasn't the only publisher to notice the

235

renewed interest in the superheroes published by DC Comics. Other organizations jumped into the mix, as well, especially once Marvel started gathering heat. And some companies gladly mimicked the look and feel of Marvel.

A random sampling of some of the dozens of comics (many licensed from TV and movie properties) that were fighting for attention on newsstands with Marvel's in 1961–65 would include:

DC's Superman, Batman, and Wonder Woman titles, as well as their other superhero comics, such as *Flash, Green Lantern,* and *The Atom.* And of course, *Justice League of America.*

Dell's *Ricky Nelson, Bonanza, Leave It to Beaver, Uncle Scrooge, Dracula,* and *The Beatles.*

Archie Publishing's Archie-related comics, as well as their superhero comics *The Fly* and *The Jaguar.* The Archie superhero line would hire Superman cocreator Jerry Siegel to help rebrand their heroes as "Mighty Comics," which imitated Marvel's look and feel, but not seeming to grasp what made Lee's line work.

Gold Key's comics line, which included *Doctor Solar, Magnus Robot Fighter,* and *The Phantom.*

ACG's *Forbidden Worlds,* which featured Herbie, the Fat Fury, and its *Adventures into*

236

the Unknown, which starred the superhero known as Nemesis.

Harvey Comics' humorous *Sad Sack, Casper,* and *Richie Rich* comics.

Charlton's *Teenage Hotrodders* and *The Young Doctors* (cashing in on the popularity of TV medical dramas like *Dr. Kildare),* and the Ditko-drawn *Captain Atom.*

In the culture surrounding the comics creators and their audience in the 1960s, between music, movies, TV, and the seemingly endless shock brought by each day's nightly news and morning headlines, there was a continuous supply of inspiration. The zeitgeist was full to the bursting point with fast-changing events performed by a wide array of colorful and controversial characters. Were the '60s really more tumultuous than the previous decades of the twentieth century, which had included two world wars, at least two major genocides, the Russian Revolution, and the Great Depression? Probably not. But by the same token, the immediacy and ubiquity of media exploded in the '60s and made it quite clear that the times were indeed a-changin'.

A brief checklist of some of the many cultural phenomena, real and fictional, which formed the media mix assaulting and informing Americans — and shaping the sensibilities of the baby boom generation that was

237

coming into its own — would include:

The assassinations of John and Robert Kennedy, and of Martin Luther King Jr.; the Great Society; the War on Poverty; the civil rights movement; the Beatles; Bob Dylan; *The Man Who Shot Liberty Valance; The Hustler;* James Bond movies and *The Man from U.N.C.L.E.* TV series; *Rawhide* and the whole then-still-thriving Western/cowboy genre; PT 109; *The Beverley Hillbillies;* Johnny Carson taking over *The Tonight Show; The Twilight Zone; Goodbye, Columbus, and Other Stories; Last Year at Marienbad;* the birth control pill; the Vietnam War; the Berlin Wall; the Cuban Missile Crisis.

Whether you lived through them or not, you probably have your own '60s montage in your head. It may be your own personal golden age, your own bête noire that you've vowed to erase, perhaps just an era and a state of mind that you're sick of hearing about from your parents or grandparents, maybe an era you long to have lived in, or possibly you were there, but feel like you missed out on all the action.

For a lot of people, the early adventures of Spider-Man, the Hulk, the Fantastic Four, Thor, and the rest of the Marvel heroes are a big part of what the '60s were about. Even at the time, magazines like *Esquire* had a sense that these characters were an integral part of

238

the current conversation. It named Spider-Man and the Hulk as two of the "28 People Who Count" on college campuses in its September 1965 issue.

Noticed and taken seriously by campus activists and tastemakers, rock stars, and movie directors (if not yet by Hollywood executives, serious novelists, and college professors), Stan Lee and his artistic collaborators had stumbled onto something that resonated with populations well beyond comics-reading children and the tiny population of nostalgic adults who had maintained an interest in continuing the comics hobby they'd started during their World War II–era childhoods.

Jules Feiffer's 1965 book, *The Great Comic Book Heroes,* was aimed at an audience of adults who were interested in taking a mature look at what had fueled their childhood fantasies. While it found that audience, it also achieved a perhaps unanticipated goal of fueling the imaginations and sense of history of the boomer kids who were reading Marvel and the other publishers' output and were intrigued by Feiffer's stories of what the comics companies — especially Marvel and DC — were doing before they were born. Far from confusing modern readers by bringing up a buried history, it *intrigued* them and made them, if anything, *more* eager to find out the backgrounds of not just the charac-

239

ters, but of the creators and companies behind them. They not only didn't want to "ignore the man behind the curtain" — they wanted to know all *about* him!

Strangely, because of the dire straits into which the comics business had fallen during the 1950s, many of the same people who made those "Golden Age" 1940s comics were still, especially at DC Comics, making them in the early '60s. There wasn't much incentive for newcomers to try to enter the field in the late '50s and early '60s. For industry veterans — feeling older, shut out of other fields, condemned to creating piecework as freelancers, or stuck in seemingly dead-end, if somewhat secure, staff career paths like Lee's — the '60s breathed new life, or at least some sense of steadier employment, into their worlds.

Many of DC's editors, writers, and artists were holdovers from the '40s. Editors Julius Schwartz, Mort Weisinger, and Jack Schiff had started their careers then. So had artists Gil Kane and Carmine Infantino. The DC editors had their private fiefdoms of titles and creators, and seemed content to rule within them, fiercely protecting their talent from being "poached" (although as freelancers, they could, in theory, have worked for whomever they liked) by their fellow editors, as well as by other companies. These editors answered to executives Jack Liebowitz or Whitney

240

Ellsworth or Irwin Donenfeld, depending in the particular time frame and issue at hand.

They had — or believed they had — a certain amount of job security and didn't seem to be interested in rising above their comfortable stations. Nearing fifty as the '60s unfolded, their mandate was to produce short, plot-driven comics stories, much as they had been doing for two decades. Ambitions they might have had beyond editing comics were attended to in ways that didn't threaten the status quo. Weisinger had a wide-ranging freelance writing career, consisting largely of articles for national magazines. Robert Kanigher wrote many comics for DC, as well as editing them. (He wrote and edited *Wonder Woman* for two decades and, notably, had penned the 1956 Flash story that heralded DC's superhero expansion.)

As parts of such an entrenched bureaucratic structure, none of these editors had the relative autonomy of Stan Lee — nor the mixed blessing of working for a relative, a Damoclean sword regularly brushing the remaining hairs on his head, threatening, if not his employment, then at least the department he ran.

At Marvel, interestingly, with the exception of Kirby, many of Lee's artists were comparatively young, having started their careers in the late '40s to mid-1950s, though they still took their creative lead from "old-timers" Lee

241

and Kirby.

Still, it wasn't by any means automatic that something as dynamic as Marvel Comics should have emerged from the offices of Stan Lee and Martin Goodman, who had both been in comics even longer than most of DC's staff. And Kirby, after all, had been working for DC, so it's not as if they were denied the opportunity to make use of his skills and genius. And yet, nothing he did there caught fire the way Marvel would.

Lee was seven or so years younger than DC's editors — yet with as much or more experience than most of them. Perhaps that comparative youthfulness, combined with thousands of comics stories of all kinds under his belt, was crucial to his being able to fruitfully mix the currents of the times with his own and his artists' talents and abilities. Perhaps also significant was Goodman's unique combination of insight, business acumen, and sensitivity to the zeitgeist. As a two-man show, it was no small thing that Lee and Goodman could make decisions and have them *immediately* enacted. They could respond to any perceived change in the marketplace or in audience taste with no lag time for memos, meetings, and other bureaucratic baggage.

Timely/Marvel — and hence, Stan Lee — also had the unique circumstance of having been enormously successful, if not especially

242

original, only to lose everything suddenly, but then to survive — barely — as a shrunken, battered company with a shell-shocked editor. Perhaps that's what made it the perfect place to come up with traumatized superheroes, characters who were inherently attuned to the fact that anything could be lost at any time. The trauma of the late '50s at the company made Lee's antenna sensitive enough to the times that — when presented with talents like Kirby and Ditko laid at his doorstep — he could, with those creators, make something that the comfortable, solid professional editors at DC couldn't.

Important, too, is that though by the late '60s Lee would attempt to present himself as some version of "hip," in the formative years of Marvel, he was intuitive enough to present a public image that was a version of who he really was: a square suburban dad, but one who hadn't forgotten his inner child; a guy who was still able to have fun, and to create fun for others in the pages of the comics. He had a sense of what was exciting and interesting to kids, but was also willing to learn *from* them what was modern and, what he couldn't intuit or remember from his own childhood. He conveyed enthusiasm that didn't seem to be faked. While he longed to go on to *bigger* things, he didn't seem to want to go on to *better* things. In other words, he loved telling stories in collaboration with other people for

243

a living. Did he yearn for a larger, more widely viewed, more lucrative canvas to do it on? Of course. But the basics of what he did — making up stories and interacting with creative, interesting people — was something he could truly get excited about.

Stan Lee was simultaneously comfortable and antsy, ambitious but too practical to walk away from the familiar. With a personal history that would not have been unfamiliar to the cast of an Odets or Chayefsky play — the luckless father, the dying mother, the traumatized brother — even if he couldn't pull out of himself the Great American Novel, he could bring to his comics work an understanding of tragedy and brokenness and, it would turn out, an ability to express them in ways relatable to readers.

That, of course, is where the X factor of *talent* comes in. Lee and his collaborators had that, and he had been practicing his craft for more than twenty years. He was ready to move to another level, if not with syndicated comic strips, then within the milieu with which he was most familiar. As he told the reporter whose byline was "Peter Parker" in the March 29, 1966, issue of the Berkeley independent newspaper, *The Daily Californian,* "I take it [my work] very seriously. . . . 20 years ago I didn't take it seriously and the books were never so good. . . . [The books] are better now than they were a year ago, and they were better [then] than they were five years ago."[7]

Likewise, something in Kirby and Ditko — and in Larry Lieber — was ready, too. They had been getting ready for Marvel, without realizing it, for several years. The work they produced with Lee, however they produced it, was different and compelling.

As innovative comics artist and writer Neal Adams observed:

You have Spider-Man [for instance] who was a shitty brat kid who gets these super powers . . . and his own miserable ego allows his Uncle Ben to die, and he finally turns into a hero. These are new directions for comic books. Over at DC Comics, all they had were basically chiseled-jawed, shiny-toothed good guys who were good guys *before* they became heroes, and good guys *after* they became heroes.[8]

Adams went on to note about Marvel's heroes that:

You can say, well, they're developed characters who have personalities. Well, no they're just rotten people. [But] over at DC, they basically had *no* personality. They had *zilch.*[9]

So, Marvel's heroes start out flawed, usu-

245

ally by arrogance — they weren't perfect like DC's heroes — and are transformed by getting superpowers. But their basic character flaws don't disappear. They become heroes by *rising above* those flaws. This is the classic hero's journey as described by Joseph Campbell and others. A flawed individual tries to overcome his or her shortcomings, and the character's heroism isn't in simply doing good but also — if not primarily — in overcoming the human desire to do selfish, spiteful things, which would be *especially* tempting should one acquire superhuman abilities. Marvel's heroes were tempted by the darkness in a way previous superheroes rarely had been. The struggles with their inner demons marked them as imperfect — flawed, damaged, and hence, relatable — and doubly heroic, fighting inner as well as external battles.

We hear it so much that it long ago became a cliché, but in the early '60s, the idea of "heroes with feet of clay" was a new and exciting thing in comic books. The broken hero was not a new idea in fiction, but it certainly was in comics. Marvel's heroes were the comics equivalent of Bogart's Rick Blaine in *Casablanca,* perhaps, or Raymond Chandler's Philip Marlowe: cynical characters, idealistic at heart, but hurt in life or love, battered by circumstance. Charles Foster Kane, having it all but really having nothing.

Montgomery Clift or James Dean in pretty much every role: tormented inside and out, tempted to do the wrong thing, but compelled by some core strength of character to, eventually, do the right thing. And doing the right thing not simply because it's the right thing (as any superhero would do), but because the thought of living with yourself after *not* doing the right thing is unbearable. To not do the right thing would make you, well, a *villain* — and many of Marvel's villains had origins not unlike those of its heroes. The lessons the villains learned from their traumas, though, were much different from what the heroes took away from theirs.

Of course, superheroes had been "flawed" up until then, but not in ways that *really* mattered to their inner character, to what reached out to audiences emotionally. Superman was vulnerable to Kryptonite. Green Lantern's ring couldn't work on anything yellow. And, yes, Superman and Batman were survivors of great traumas, but you wouldn't know it for most of their careers into the '60s. Nothing really seemed to faze these characters. "I'm the sole survivor of an exploded planet? Oh, well. I must get back to making sure Lois doesn't discover my secret identity. And I have to carve a giant granite key for my secret arctic clubhouse. No morose reflecting for me."

Marvel's characters, on the other hand, had

247

flaws — hell, *embodied* flaws, weaknesses, vulnerabilities — of personality. You could find their diagnoses throughout the various editions of a psychiatrist's *DSM* diagnostic handbook. They had tragic pasts that they actually acknowledged, reflected on, and were motivated by! Their origin traumas were thematically integral to all their best stories. Many of them were arrogant to the point of hubris: Reed Richards takes his friends into space on a faulty rocket ship; Stephen Strange only operates on rich people; Peter Parker gets spider-powers and immediately seeks to cash in on them; Thor is so full of himself that Odin traps him in the body of a crippled mortal. And their comeuppance for their hubris is always profound, always eliciting endless regret. If they could only go back and do things over, save someone, make a better choice . . .

Not only were Marvel's heroes riddled with flaws of Shakespearean level, but so, as mentioned, were its villains! What made the heroes *heroes* was their transcending their flaws and traumatic pasts. If they could do it, so could you! And if some villains like Hawkeye or the Scarlet Witch and Quicksilver could transcend their pasts and become heroes — then maybe there was hope for you, too, no matter how many times you screwed up. Hard-core villains like Dr. Doom, Dr. Octopus, and the Mole Man were flawed individuals who used their powers to *get even* with the world, to get rich, to abuse others. The heroes — eventually, and with great struggle — rose above such base responses to life's adversity. That's what made them heroes. (Marvel's villains, of course, were not without a certain tragic nobility, too, which made them appealing and sympathetic, despite their horrific actions. This more sophisticated approach to "bad guys" was another leap forward for comics.)

Marvel's good guys were, indeed, the heroes "who could be you." Not because you might have a chance encounter with an irradiated spider or an exploding gamma bomb, but because they dealt with their burdens the way you had to deal with yours. They didn't want to have to face their daily challenges any more than you wanted to face yours. They wanted to give up. They wanted to blame somebody else for their problems. And they would, indeed, sometimes do that. But in the long run, they figured out the right thing to do — and then they *did* it! Just like you do, or try to do. And then, every time they solved a problem or overcame a challenge — a *new* one popped up. Just like happens in *your* life. Lee, Lieber, Kirby, Ditko, et al. had hit on something big.

But what, exactly, had they hit on?

To discover that, let's pause for a moment to

249

move to a higher altitude, to get a wide overview.

Lee and company didn't simply invent characters that were visually compelling and who had interesting backstories. And they didn't just stumble onto the idea that the characters would exist in a shared universe so that they could, when appropriate, cross paths with each other, whether as allies or as adversaries. And they hadn't invented big action (although they certainly took it to the extreme).

What they came up with — and it's hard to not attribute this to Lee, even if he possibly only realized where the train was heading while it was already in motion — was a fictional world where the sense was, as in the modern Marvel movies, that all this was leading to something, even if, as in real life, that something would never be reached. There might be periodic pauses-disguised-as-endings, but, like life, things just kept going. The journey — and its accompanying transformations — was indeed the point.

By the 1960s, DC Comics had put out hundreds of stories featuring Superman and his supporting cast. And yet there was little if any forward character growth or development of the various situations in that universe. Superman foiling a bank robbery in one issue would be very much like Superman foiling a bank robbery ten years later. That was all well and good, especially if you assumed that the readership turned over every two or three years and the audience for the two bank robberies wouldn't know or care that the stories were virtually the same. Superman stopping armed crooks is cool to look at and read about.

What Marvel's stories and characters did was *develop* over time. They changed and grew from issue to issue, year to year. Lee and his collaborators were incrementally creating some form of literature. As the characters developed, both the readers and the creators got to know them better. While not stinting on action, the creators, along with the readers, got to know the characters and their universe, got to witness a semblance of what real people in such situations might do if they had superhuman powers. Heroes and villains and supporting casts developed deeper and more nuanced personalities, grew complex in a way more familiar to readers of serious prose than of comic books.

As more attention was focused on *why* characters did things, Marvel's stories grew to have more and more in common with real lives — or at least, with lives as portrayed by creators of novels and plays and movies that dealt with human growth and development.

Even more, since the comics stories were *serialized,* they could develop from issue to issue. This was in part due to the simple need

251

to stretch ideas and story points beyond one twelve- or twenty-page story. The need existed on two levels. Ideally, a story could be interestingly explored for several issues without seeming padded. But padded or not, continued stories meant that the creators had to come up with fewer new ideas, an important thing when working with a small staff that needed every shortcut they could find. But the lengthening of story lines meant that stories, subplots, and especially *characters* could be developed as never before. Romances could begin, grow, encounter snags, and then flourish or perhaps dramatically end. Villains could, like the heroes, be found to have relatively complex motivations for what they did.

Lee and Marvel's artists took great advantage of these possibilities. And as they did, sales and reader feedback showed general approval of this approach. TV shows and movies of the '60s were showing similar advancements. While there was no lack of mindless sitcoms, there were also plenty of TV series and movies that displayed depth of characterization. Shows like *Dobie Gillis, Bonanza, The Defenders,* and *The Fugitive* demonstrated that people would respond positively to entertainment that made them stretch their minds a bit. Cartoons like *Rocky and Bullwinkle, Peabody and Sherman,* and *Dudley Do-*

252

Right showed that even some children's programming had acquired an edge. Such shows — adults' and children's — could be enjoyed on a basic level of understandable plots, but could also provide multiple levels of humor and insight for those equipped to catch them. Even those who didn't know they were being given dense entertainment somehow understood that there was more to what they were getting than met the eye.

Similarly, Marvel's comics went from being simplistic, one-off adventures with perhaps some kind of lesson or moral to larger, more complex tapestries. *Spider-Man* and *Fantastic Four* grew more sophisticated with each issue. "The Brutal Betrayal of Ben Grimm" in *FF* #41, cover-dated August 1965, explored the toll that becoming the Thing really took on Grimm. The *Spider-Man* continuity explored secret pasts for supporting characters such as Betty Brant, showing her to be much more than just J. Jonah Jameson's secretary. Thor revealed his secret identity to his love interest and took her to Asgard to meet his father, Odin, ruler of the Norse gods, and demand that she be granted superpowers — a development that ended in bittersweet tragedy for all concerned.

Such nuanced, psychological angles had never been portrayed in superhero comics before. These elements weren't included because of focus group–derived calculation but rather by an instinctive understanding of what the audience would respond to. It was almost magical.

Lee, Ditko, and Kirby, all proficient in their crafts, could now flex their creative muscles — discover muscles they didn't even know they had — and expand the boundaries of comic book storytelling, even within the boundaries of the genre.

What they *didn't* do was settle into routine modes of storytelling. (That would happen, but not for another half decade.) Virtually every month, something new in terms of content or visual style was being introduced in Marvel's comics. And while all this was going on in the stories, Lee was developing and embroidering the company's ongoing relationship with its readers within the letters pages and Bullpen Bulletins and even in the story footnotes! Even when he was selling you stuff, he was doing it in an entertaining, humorously self-aware way, bonding readers even more closely to the company — and to its voice: Stan Lee.

Marvel's stories and everything surrounding them were evolving, subtly inviting readers to grow, too. This was a large part of what made Marvel so irresistible to those on its wavelength. And there were more and more people on its wavelength all the time.

So Marvel's achievement wasn't to publish one great story, or even many great stories, or a particularly resonant piece of text. It was to create a *phenomenon* that, for many, lived up to the hype surrounding it. Like few popular culture touchstones — the Beatles come to mind, and perhaps the novels of Kurt Vonnegut or the films of Robert Altman — Marvel kept on living up to its hype for far longer than most explosions of pop culture.

Stan Lee, in the first era of Marvel's 1960s success, was able, after helping create it, to recognize, exploit, and maintain, for a full decade, this phenomenon's first incarnation, and to plant the seeds for it to regularly renew itself.

So then, whoever "really" invented the specific first wave of Marvel characters, however the stories were developed, there was one consistent, singular — call it *omniscient* — voice telling you the stories and, as importantly, welcoming you into the world of Marvel. That voice had a name in the real world and in the magazines' pages.

That name was Stan Lee.

It was the voice that told you — starting with its third issue — that *Fantastic Four* was "The World's Greatest Comic Magazine!"

It was the voice that asked, on the cover of *Amazing Spider-Man* #14, "Does the Green Goblin look cute to you? Does he make you want to smile? Well, forget it! He's the most

255

sinister, most dangerous foe Spidey's ever fought!"

It was the voice that introduced issue #15 of the same title by saying, on the first page, lettered inside a giant arrow pointing at Spider-Man:

For any of you who may have been living in another galaxy for the past two years, we'll explain that this is Spider-Man . . . and this is certainly the most exciting Spidey adventure we've ever presented! (*Since the last one!*) It's got villains, heroes, action, a mishmash of everything — and it's told in the Marvel manner! 'Nuff Said!

It's the voice that, in the same issue, listed the credits thus:

Written by STAN LEE (because we couldn't afford Mickey Spillane)

Illustrated by STEVE DITKO (because Picasso was out of town)

Lettered by ART SIMEK (because his name fits the space)

It's the voice that, on the cover of issue #16, wherein Spider-Man first meets Daredevil, advised:

Warning!! If you don't say this is one of the

256

greatest issues you've ever read, we may never talk to you again!

This omniscient, fourth-wall-breaking, friendly, self-deprecating voice was the voice of Marvel. It was written as the editorial "we" and portrayed as the collective voice of Stan and Jack or Stan and Steve, or the voice of the entire Marvel bullpen. It was sometimes even acknowledged as the voice of Stan Lee.

In letters page responses and special announcements, the voice could say things like this, from Amazing Spider-Man #20:

One thing we get a kick out of is the occasional fan who writes in to demand that we give sunny Steve some more strips to draw! Poor ol' darling Ditko does about twenty pages of Spidey each month — plus ten pages of Dr. Strange — plus ten pages of the Hulk — and he *still* finds time to argue with Stan for a few hours each week!

(Was this a witty remark? An accurate description of Lee and Ditko's relationship? Both?)

The voice could also say things like this, from Spider-Man #21:

We haven't seen the sketches for Spider-Man #22 yet, but Stan and Steve have been walking around chuckling to them-

257

selves and patting each other on the back for days! So they must have something pretty special cooked up. Anyway, when these two characters go to town, how bad can it be? So live dangerously . . . try us again next ish! Who knows — you might even like it!

This was a remarkably clever way to say that they — by this point, most likely just Ditko — hadn't plotted the issue yet. It created the illusion that someone other than Stan was reporting on those wonderful guys, Stan and Steve, and that Stan and Steve were great pals who so enjoyed their collaborations that they walked around "patting each other on the back for days!" And by golly, it did make you want to come back next issue to see what they'd come up with!

Or take this "special announcement" from the letters page of *Fantastic Four* #23:

We needed a name for the villain of X-MEN #3, and Stan and Jack were kicking a few around when a boy delivering sandwiches walked in and jokingly said, "He looks like a big blob! Call 'im The Blob!" . . . Stan and Jack looked at each other and said, "Why not?"

In one paragraph, Lee switches from being the *teller* of the anecdote to being one of the

258

people being *told about* to doing an apparent mind-meld with Kirby where the combined Stan-Jack is willing to take advice from a regular working stiff — a "boy delivering sandwiches," no less. Did this story really happen? Did a delivery boy get to name a villain? Were Stan and Jack actually there to agree that it was the perfect name? (And of course, where is the moment where editor Stan or publisher Goodman had to approve a decision made by the writer and artist?)

This is the same voice that can also get plenty serious, as in the letters page to *FF* #24, when it declares:

Many readers say they don't like referring to our mags as "comic" mags . . . but we must disagree! It is our intention, here at Marvel, to produce comics which are so well-written and well-drawn, that they'll elevate this entire field in the mind of the public!

Stating this thought this way was a major step. In an era before widespread consideration of comic books as art — and less than a decade after Wertham's *Seduction of the Innocent* — no one inside comics, and few outside it, thought of them as anything beyond craft, and fairly low-level craft, at that. Only Will Eisner had spoken on the

259

record of comics as art — and that was in 1941.[10]

Lee's bold statement was followed, lower down on the same letters page, while signing off for the issue, with:

And so, till next ish, remember — we're working night and day to bring you the best in story and art — to make you PROUD of the comic magazines you read!

Imagine this voice, in this intimate medium, making you laugh, giving you insider stories, ballyhooing the very issue you're reading, promoting the upcoming issue, adding narratively unnecessary but fun-as-hell verbiage and wordplay — extending your time reading the comic, so also adding to its value as entertainment time purchased — and complimenting you on how great *you* are for simply reading and, of course, enjoying (not to mention *buying*) the comic! Imagine experiencing this multiple times a month in the various Marvel comics! Your parents, your older siblings, your non-comic-loving friends — they might all make fun of, or simply just not understand, the hold these gaudy pamphlets have on you. But the voice of Marvel does. The entity that is Marvel does.

Stan Lee does.

Stan Lee had become the literal and figurative voice of Marvel.

As Spurgeon and Raphael observed:

[Stan's voice was] that of the kindly "with-it" uncle. It added another layer of enjoyment to Marvel's superhero titles. . . . Lee's showy writing also helped him transcend the traditional writer and editor roles to become Marvel's host. . . . Lee was offering up the Greatest Show in Pulp.[11]

Later, they continued:

More than any figure in comic-book history, Stan Lee maximized every opportunity to forge a deeper connection between reader and comic book, with himself as intermediary.[12]

Indeed, while promoting Marvel's comics and characters, Lee had refined a friendly, welcoming, charming persona — already evident in his letters and memos and editorials from the 1940s and onward — that was a reflection of his best self. He brought that persona to bear as the voice of Marvel Comics and in so doing made himself indistinguishable to readers from the encompassing experience that was Marvel.

Of course, as can't be stated enough, all this interaction and bonding with readers wouldn't have been worth much of anything if the stories themselves didn't pay off in

261

satisfying ways issue after issue, month after month. Were they all gems? Of course not. But many were, many were very good, and some were, inevitably, forgettable — but relatively few. And the *voice* was always there, often self-deprecating (so you wouldn't think it was getting too full of itself, despite its frequent bragging), which made it hard for a reader to be angry, even if there *was* the occasional clinker of a story. These were your pals in the bullpen, doing their best to tell you an engrossing story, and if it wasn't a home run every time out, well, hey, even Mickey Mantle only got a hit one out of every three times at bat! These were your friends: Stan, Jack, Steve, Larry, Don, Dick, Flo, Sol — even the sandwich delivery kid. They were trying their best every time. Just like *you.*

Asked, in 2017, "How did you figure out that the best way to promote Marvel would be with some version of 'Stan' as the focus?" Lee responded:

It just came naturally. I wasn't saying, "What is the best way to promote Marvel?" But since I was the editor, I was writing little messages to the readers . . . and I felt it was very important to stay in touch with the fans and have the fans think they knew us, and think we're a great bunch of guys, and we're fun to be with, and so forth. I wanted to make everything very enjoyable. And I

262

loved the fans. Without them, we had nothing.[13]

Intentionally, or as something that "just came naturally," Stan Lee had become the living incarnation of Marvel Comics. Promoting Marvel became promoting Stan Lee.

It was only a matter of time before unforeseen repercussions of that reality would be felt.

10
THE TIES THAT BIND

Only Stan Lee would have accepted the Silver Surfer. If you took the Silver Surfer to a DC editor, he would have laughed at you. . . . Stan Lee not only accepted it, he ran with the ball and made it even better.

— John Romita[1]

In the July 4, 1963 issue of *South Shore Record,* a local Long Island newspaper, Roslyn Davis's "Roslyn Reports" column notes:

A gay poolside party and buffet supper Saturday evening was hosted by Writer-Art Director Stan Lee (Lieber) and his beauteous British-born wife, Joan, at their 125 year old Colonial home on Richards Lane [in Hewlett Harbor]. . . .

Always decorative, Mrs. Lieber, her blond tresses piled high, received in a long black and white checked gingham dishabille du soir caught at the waist with a cluster of daisies.

264

The interesting, attractive and talented company included David Mansure, painter here from Columbia, S.A., on a Guggenheim Fellowship; Magazine Publisher Martin Goodman and his wife Jean; Mr. and Mrs. Kenneth Bald (he's the artist for the Dr. Kildare Comic Strip); TV Commercial Announcers Kay Dowd and Stanley Sawyer, Sheila Sawyer . . . Attorney Jerry Perlis [sic] and his talented wife Blanche . . . By the way, Stan Lee's second book of hilarious captions, "More, You Don't Say", has just been published.[2]

In that July of 1963, while *The Avengers* and *The X-Men* were debuting on newsstands around the nation, Stan "Lee (Lieber)" was being presented to the world, or at least the south shore of Long Island, as a "Writer-Art Director," although writer-art director of *what* exactly would be left unspecified for the readers of *South Shore Record*. While the "gay poolside party" was attended by a sizable crowd, many of the attendees listed — the Goodmans (Stan's relatives and employer), the Balds (Stan and Joan's close friends), Kay (actually Kaye) Dowd (sister of comics artist Vic Dowd, and also Ken Bald's wife; she gets mentioned twice), the Sawyers (longtime friends of Stan and Joan), and Jerry Perles (Goodman's lawyer) — were certainly no strangers to the unnamed area of publishing

265

that Lee was an apparent big shot in.

The purpose of the account of the Lees' party, which takes half the column, seems to be, ultimately, to promote Lee's second volume of *You Don't Say*, published by Goodman. (The upper half of the column is devoted to promoting Guy Lombardo's production of *Around the World in Eighty Days* at the Jones Beach Marine Theater, as well as Lombardo's East Point House restaurant.) While the Lees and the Goodmans were longtime residents of the area, it does seem a bit strange that so much newspaper real estate would be devoted to proclaiming what great parties the Lees gave and plugging *More, You Don't Say,* while neglecting to mention what kind of publishing Martin or Stan were involved with or to mention any but one of their publications by name.

In any case, here, in the early — but not earliest — stages of the Marvel Age, Lee's presentation of himself is still ambiguous, still in transition. The only photo in the column — on the entire page — is a headshot of Joan, with the label: "Joan Lieber." Who are these people at the party? Are they establishment publishing professionals? If so, then why all the vagueness? And what the heck is a "book of hilarious captions"? Captions to *what*? Why is the only comics-related credit for any of the guests Ken Bald's for the (much more respectable than comic

266

books and TV hit–associated) *Dr. Kildare* comic strip? This seems to have been some kind of strangely specialized name-dropping gossip column.

Stan Lieber had, starting in 1941, presented himself to comics readers and professionals as "Stan Lee," while in his nonprofessional life holding on to his identity as Stanley Lieber. There were now two versions of this person. But the fictional one was slowly but steadily evolving from within the real one and *becoming* the real one. It wasn't that Lee was abandoning an outmoded self. It was more like he was learning to deploy his already charming, engaging private self in a wider arena.

By 1963, Stan Lieber was living an upwardly striving suburban life, while Stan Lee was working overtime, trying to keep the recently captured lightning in a bottle while chasing more lightning with more bottles. The lightning wasn't just the characters and stories. The lightning was in large part Marvel's relationship with its readers. And Marvel was becoming synonymous with "Stan Lee."

Through an uncanny combination of instinct, observation, and experience, Lee had created a relationship between himself and his readers that went wider and deeper than just telling them that if they liked what they were reading, they should try these other things the company was putting out. Starting with his relationship with the fan press and then extending it to the readership at large, Lee engaged in a one-man advertising and promotion campaign for Marvel, its characters, and its creators. Lee recalled his own experience of having been a fan of Poppy Ott and the other Leo Edwards book series of his childhood, remembering how Edwards created a bond with his audience through supplemental text pieces and letter columns in which he responded to his fans' questions and concerns. He was also well aware of the way that Bill Gaines's EC Comics had created a connection with those comics' readers through informal text and letters pages. And, ensconced in Marvel's Madison Avenue offices, Lee was a longtime student and admirer of advertising campaigns. So he had a keen awareness that, if you could bond with your readers, you could at the very least sell them more comics.

But it went deeper than that. While Magazine Management might have had specialists in various promotional roles, there was, at the beginning of '60s Marvel, no such staff for the comics. While even the smallest media companies have entire departments devoted to promotions, public relations, consumer outreach, advertising, branding, and so on, Marvel Comics only had one person able and willing to do all that: Stan Lee.

Lee intuited that what he was selling was not just the contents or the quality of the comics. Those were subjective elements that varied from issue to issue, story to story. You couldn't control what a person would or wouldn't like or what they would forgive regarding things that didn't work for them in a given issue or story. Lee figured out that he needed to create a loyalty that went beyond a single, or even a series of, satisfying reading experiences.

So of *course* he wanted you to love the comics. But as much as stories and art and characters, Stan Lee was selling personal relationships. He was selling relationships between the readers themselves (constantly reminding them that they were a "new breed" of reader, that just by reading that comic book in their hands they were members of a special club); he was selling personal connections between the readers and the artists, letterers, and staff members — the "bullpen"; and he was selling relationships between Marvel and the entire world of popular culture. Hence the continual name-checking of cool writers, musicians, and filmmakers, most of whom the majority of his audience had only the faintest notion even existed.

But these were names that were in the air, mentioned in classy magazines and on late-night talk shows. By associating Marvel with

269

the new, the hip, even the snobbish, he was telling you that you were *more* than a ten-year-old kid whose biggest upcoming excitement was a midterm exam you weren't prepared for. No, you were a member of an elite that, sure, appreciated Marvel comics, but you were also — somehow — hooked into a sophisticated world of New York culture. You were in on the same jokes that Stan's high-class Princeton University fans were privy to.

Of course, underneath it all, Stan Lee was developing a connection — relationship, friendship — between the readers and *himself.* Stan Lee's was the voice in the cover copy, in the narration of the stories, in the footnotes, and especially in the letters pages. Stan Lee had managed to make himself and Marvel Comics synonymous.

Not everyone was wild about that idea — Martin Goodman, for instance, who was worried that the company was becoming too dependent on Lee.[3] But no one seemed to have a better one.

If you loved Marvel Comics, you loved Stan Lee. If you had a hard day at school and you ran home to read a Marvel Comic to forget about whatever terrible thing had happened, you were comforted by Stan Lee. If you wanted to know what was going on behind the scenes at Marvel, Stan Lee told you. If you were in the mood to just hear some silly

270

story about Sol Brodsky moving, but just to a *different apartment* in the same Brooklyn building, Stan Lee told you that story. Marvel Comics told you that story. Stan-Marvel, Marvel-Stan told you that story. It was a recognizable voice, the sound of someone writing you a letter or letting you peek into their diary. It was a friend's voice. It was a voice that even enabled you to forgive comic stories that weren't great, because, as he assured you, Marvel — your pal — was always trying. Unlike your real father, brother, teacher, friend — *Stan Lee would never let you down.* Because if he did, he wouldn't just be letting *you* down, he'd be letting himself and his coworkers down. He'd be letting down everyone who worked so hard to get you the best blamed comics they could, on time and on a regular basis. And that, you just knew, the voice would not let happen.

The voice understood, just like Peter Parker did, the importance of being responsible. Friends don't let friends down. Ever.

So from the front cover promotional copy to the telling of the stories inside the covers, to the answers to the letters and the plugs for the company's other products, to the name-dropping of celebrities large and small, to the gratitude expressed for what great people the readers were, to the idle complaining about the eyestrain caused by the hundreds (hundreds!) of letters they received every day, to the wisecracks about "Marty" Goodman's golf game — it was like nothing readers of the era had ever experienced before. This merging of the personae of an individual and a company in a medium as intimate — especially to a child, but also to older readers — as comic books was an incredible gift to be given.

That this person — this Stan-Marvel — was not just telling you a great story, or even sometimes a not-so-great story, but was then chatting and joking and gossiping with you — and that he was indebted to you for simply handing over your twelve cents for what, even for a fast reader, was at least twenty minutes of intense engagement, was as magical as any entertainment experience anyone could ask for. And it was far more than an entertainment experience. It was, let's be frank, a *family* experience. Stan was your family without the pain-in-the-ass aspects of your real family.

Where did this sudden ability to engender connection with the readership come from? How did a lifelong media professional entering his forties suddenly develop the skill set to link with a wide swath of readers, from kids to teens to college students and GIs? How did Stan Lee step out from behind the curtain and become not just his own personality but that of an entire company?

The answer seems to have to do with him

272

realizing that what had worked for him behind the scenes could work for him in front of the curtain, as well. It wasn't a matter of inventing a personality. It was a matter of sharing that personality, of developing a version of it for the readers. This "new" Stan Lee voice was evident in his letters to Toni Mendez and others in the syndicated strip world of the '50s. It was the voice in letters sent to fans like Jerry Bails. It was the voice that showed up occasionally in blurbs for *Menace* and other comics published by Atlas throughout the '50s. It's the voice of the personality that had become familiar to those in his various circles since "Gabby" Lieber had scrawled "Stan Lieber is God" across the ceiling at DeWitt Clinton.

If, even in its high-volume heyday, Goodman's comics line had lacked individuality, then the closest it ever came to having a personality, even then, was Stan Lee's. The company's '50s comics, though, seemed to be intentionally nondescript as far as branding, often imitating Goodman's own or other companies' products. From the '40s through the '60s, freelancers would sometimes say they were doing work for Timely (never Atlas, which is a name used in retrospect). Once in a while, some might have said they were doing work for Marvel, which is a name the company used off and on before the '60s. But mainly, they would say they were doing

273

work "for Stan Lee."

So the mechanism was in place for people to identify Marvel and Stan Lee as one and the same entity. It was just a matter of Lee's understanding the significance of that phenomenon and making use of that reality in a public — as opposed to behind-the-scenes — forum. The idea of Stan Lee and Marvel as one entity had to be exploited. The curtain had to be opened to reveal the man behind it. Unlike the Wizard of Oz, the trick involved clearly *seeing* the person behind the curtain — but *still* buying into a variety of pleasurable illusions.

The illusions would become simultaneously more complex and more simplified. Stan Lee didn't own the company, didn't draw the stories, often didn't fully plot the stories, and yet *his* was the animating spirit of the company and its products. This confusion/ confabulation of Lee with his collaborators and coworkers, as well as with the company itself, would lead to some of Marvel's and Lee's greatest triumphs, as well as its most enduring controversies. Stan Lee was charismatic and affable in person. On behalf of — and combined with — Marvel, he launched a charm offensive whose effects endure to this day. It started in the comics, which led to bonding with readers, which led to increased sales, which led to increased visibility and respectability for him and for Marvel, which led to increased business opportunities, which led to larger and better-paid staff and freelancers, which led to more and bigger everything, for Marvel and for Stan Lee.

And significantly, while all this was developing, Marvel's stories and art — the bringing into existence of incredibly exciting and compelling superhero adventures — continued apace. All cylinders were firing at once in a manner rarely, if ever, seen outside, perhaps, MGM studios in its prime. As Raphael and Spurgeon have said of Lee:

> He rooted out the essence of what was appealing to the readers, distilled it, and communicated it successfully to a wide variety of artists and writers. . . . He also did the best writing of his career, both in service to ideas from other artists and working with artists whose creativity was subsumed into Lee's own. No pop culture phenomenon has ever offered its readers more than Stan Lee's Marvel gave comic-book fans in the 1960s.[4]

Throughout his career, Lee had been inspirational to many writers, artists, and staffers, often thanks to the same personality traits and editorial practices that would also alienate some of them. With success building upon success as the '60s progressed, Lee's momentum and enthusiasm, in the stories and with

275

the artists, fed his approach to the readers in the text pages as well as in the stories and even the footnotes. With gal Friday Flo Steinberg culling through the hundreds of daily letters, Lee would then sort through her choices to pick ones that would set him up to give clever, entertaining, and informative responses, significantly supplemented by special announcements and promotional blurbs.[5]

By the December 1965–dated comics, the most interesting or important special announcements, as well as the Marvel Checklist of comics on sale that month, were formalized into the Bullpen Bulletins page. Lee well understood that a letters column or Bullpen page was as important in promoting the comics as any official house ad or story page. The fun of reading Marvel comics had to be communicated *everywhere* in every issue. Even the strange array of small, cheap ads that the company printed for pay in the comics — for everything from offers to set your poetry to music to buying an "atomic sub" for $6.95 (a pretty good deal!) — somehow added to the carnival atmosphere of the entire comics package.

One couldn't say that Lee planned overly much — at least at first — for this phenomenon of fan outreach and interaction. When Atlas was putting out its genre 1950s fare, there was virtually no fan mail, even when

276

circulation was massive. While DC's superhero comics were printing regular letter columns and awarding original comic art pages (which then had little or no value) to writers of exceptional letters, virtually no one was writing to Timely's editor. Apparently, the generic stories they were printing, no matter how exciting the art or clever the dialogue, were considered mere time killers for which no one would take the interest or the time to write a letter or postcard to praise or pan. These were stories for kids who read comics as a way to alleviate boredom. Who would become passionate enough to write a letter about them? By the same token, little effort was made by the company to encourage the readers to comment, except in girls' fashion comics like *Millie the Model,* where readers were urged to send in clothing designs for the characters. Another exception was 1952's *Menace,* which encouraged readers to comment on stories, even offering a prize — "a picture of 'The Men with Two Heads' . . . autographed by artist Bill Everett." Historian Michael Vassallo believes this "picture" must have been some kind of print.[6]

And yet there were enough letters about *Fantastic Four* #1 to print a letters column in issue #3. Catalyzed by the DC superhero revival, a small core of fans had become excited that Timely was doing a new superhero book. True, there was a lot of extra space

277

surrounding the issue's published letters, and one obvious fake letter — from staffer Sol Brodsky. But the rest seemed genuine enough, including one from future comics artist Alan Weiss. Issue #4 again printed real-seeming letters, with the exception of one from Timely artist and colorist Stan Goldberg. Issue #5 contained authentic letters from fans, including ones from future Marvel writer and editor Roy Thomas and fellow fandom force Ronn Foss. At the end of that column, Lee wrote:

We're learning a lot from your letters. We learned that you do like the name 'MR. FANTASTIC' and that you don't like it. You do like the Thing and you don't like him. Well, we can't please everyone. . . . Keep your letters coming, don't get too angry at us, and always face front!

Interestingly, that one blurb encapsulated what would soon become the Marvel approach — that is, the Stan Lee approach — to comics and to fans. Approach them like friends who can thrill to an exciting story one minute, then share a joke (and an "insider's" ironic perspective) with the editor (unnamed at this point) as he gives you a peek behind the curtain. The editor then ends with a catchphrase — "face front" — that will come to be associated with him, but is also,

278

like a number of Lee's slogans, derived from army slang, bonding Lee to veterans and their kids but also inventing a special Marvel insiders' lexicon. The one "plant" letter in the column may be one from Jon Davidson, who describes himself as "an English schoolboy." The schoolboy is from Joan Lee's hometown of Newcastle-upon-Tyne, and in his response, Stan says, "We hope you'll continue to enjoy the adventures of your American cousins!"

In *Fantastic Four* #10 (which featured fictionalized versions of Lee and Kirby as part of the issue's main story of the FF battling Dr. Doom), the letters page opened with this announcement:

Look, enough of the "Dear Editor" jazz from now on! Jack Kirby and Stan Lee (that's us!) read every letter personally, and we like to feel that we know you and you know us! So we changed the salutations in the following letters to show you how much friendlier they sound our way!

In a truly game-changing move that would forever alter relationships between comics fans and professionals, Lee performed an elegant tonal shift. He edited his readers' letters to teach them a new way of thinking of the Marvel staff. Every letter in the column now began, in all capitals:

"DEAR STAN AND JACK."

279

With this one insightful action, Lee upended the producer-consumer relationship between Marvel and its readers. No longer would a reader be addressing an employee at a company. That reader was now engaging in an interactive communication with a couple of friends.

Moreover, Lee pivoted the mental image he wanted his readers to have of who exactly they were writing to. If he had just simply wanted to informalize the salutations, to just make Marvel seem a bit less stuffy than DC, then the logical revision from "Dear Editor" would have been "Dear Stan." But it was obviously important to him to include Kirby in the equation. And the Stan-Jack construction would come to take on a multitude of meanings. Depending on context, it could mean either or both Stan and Jack, but also any or all members of Marvel's creative or business departments.

What Stan-and-Jack could offer readers that the DC editors could not was the reality that there was, at Marvel, no gulf between the creator voice and the editorial voice. If a comic magazine could speak, Stan-and-Jack was what it would "sound" like. There were no buffers between you and the people who created the comic you were reading. Lee cooked up an authorial voice that spoke from the heart of Marvel to the hearts of its/his readers. Thinking of Stan and Jack as two guys — pals with each other, pals with you — collectively addressing each letter writer (each of whom was an avatar for many readers) created a sense of a special club that the reader belonged to.

Did he and Kirby, as stated, "read every letter personally"? Certainly, when there was a trickle of letters, this might have been possible, less likely as time went on and the volume of mail seriously increased. But whatever the degree of participation Kirby — and for that matter, Ditko — might have had in evaluating the fan mail, it's pretty clear that the voice and attitude of the entity calling itself "Marvel" was coming directly from the mind, pen, and hunt-and-pecked typewriter of Stan Lee.

Just for one example of the embracing nature of the letters columns' seemingly genuine intimacy is this, from *Fantastic Four* #23. In a burst of calculated, yet authentic, frankness, Lee wrote:

We can't tell you what the next *FF* will be because we haven't decided on a plot yet. . . . All we'll say is — we've got to dream up a story in the next couple of days, and have it drawn pronto if we wanna make our deadline! So to find out if we've succeeded . . . don't miss *FF* #24.

But after that candid admission, laced with

281

humor and humility (but also counting on the reader assuming that whatever they come up with will be great), Lee added this sardonic kicker:

Incidentally, if we DO miss our deadline this month, forget about addressing your next letters to Stan and Jack — there'll probably be a crop of NEW names here next time!

Here again, the "regular guy" side of Lee comes through, even as he's supposedly speaking on behalf of both himself and Kirby. Sure, everyone reading knew that the odds of Stan and Jack either failing to produce or getting fired for that hypothetical failure were slim to none. But the idea that, like the readers' parents and even their teachers, the people making the comics were human and fallible and, given the right — or wrong — set of circumstances, could lose their jobs . . . ! These comics are entertainment for you, he was telling the readers, *but they're how we make a living!* You know — the way your dad and mom could lose *their* jobs? So could *we*!

This bonding with the readership, combined with the comics' growing creative and sales successes, would lead, in what — at least in its beginnings — seems a relatively unplanned, unstrategized way, to a heady circle of growth and expansion at the company. The press was now paying attention to Marvel, both the comics and the voice that spoke on the company's behalf. They wanted to meet that voice. And the person they ended up meeting with was, of course, Lee. Outgoing, convivial, and in the office regularly, Lee was the natural choice to speak to when reporters or fans came calling. And he was the natural choice for fans — especially college students — to invite to address them on their home turf.

Bard College students J. Geoffrey Magnus and Isabelle Kamishlian, both on the "Special Committee Programming Bard College Science Club Lectures," in a letter dated March 24, 1964, were the first to ever invite Stan Lee to speak at a college.[7] They offered him an honorarium of fifty dollars and a meal at local Italian restaurant. They might also have thrown in train fare.

Kamishlian, a chemistry major — a rarity at the liberal arts–oriented Bard — who went on to work in quality assurance for Coca-Cola, recalled Lee as being entertaining at the dinner and the lecture. "We started something," she said in 2017. "People were 'out of the closet' and weren't afraid of reading comics like they had been." She recalled that Stan was perhaps "confused" about why he would be invited to speak at a college. The students, as she recalled, had invited him "as a lark." According to Kamishlian, Lee's appearance was the most popular meeting the

283

Science Club ever had, drawing about fifty people, the same as the school's Film Club's attendance.[8] They had billed the June 5, 1964, speaker as "Dr. Stan Lee."

Bard College wasn't just any college. While what we think of as the 1960s long-hair, tie-dyed era of hippies and wannabes didn't gain full hold on the cultural imagination till around 1967 and the Monterey Pop Festival and San Francisco's "Summer of Love," Bard was a center of the early blossoming of various countercultures of the era. Ninety miles north of New York City, it was a famously liberal school, its students known for being on the cutting edge of political and cultural upheaval. Certainly, to invite a comic book writer-editor — but more importantly, the embodiment of Marvel Comics — to speak was simultaneously bold and also likely ridiculed. With the choice of every political and cultural figure in the New York area, Magnus (who passed away in 2015) and Kamishlian decided that Stan Lee was someone they had to invite to speak.

Similarly, in an article by Jonathan Wax (a Princeton student and the son of a prominent Memphis civil rights activist rabbi) in an issue of the *Trenton Sunday Times-Advertiser* from March 1966, an unnamed Princeton English major declared: "We think of Marvel Comics as the Twentieth Century mythology and you [Stan Lee] as this generation's

284

Homer." Lee had been to the school to address the university's "Whig-Cliosophic Society," who were the first to find out that Ditko had left the company[9] and who made Lee an honorary member in a later ceremony at Marvel's offices.[10] (It seems likely that Wax himself was the unnamed Princeton English major. Otherwise, why not name him?)

This was a new phenomenon. Hip, smart, educated young adults were finding inspiration in Stan Lee's Marvel Comics. While they knew of and admired the artists, whom they assumed must be spending at least parts of their days high on various psychedelic substances, it was Stan who had made himself the voice and face of Marvel and whom they came to see. Even at that early stage, Lee represented not just himself but the entire Marvel — perhaps the entire comic book — phenomenon.

But while spreading the word about Marvel and devising numerous ways to maximize sales and interest, the day job that Lee was getting paid for was editing the comics. No longer having the time to edit and script all the comics and also do the promotional work, Lee needed to add people, both inside and outside the office. He had hired Flo Steinberg in 1963 as his secretary (and there had been at least one person in that role preceding her, once Goodman allowed him to hire someone) and, in 1965, Steve Skeates as an

285

editorial assistant. And as the months went on, slowly but steadily, the freelance ranks were growing, with writers like Robert Bernstein and Leon Lazarus and artists like Bob Powell and Werner Roth (as Jay Gavin) showing up in the credits.

In July 1965, shortly after Skeates had started, überfan Roy Thomas had a meeting with Lee. Thomas, on the verge of embarking on graduate studies in political science, had instead recently accepted an offer to be the assistant to DC editor Mort Weisinger. Their match was hardly one made in heaven. Thomas was miserable working for the difficult *Superman* editor. Not thinking of quitting yet, he had made an appointment to see Lee, with whom he had corresponded. Lee was pleased with Thomas's rave review of *Fantastic Four* #1 but otherwise knew little about the young Missourian. Thomas had taken the Marvel writing test — creating dialogue over some unscripted Kirby pencil art — and thought that perhaps he and Stan would discuss it.

At their meeting, Lee didn't mention the test — but offered Thomas a job as "staff writer." Thomas jumped at the opportunity and, ejected from DC as soon as he told Weisinger of his offer from Lee, was working at Marvel that same afternoon. His job would soon morph from staff writer to assistant editor who also did freelance writing.

286

Thomas's arrival enabled Lee to hand off some of his editorial and writing work to the younger man. This gave Stan more time to concentrate on the editorial big picture and also to do more traveling and speaking, which, he realized, could help Marvel sell comics and would also provide him with an income stream as a speaker that could replace — and exceed — any writing work he was relinquishing.[11]

Thomas's recollections of his first days at Marvel paint a fascinating picture of the company in mid-1965:

> Marvel didn't have much in the way of offices; just three or four little rooms. Stan's office was as big as everything else put together, and Sol Brodsky, Flo Steinberg, and Marie Severin were crowded into two other little rooms. . . . Ditko and Stan weren't speaking . . . so Ditko would come in, deliver his stuff to Sol, Sol would take it in to Stan. . . . Jack and Stan were still getting along pretty well. They'd go out to lunch together occasionally.[12]

These offices were a step up from the tiny, humiliating office author and screenwriter Bruce Jay Friedman recalls Lee having post-1957[13] and were larger than the space that Steinberg described in her memories of the earlier Marvel circa 1963.[14] Things were

287

slowly improving for Goodman's comics division.

Skeates would leave before too long, and Thomas would soon be joined by fellow Missourians Dennis O'Neil and Gary Friedrich. O'Neil would last about six months at Marvel, then depart to legendary accomplishments at Charlton and especially DC Comics. Friedrich would stay at Marvel as a writer for over a decade. But Thomas would be the most significant writing and editing newcomer of the era. His day job now having evolved into a major editorial role, he would also do large quantities of freelance writing, paid separately from his salary. Lee would, at first, heavily rewrite Thomas's scripts but would eventually leave his writing mostly as it was submitted.[15]

Shortly after Thomas's hiring, John Romita, who'd spent eight years drawing romance comics at DC, was lured back by Lee after a couple of earlier attempts by Stan to get him in '63 and '64. Left without steady work by an executive policy decision at National, Romita had done some inking for Lee but didn't want to do any penciling, which he found more difficult. (Apparently, his feelings toward Lee and Marvel had grown more positive since his 1957 direction to his wife to tell Stan to "go to hell.") Having worked with Romita on *Captain America* and other features in the '50s, Stan was eager to have

288

this talented, dependable, and even-tempered artist back at Marvel. With artist/writer Wallace Wood's recent angry departure over his teaming with Lee on *Daredevil,* and Lee and Ditko on nonspeaking terms, it made perfect sense to want to have such a figure added to the Marvel roster.

Romita recalled in a 2001 interview conducted by Thomas in *Alter Ego* that he had accepted a job at prominent ad agency BBD&O, doing storyboards

> but when he [Lee] asked me to pencil, I told him, "No, I don't think I can." . . . he said, "Come on in, I'll take you to lunch." So we went to lunch and he spent three hours browbeating me. . . . "Why do you want to be a little fish in a big pond when you can be a big fish in a little pond? I'll guarantee you to match their salary."[16]

With comics, especially action-adventure comics, his first love, Romita left the advertising job and accepted the drawing job with Marvel. For his own discipline, Romita requested to be able to work at the office so he could focus on his art. But being in the office, he soon ended up doing all sorts of art-related chores in addition to drawing his assigned comics. In this way he became, at first informally, but at a certain point officially, Marvel's art director, though he was

289

still also committed to drawing at least one twenty-page comic a month.

In the beginning, he was drafted to replace Wood on *Daredevil*. At first working from Kirby's rough layouts to acclimate him to the dynamic approach that Lee favored, Romita was soon doing his own outstanding pencils on the title. His first issue was #12, dated January 1966, on sale in November 1965. Interestingly, sell-through percentages on his issues significantly increased from previous issues.

Very likely with the idea in mind of shifting Romita to *Spider-Man* if Ditko were to leave, Lee had the web-spinner guest star in *Daredevil* #16 and #17. Romita would only draw two issues of *Daredevil* beyond that, because Ditko did indeed leave *Spider-Man* (and the company) with issue #38, which was cover-dated July 1966. Romita, believing Ditko would realize he'd made a mistake and return to *Spider-Man* — and *Dr. Strange* — tried his best to imitate Ditko's approach, which was diametrically opposed to his own more traditionally heroic style, populated with handsome, muscular men and Hollywood-beautiful women.

Frustrated in his eggshell-walking relationship with Ditko, Lee was glad to again become heavily involved in plotting Marvel's second-highest-selling title. To make sure readers stuck around, the first Lee-Romita

290

Spider-Man story was a two-parter in which the Green Goblin was unmasked as Norman Osborn, industrialist father of Peter's classmate Harry Osborn. Indeed, the senior Osborn and Spider-Man would each discover the other's identities in these issues, which climaxed a long-running story line. Lee — and Marvel — had seemingly weathered the storm of Ditko's exit.

Much of the campus excitement about Marvel, as well as the excitement for it exhibited by children and teens, was exemplified by the popularity of the Merry Marvel Marching Society, a fan club invented in 1964 by Lee, modeled perhaps on Timely's Sentinels of Liberty fan club of the 1940s, on fan clubs of his youth, and likely on an awareness of the popularity of pop star fan clubs, especially the Beatles', whose rabid admirers were legion. By the early '60s, the only well-known comics-related fan club was DC's Supermen of America. For a dime, a kid would get a letter signed by Clark Kent, a button, and a decoder for secret messages printed in the comics — usually promotional messages about other comics.

The M.M.M.S. cost a dollar to join — the amount you'd pay for eight comic books — so a lot for a kid. But for that buck, you'd get all sorts of swag, most interestingly a flexible 45 RPM recording of Stan, Jack, Sol, Flo, and other bullpenners — notably not Steve Ditko — making jokes from an intentionally corny script written by Lee. With fans knowing the work, quirks, and faces of the Marvel creators from the comics, now they could hear them in this pre-internet, audio treasure trove. Despite its hefty fee, the M.M.M.S. was astonishingly popular — boasting more than fifty thousand members. The Marvel offices were flooded with dollar bills sent in for membership.[17] Significantly, part of the membership agreement was that Marvel would print the name of every single member in an unspecified issue of a Marvel comic — an inspired way to sell more comics. The comics' letter columns were filled with messages from college students who had formed M.M.M.S. chapters at their schools. Lee had again touched a rich vein of enthusiasm. Interest in the comics fueled interest in the club, which fueled more interest in the comics, and on and on.

But why all this growing excitement about what, on the surface at least, seemed to be simply some good stories and clever marketing spawned by a publisher of a small roster of magazines featuring stories of garishly clad characters punching each other? Why was an audience of such a diverse nature so taken with Marvel Comics and with Stan Lee? There can be a hundred plausible explanations having to do with the baby boom and the JFK assassination and the threat of nuclear devastation, but, of course, the reasons are unknowable, aside from the obvious one of being in the right place at the right time with the right products. (Equally fascinating, it would seem, is the question of why Marvel's superheroes have not just sustained but have immeasurably expanded their popularity well into the twenty-first century, albeit now largely in movies and on TV?)

In any case, in 1966, there was no general-interest magazine that was considered hipper and more taste-defining than *Esquire*. Its college-themed issues especially were thought to have a finger on the pulse of young (male) Americans with disposable incomes. In its September 1966 issue (having the previous year named Hulk and Spider-Man as two of the most important figures on American college campuses), the magazine featured a spotlight on Marvel Comics, especially about the comics' popularity in colleges.

In it, student Jack Marchese of Stanford University said, "The stories, heroes and villains all have character — they are real. They are governed by emotions and ideals. In other words, the Marvel heroes are not witless put-ons, but rather they are personable human beings. Spider-Man . . . is one of us."[18]

In the same article, Richard Weingroff, a contributor to comics fanzines and a student at the University of Maryland, declared: "Spi-

293

dey is comicdom's Hamlet, comicdom's Raskolnikov. The uninitiated have disagreed about this of course — but we don't feel we should hastily appraise Hamlet and Raskolnikov just because they are from literature."[19]

Looking back in 2010, Weingroff reflected that "I was one of the Baby Boomers who wanted the larger culture to take comic books seriously. . . . Looking back on my quote four decades later, I see that I wasn't trying to be serious. . . . I was exaggerating to make my point . . . that Marvel had changed the superhero stereotype and deserved to be taken a little more seriously than society usually did. . . . One thing was certain: By revitalizing the superhero concept, Lee and his fellow creators allowed Marvel's comics to retain their appeal as readers grew older."

Significantly, Weingroff concluded his recollection by recounting how, in 1966, at an early comics convention in New York

I met Stan Lee as he was entering the meeting area. . . . When we shook hands, I was amazed that he knew who I was and recalled one of my articles. It was one of the high points of my years in comic fandom.[20]

Here we have another insight regarding the wide popularity of Marvel Comics, which, truly, was inseparable from the popularity of

294

Stan Lee: Lee paid attention to people who were important to him and to Marvel. Sure, any decent businessperson pays attention to his customers. But real or not — and much of it seems indeed genuine — Lee's attention was based on some kind of sincere care about the quality of the product he was providing, and further, one can argue, caring about the people for whom he was producing the work, especially sophisticated ones like Weingroff, who got what he was doing.

Something in the gray area between earning a living and the sheer joy of creating stories — as well as the sheer exuberance of realizing that he and his coworkers were creating a phenomenon — seems to have inspired Lee. Whatever motives one cares to ascribe to it, there was something going on at Marvel different from creating the rote superhero adventures being produced, often at a high level of craft and competence, by DC and other companies. Inspiration? Genius? Luck? Whatever it was, people were talking about — and buying — Marvel comics.

You could thrill to Kirby's dynamic drawing, inventive plotting, and astonishing characters. You could be enthralled by the moody angularity and intense hyper-normalcy of Ditko's drawn world. But it was Stan Lee who put the words in the characters' mouths and who narrated their stories. It was

Stan Lee who made you feel that every story was, if not great, then at least worth reading — and *re*reading — because the authorial/editorial voice was a voice that cared about *you*, that remembered you in the midst of a great crowd — as he did with Richard Weingroff — and that made every visitor to the offices feel like a special guest, not like an annoyance or a distraction from "real work."

Little by little, Lee was making himself and Marvel into celebrities. By taking credit and giving credit, by mythologizing what he and his peers did for a living, by making himself and them as important as the characters whose stories they told, Lee had done what no comic book creator had achieved since Jerry Siegel, Joe Shuster, and Bob Kane had, decades earlier: become a celebrity. Now in the age of television and, to a lesser degree, early talk radio, with their endless need for content, Lee had tapped the vein of celebrity ore, a brave new world for him and the company he embodied but didn't own. Stan Lee was becoming a celebrity. As he would learn, that role came with its own set of powers and responsibilities.

Lee might have been courting — and achieving — celebrity. But he certainly couldn't be accused of neglecting the comics for fame's sake. Indeed, he focused with more intensity than ever on the comics, even as he was

296

delegating more of the actual plotting work to his collaborators. As he wrote in the March 1966 Bullpen Bulletins (appearing in December '65's Marvels), speaking of himself, as usual, in the third person:

> All Stan has to do with the pro's like JACK "KING" KIRBY, dazzlin' DON HECK, and darlin' DICK AYERS is give them the germ of an idea, and they make up all the details as they go along, drawing and plotting out the story.

Simultaneously, though, while keeping a close eye on the stories, whatever stage he entered into them, Lee (with Goodman's approval, of course) was also building an institutional infrastructure designed to sustain the comics' ongoing innovation and breaking of creative barriers, all while growing Marvel's cultural and economic footprint. And as a bonus, he now got to be famous. He was glad to take his collaborators along for the ride, but he made sure everyone knew that Stan Lee was driving.

Already embarked on a college speaking career, Lee was now even more the lightning rod for media attention paid to Marvel. On November 3, 1965, legendary Italian director Federico Fellini — and an entourage — came to meet Stan and see Marvel. So, in the spring of '66, did rock musician Peter Asher of the popular British folk-rock group Peter and Gordon. Asher told Lee that his pals, the Beatles, were also Marvel fans. In the August '66 Bullpen Bulletins, Stan told of Asher's visit and of the mop tops' Marvel love, and continued . . .

Believe it or not, [Peter's] opening a book store in jolly ol' London, and wants to sell our Marvel masterpieces — as well as the works of Shakespeare, Sartre, Salinger and other equally well-known literary lights!

As had become second nature, Lee managed to associate Marvel and himself with an alliterative list of writers that would subliminally assure readers that he and Marvel were thought of in the same sentence as the Bard, the Existentialist, and the enigmatic bestselling author. The author of *The Catcher in the Rye* and the writer of *Amazing Spider-Man* were now, literally, on the same page.

Nineteen sixty-six also seems to be the year that French director Alain Resnais — like Fellini, a comics fan and a Marvel fan — first came to visit Lee. They would become close friends and would go on to work on film projects together several years later.

Nineteen sixty-six was also when a *New York Herald Tribune Magazine Section* article about Marvel appeared in the January 9 edition of the paper. The piece described a *Fan-*

tastic Four plot conference between Lee and Kirby, with Thomas in the room, taking notes, and *Herald Tribune* reporter Nat Freedland there to witness the action. While there was some resemblance to an actual Lee-Kirby story conference, and the meeting seems to be about what would be *FF #55*, there was clearly one participant who was much more at ease in this situation that was at least partly staged.

While the article described the outgoing Lee as "a rangy lookalike of Rex Harrison, with the brightest-colored Ivy League wardrobe in captivity and a deep suntan," it described Kirby as looking like "a middle-aged man with baggy eyes and a baggy, Robert Hall-ish suit," who might be mistaken for "the assistant foreman in a girdle factory." Lee was portrayed as dynamic and active, spouting ideas and suggestions, Kirby as taciturn, muttering an occasional terse response.

When the Kirbys — especially Jack's wife, Roz — saw the article, they were livid and accused Stan of somehow arranging for Freedland's take on the meeting. Lee felt terrible about it. There are those, including Thomas, who see this as the beginning of the end of the Lee-Kirby partnership.

It's unknown if the Kirbys were at all mollified by this item in the September 1966 Bullpen Bulletins, published in June and likely written in April or May. It's narrated by someone who refers to himself as "we," and who speaks of "Stan" in the third person, but is no doubt Lee himself:

King Kirby walked in after having finished an hour-long story conference with Stan. . . . Jack was heard to mutter: "Well, we just polished off a few holocausts [before the word was commonly used to refer to the Nazi murder of European Jews], and a cataclysm or two! Now I'll . . . relax by dreaming up a few simple disasters!" . . . Ever wonder what it's like to illustrate galactic wars, battles between gods, and cosmic adventures day after day?

Perhaps the entry wasn't a direct compliment to Jack beyond the use of the nickname *King Kirby* and the idea that Jack will be "dreaming up a few simple disasters" (i.e., plotting how they develop), but the subtext is clear: Jack Kirby is a genius.

Kirby's former partner, Joe Simon, took a shot at Lee's growing celebrity later that year. In the Simon-edited humor magazine *Sick,* issue #48, from Crestwood Publications, Simon wrote a story, drawn by Angelo Torres, called "The New Age of Comics," in which a no-talent egotist named "Sam Me" runs a popular line of hackneyed superhero comics, where he takes credit and payment

300

for other people's work, signing his name to everything. Sam Me is even shown to be guilty of stealing a character called "Captain American" from its creators, evoking echoes of Simon's hard feelings about Goodman's usurpation of his and Kirby's character. (Despite this fairly mean satire, Simon, in his later years, anyway, seemed to actually be quite fond of Lee, and vice versa. But it does seem that, for all his savvy and experience — or perhaps simply because of his anger over Captain America — Simon couldn't or wouldn't take seriously the innovations that were going on under Lee at Marvel.)

Marvel's early successes spawned widespread imitation. The comics racks were, by 1965, filled with superhero comics, many of them blatantly imitating Marvel's, including a line of heroes, dubbed "Mighty Comics," published by Archie, and edited by Superman cocreator Jerry Siegel. While using some of Marvel's artists and writers — and Siegel himself — to create their superhero tales (many using updated versions of that company's own 1940s characters), they were nowhere near the quality of Marvel's comics in the eyes of most consumers.

By 1966, DC's comics were still overall outselling Marvel's. The *Batman* line had been near cancellation, but with editor Julius Schwartz having taken them over and ushering in a much-heralded "new look" for the character, sales were going up. Then, with the popularity of Marvel comics among not just kids, but with teens and adults, at the same time that the pop art movement was making use of comics-derived images, superheroes became a fad beyond comics. A campy *Batman* TV series, starring Adam West, was launched to high ratings in January 1966. So popular were superheroes that a Broadway musical featuring DC's flagship character — *It's A Bird . . . It's a Plane . . . It's Superman* — starring Bob Holiday as Superman, as well as Linda Lavin and Jack Cassidy (father of future teen idol David Cassidy) debuted on Broadway that same year.

Marvel's response to this competition was, logically, to double down on their business and creative initiatives. In the October '66 Bullpen Bulletins, Lee mentions that — in addition to the burgeoning M.M.M.S. — there are out now, or due soon, Marvel-branded paperback books, record albums, plastic model hobby kits, hats and hoods, Halloween costumes, jumbo character buttons, mini-books, pins, bubble gum trading cards, toy rings, action dolls, board games, jigsaw puzzles, T-shirts, sweatshirts, flicker rings, charms, and sticky labels. And on the same page, he announced:

Marvel super-heroes are on TV! . . . Our

first stations will begin showing animated films of five — yep, FIVE — of our Marvel heroes in the middle of September [1966]. The characters to be featured will be: Captain America, Iron Man, Thor, Sub-Mariner, and the Hulk — all in full color! . . . Production is under way right now at the famous Grantway-Lawrence Animation Co. in Hollywood.

The Marvel merchandising bonanza was well under way. Keeping things in the family, Goodman had assigned his son Chip to oversee these licensed treasures. Indeed, in the December Bullpen Bulletins, Lee would inform readers of this turn of events:

Wait, whom have we here? Who sits thus spinning records, watching TV, fondling plastic super-hero models, inspecting sweatshirts and bubble gum cards with equal aplomb? 'Tis none other than Cheerful Chip Goodman, Master of Marvel merchandising, who daringly dispenses our goodies to all the aesthetic areas beyond the printed page!

In the story pages of the comics themselves, the momentum was no less exhilarating. While Lee and Romita were reenvisioning Spider-Man, Lee and Kirby were introducing, in *Thor* (formerly *Journey Into Mystery*),

303

the science fiction–infused Norse mythology that would bring Ego the Living Planet and the High Evolutionary to life. In the Lee-Kirby Captain America serial in *Tales of Suspense,* the master villain, the Red Skull, was reborn in the present day and had gained control of the terrifying wish-granting power of the Cosmic Cube. Each of these stories — indeed, most of the Marvel line — raised the stakes, issue after issue, to "can-you-top-this?" levels of excitement.

Perhaps the most ambitious and thrilling stories were being told in Marvel's flagship title. The Fantastic Four were facing the planet-devourer Galactus — and his dreaded herald, the Silver Surfer — in a three-part story (in issues #48–50) that has come to be known as "the Galactus Trilogy." Lee has always said that Kirby had created the Surfer without discussing it with him, the artist reasoning that someone as powerful as Galactus would have a herald to announce his arrival. Although Lee was at first less than pleased with this potentially absurd figure who looked like an Oscar statuette, surfing without any actual water in sight, and referred to him as "a nut on some kind of flying surf board,"[21] he and Kirby made the Surfer work. Both men would end up taking a proprietary attitude toward the character.

Lee and Kirby (and inker Joe Sinnott) followed up the Galactus Trilogy with a year of

304

equally stunning story lines, including the classic "This Man . . . This Monster" story in issue #51, the introduction of the first black superhero, the Black Panther, in issue #52, and a transcendent four-part story, generally referred to as "Doomsday," in issues #57–60, wherein Dr. Doom steals the Silver Surfer's cosmic power and uses it in an attempt to kill the Four and conquer Earth. While the plot is reasonably straightforward, the character development and rise and fall of dramatic tension was equal to, if not possibly even more intense than, that in the Galactus Trilogy. (And proving that they didn't take themselves too seriously, the following year, Lee and Kirby did a hilarious parody of Doomsday in "The Saga of the Silver Burper" in the first issue of Marvel's 1967 satire comic *Not Brand Echh*.)

The Marvel juggernaut — as shepherded by Stan Lee — was at full power. In terms of sales and creativity, as well as penetration into areas beyond comics, the company was becoming synonymous with cutting-edge entertainment for a wide demographic, as well as the source of a plethora of merchandising items. Despite the potentially devastating losses of Wood and Ditko, Lee was at the helm of a pop culture phenomenon.

If the *Herald Tribune* article had angered Kirby, indeed if, as artist Gil Kane had theorized, all of Kirby's "frustration [with

305

Lee] came out in the work, which obviously made it richer," then that rage was indeed paying off in spades for Lee and Marvel.[22] And if the success of the *Batman* TV series was selling comics for DC — well, Marvel's sales were rising, too.

But in the midst of so much success in 1966, that year also brought lawsuits against Marvel by two of its founding creators. Those court actions threatened to undo everything that Lee had accomplished in the past five years.

While modern Marvel's early success started in 1961 with *Fantastic Four,* its roots were in Timely's comics of the '30s and '40s. The major Goodman superheroes of that era — as well as the ones briefly revived in the 1950s — were the Sub-Mariner, the Human Torch, and Captain America. It was largely on these characters that Stan Lee learned the ropes as editor, writer, and art director.

Now, in the mid-1960s, with Marvel on the rise, two of the company's more high-profile titles were *Fantastic Four* and *The Avengers.* The former counted the new Human Torch as a team member. And among the team's primary adversaries was Prince Namor, a.k.a. the Sub-Mariner (who by 1965 had his own ongoing feature in *Tales to Astonish*). Meanwhile, the Avengers were being led by the literally and figuratively revived Captain America. Namor, the Torch, and Cap were important parts of the modern Goodman comics publishing venture and certain to be of value to anyone contemplating buying the company. Goodman owned the copyrights and trademarks to these characters, as he did to all the Marvel characters.

But a legal window for the original creators to claim them was approaching, and at least two of those creators were determined to do just that. Carl Burgos, creator of the Human Torch, and Joe Simon, cocreator of Captain America, initiated — independently of each other — legal actions to take ownership of their characters.

How far, if anywhere, Burgos's lawsuit against Marvel ever got is unclear in history. Carl Burgos had not disappeared into non-comics fields after the Golden Age. He had worked regularly and unceasingly for Lee and Goodman throughout the 1950s on comics, humor magazines, and pulps — writing and drawing stories, as well as designing, drawing, and reworking countless covers — to the point where historian Michael Vassallo has coined the term "Burgosized" to refer to art drawn by others but heavily reworked by Burgos.[23]

After the sudden narrowing of the Goodman comics line in 1957, Burgos then worked in commercial, non-comics art. In 1964, though, he briefly returned to Lee's employ to draw a few stories — including a Johnny

307

Storm / Human Torch story with cameos by himself and Lee. But at some point between then and the summer of 1966, he initiated a legal action of some indeterminate kind against Goodman for the rights to the original 1939 Torch. Likely as a way of cementing Goodman's ownership, that "original" Torch reappeared for the first time since the '50s and battled the modern version in the 1966 *Fantastic Four Annual #4.*

During that summer, Burgos's daughter Susan — age fifteen at the time — recalled that her father had gathered all his old comic books and other unspecified vestiges of his comics career into a pile in their yard in order to dispose of it all, even insisting she bring back to the pile the few comics she had tried to rescue. Susan's memory from that day is that this must have been the day he settled — unsatisfactorily — whatever legal action he had taken against Goodman. While it would be tempting to think Burgos intended to "torch" the materials, he seems to have just disposed of them in a more suburban-approved manner — putting them out for the trash collectors.[24]

Probably, but not definitively, connected, Susan Burgos also recalled that, around the time of the lawsuit, "for months he [Burgos] mumbled comments about Stan Lee under his breath. Before that day [that he tossed out his Golden Age material], I knew he was unhappy and that something was going on, but I didn't really know what was happening. . . . It really upset him that Stan Lee completely revamped the Torch."

So, aside from whatever ownership issues Burgos might have had with Marvel, there seemed to be something that rubbed him the wrong way about the Johnny Storm version of the character. Whatever the issues, as far as Carl Burgos was concerned, they were not resolved justly.

Interestingly, Burgos would go on to draw a version of Captain Marvel for publisher Myron Fass's M. F. Enterprises in 1966. With Fawcett Publications' trademark on the original Captain Marvel having lapsed, Fass jumped on the name and published several issues before Goodman bought the rights from him and, in 1967, published Marvel's version of Captain Marvel, written by Lee and drawn by Gene Colan. The cover of Fass's *Captain Marvel* #4 (cover-dated November 1966) was Burgos's last-known comic book work, although he stayed in comics as an editor for Fass's Eerie Publications (not to be confused with Warren Publishing, who published a title called *Eerie*) and Harris Publications, until his 1984 death.

Joe Simon, always savvier about business than most comics creators, and still smarting from Goodman's broken 1940 promises of profit

309

sharing on Captain America, would be harder to deal with. Likely not by coincidence, Marvel had started reprinting Simon and Kirby's 1941 *Captain America* stories, but with Simon and Kirby's credits removed — notable for a company that made a point of giving even its letterers credit. Whether or not this was a preemptive move by Goodman to retain ownership and control of the material, Simon did indeed file suit. As he wrote in *My Life in Comics,* "I submitted the appropriate paperwork, but didn't include Jack Kirby because he was working for Marvel at the time, on projects that included Captain America. I thought it would constitute a conflict of interest [for Kirby]."

In 1966, Simon sued in New York State Supreme Court over the Goodmans' (Martin and Jean — they were both listed as owners of the corporate entity Simon was suing) "misappropriation of his state law property rights," and in '67, he filed a similar action in the United States District Court for the Southern District of New York. In the latter, he claimed that he "as the author of the Works, had the sole and exclusive right to the renewal terms of the copyright" and "also sought . . . to prohibit the Goodmans from applying for renewal registration of the Works."[25]

The Goodmans countersued, claiming, according to Simon, that Lee and Kirby had

310

"created the character while working in the office on staff, so it was company property." In addition, Simon added, Marvel had convinced Kirby to testify on the company's behalf. That, combined with a contemporaneous case that went against Theodor Seuss Geisel (a.k.a. Dr. Seuss), who was suing *Liberty* magazine over ownership of work done for them in the 1930s, convinced Simon to eventually, in 1969, settle out of court. Marvel ended up with definitive ownership of Captain America, at least until Simon would again initiate action decades later.

As for the Sub-Mariner, Bill Everett had been back working sporadically at Marvel since 1964's *Daredevil* #1 and then regularly since 1966. According to Roy Thomas, Everett was dependent on the company for regular income, which — with his erratic relationship with deadlines — he was glad to have. As Thomas further explained:

That was another good thing about Stan . . . he felt a loyalty to longtime pros like . . . Everett; and though he couldn't make room on the Ark for everybody, he felt that they deserved a chance. Stan didn't think artists should be tossed on the scrap heap simply because they might not be at the top of their form anymore.[26]

In addition, Goodman had given Everett a

311

sizable loan for which, according to Thomas, no repayment was expected. The loan, according to Everett biographer Blake Bell, was probably for some serious health issues Everett was dealing with. Bill Everett was not going to sue Martin Goodman.[27]

While it's never been definitively established that the reprinting of the iconic Timely characters was undertaken by Lee at Goodman's behest, and thereby done specifically in order to establish that they belonged to Marvel, it's hard to imagine, if such was the case, that Lee, after twenty-five years in the business, didn't understand what was going on. It's also hard to fault him for going ahead and publishing what was in the company's best interests (and what many fans were actually grateful to have a chance to read). In the final analysis, Lee was, indeed, a management employee of Marvel Comics and Magazine Management, and he was, indeed, Martin and Jean Goodman's cousin.

And so, several potential impediments to Marvel's — and Stan Lee's — progress were avoided and contained. The next few years would only accelerate the pace of growth of the man and the company.

While there would be dramatically more lucrative and higher-profile eras for Lee and for Marvel, the next several years would bring what many would consider the peak of cre-

312

ativity and inspiration for both. And all this would be accomplished during the coming-of-age years of the earliest baby boomers, in the midst of political, cultural, and social upheaval in the United States in particular and across the entire world.

It was a period that would place confusing yet stimulating demands upon the members of Stan Lee's generation. Lee's response was typical of Greatest Generation members and yet unique to someone of his specific talents and temperament, and to his roles as, simultaneously, reflector and shaper of the developing streams of the culture that surrounded him.

The baby boomers were coming into their own and, though decades older, so was Stan Lee.

More than ever, Stan Lee's unique position in the culture would present him with challenges that neither he, nor anyone else in the comics business, had ever really had to grapple with. Like the challenges, his responses to them would be multifaceted and not always consistent, but they would be uniquely his.

11
BOOM BOOM BOOM

ITEM! Didja hear about STAN THE MAN rapping for hours with JOE McDONALD, BARRY MELTON, and their manager, ED DENSON? Or maybe you know them better as COUNTRY JOE AND THE FISH!
— Marvel Bullpen Bulletins
in comics dated June 1970

Joe McDonald, born January 1, 1942, was a pre-boomer, as were many of his fellow rock musicians of the late '60s, entering the world before the baby boom starting gun of 1945. He and his band, Country Joe and the Fish, addressed charged topics of the late 1960s, including in "Superbird," a 1967 song that portrayed Marvel's superheroes — specifically the Fantastic Four and Doctor Strange — as representing new-era thinking that would topple the outmoded philosophy of the eponymous Superbird, an alternate identity, according to the song, for then-president Lyndon Johnson.

Interestingly, in the song, Johnson is portrayed as a version of Superman gone mad, not a villain so much as a cracked hero. One could also see the Superbird figure as an outdated hero of an older generation, while the ones who will help the narrator of the song — either the Fish themselves, or possibly the entire generation the Fish represents — have their "brand new day," are the more modern superheroes from Marvel's comics.

In a 2018 interview with the *Aquarian Drunkard* website, McDonald, fifty years later, recalled the connection between the comics and the song:

> It was the beginning of Marvel Comics and that comic book hero, ironic humor, so [the idea] was to turn the president into a comic book character. We just did it and thought it was funny.[1]

While the Fish were never as popular as other San Francisco Bay Area bands of the era like the Jefferson Airplane or the Grateful Dead, they were quite well known in their heyday and, though they played their share of love songs and feel-good rockers, did tend to wear their politics a bit more on their sleeves than many of their contemporaries.

Their best-known song was the sardonic anti–Vietnam War "I-Feel-Like-I'm-Fixin'-to-Die Rag," written by McDonald, and released in November 1967, which darkly sang from

315

the point-of-view of the era's soldiers that, "whoopee, we're all gonna die." McDonald would make the song most famous in his solo set at the Woodstock Festival in August 1969, as well as in the 1970 movie of the festival.

The band's songs were often darkly humorous and shot through with self-mocking irony as well as with a sense of dramatic urgency.

Much like a Marvel comic book.

While many celebrities would come to visit Marvel Comics and Stan Lee, the Fish were perhaps the only high-profile, '60s-era band that were reported, via the Bullpen Bulletins, to have visited Marvel at least a couple of times, possibly even more. Plus, they actually appeared in an issue of *Nick Fury, Agent of S.H.I.E.L.D.* So while a third party, Peter Asher, had to tell Stan that the Beatles dug Marvel, the Fish demonstrated their affinity for the company, its characters, and its staff from early on, in its music and in person. The band's relationship with Lee opens an interesting window into his own growing celebrity in the late '60s.

The relationship began with a letter from the band to Lee dated May 19, 1967. This would be about a week after the May 11 release of the band's first album, *Electric Music for the Mind and Body,* which contained "Superbird." (For historical context, the Beatles' classic album, *Sgt. Pepper's Lonely*

316

Hearts Club Band, was released in the United States on May 26.) The letter was from "Country Joe and the Fish," probably written by band manager ED Denson, apparently accompanying a copy of *Electric Music,* and told Stan:

No doubt you'll be pleased to know that your creations have so entered the consciousness of the generation that they emerge, yes actually emerge, in the folk music of the times. If you listen carefully to this record . . . you'll hear and see two actual figments [Fantastic Four and Dr. Strange].[2]

Lee's response, dated May 26, was:

Hi, Piscatorial Pals!
. . . we're deliciously delighted that our somewhat forensic fame has reached as far as the hallowed harmonious halls of Berkeley — and penetrated, how'er insidiously, the liltin' lyrics of thine own rollickin' record!

What I'm trying to say, guys, is — enjoyed your tintinnabulatin' tunes — got a kick out of our mention — and are glad to dub thee — one and all — Merry Marchers in Perpetuity! . . .

Hang loose, gang — you're our type of heroes.[3]

The Fish would have a breakout perfor-

317

mance on June 17 at the legendary Monterey Pop Festival. Soon after that, sometime in "the summer of 1967," according to Marvel staff writer/editor Gary Friedrich (who passed away in 2018), during a stand in New York where the Fish played at venues, including the Café Au Go Go, band keyboardist David Bennett Cohen arranged a visit to Marvel.

As Cohen recalled in 2010:

I was the one who instigated the visit. I called Marvel Comic Books to thank them for their comics. There was just something about Marvel's comics. They were grown-up comics. It wasn't like teenage stuff, or kid stuff. Of course, it was fantasy, and it was beyond the realm of reality, but it had a maturity about it. . . .

So I called the office to thank them, and I told them I wanted to come up and meet them. I told them I was from Country Joe and the Fish . . . and I think somebody may have invited me up.[4]

Friedrich, a Fish fan, went out to the lobby to greet the band when they came to visit the office, apparently without an actual appointment. He convinced Stan, who seemed to — despite the recent correspondence — never have heard of the band, to make an appointment for them to come meet him. In 2010,

318

Friedrich recalled that despite some reluctance on Lee's end

after some arm-twisting on my part, mainly buttressed by my pointing out the value of mentioning the meeting in the Bullpen Bulletins, he relented, and a meeting was arranged.

A couple of days later, David showed up with Joe, Barry [Melton] and the rest of the band. . . . I escorted the band into the inner sanctum and we were greeted by the ever-smiling Stan. He was very cordial, as always. . . . The meeting didn't last long. Joe asked Stan a few questions . . . the band was somewhat awestruck. I think Stan, as always, just wanted to get back to work, though he'd never have let his guests know that.

After a few minutes, Stan very graciously broke it all up, shook hands all around, and the big meeting was over. . . . Stan would light up the room with his smile for guests, make them feel perfectly at home and that they could spend the day if they wanted. Then, in no time flat, he'd wrap it up, shake their hands and move them out so he could get back to work. And I never talked with one of Stan's guests after one of those meetings who didn't feel they'd been treated royally and that this had been one of the highlights of their lives. It was the same with CJ and the Fish.[5]

Cohen would say of the meeting:

Stan Lee made an impression in my life. Meeting him was almost anticlimactic, because, you know, those comics really sustained us a lot of times.[6]

As band cofounder Barry Melton said in 2010:

Of course I remember meeting Stan — I could never forget meeting one of the greatest creative minds and inspirational human beings of my generation. . . . Dr. Strange and the Silver Surfer, and to some degree, the Fantastic Four, were just part of our subculture in San Francisco, which ultimately became the subculture of the country's young people. . . .

I remember Stan being really encouraging. I thought he must be an old beatnik or something, because he wore dark glasses. . . . Marvel comics, sociologically, was part of the youth movement of the Sixties. . . . I am totally enamored of Stan Lee and the impact he's had on our culture. I mean, the guy was truly a giant.[7]

The Fish, it seemed, were indeed Stan

320

Lee's "piscatorial pals." Cohen's memory was that the band members at the meeting that day were just him and either Gary "Chicken" Hirsh or Melton, as opposed to Friedrich's recollection of the entire band showing up, and that the whole band was there for at least one subsequent visit. Obviously, time has blurred some of the details of the band's visits to Marvel.

Lee's recounting of that meeting, though, seemingly didn't make the Bullpen Bulletins until the September 1967–dated comics, out in June, so the entry was probably written in April, when Lee signed off his "Stan's Soapbox" editorial with: "And now we've gotta cut out — Country Joe and the Fish just arrived to visit us — and we don't wanna keep 'em out of the water too long!"

The Fish then appeared as part of the story in the November '69–dated issue #15 of *Nick Fury, Agent of S.H.I.E.L.D.,* written by Friedrich, with art by Herb Trimpe, Dick Ayers, and Sam Grainger. In the scene, the band played "Not So Sweet Martha Lorraine" and the superhero-name-dropping "Superbird," both from *Electric Music for the Mind and Body.*

Their next appearance in the comics was in the June '70 Bulletins, out in March, probably written in January or February:

ITEM! Didja hear about STAN THE MAN rapping for hours with JOE Mc-

321

DONALD, BARRY MELTON, and their manager, ED DENSON? Or maybe you know them better as COUNTRY JOE AND THE FISH!

Such were the times that the visit of a fairly politically radical band to see Lee was not only allowed but was trumpeted in the Bullpen Bulletins. Lee might not have fully understood the times, but he was somehow in tune with them, or was at least making the effort to be. Equally of note was the counterculture's fascination with Lee's superheroes, who, even as hip Marvel versions of such figures, were essentially vigilante power fantasies.

And, of course, the parade of celebrities to the offices was a mere trickle compared to the endless stream of fans, often children, who would come by to try to catch a glimpse of the creators of their superhero fantasies (not realizing that most of them worked at home), as often as not stopped by the gatekeeping — usually verbal, sometimes physical — of "Fabulous" Flo Steinberg.

The summer of 1967 was the Summer of Love in San Francisco, when young people from all over the country flocked to the slums of Haight-Ashbury, intent on living out some kind of hippie dream. It was also the year when "underground comix" started appear-

322

ing in strip form in alternative newspapers, such as *The East Village Other* and *Berkeley Barb.* The work of pioneer underground cartoonists like Robert Crumb and S. Clay Wilson was not yet as well known as it would be, so the energetic and colorful Marvel Comics of the era would be a natural to appeal to people looking for some kind of "outlaw" cultural fix, sometimes in conjunction with usage of mind-altering substances. (By early 1968, though, the first true underground comic books, such as Crumb's *Zap Comix,* would appear and would before too long have a curious effect on kids' adventure comics publishing companies, as we shall see.)

Though beloved by many, comic books were still generally considered junk, at least a decade away from most mainstream cultural arbiters even being willing to consider they might be some kind of legitimate art form. So the "outlaw" appeal of mainstream comics to youth culture lingered and became especially strong when idiosyncratic visual innovators such as Jim Steranko came on the scene.

Steranko, born in 1938 (the same year that Superman debuted in *Action Comics* #1), had been with Marvel since 1966, when, through sheer force of personality, combined with astonishing talent, he had, shortly after

323

Ditko's resignation, made his way past gate-keepers Steinberg, Brodsky, and Thomas to a meeting with Lee. Steranko had walked out with a regular assignment to be the penciler and, within five months, the plotter and scripter on the "Nick Fury, Agent of S.H.I.E.L.D." series in *Strange Tales.*

One of the few new creators to enter the field in over a decade, Steranko, hardly a hippie, nonetheless brought a breath of fresh air into the comics mainstream, with a sense of what was current in design and a style that absorbed and synthesized the greats of the business — Eisner, Kirby, Infantino, Kane — and infused them with his own passion and wide-ranging life experience. Steranko would be one of the people through whom Lee would reduce the workload he and Kirby labored under. His youthful enthusiasm and boundless talent began the process that would gain steam and come to full fruition by the '70s, whereby veteran talent would be supplemented by younger creators who realized that not only were comics expanding in terms of employment opportunities as well as content but that they were, if not yet a respectable career choice, then at least not as great a source of shame as they had been.

Lee, perhaps smarting from losing Wood and Ditko, was willing to give Steranko the kind of creative freedom and explicit credit he wouldn't fully grant Kirby. Or perhaps he gave it because Lee really didn't care that much about *S.H.I.E.L.D.* — Steranko has claimed that he asked Lee to give him his lowest-selling series — and figured there was nothing to lose by letting Steranko take credit (or blame, if such was needed) for whatever the newcomer would do with it. On the other hand, with his favorites such as *Fantastic Four,* Lee still took enough pride of authorship to let the credits say only "by Stan Lee and Jack Kirby." (This wording was a concession made to Kirby, where the ambiguous attribution would mean that Kirby was no longer relegated to being credited as "just" the penciler. The credit also echoed collaborations of earlier in Kirby's career, which were announced as being by "Joe Simon and Jack Kirby.")

While certainly not an underground artist, Steranko brought a modern look and feel to his work that, while it was well in the ballpark of what readers associated with Marvel, brought a caffeine jolt — and a dollop of psychedelia — that most of the regular Marvel creative crew, at least the artists, wasn't able to summon up. Though the younger *writers* like Thomas, Friedrich, and O'Neil were each, in their own way, connected to the ever-elusive zeitgeist, their stories were inevitably drawn by established, talented, but older professionals who were not. It was the rare middle-aged artist who, like Kirby, could plug

325

into the zeitgeist or, if need be, invent his own.

Steranko had been freelancing around, including for Joe Simon at Harvey, but had run into resistance to his innovations at other companies. But his work had a raw energy that Lee had been looking for and had, indeed, always been open to. Here, again, Lee's relative freedom to act on his editorial instincts served him well. As he told radio host Neal Conan (then an eighteen-year-old at the beginning of his illustrious career) in a 1968 interview:

> Jim Steranko, he violates all the rules, and whenever he does, the job is beautiful. I'm not even really an editor where he's concerned. . . . The nuttier it is, the more I say "Go ahead and do it."[8]

If, as Spurgeon and Raphael say, Lee was by this period "a great comic book editor, perhaps the most successful in the medium's history,"[9] it was instinct-based decisions, like giving Steranko relatively free rein, that were part of that success. Lee was autonomous enough in his position to be able to take calculated risks that other editors couldn't or wouldn't.

Born the same year as Jack Kerouac, Lee could have plausibly been, as Barry Melton

326

thought, an "old beatnik." (Lee would have been forty-four at that first 1967 meeting with the Fish.) Of course, he, Kirby, and Ditko were about as far removed from being participating members of bohemian counter-cultures as it was possible to be.

While the Marvel writers and artists worked in a creative, albeit marginalized, field, their lives caught up in telling stories, their actual day-to-day existences, away from their drawing boards or typewriters, were involved in things that hippie boomers and pre-boomers could hardly have found especially interesting. Lee and Kirby were suburban dads, preoccupied with supporting their families and with the traditional trappings of success. And Ditko's Randian philosophy was anathema to the collectivist leanings of many in the counterculture. The Fish and other popular music groups were, of course, pursuing careers and success as much as Lee and his peers but were perhaps more conflicted about it, trying to thread the needle of having successful careers while staying true to an amorphous, but generally nonmaterialistic, set of ideals.

Of course, no generation is all one thing. While many young people were active in the civil rights and anti-war movements, many were on the other side of the fence. And as always, most young people were just trying to get by in school and develop some kind of social life. But the ever-escalating war in Vietnam and the military draft were impacting daily on the lives of young people, whether they were massing in Golden Gate Park or shipping off to Saigon. Generalizing about a generation — or multiple generations, which the baby boom encompasses — is always tricky, and yet generalizing is ultimately what the art, craft, and business of popular culture are all about: finding something that will appeal to and excite a large segment of a demographic while offending or alienating as few as possible. Marvel's comics were achieving that, offering stories that could be interpreted in multiple ways.

Sure, children were, as always, buying and reading comics. But here was a new phenomenon. Hip, smart, educated young adults — people who might well have been listening to bands like the Fish while they were reading Marvel's comics — were enamored of Stan Lee and Marvel. Whether they had followed their dreams to become celebrity musicians or were taking more traditional routes by pursuing professional educations or serving in the military, young Americans were finding inspiration in Marvel Comics. And like Cohen and Melton, they were finding that inspiration embodied in Stan Lee, who had become the physical incarnation of Marvel.

It must all have seemed like a dream to Stan

Lee. Starting at a job at age seventeen in 1940 — one that likely seemed to be just another temporary gig like the many he'd gone through since graduating DeWitt Clinton the previous year — he had now progressed, after a twenty-five-year career that encompassed the ups and downs of the comics business, to an extraordinary position. He'd become the head editor of Timely Comics at age eighteen and had presided over what had been, until 1957, one of the largest-volume producers of comics in the country. He was well known in the field, and generally well liked, even admired, by his peers. But in the '50s, he was by no means famous and certainly not considered any kind of influence on the overall culture, popular or otherwise, and not even really on comic books outside of the ones he oversaw.

He then weathered the implosion of 1957, and, in its wake, gathered his wits and his forces to improvise the phenomenon of Marvel Comics. The comics were successful and were being noticed *not* just by children — as rabid in their love for the stories and the characters and the creators as they were — but by college students. In addition, they were being noticed by adults who had loved the comics of their childhoods and now were interested in what Marvel was doing — highly educated adults like Roy Thomas and Dr. Jerry Bails. And celebrities like Federico

329

Fellini were noticing, too.

So Stan Lee, who had been eager to leave comics — and nearly desperate enough to actually do so — was now busy reconstructing comics (and himself) into something new. He was even regularly speaking to large crowds at colleges and universities all over the country. No comic book editor or writer had ever been in exactly this position. The entire world was in flux in the late '60s, and many people seemed to want to know what Stan Lee thought about the political and social upheaval that was going on. What an odd thing.

For whatever reason, Stan was no longer just selling stuff. Of course, his livelihood and lifestyle *depended* on him making and selling stuff. But now, added to what would turn out to be a lifelong compulsion to tell the truth (even if that truth was disguised with casual wording and surrounded by hype) was the desire to say — in person and in print — things that had *meaning*. Comic books, which had given him a pleasant way to make a living, had suddenly made him a figure whose opinions people wanted to know. But did he want to share his opinions in public — not just at lunch with his pals or in the relative intimacy of a college auditorium, but in the same pages of the same magazines where Marvel's characters fought supervillains and emoted grandly?

330

Well, apparently, he *did* want to share his feelings and opinions, because that's exactly what he did. Apparently, he felt he had something to say that *needed* to be shared. But whose opinions would he be sharing? Stan Lee's or Marvel Comics'? Because they were now, in many ways, one and the same — except, of course, for the small detail that he was neither the owner nor the publisher of Marvel Comics. Nonetheless, share he did.

For Lee, this would be another "learn while you earn" situation. He would state some usually mild but heartfelt feelings, as he'd already been doing in the letters pages and Bullpen Bulletins, but there using some variant of the editorial "we," or speaking of "Stan" in the third person. Now, though, he would make it clearer whose opinions he was stating as he introduced the Stan's Soapbox column into the Bullpen Bulletins, the first appearing in the comics dated May and June 1967. His debut Soapbox topic was "the Marvel Philosophy," of which he wrote:

We do have a motive — a purpose — behind our mags! That purpose is, plain and simple — to entertain you! . . . If we can also do our bit to advance the cause of intellectualism, humanitarianism, and mutual understanding . . . that won't break our collective heart . . . !

331

Admittedly not an especially controversial editorial. By the same token, no other comic book company was advocating "the cause of intellectualism, humanitarianism, and mutual understanding." It's unlikely that such advocacy had come as a mandate from Martin Goodman. No, this was coming straight from Stan, even if it was cloaked in the ambiguous disguise of "we."

By the November '67 cover–dated comics, the Soapbox informed us:

We do cater to a special intellectual level. Our rollickin' readers, no matter what their ages, have proven to be bright, imaginative, informal, and sophisticated!

Again, perhaps not the most risk-taking passage, complimenting his readers as it did. Still, there were no doubt those who didn't like being told they were some kind of elite, snobby person of a "special intellectual level," who might even have harbored ill will toward that kind of person. It could be seen as a slight but real risk to make such a statement.

In the April '68 cover–dated comics, Lee stated in the Soapbox:

Didja know that more than a dozen college professors throughout America now use Marvel mags in their English Lit courses as supplemental material? It's

332

only a start — but we're getting there, gang!

What percentage of the audience cared about that? What the heck is "supplemental material," anyway? (And where was "there," exactly?) Clearly, though, it was important to Lee to get the point across.

In the September '68 comics, Lee started dancing among some land mines. Noting that some Marvel employees were Democrats and some Republicans, he continued:

> As for Yours Truly and a few others, we prefer to judge the person, rather than the party line. That's why we seek to avoid editorializing about controversial issues . . . because we share the same diversity of opinion as Americans everywhere.

People were not expecting *that* from their escapist fantasy in 1968.

And then Lee immediately followed that, in the same Soapbox, with the following, which perhaps might have made some readers think he himself had been indulging in some kind of substance experimentation:

> We believe that Man has a divine destiny, and an awesome responsibility — the responsibility of . . . judging each fellow

333

human on his own merit, regardless of race, creed or color . . . and we'll never rest until it becomes a fact, rather than just a cherished dream!

Where did *that* come from, suburban dad who claims to just be concerned about earning a living? Marvel — Stan — *somebody* — would "never rest" until humankind fulfilled its "divine destiny"?

As a certain Kryptonian refugee might have said: "What th— ?!"

By the October-dated comics, Lee reported in the Soapbox that most readers who responded *did* want Marvel to editorialize. Which led to the November '68 Soapbox, on newsstands in August, which declared:

Let's lay it right on the line. Bigotry and racism are among the deadliest social ills plaguing the world today. . . . Sooner or later, if man is ever to be worthy of his destiny, we must fill our hearts with tolerance. For then, and only then, will we be truly worthy of the concept that man was created in the image of God — a God who calls us ALL — His children.

And in case you were wondering who he was speaking for, it was signed, using the

334

Latin for "peace and justice":

Pax et Justitia,
Stan

It's not so much the denunciation of bigotry that's remarkable in the above. It's the *tone* and *passion.* This was far beyond the tongue-in-cheek humor of the Merry Marvel Marching Society or the name-checking of celebrity visitors to the bullpen. This was a man with something to say and, thanks to his own accomplishments, a forum in which to say it. The EC Comics of the 1950s had taken stands, in their text pages, against censorship, that, like the Soapboxes, might have gone over the heads or against the philosophies of significant numbers of readers. But the primary aim of EC's editorials was survival. They were in the crosshairs of enemies within and without the comics industry, and their goal was to invalidate their critics and live to publish another day.

But this was something different. There was no perceived gain for Lee personally or Marvel collectively to start pontificating on issues, even on something as seemingly noncontroversial as bigotry, or, for that matter, on the subject of editorializing itself. But somewhere inside him, with a schedule overbooked and overextended, Lee decided that expressing his deepest feelings — and

335

conflating them with Marvel's "feelings" — was an urgent thing to do. If it wasn't sincere — if it was some kind of pandering to an audience that was already hooked on the company's comics and merchandise — it seems like a lot of trouble to have gone to simply in order to *pretend* to care.

Nothing happens in a vacuum, of course. As Lee's personal universe was convulsing — not unpleasantly — so was the country and the world around him. To say that Lee was compelled to respond to surrounding conditions is a truism. *Everyone* must respond to the world around them. But Lee had been given a chance to become a role model, and he had not shied from the challenge. He clearly relished the idea that people would look to him — both to his work and to him, personally — for guidance in perplexing times.

Sure, there were figures of Lee's generation who were popular with boomer kids, such as local New York kids' show hosts Sonny Fox and Chuck McCann, and national figures like Bob Keeshan, a.k.a. Captain Kangaroo. There was also the phenomenon of Soupy Sales, whose popularity crossed over from kids to teenagers and college students.

But Stan Lee's situation was different. No one cared what Captain Kangaroo thought about the war in Vietnam.

There were also figures around Lee's age popular on campuses — Marshall McLuhan and Allen Ginsberg, for instance. William F. Buckley Jr. and Abbie Hoffman. But *their* job was to confront people with their opinions. Lee was clearly not in that mold, either.

If there were ever a sui generis figure, it was Stan Lee. There was no one in the culture in a similar role: a highly placed (but not top) employee of a publishing enterprise whose products were consumed primarily by children felt he had to speak out on the issues of the day. As his public persona was coming into focus in the late 1960s, somehow or other, Lee had taken it upon himself to be, not a wannabe peer to the boomers, but rather some kind of philosopher-cheerleader, a hip-but-square parent, an adult who hadn't thrown in the towel on idealism but who also wasn't a doctrinaire partisan.

Stan Lee said out loud that he was opposed to bigotry. As history has shown us, not everyone is even that brave, especially not someone whose job is, ultimately, to sell stuff.

Baby boomer navel-gazing is beyond a cliché. And yet there seems to be no better way to explain Marvel's popularity and Stan Lee's celebrity than as a factor of boomer culture. A significant number of kids, who were hooked by Marvel from early *Fantastic Four* and *Spider-Man* and the rest, grew from

337

childhood to adolescence, or from adolescence to adulthood, during the period from 1961 to the late '60s and maintained an interest in Marvel's characters and creators over those years. Of course, most adolescents dropped comics, but a fair number now *did* stay with them, including college students, and as Kirby was bursting boundaries of concepts and vision, Lee was doing the same with writing, editing, and promotion.

Certainly, the fact that both men had boomer children could well have been a factor in what they were thinking and storytelling about. They had literal skin in the game. The world in which their children were growing up was knocking constantly at their doors. "Sex, drugs, and rock and roll" wasn't just a glib slogan to them; they were realities that their kids faced daily at school and on the streets and, for that matter, on TV and in the movies. It was what everybody's kids faced. There were seventy million boomers in a country of around two hundred million. A third of the country's population were the test subjects for the various experiments of the ever-evolving societies of the United States and the world. (And while Steve Ditko was neither a boomer nor the father of one, he did seem to have never lost touch with the Johnstown High School teenager he had been or with the timeless verities of adolescence.)

So the audience that had been in grade

338

school in the early to mid-1960s was now heading for college or Vietnam. Or the Peace Corps. Or Canada. Or Haight-Ashbury. Or a factory or an office. And many members of that audience kept up with Marvel's comics, as well as the underground comix, and with the movies and, especially, the music of the era. And many of them wanted to know what Stan Lee thought about what was going on.

Why? Largely because Lee had happened upon a personal connection with Marvel's readers, many of them from the time they were kids — and Lee was synonymous with Marvel. Stan Lee — an actual person with a voluble public persona — was the voice and face of Marvel in a time when, well, Superman and Batman were the voice and face of DC, and no one was really the voice and face of any other comics company.

So it didn't really matter to most readers what DC editors Julius Schwartz or Bob Kanigher or Mort Weisinger thought about the issues of the day. Those men, whatever their personalities, didn't think of themselves as publicists or cheerleaders or spokespersons. Their job was to put out entertaining comic books that sold well enough for them to keep on putting out entertaining comic books that sold well enough.

Stan Lee had decided that his job description was something else. A child of the Great Depression and of the peregrinations of the comics business, he seemed to instinctively realize that his desperation-move to provide Marvel with a friendly face also gave him a launching pad for becoming a celebrity who had opinions and feelings and passions, passions that related both directly and tangentially to a medium and a company that he thought he had long ago ceased caring about.

Lee took to this new celebrity like the proverbial duck to water. He developed a new look that involved fashionable suits, a neatly trimmed beard, and a stylish, well-sculpted toupee, as would befit a man now so much in the public eye. It had become clear that, so long as Marvel was prominent, he would be prominent. And if Marvel ever lost its cachet or if it decided it didn't need Stan Lee anymore, he was now in a position to take his celebrity and do with it whatever he felt necessary and appropriate. Sure, he was in the comics business, but he was now also in the larger entertainment business.

Most important, he was in the *Stan Lee* business. And that, it would turn out, would be a very interesting business. It was a business that would be the key to pretty much everything professionally — and often personally — that would happen to him for the rest of his life. If there were ever someone in the right place at the right time with the right skill set, experience, and personality to make the most of the possibilities presented to him

— and created by him — it was Stan Lee.

Marvel's 1961 creation of an evolved super-hero genre was an incredible turning point in Lee's life. He took the opportunities offered by this new approach to comic book storytelling that he'd helped invent and made the most of them. By 1967, and certainly by 1968, the creative and business potential of the Marvel juggernaut was a certified cultural phenomenon. Those two years would also prove to be some of the most tumultuous in American and world history.

With his and Marvel's growing cultural footprint, it was inevitable that Lee would become caught up in the extreme developments of the era. It would prove to be a wild ride for all concerned.

12
REVOLUTION IN THE AIR

Beware the fanatic! Too often his cure is deadlier by far than the evil he denounces!
— Narrator (Stan Lee) in *X-Men* #16,
January 1966

As much as anyone, Stan Lee helped create the popular culture of the 1960s. And yet for someone responsible for fueling so much of the era's imagination, Lee seemed to be as puzzled as anybody by the forces at play during that tumultuous period, which by 1968 would present him with great opportunities as well as perplexing challenges.

One thing he did understand was the power of mass media — comics, of course, but especially *radio.*

Stanley Lieber had loved radio as a kid. In later years, he would speak fondly and often of the radio shows that had fired his imagination. Shows like *Chandu the Magician* and *The Charlie McCarthy Show* were among his favorites. Along with feature films — especially those starring Errol Flynn — and

342

Saturday morning serials, as well as his favorite kids book series, such as Bomba, the Jungle Boy ("With Bomba, to think was to act.") and the series featuring Jimmie Dale, the Gray Seal, Stanley's imagination was continually fueled. Much of the edifice of the Marvel Universe was built on the foundation of preadolescent Stan's immersion in — and analysis of — the popular culture of his childhood.[1]

By the mid-1960s, television had long ago taken over radio's function in kids' lives. For better or worse, children got their story-oriented entertainment more and more from TV, less and less from books, and virtually not at all from radio. But radio had by no means gone away. The medium had, at that point, become the vehicle for popular music, most recently rock and roll, which was transforming from a fad that wouldn't go away to a tribal bonding soundtrack for both mainstream and fringe youth cultures.

But as more and more listeners were buying radios that carried FM, as well as the more-established AM signals, station owners found themselves with this underutilized, new bandwidth, FM, that was well suited to carrying stereo, high-fidelity music, which was exactly what was demanded by an audience becoming more and more finicky about the quality of sound reproduced by elaborate home stereo systems. So FM radio became the place where people would hear crystal-clear music of every variety, from classical to jazz to the newest psychedelic hits. Top 40 music and ethnic music were still plentiful on the AM band, as was the new fad of listener call-in shows. But the wave of the future for serious music aficionados (and the mellow-voiced announcers who introduced the music) was FM.

In more practical terms, radio's virtual doubling of its available program hours meant that its time had to be filled. So there was more music, more news, more traffic reports. And, of course, more talk.

Radio stations needing to fill time and hold listeners' attention added talk shows, often with opinionated hosts. The stations were eager for interesting guests with outgoing personalities and the gift of gab, involved with things that people wanted to hear about, perhaps with products they would want to buy. And if such guests lived or worked near the radio station so they could drop in on short notice and not require any elaborate or expensive arrangements to get them to the studio, so much the better.

It was a ready-made paradise for Stan Lee, who worked (and would soon live) in mid-town Manhattan, close to every radio station in the New York metropolitan area.

New York radio in the late 1960s was populated by progressive rock, all-news, top

40, college radio, and talk shows with hosts of a variety of political stripes. One station of note was left-leaning WBAI. A station in the tiny Pacifica network, WBAI had become the nexus of New York area '60s counterculture. It was pretty much the central clearinghouse for information for people planning to protest in Chicago at August 1968's Democratic National Convention. During a heated, local teachers' strike, it had, in the name of free speech, broadcast an anti-Semitic poem written by a black schoolchild. The broadcast had prompted Meir Kahane's Jewish Defense League to occupy the station's headquarters in protest.

But as a center of various alternative cultures, WBAI was also a place where fans of nonrespected media — such as comic books — could host free-form talk shows that featured their culture heroes — for instance, the former Stanley Martin Lieber.

Never one to pass up free publicity — and working within walking distance of the station — Lee knew that, as much as he needed that exposure, the station needed to fill time, especially the late-night/early-morning hours. So WBAI it was. Not the political shows. Not the black power or feminist shows. But the hippie-culture shows, hosted by budding radio personalities, amazed that they could get the voice of the comics that meant so much to them to be on their radio programs.

345

Did it bother Lee to be on a station so identified with radical politics? Did he even know that it was? In any case, Lee was a regular on WBAI. Neal Conan, who would go on to be a prominent NPR personality, in 1968 did one of his first interviews with Lee on WBAI. A year earlier, a science fiction freak named Mike Hodel had interviewed Lee and Kirby on *his* WBAI program.

On the other end of the political spectrum, there were local New York talk show hosts such as Barry Farber. A gentle-spoken Southerner, Farber was a political conservative, with a love of language and an appreciation for people who, like Lee, could turn a phrase and who could fill up the long stretches of an overnight talk show — this one originating from New York's WOR — with entertaining chat. Farber also liked a good fight, so he was glad to mix and match his panelists and let them go at it — guided by questions and comments from Farber himself, playing the concerned, not-so-innocent bystander.

And in the divide between those extremes, there were assorted radio hosts, including those on New York area college radio stations, to also provide a forum for Stan Lee, where he could reach the college students at whom Marvel was increasingly aiming its comics. Not only had college students caught on to Marvel from the beginning, but the children who were reading his comics in '62 and '63 were now themselves college students, interested in sex, drugs, rock and roll, and politics. Radio would be a big part of continuing and growing Marvel's connection to its audience.

Lee and Kirby's WBAI radio appearance occurred during a significant period in Marvel's development. In early 1967, Marvel's creative and sales pictures were outstanding. There were toys and cartoons and other merchandise based on the Marvel characters, and it seemed unimaginable the company would ever be worth more. After all, Spider-Man might have been popular, but he'd never be in the same league as, say, the Walt Disney characters.

Stan Lee believed that there were two factors that had been part and parcel of the company's success over the six years since the 1961 debut of the Fantastic Four, factors that he had been canny enough to understand and capitalize on. And he wanted to be sure that the world — including Martin Goodman and any potential purchasers of Marvel — knew exactly what he had contributed to the phenomenon that was Marvel.

One factor Lee felt was important was that no matter how successful Marvel was, it should never stop acting like it was "the little engine that could." To admit — much less boast — that its ratio of sales compared to what they printed was far outstripping top competitor DC's (although DC still reigned supreme in total copies sold, albeit with many more titles than Marvel produced) was something Lee believed would be commercial suicide. True, Goodman was trumpeting Marvel's success in trade magazine ads. That made sense from the perspective of ad rates and sales — and the value of the company to a suitor. But certainly it would be foolhardy for Lee, or anyone else besides Goodman, in any mainstream context, to make such statements.

So on March 3, 1967, on Mike Hodel's WBAI radio program (found in Lee's University of Wyoming archives), when Lee and Jack Kirby made a joint appearance, Lee articulated his feeling about how he thought the company should present itself — simultaneously pulling off the neat trick of letting the audience in on some "behind-the-scenes" strategy. Prompted by Hodel to resume a disagreement he and Kirby had been having before the show went on the air, Stan opined:

I don't want to lose our image of being the underdogs, which we've had for years, the little outfit that came along and we're challenging the big fellows. The American public being the way it is, once we're known to be the leaders, they're liable to sympathize with another outfit, so . . . I'd like them to think of

348

us as the little, homey, fun outfit that, you know, we're not quite that big and successful, we're not that fat-cattish yet. Jack feels differently, though, I think.[2]

Kirby certainly did feel differently. He responded passionately to Lee's comments, saying that Marvel has

content that is superior to any of the magazines on the market, and I, as a reader, would like to read Marvel. And when I do a strip for Marvel, I feel that I *am* a reader. . . . So I feel that we are number one, we should be number one, and *say* we're number one, and have no regrets about it.

Doing his best to placate star-artist Kirby, Lee assured the listeners that he agreed with Kirby, but:

The public generally likes an underdog, and . . . I think it's more fun for the reader to think he's latched onto something that is sort of his little discovery. . . . But the minute the reader feels everybody knows about Marvel . . . they may try to find something else . . . to lavish their affection on.

In February '68, Lee would articulate what he felt was the second crucial factor that he brought to Marvel, something perhaps even

349

more important than his approach to Marvel as an underdog ad campaign. In an interview with New Jersey's Rutgers University radio station (also found in Lee's University of Wyoming archives), he would opine:

We've done stories that were quite successful with the readers . . . [and] I would say to myself, "Well, the story was really nothing. It was just the hero meets a villain, fights him. . . ." But I suspect it was the little subplots, and the little asides, and the characterization that . . . makes our books a little better than some others. . . . It's practically the same plot all the time.[3]

"The *dialogue*," he continued, "I have always felt, is the most important thing . . . the thing that gives a story realism is having the characters talk and react . . . like real people. Therefore, the thing that we spend, I guess, about 99 percent of our time on is the dialogue. I will rewrite one sentence a dozen times if I don't feel I've got it right."

In other words, though by his own admission over the years that artists like Kirby and Ditko were heavily involved in creating the plots of the stories they drew, what Lee brought to the table was, as he saw it, *the most important thing,* the thing that made Marvel *Marvel:* dialogue as only *Stan Lee* could write it, that could make stories that

350

are "pretty much the same from issue to issue" reach out and grab a reader by the throat. However beautiful the pictures, they were telling the same old story until Lee was able to bring his signature point of view to the visuals.

And who's to say he wasn't right? An argument can be made that, if the artists were the heart of Marvel, Stan Lee was its *soul* — its literal and figurative voice, the element that bonded readers with the comics. It's an unwinnable argument, of course, but one that rages to this day.

As 1968 rolled on, one shock wave after another was unleashed on the American public. Still not fully healed from the assassination of President John F. Kennedy on November 22, 1963, the nation had been rocked by events that we have now compartmentalized into neat boxes — the Vietnam War, the civil rights movement, the assassinations of Robert Kennedy and Martin Luther King — but that, as they were happening, felt as if they were rending the country asunder.

And on November 5, 1968, Richard Nixon was elected president, defeating Hubert H. Humphrey, and embodying liberal New York's worst nightmare. As Gloria Steinem put it in "Learning to Live with Nixon," her *New York* magazine piece that had come out

351

just before the election, "We were going back to the '50s again. . . . It hadn't been very pleasant at the time, and having come so close to basic social changes made it, as Bobby Kennedy would have said, *unacceptable.*"

A week later, on November 12, Stan Lee found himself on *The Barry Farber Show,* matched against a lauded psychiatrist and educator, Dr. Hilde Mosse, close associate of Dr. Fredric Wertham, whose 1950s attacks on comics had decimated the industry, put scores of Lee's colleagues and friends out of work, and nearly ruined Lee's career, as well. Mosse was from a once-prominent German-Jewish publishing family that had been attacked by the Nazis and forced to flee Germany in 1933.[4]

Farber pitted Lee and Mosse against each other, ostensibly because, as Farber says in the show, "I was first interested in this because I wonder how I survived my earlier children's films." He also knew radio that would attract listeners, and that controversies over the effects of media violence on children were again big news. Congressional hearings on the topic had been held earlier in the year.

Although it was more than a decade since Mosse and Wertham had savaged the comics industry, although through Marvel Lee had helped regain some — but by no means all — of the creative and commercial ground

352

laid waste by Wertham's bestselling 1954 *Seduction of the Innocent* — for the several hours the two debated each other (with Farber and animation veterans Dennis Marks and Barry Yellin occasionally chiming in), it was as if it were 1954 all over again. Worse, to Lee it must have felt like *1957* again, when he was forced to let most of his artists and writers go, and he survived as "a human pilot light."

It might have felt like an even earlier year to the combatants. In 1948, Mosse had participated in Wertham's Psychopathology of Comic Books symposium, where comics were savagely critiqued by Wertham, Mosse, and other prominent social critics.

For her part, if Mosse didn't specifically know who Stan Lee was, she at least admits on the program to having read his comics — even mentioning Spider-Man as being a little more "intelligent" than the others — and she knew that the character symbolized everything she hated about violent popular culture. As Leonard Rifas noted in his article "Especially Dr. Hilde L. Mosse: Wertham's Research Collaborator": "Her [Mosse's] work with children and her research on children's media were colored by the political perspective she developed while watching the Nazi rise to power."[5] And indeed, that seemed apparent during the program.

(Interestingly, notes found by comics historian Carol Tilley in Wertham's archives at the

Library of Congress show that he was listening to the Farber program and jotting down what he saw as key points the participants were making. It's unknown what, if anything, he intended to do with the notes or whether he discussed Mosse's appearance on the show with her before or after it aired.)[6]

For Lee, this had clearly become something more personal and profound than simply an opportunity to promote himself and Marvel. It was 1968 now, and Stan Lee wasn't going to let himself be the victim of comics-hating crusaders again, no matter how well intentioned they may have been. And so Mosse and Lee faced each other on Farber's show. They each spoke with conviction as well as a desire to publicize their respective causes, polite but unwilling to compromise. (Adding a surreal touch to the argument was the fact that, although she was a genuine victim of Nazi oppression, Mosse, a native of Germany, spoke with an accent that American listeners had come to identify with every movie Nazi they'd ever heard.)

Lee saw Mosse as embodying the same old anti-comics arguments brought by the same old arguers. Perhaps unsurprisingly, if she seemed to see Stan as a reminder of a Nazi philosophy that "might makes right," he — a Jewish World War II veteran — conversely saw something similar in her. For instance, at one point, he reported:

354

I, myself felt like this whole thing is a little bit like this thing with Hitler in Czechoslovakia. I think the minute you start giving in to this kind of thing [censorship], then you're in even more trouble. . . . Dr. Mosse still condemns what's being done when we've tried to live up to the [Comics] Code.

After Mosse, in a dismissive and condescending tone, made some broad points about how children imitate violent media, Lee fired back:

For the past twenty years, I have heard this particular speech. I have heard the same arguments, and the same answers. Dr. Wertham and his followers . . . have never swayed from their point of view. . . . If you had your way completely, it would not be a healthier world . . . if there were no comic books, and if every television show . . . with violence, were taken off the air, I do not believe the mental climate in this country would be improved one iota, because . . . other things, which are far more serious, would then affect the children even more, and there'd be no relief in fantasy.

"The thing that I fear," he continued, "is a fanatical do-gooder. I fear that terribly. I fear the person who knows what's right and wrong for my child. I fear the person who,

355

when I write a story that I think is amusing and entertaining — and I really think I'm as good a judge as anybody else, and I know I'm *not* a villain — I fear the person who says, 'That's bad because I say so.' "

After vigorous back-and-forth over whether or not children imitate violence they see in media and whether the Bible or classic mythology were better or worse than super-hero comics, Mosse at last came to the point that seemed most important to her:

Spider-Man, Superman, Batman, they are all the same. Psychologically the exact same type of character. They are the very powerful muscle-type men, heroes who solve every problem by physical violence or weaponry. . . . The law does not exist, because they take it in their own hand to solve whatever conflict they are in. They are the antithesis of democracy, because they are the muscle-Superman, they are the adoration of physical violence and power. They are exactly — *exactly* — what anybody who knows anything about what fascism stands for, what Nazism stood for, they are the ideal that people had in the Hitler era.

And so the argument went on, each combatant scoring points for their side. The calendar might have said 1968, but for Lee and Mosse, it was also 1948 and 1954 and 1957 — and even 1933. If Barry Farber had wanted great radio, he certainly got it that night.

Lee might have walked into Farber's studio thinking it would be just another chance to plug his comic book line and be adored by the fawning fans who would be listening to the program. But in the course of the evening, he dropped the cheerleader mask and took dead aim at Mosse, whom he saw as someone whose idealistic — and, to him, unachievable — goal of a violence-free world was in the end a threat, not just to his livelihood, but to the principles — which, evidently, they both shared — of freedom of speech and thought.

It's unlikely that Lee or Mosse convinced each other of anything that night, but for better or worse, by the end of the show, Lee had stepped that much further into his role as industry spokesman. It was a self-appointed role, but one no one else seemed to want or be capable of fulfilling.

Maybe he was reading too many comic books — believing his own hype — but somehow, in some way, Stan Lee seemed to be transforming, intentionally or not, into a man with a mission.

13
SURFING THE WAVES

Here . . . on this lonely little world . . . I have
found what men call . . . conscience!
— Silver Surfer, in *Fantastic Four* #50,
May 1966

Jack Lieber died on February 26, 1968.

Stan's recollection of the event, in *Excelsior!*, read thus:

An unexpected phone call from my brother
Larry told us, in a voice trembling with sorrow, that my father, who never remarried
and had been living in Manhattan all these
years, had died unexpectedly.[1]

Lee went on to say that the death inspired
him and his family to move back into Manhattan from Hewlett Harbor, especially since
the now-eighteen-year-old JC was eager to
live in the city.

And that is the entirety of the discussion in
Lee's memoir of Jack Lieber's death. It seems
to be all Lee has ever said on the record

358

about the topic. It's reasonable to imagine that his father's death had a powerful effect on him. Certainly, Jack Lieber's passing could not have come at a more eventful and pivotal year in Lee's life, not to mention in the histories of the United States, and the world in general, for that matter. At eighty-one years old, Jack's death might have been unexpected — indicating that his health had probably been stable — but, especially by the standards of 1968, eighty-one was by no means a short life.

It's hard to know what, if anything, to make of Lee's decision to return to Manhattan, where his father had been residing and where Larry still lived, in the wake of their father's passing. Certainly, had his daughter simply wished to move into Manhattan after a life in the suburbs, it would have been fairly simple for Stan and Joan to provide her with a nice apartment in a secure building in a safe neighborhood.

Perhaps it was simply Lee's increasing workload that made it make sense for all three of them to return to Manhattan. Stan Lee's world in the late '60s and into the early '70s was astonishingly event-filled. That kind of busyness can divide someone's attention into a thousand pieces — and the sudden loss of a loved one added to that could distract even the most focused person, perhaps lead him to not notice things that you'd think he would have . . .

. . . such as Jack Kirby's feelings about the Silver Surfer.

During their careers, Stan Lee and Jack Kirby had each created or cocreated hundreds, if not thousands, of characters. In the course of their collaborations, they came up with dozens, if not hundreds. Issues of ownership and financial value aside, it's interesting to try to figure out which characters might reflect more of one or the other creator's personalities and sensibilities. Is Reed Richards more the wordy Stan, or is he Jack, whose head was always in the clouds? Is the Thing more Kirby because his affect is that of a Lower East Side street kid, or is he more Stan because of his endless need to crack wise?

With many of their most famous creations, the history of who actually came up with the initial idea is fraught with ambiguity and contradiction. Strangely enough, one of the few characters Lee has, from the beginning, unambiguously credited as being created by Kirby is the Silver Surfer. Nonetheless, from the beginning, there was something about the character that strongly appealed to Lee. He enjoyed writing melodramatic dialogue for this ultrapowerful naïf from beyond. And he found the Surfer to be an appealing vehicle through which to express his personal philosophy.

Indeed, as Lee told Neal Conan in the 1968 WBAI radio interview, the Silver Surfer

doesn't have to have that surfboard, and he doesn't have to be silver. . . . The important thing is that he's a character who represents something, and stands for something. . . . And there is a lot of philosophy, and a lot of moralizing, and there's something you can sink your teeth into if you feel like reading something with meat and possibly, even with a message.[2]

Earlier in the program, he had told Conan, about speaking at colleges:

These college kids are terrific. And I'm always amazed at the questions they ask, always on a philosophical plane. . . . I have to become something of an amateur philosopher, myself, in order to have these little lectures.[3]

And in early 1970, Lee told Mike Bourne in *Changes* magazine:

As I realized that more and more adults were reading our books and people of college age (which is tremendously gratifying to me), I felt that now I can finally start saying some of the things I would like to say . . .

361

about drugs and about crime and about Vietnam and about colleges and about things that mean something.[4]

Later on, in the same interview, he confided to Bourne:

I like to moralize [in the comics stories] as much as possible. I'm always a little nervous and hope I'm not overdoing it and turning people off. But maybe I'm naturally half a preacher at heart. I find I enjoy it. And it's funny, because it seems that people enjoy it.[5]

So if he hadn't yet written the Great American (or any) Novel, Lee was feeling creatively ambitious enough to want to somehow leave a record of his thoughts and feelings about the human condition. The Silver Surfer called out to him as the perfect vehicle for those thoughts and feelings.

Of the Surfer, he told Bourne that his instruction to John Buscema for how to draw the Surfer was:

The closer you come to Jesus Christ, the better.[6]

As Spurgeon and Raphael have noted:

Lee made the Silver Surfer a poet, a street-

362

corner Romeo tossing out pained commentary on mankind and his own miserable fate . . . Lee had taken a character with godlike abilities and made him noble but tragic.[7]

If Lee's affinity for the character wasn't clear in the *Fantastic Four* Surfer stories — where it could be Kirby's concept of the Surfer as much as Lee's that readers experienced — then as early as the Hulk feature in 1967's *Tales to Astonish* #93, drawn by Marie Severin, it had become clear that Lee felt a special connection to the Surfer. And the Lee-Kirby Surfer backup from the same year's *Fantastic Four Annual* #5 — the first solo Surfer tale (perhaps a prototype for a Surfer series) — seemed to be setting the stage for an eventual Surfer series. And who else but Kirby — the acknowledged creator of the character — would be the natural partner with Lee to chronicle the Surfer's philosophy-tinged adventures?

And yet the assignment to draw the Silver Surfer series did not go to Jack Kirby. It went to John Buscema. Why it did remains a mystery.

Kirby's friend and biographer Mark Evanier offers several possible explanations, all of which make sense.[8]

For one thing, Evanier feels, it's possible that Lee did mention to Kirby that he wanted to do a Surfer series, but briefly and off handedly and, when he got no strong response from Kirby (who might have only been paying partial attention), assumed that Kirby didn't care who would be drawing it. It's also possible that Lee might have figured that, with so many characters to his credit, why would Kirby especially care about the Surfer?

Evanier also hypothesized that it's possible that the schedule-aware editor in Lee didn't want to take Kirby from any of his regular assignments by giving him another that would require him to jettison a feature that was already running smoothly.

It's also possible that it might have been a case of yet another Lee and Kirby disagreement over story or character direction, where Lee prevailed because he was the editor. Both Lee and Kirby sensed the Surfer was something special, and each somehow identified with this literal tabula rasa of a character, but their ideas for the character's origins and direction diverged, and Lee decided that he didn't want to compromise on this one.

For whatever reason, Lee launched a Surfer series with Buscema that Kirby only found out about, according to Evanier, thanks to an off hand mention of it from an unnamed Marvel staffer.[9]

The miscommunication on this topic between the two men was apparently so great that Kirby — who, according to Sean Howe, was anticipating involvement in an eventual

364

Silver Surfer series[10] — had even begun work on an *FF* story line that would explain the Surfer's origin and was forced to abandon it. The Surfer story that did appear in the likely period where the origin would have gone was presented in 1968's *Fantastic Four* #74–77. It involved the Surfer, fleeing Galactus, who wants him back as herald, and his eventual reuniting with Galactus, the Surfer now pledged to keep that force of nature from consuming planets populated by sentient beings. In effect, Kirby was tasked with creating a prequel — a tale of a noble but doomed attempt to escape one's fate — to the Surfer series that he was not to draw. The final issue of the *FF* story line even contained a plug for *Silver Surfer* #1, on sale at the same time.

It's tempting for readers to sometimes ascribe more import to certain creative decisions than they warrant. Sometimes a cigar *is* just a cigar — and a comics assignment is just another job. But in this case, it does seem that not getting to do the Surfer series was perceived as a significant slight by Kirby, taking a fair amount of wind out of his sails. As Evanier said, "Kirby especially didn't like that he hadn't been given first refusal on doing the new [Silver Surfer] book. His idea had been taken from him in every possible sense."[11]

In retrospect, Kirby's declining interest in providing innovative visual storytelling can

365

be seen by this point in the pages of that *FF* story line. While filled with action and soap opera to spare, the overall feel of those issues, and certainly the ones that followed, gives the sense that old ideas are being recycled — recycled well and powerfully, to be sure — but lacking the aura of novelty that earlier *FF* stories had possessed.

For his part, Lee filled the four-part *FF* story with copious amounts of engaging dialogue and captions, as well as with witty footnotes and asides, making, for most readers, a seamless continuation of the saga that had started with the title's first issue. What the four issues lacked in novelty — and they only "lacked" compared to previous issues — was made up for by the deft wielding of craft by Lee, Kirby, and inker Joe Sinnott.

So, whether through carelessness, ruthlessness, or plain miscommunication, *Silver Surfer* would debut in mid-1968, in the middle of Lee's and Marvel's evolutions. The details of the character's origin story, as envisioned in the issue by Lee, altered what little was known of the Surfer's backstory in an effort to make him more relatable and sympathetic. He was established now as a humanoid alien who joined Galactus to save his homeworld of Zenn-La, and he had, from the beginning, kept Galactus from devouring planets with sentient populations. This was a blatant revision of the unique role Earth had played in the Surfer-Galactus relationship. Concern for the planet was what had made the Surfer rebel against his master, Galactus. The Surfer realized it had been wrong to lead Galactus to sentient-inhabited worlds in the past.

Kirby's concept of the Surfer as a stoic being of pure energy — as opposed to Lee's vision of him as a troubled, tragic humanoid alien granted cosmic power and a silver coating — would likely have been too much at odds for a compromise to have been reached if the two creators had discussed it.

And it did seem that Lee genuinely had big ideas he wanted to express, even if they boiled down to permutations of the Golden Rule. Maybe it was the sense that this was indeed his chance — perhaps the only one he'd ever have — to make his mark on the world as something other than a word-slinger in a disdained branch of publishing. His father was gone, having left no discernible mark in the world. That was a fate to be avoided. Lee was now in his forties. He had not written novels or screenplays. The greatness he longed for, the literary achievement he dreamed about, despite his undeniable impact on the overall culture, was still out of reach. Perhaps, somehow, the Surfer would give him, for lack of a better word, *class*.

After all, crowds of college students — students from prestigious universities —

wanted to hear what Stan Lee had to say. Whether many had much interest in his thoughts beyond the hour or so that his lecture and Q&A sessions lasted is hard to judge. But the fact is, they *did* turn out to hear him, and many of them *did* ask him about the deeper meanings of his comics. Apparently, all this attention did get him thinking, and either he solidified thoughts and ideas he'd been mulling for a while, or he decided he needed to come up with answers that were more than wisecracks — and *Silver Surfer* would be his comic book outlet for expressing his deeper views on life.

One of the clearer examples of Lee's usage of the *Surfer* comic as a podium can be found in issue #5's story — cover-dated April 1969 — "And Who Shall Mourn for Him?" In it, a courageous African American physicist, Al B. Harper, brings the Surfer — knocked unconscious trying to free himself from the Galactus-imposed barrier that keeps him from traveling into space — to his home to recover. Later, he explains to the revived hero that he did it because he "knows how it feels to be pushed around." Though Lee portrayed Harper as a guy who just happened to be black, with that remark, the writer briefly hinted at a difficult past the character had had to overcome. At the story's climax, Harper sacrifices his life to save Earth.

In a letter about the story, in issue #7's let-

368

ters page, a reader complained that

> there has been a recent trend by Marvel to put the Negros [*sic*] in the spotlight. . . . when you start your own civil rights protest, well, I'm against that. . . . For months you've been knocking "us" (you know who I mean). . . . I'm not a racist, just a concerned Marvelite who doesn't want his favorite comic company to be ruined.

An editor doesn't run such a letter unless he or she has a specific response in mind. And, indeed, the response from the editor — if not written by Lee, then undoubtedly read and approved by him — could as easily have come from the Surfer himself:

> But such matters as racism and equality *do* concern us . . . We think that many people . . . have too long turned their backs or averted their eyes to the more unpleasant things that are going on every day. Maybe we felt we could do something . . . to change things just a bit for the better.

Lee's point was clear. Marvel Comics — *Stan Lee's* Marvel Comics — were not going to ignore "the more unpleasant things" that were "going on every day."

On a certain level, Lee could be accused of taking himself too seriously, not to mention

369

risking alienating segments of the buying public. By the same token, though, this was new territory for Lee and for comics, so *serious* might well have been the appropriate approach to take. Choosing to run that letter and then giving the response that was given was no small step. But what was it a step toward? That would remain to be seen.

It definitely was, though, another step *away* from an editorial stance that played it safe. Was Lee here expressing a genuine, personal point of view, one that — because it was the right thing to do — he didn't care who liked it or not? Or was he just putting forth views that he thought would go over well with his college audiences? It would take an extremely cynical evaluation to find no sincerity in his words at all.

Was showing in the comics some measure of his true feelings the right step for Stan Lee to take? Well, eight years earlier, Marvel nearly ceased to exist. Eight years in the future — who knows? — it might be just a memory. There were no guarantees for anybody. Why *not* let the Surfer be a vehicle for Lee to express his personal beliefs? If he couldn't take a risk like that now, when would he *ever* be able to?

In the entertainment world of 1968, Marvel Comics was still the proverbial small pond, even if Stan Lee was getting to be a bigger

370

fish in it with each passing day. But outside that pond, there were still plenty of people who, even when they saw the value of associating with Stan Lee and the Marvel phenomenon, took neither of them particularly seriously.

For instance, Lee made one of his first national TV appearances on the May 30, 1968, episode of *The Dick Cavett Show,* a New York–based talk and variety program on the ABC network. On it, regular guest Pat McCormick had facetiously remarked, "One thing I like about those comic books is that they're easy to turn while you're sucking your thumb with the other hand."

Lee seemed to let the insult slide off his back, simply parrying with, "Can I change seats?" But later on, when Cavett asked McCormick, "Have you ever seen a copy of *Mighty Thor,* Pat?" Lee cut in with, "It has two-syllable words, so you might have a little difficulty."

Interestingly, the famously intellectual Cavett himself treated Lee with a reasonable amount of respect and seemed to have some familiarity with the comics. He and Stan had this interesting exchange:

CAVETT: Do you ever worry about the amount of power you have with that gigantic circulation?

LEE: Well, no, not really. We kind of enjoy

371

it. I like to think, if somebody has to have power over the young people today, and a degree of power, it might as well be us. . . . We're trying to do whatever we can to make things a little better.

So here was Stan Lee, holding his own against Harvard-educated Pat McCormick — a well-known comic and comedy writer, and a large, physically imposing individual — and making sparkling conversation with Yale alumnus Dick Cavett, while getting across the message that Marvel comics contain philosophy, satire, and commentary that mark them as more than mere kids' stuff. And all this while also answering questions from fellow guest Diana Sands (who had recently starred in an acclaimed production of George Bernard Shaw's *Saint Joan*) about *Little Lulu.*

Lee was in the big leagues now. The *Cavett* appearance wasn't exchanging quips with Sol Brodsky and Marie Severin. It wasn't even arm wrestling over plot points and ethical undertones with Kirby and Ditko. And it wasn't even negotiating around Martin Goodman's moods and whims. Those were all done in the familiar confines of the Marvel offices. And even the smartest college students he would pontificate to were still kids, still in awe of seeing Stan Lee in person.

No, this was a whole different thing. This was a whole different Stan. Or at least, an *evolved* one, moving onto a national and world stage. But there seemed to be more to it than simply the pursuit of money and fame. It was evident in what he wrote in the comics stories themselves. It was evident in what he was writing in the Bullpen Bulletins. And it was evident in the unusually proprietary interest he took in the Silver Surfer's development as a character.

Something was happening to Stan Lee. Maybe it was yet another midlife crisis. In 1968, he was forty-five years old. He had transformed a reasonably steady, but somewhat lackluster, career into a small amount of celebrity. While Marvel comics readers had some vision in their mind of who Stan Lee was, the general public — like Pat McCormick — didn't really know or care. If his silly comic books were a little more sophisticated than some of the others on the stands, that still wasn't a big deal and didn't even register with most people.

And yet these comics had given him a chance to elevate himself — as well as the medium in which he had toiled for nearly three decades — at least somewhat into the category of "things to be taken seriously." Now was his chance to . . . well, to do what, exactly?

Even by the standards of the '60s, a decade famous for change, 1968 was a head-spinning

373

year. The country was buffeted by assassinations, riots, civil unrest, seismic cultural shifts, and the ongoing war in Vietnam. But closer to home for Stan Lee, besides the death of Jack Lieber, things were shifting in ways both personal and professional.

In the world of business, the late '60s were characterized by corporate acquisitions, where conglomerates would add to their portfolios, with charm-bracelet randomness, companies that had often little or no synergy with each other. National Comics had been recently purchased by Warner Communications, which had been purchased by Kinney Parking, which was originally a funeral home and limousine rental operator. As part of the new order at DC, where sales were softening, veteran artist Carmine Infantino, who had been designing the company's covers, was chosen to run the editorial department. Infantino would bring a sensibility to DC's comics that was more visually driven than had been that of past regimes, which were run by editors who were not artists.

Around the time of this changing of the guard, a number of DC's long-time freelance writers and artists decided that it was appropriate to politely demand that they be given some basic benefits, such as health insurance and pensions, despite the fact that they were not technically staff members. Before too long, most of these creators found

374

that not only were their demands not met, but they were also no longer receiving regular assignments, while younger freelancers started showing up in the credits. Insiders differ on whether this was a calculated reprisal by management or simply a response by the company to changing audience tastes. Either way, it was made quite clear to the veterans — and anyone else in the comics business — that comic book creators were expendable and replaceable, no matter how many years of high-quality work they had provided.

It was also plain to industry observers that Martin Goodman was shopping Magazine Management around. And in large part because of the success of Marvel's comics, Goodman had found a buyer for his entire publishing operation who was willing to pay what Goodman felt was a fair price. Relatively young — he was sixty years old in 1968 — Goodman had been in publishing for close to forty years. Ads in trade journals bragging of Marvel's high sales were thinly veiled For Sale signs. With the glamour of Marvel's comics leading the way, the company was ripe for picking. To sell, Martin had a demand that seemed to have been as important to him as the money offered. He wanted to ensure a future for his son, Chip, who had already been working at the company. Martin wanted Chip to succeed him as publisher.

375

So when Perfect Film & Chemical Corporation offered $14 million and agreed to make Chip publisher after Martin himself would serve in that role for another four years, Goodman took the offer. Part of the assurance that Perfect Film (later to rename itself Cadence Industries) wanted in order to make the deal was the guarantee of the continuing services of the one comic book professional whom they considered irreplaceable: Stan Lee.

According to Lee, Goodman made him verbal promises — including of a grant of "warrants" in the company that would set him up for life — to induce him to sign a multiyear contract. Not insisting that the promise regarding the warrants be put in writing, Lee went ahead and signed the contract, anyway. Beyond a pay raise, the promises would never be kept.[12]

Was Lee naïve to sign? He has said, in his memoir, that his close friend, businessman Marshall Finck (whose wife, Edith, was said, in her 2017 obituary, to have been the model for the FF's Susan Storm), advised Lee that he could use his leverage to get Goodman to sign off on just about anything he wanted. And yet he didn't push Martin anywhere near as hard as he could have. That could certainly be seen as naïve, as well as one of the pitfalls of working for a relative. By the same token, not that long ago, Goodman's entire comics

376

division had been on the brink of extinction. To have not just survived that period, but to have thrived in the ensuing years, must have seemed like some kind of miracle to Lee. Would asking for more have seemed greedy? Would it be tempting fate?

To add another twist to the entire situation, Goodman himself had signed an agreement to stay on for four years as publisher. He would have the supervisory power he'd had before, but none of the risk. The company would be owned by a conglomerate but would still seem like the same family operation. The number of Goodman relatives employed by Magazine Management would stay exactly the same as it had been before Perfect Film & Chemical bought the company. Day-to-day life would be much the same as it had been.

Except it wouldn't.

Lee was now in unexplored territory. He had security for three (or by some accounts five) years — but then what? By the time the contract expired, he'd be pushing fifty. What then? Anything could happen by the end of that contract — and there would be no relative to backstop him then.

And what would become of his audience — including the college students? They still seemed to love Marvel's comics. But there were now underground comics (or "comix") that were exploring topics that Lee and

377

Marvel couldn't — and wouldn't, even if they could, if simply because they didn't understand them. It was one thing to be admired by rock bands and filmmakers, but there seemed to be a secret youth language, something *truly* underground, that was clearly something that a trendy beard or stylish toupee couldn't help you translate. Publications like R. Crumb's *Zap Comix,* which debuted in early 1968, were appearing, with the potential to change everything. It wasn't just the freedom to portray more explicit sex and violence that those comics possessed. It was an insider's familiarity with the ever-evolving youth culture, a culture that was impenetrable to most people over thirty.

Perhaps nothing symbolized the conflicting currents at Marvel — the pull to explore new areas versus the imperative to not rock the boat — so much as the departure of Flo Steinberg. A genuinely beloved, highly competent employee, Steinberg had also become a part of the Marvel mythos, thanks to Stan's creation in letters pages and Bullpen Bulletins of Fabulous Flo. Fans cared as much about her as they did any of the artists and writers that Lee had made familiar names. Equally significant, Steinberg counted among her social circle the very underground cartoonists and downtown tastemakers that a company like Marvel needed to stay current. And yet, reportedly over a request for a five-

378

dollar-a-week raise, Goodman chose to let her go, his logic being that her position in the company structure mandated she could not earn over a certain set amount, no matter how important she was to Marvel's functioning and image.

And so, in the September 1968 Bullpen Bulletins, it was announced that

> with heavy hearts, we announce the departure of one of the Bullpen's most popular pixies — Fabulous FLO STEINBERG who bids us a fond farewell to seek her fortunes in another field of endeavor.

In other words, she was so annoyed at being denied the raise, she left without having a job to go to.

In a conciliatory gesture, the Bulletins would announce in the February 1969 dated comics that

> Fabulous FLO STEINBERG, our former Gal Friday, has a great new job at Rockefeller Center, not too far from our own offices here — and wants to thank her many friends out there in Marveldom for their letters and good wishes.

Flo's replacement was a woman named Robin Green, who would go on to write a 1971 article for *Rolling Stone* magazine about

379

her time at Marvel and would notably go on to write and produce TV shows such as *Northern Exposure, The Sopranos,* and *Blue Bloods.* In her *Rolling Stone* article, she said of Stan:

Because he worked so hard, tried so hard, was so enthusiastic, you'd want to make it easier for him. He's got a one-man show going, he won't delegate, which is why he works so hard.[13]

Interestingly, while Lee would have numerous assistants over the years (Green only worked for him for about six months in 1968), he would never again grant any of them the pivotal role in the imagined bullpen that he had given to Steinberg.

And so, in this work environment that was in transition from family business to corporate behemoth, Stan Lee found himself in a situation that was at once secure and yet precarious. There were two things that seemed certain, though.

One, of course, was that the comic books had to keep coming out. As a matter of fact, even *more* comic books had to come out. Several months prior to selling the company, Goodman had negotiated a better distribution deal with Independent News. He was now free to increase his comics line, which had been gradually growing all along. And before too long, Cadence would own Curtis Circulation and be free of Independent altogether. Lee was now overseeing more than twenty titles a month, as well as experimenting with different formats, such as a *Mad* magazine–sized comic magazine staring Spider-Man.[14]

The other thing that seemed certain was that he had to keep advancing the Stan Lee brand. The new owners' needs and the public's tastes and desires were impossible to predict. Hell, the entire world seemed to be changing before his eyes. The change all seemed to be coming from kids — teens, twentysomethings — many of whom were inclined, at least for now, to think that Stan Lee had something to offer them. But how long could that last? Besides, having a plan B had long been part of his career strategy. Now that he was some kind of celebrity, why not see where it could lead?

Stepping beyond the bounds of the comics pages, Lee took a tentative step into an unfamiliar but logical seat in the fall of 1968: television talk show host. In that period, sometime after the summer's Republican and Democratic presidential nominating conventions, but probably before the election of Richard Nixon as president, Lee was the host of a pilot for a political / current events TV talk show. The pilot focused on a discussion of, among other things, the Columbia Univer-

381

sity student protests of April and May of '68, as well as the August conventions, and alludes to the assassination of Robert Kennedy.

Panel-style topical talk shows were popular on TV in that era, running the gamut from the erudite intellectualism of David Susskind and William F. Buckley Jr. to aggressive provocateurs like Alan Burke and Joe Pyne. In the pilot, Lee seemed to be leaning more toward the first type, positioning himself as what he was: a concerned, aware suburban dad who was trying to understand just what it was "these kids today" wanted.

He had addressed that topic to some degree in *Thor* #154, which was on sale in April, in which the Thunder God chides a group of hippies for dropping out of society:

'Tis not by *dropping out* — but by *plunging in* — into the maelstrom of *life* itself — that thou shalt find thy *wisdom*! There be *causes* to espouse!! There be *battles* to be *won*! There be *glory* and *grandeur* all about thee — if thou wilt but *see*!

As he said of the sequence on the *Cavett* show:

At the time the little page was written [likely in February], it was a good little sermon. Today, fortunately, I don't think it is as necessary. Youth today seem to be so much

382

more activist, which I think is a healthy thing. This business of dropping out seems to have gone by the boards for the most part.

It was a sign of the times that Lee's observations about "youth today" could change so significantly over just a few months, from the February writing of the dialogue to the late May *Cavett* show.

The "youth" that were on the pilot with him were definitely *not* the dropping-out types. The show (viewable on YouTube), was a panel-type program, shot in black-and-white.[15] If it had a title, that has been lost to history. On the show, Lee sported his full beard and a genuine-looking toupee. Forty-five years old, he could pass for a decade younger. (Asked about the pilot in 2017,[16] Lee had no memory of it at all, even after viewing it, so could shed no light on how it came to be.)

Clearly, someone had in mind that articulate, quick-witted, affable, and charming Stan Lee could be the host and moderator of a current events discussion show. The show, it seems, would cover topics having almost nothing to do with comics, aside from the fact of them being the source of Lee's celebrity and credentials. Based on the pilot, the show was intended to cover events that would probably be of interest to Marvel's audience,

383

especially its older members, but would also appeal to anyone with an interest in society and politics, perhaps even Lee's fellow confused parents.

Lee's guests on the show were Jeff Shero, editor of the underground newspaper *Rat Subterranean News;* Chuck Skoro, managing editor of the Columbia University student newspaper, *Columbia Daily Spectator;* and Skip Weiss, editor of *The Daltonian,* the student newspaper of the elite Upper East Side Dalton School. With all present being editors, Lee was the only one *not* helming a newspaper of some kind. But he wasn't trying to compete with his guests' journalistic specialization. He was, for the most part, playing the "everyman" role. The conversation, if anything, was representative of countless conversations of the era, held around countless dinner tables.

Here's how Lee, in his opening remarks on the pilot, described his and the show's mission:

I'm Stan Lee. I've been writing stories for the younger generation for thirty years, and . . . I have received about two to three hundred fan letters every day — probably as much as the Beatles. I spend most of my time reading the mail, and quite a lot of time answering it.

I think I've learned a lot about what

384

younger people think. More importantly, I think I've learned a lot about what young people *are.* Today, we've come to a time in history when there definitely is a generation gap. It seems to us that perhaps anything that can be done to bridge this gap, anything that can be done to help present the point of view of these young people . . . would be . . . beneficial . . .

Today's show will cover topics that we feel are uppermost in the minds of young people.

So the aim of the pilot (and, we can assume, of any ongoing series that would have emerged from it), was to give a voice to young people — with Stan representing the older generation.

Like many talk shows — and many dinner-table conversations — the show's back-and-forth was wide-ranging and free-flowing, with many of the panelists' contributions turning into speeches or pronouncements. And yet it's possible to hear, in Lee's moderate moderating, the same voice that informs the Bullpen Bulletins and Stan's Soapboxes, with the notable lack, for the most part, of Lee's trademark wisecracks. The show is remarkably devoid of humor, a sign of the times, perhaps, but also of Lee's needing to have the show — and himself — taken seriously. He might also have been concerned that the panelists might have perceived more than

385

token attempts at humor by Lee as him — representing the Establishment — not taking *them* seriously.

Some excerpts from the episode give a sense of the generational rift. For instance, in this exchange between Lee and *Rat*'s Shero about putting across messages in print:

STAN LEE: If I were editing an underground newspaper . . . and I had some sort of a message . . . I would want to present it in a way that would give me the widest possible audience. Now, the magazines that I edit have all sorts of subliminal messages . . . but we don't do anything . . . that would turn any segment of the readership away from us.

JEFF SHERO: I think that's an old-fashioned view, because it assumes that people have power. . . . The only people that have any effect on where the country is going . . . are people that have committed, and people who sit at the top and have the reins of power. It's only young people that are committed to changing society, and so the *Rat* is attempting to talk to young people.

Shero was the most radical — and most talkative — of the bunch, the one, perhaps, most connected to the self-described "counterculture." The other two were students, but Shero was a working journalist, who had started the edgy *Rat* that spring.

Lee attempted to challenge Shero's radical notions:

JEFF SHERO: Law and order means keeping down black people.

STAN LEE: Isn't it possible that law and order could *mean* law and order? People feel there is too much crime in the nation today and they would like law and order. Why does this necessarily have to be a racist remark?

Shero, needless to say, was not convinced.

In the most heated exchange of the show, Lee and Shero demonstrated just how far apart their sensibilities were:

STAN LEE: I think I'm a member of the Establishment [and] I find that at root, there isn't that much difference between what the Establishment wants and what you young people want.

JEFF SHERO: I think that's absolutely wrong. The Establishment doesn't want to end the [Vietnam] war. You talk about the corporations —

STAN LEE: Well, wait a minute. How can you possibly make a remark like that?

JEFF SHERO: How can I make that re-

387

mark? Because the war has been escalating consistently over the last five years — because the peace candidates, who had the popular following, were eliminated from the election.

Here, Lee — intentionally or not — failed to take the bait of Shero's loaded remark about the "peace candidates" being "eliminated from the election." The peace candidates were Eugene McCarthy and Bobby Kennedy. Shero was implying that the former was somehow not allowed to win the Democratic nomination by "the Establishment," and, more darkly, that the latter's assassination was committed at the *behest* of that Establishment.

During the pilot, although he would never do this in the pages of the comics, Lee took a definitive stand on the Vietnam War:

STAN LEE: I must admit, I would never defend the war in Vietnam. I think it's an utterly indefensible war. I think it's a ridiculous war. I think I agree with the word you used before, I think it's an obscene war. . . . But I think you're being equally obscene when you say that the Establishment . . . doesn't want the war to end, I think that's just a ridiculous statement.

388

JEFF SHERO: What concrete steps do you see?

STAN LEE: Well, isn't it possible that, just as the young people today are floundering . . . that the Establishment is [also] confused . . . I think the only way we can be led out, and certainly the young people are the only hope for the world, but only through a legitimate legal manner. I don't think anarchy is the answer.

Shero and Lee then agreed that it would be difficult for America to just abruptly leave Vietnam, although Shero attributed that to more nefarious reasons than did Lee:

JEFF SHERO: The problem with the politicians that run the country [the United States] is, are they going to recognize the legitimacy of the National Liberation Front? And are they going to turn over control to them? . . . Bringing about peace in Vietnam means turning over the country to those people. And so it's a contradiction that the politicians can't deal with.

Shero even called Lee's entire career into question:

JEFF SHERO: You edit Marvel comic books, and if your private opinions were

389

reflected in Marvel comic books, you'd be in a hot spot. Your comics, for instance, build up war and the excitement of battle . . . and you're saying you're against —

STAN LEE: We present war in some stories, but we don't try to make it fun.

JEFF SHERO: Some really do kind of exalt it.

Lee's attempts at bringing a "realistic" adult point of view were constantly challenged during the broadcast, here by Columbia's Skoro:

STAN LEE: My sympathies, really, are with the liberals, but the minute the liberals get too much power . . . or become too much of a threat, the nation will swing toward conservatism, and the very things I think you're trying to accomplish are apt to be crushed.

CHUCK SKORO: *Liberal* is sort of a dirty word in the radical movement. To call someone a liberal, if you happen to be a member of SDS, is like really calling him a nasty thing. . . . A liberal is a person who saw kids in the streets getting beaten savagely [outside the then-recent Democratic convention], and said, "Well, . . . they deserved it."

STAN LEE: I thought of a liberal, obvi-

390

ously, in a different way. . . . To be a liberal is almost to be a conservative, by your definition.

Shero, in a 2016 Facebook message to historian Sean Howe, recalled about the video that "it was shot as a pilot for a Stan Lee show, but they said he let me talk too much and didn't express his opinions enough . . . so the show was a no go." (Who the "they" Shero refers to was, is unknown. In the pre-cable, pre-internet days of 1968, it's likely that would mean a production or syndication company hoping to sell such a show to independent TV stations, such as New York's WPIX or WOR.)

The problems with the pilot that Shero cited don't seem like they'd necessarily have been insurmountable. Lee didn't seem hesitant to counter his guests' remarks, although his statements — like theirs — did seem to regularly devolve into vague, albeit profound-sounding, jargonizing. By this point, though, Lee had had lots of experience verbally sparring with college audiences. It's not inconceivable that he could have learned to further polish his style for an ongoing TV show.

It's harder to imagine, though, that he'd have been comfortable having to live with the consequences — financial and personal — of the likely alienation of large segments of his comics-reading audience that would result from his regularly and consistently taking even mild stands on the issues of the day, much less espousing an all-out condemnation of the Vietnam War.

That he did make the effort to do such a show indicates a willingness by Lee to try to redefine himself or at least to stretch the possibilities of what his ever-developing position in the culture could be. Concern over what to do with his newfound celebrity, and with his seemingly genuine concern for where his society was going, marked Lee as more than simply the overseer of a line of comic books. But who and what he would evolve into was yet to be seen.

Shero, today known as Jeffrey Shero Nightbyrd, has stayed true to his countercultural roots and writes of them on his website. Charles Skoro died in 2016 at age sixty-eight, having spent a career first as chairman of the Economics Department at Boise State University in his native Idaho, and then as campus minister for Saint Paul's Catholic Student Center on the university campus and as a deacon at Our Lady of the Rosary Parish. Skip Weiss's life story and career are unknown.

For his part, Stan Lee would eventually host TV shows that made it to the air, but never again would he attempt to do so outside his popular culture / entertainment comfort zone. It was a limit that he would rarely step beyond.

Indeed, in art, as in life, real and metaphorical limits — and the struggle against them — would come to define Lee's career.

In the 1966 Lee-Kirby Galactus Trilogy, the Silver Surfer's punishment for doing the right thing — turning against his master in order to save the Earth — was to be banished forever to Earth and the skies surrounding it. An invisible barrier now kept him from realizing his full potential to experience the boundless freedom of space. In his subsequent appearances after that, he bemoaned being trapped on "the mad, orbiting *prison* which men call *Earth*," as he would refer to the planet in the August 1968–dated *Fantastic Four* #77. The same month, in *Silver Surfer* #1, by Lee and John Buscema (with inks by Joe Sinnott), the Surfer lamented that

trapped upon this world of *madness* . . . stand I! How much *longer* am I destined to endure a fate I cannot even *comprehend*?

So strongly did Lee feel about the Silver Surfer that, for the next two decades, he mandated that he would be the only writer allowed to script the Surfer's adventures. And for those two decades, the Surfer would remain imprisoned on Earth. His potential would be limited — though within those

393

constraints, he would see and achieve much. And yet, he would always yearn for what he imagined were the endless possibilities of a larger — an infinite — field on which to play.

Perhaps this straining against limitations was the part of the appeal to both Lee *and* Kirby of the character, why both so closely identified with him. The Surfer's greatest challenge was not other superpowered beings or tormented interpersonal relationships, though he had both. It was the limits placed upon him, against which he endlessly struggled — and which Lee chose not to remove.

Lee and Kirby both felt limited to, and trapped in, not just the comic book business but, specifically, Marvel Comics. Each man, in his own way, saw his career hemmed in by forces seemingly beyond his control. For each of them, the comic book business felt like a confining, albeit comfortable, prison. They were the biggest fish in a pond that — compared to movies, TV, and novels — seemed tiny. Their fame and fortune, as well as their creative achievements, could only go so far.

Like the Surfer, they each explored and exploited their limited realm as best they could. Like the Surfer, they longed to discover and conquer new worlds, to be free of the ups and downs of comics, of the fickle moods of their employer and their audience. Their struggles became the Surfer's struggles, and

394

his theirs.

But who was their Galactus? Who was, in real life, keeping them from freedom, from reaching their potential? Or were the limits self-imposed? Were they simply afraid of taking a risk?

Lee's efforts to break free of those limitations included projects like the talk show pilot. In the coming years, he would test his boundaries both within Marvel — experimenting with different formats and types of subject matter — as well as outside its confines. But could he ever completely leave?

For his part, Jack Kirby, in early 1969, moved his family from Long Island to Los Angeles, spurred largely by his daughter's need to live in a dry climate. Even three thousand miles away, though, he was still in Marvel's orbit, still bound by invisible barriers.

But Passover, the Jewish festival of freedom, commemorating the Children of Israel's escape from bondage, was approaching. And while Moses wasn't coming to the Kirbys' family seder, someone almost as good was.

His name was Carmine Infantino.

14
TENSE TRANSITIONS

I would say that the comic book market is the worst market that there is on the face of the Earth for creative talent, and the reasons are numberless and legion.
— Stan Lee, at a 1971
National Cartoonists Society panel

Knowing of Kirby's growing dissatisfaction at Marvel, DC editorial director Carmine Infantino made a point of making time to accept Kirby's Passover invitation. And sometime after the seder had wound down, Kirby invited Infantino to his studio to see the characters he'd been developing that he was holding back from Lee and Marvel.

Infantino was impressed, but even if he was not, here was a golden opportunity. Jack Kirby was a *very* large part of what made Marvel *Marvel.* And while Jack was not the world's best self-promoter, he had been teamed up for over a decade with a man who was not merely a great self-promoter, but who loudly blew the horn for everyone within his circle. Who, after all, didn't know that Jack Kirby was "the King"?

While Stan Lee had not given Jack Kirby his talent, and while Kirby had a wide and deep professional track record going back to the 1930s, the fact was that his current high-profile, living-legend status was the product of tireless and ceaseless promotion by the man who had been Stanley Martin Lieber. Kirby might have thought that being referred to as King Kirby was corny, but as a recognizable brand, it couldn't be beat.

Month after month of Lee telling Marvel's readers how great Jack was — making sure they identified Kirby as one of the key figures in the creation of Marvel's magic — meant that Kirby was, in the minds of readers, a part of Marvel that could not be replaced. Marvel without Kirby was unthinkable, in a way that even Marvel without Ditko hadn't been. Ditko was brilliant, and Spider-Man and Dr. Strange were unique. But *Fantastic Four* was first and had set the tone for everything else. Moreover, it was Kirby who did layouts for new and returning artists and Kirby who was drawing many of the covers. Much of the line's look and feel was Kirby's art as directed by Lee. Thanks to Lee, Kirby was considered as irreplaceable as . . . well, as irreplaceable as Stan Lee.

But Kirby still felt ill treated, still forced to bend the stories he was plotting to Lee's vision, expressed through Stan's scripting and — often last-minute — demands for revisions, changes that were often unpaid for. Whether in some abstract or even concrete way Lee's edits made the stories "better," that wasn't how Kirby saw it.

Like Lee, he was well aware that, a decade earlier, the company and the industry were on the verge of collapse. Like Lee, he had felt as if he could find no place to go besides Timely/Marvel. And like Lee, he wanted to make use of Marvel's success to widen his creative and financial horizons. Kirby was negotiating a new contract with Cadence, but was certainly well aware that being closer to the wellsprings of film and TV production could work to his advantage, one way or another. Something was going to happen with Kirby. It was only a matter of time.

With sales softening industry-wide, and with a mandate to shake things up, Infantino was ready to do anything he could to get Kirby over to DC. Eager to get free of Lee and Goodman, Kirby was ready to make a move. But it wouldn't be as easy as Carmine or Jack hoped, if only because Kirby did have a wife and four children to support and didn't want to risk a sure thing.

But Cadence had offered him a take-it-or-leave-it contract that he wasn't very happy with. They refused to negotiate. And yet, while far from perfect, it was a measure of

398

security for decent pay.

Also, although editor Jack Schiff was no longer at DC, the general feeling in the editorial and creative ranks there, more than a decade after their falling-out, was that Kirby had somehow done Schiff wrong, had been ungrateful and unappreciative. The fact that he seemed to be the powerhouse fueling Marvel's renaissance was seen at National as some kind of historical blip that would soon be corrected. The comics-reading audience would come to its senses and get over its infatuation with what most of DC's editors saw as the aesthetic of "ugly" that Kirby had brought to Marvel.

Infantino knew better, and circumstances were changing, including his own growing authority to *make* things change. Schiff had left DC several years earlier, and another Kirby nemesis — Mort Weisinger — was on the way out the door. Now it was just up to Kirby. But Jack was hesitant to leave the place and the titles where he'd been so successful. It would take him some time to make the decision to leap. But the seed had been planted.

As for Stan Lee, he was making plans for his *own* future. Sure, it was fun to drop the names of celebrities who visited the Marvel offices, or of the universities where he'd spoken, or publications and media outlets that had interviewed him. But these places

399

and people were also *contacts*. If they were interested in him . . . well, he was just as interested in *them*. Especially by 1969.

So Lee would start utilizing his contacts. His Wyoming archives are filled with cordial correspondence with celebrities, authors, academics, and poets (as well as with comics fans of all ages). Lee seemed to genuinely enjoy, beyond simple utility, corresponding with famous people — and they with him — but it's clear that keeping those lines of communication open was part of an overall strategy he had for himself (and, for now, Marvel) to keep options open. True, he would eventually think better, for example, of working on a series of anti–Vietnam War comics with poet Kenneth Koch, but his relationship with Alain Resnais, for a prime example, started out strong and continued that way until the director's 2014 death.

Resnais seems to have come to visit Lee at Marvel for the first time in '69, and he and Lee almost immediately clicked and started brainstorming projects to work on together. In a recorded private conversation between the two made in that year, Lee told Resnais:

I was loyal to the publisher [Goodman], but now that it's [Marvel] owned by another company, now I figure, for the first time, at my age [Lee is here forty-six], it's time I started thinking of other things.

I've been thinking of trying to write a play — I know some producers in this country — trying to do a movie scenario. I was even thinking of writing some poems, like Rod McKuen, and people like that, with some philosophy and some satire in them — the type of thing I put in the comics, like the *Silver Surfer,* you know, or *Spider-Man.*

I think my name may be well known enough that maybe these poems would sell. The only problem is, as long as I'm here [at Marvel], I don't have the time to write them. And if I leave, I don't get the income, which I need to keep living! So I've gotta figure out how to do this.[1]

Indeed, by 1971, Lee and Resnais would be at work on the first of two film projects they collaborated on. Lee took a month off from his comics-writing duties that year, even handing the Bullpen Bulletins off for that month to Roy Thomas, to write a script called *The Monster Maker* for Resnais. The story deals with a burned-out producer of grade-B horror movies who's had great success with genre work but now yearns to make a "meaningful" film about the dangers of pollution (a passion of Resnais's). The script itself weaves a fine line between self-parody and seriousness, and it's impossible to tell how it would have done with some rewrites and a cast that was in on both the humorous and the serious

401

aspects of the script. It was written for Filmways Inc. Lee was paid $25,000 for it, but it was never produced.

As Lee would say of his partnership with Resnais:

He came to New York because he wanted to do a Spider-Man movie, and at that time, I just wasn't in a position to give him a Spider-Man movie. I didn't have that much power. But we got to be very close friends, so we thought, "Let's do another movie, one that we can do together." And I came up with the idea of *The Monster Maker.* I wrote that, and I had never written a screenplay, so I *overwrote* it. Too much dialogue.

We brought it to someone named Martin Ransohoff, who was the head of Filmways, and he loved it. He wanted to produce it. But he said, "You've gotta cut the dialogue, Stan. You've gotta make it half the size it is." And I said, "Fine." And Alain walks over and he says [French-accented voice], "Stan will not change a word of it!" Alain loved it the way it was. And even I, an amateur, I said, "But, Alain, it's too long!" "No, you will not change a word of it!"

We had chemistry, personal chemistry. And he was so different than American people. Like, for the movie, *The Monster Maker,* he was out looking for locations, and he came to me one day. We were looking

402

for a place that was smelly, and dirty, and awful, and polluted, and he came running to me, excited. He said, "I found the place! I found the place!" I said, "Where, what?" He said, "In the East River, there's a little island called Rat Island, and none of the Americans know about it, but I found it!" I had never even heard of Rat Island, and he was so excited, and he showed me little photos he had taken. It looked like hell, so it was a good location. Anyway, that was Alain. We even went on a vacation together, he and his wife, who was the daughter of the Minister of Culture in France, and my wife and I. We went to France for a vacation for a couple of weeks, once. Had a great time.[2]

Lee would also produce a treatment of another film for Resnais called *The Inmates,* about a future where Earth was quarantined from other planets but an earthling and an alien nonetheless fall in love. Lee's plan was to write only the treatment and hire someone else to execute the screenplay, but the project never got beyond treatment stage.[3]

Even with Marvel's success, Lee was looking for options to supplement or — if need be — replace his income there. Indeed, he was looking, as he told Resnais, to use that success to enable him to move on to other things. And, as with the talk show pilot, Lee was also looking to do something "relevant."

403

Perhaps it was simply the tenor of the times, as communicated through conversations with his college audiences and with Marvel's younger staffers, that made him want to somehow use his influence to, in some way, make a difference.

Whether or not Lee knew of Kirby's contact with Infantino, he may well have been concerned about the artist's feelings. In the October '69 Bullpen Bulletins, Lee wrote:

Suddenly, the fabulous FANTASTIC FOUR have become the talk of Marveldom! First, everyone flipped over the way we playfully parodied the themes of TV's "The Prisoner" some months back — and now, the FF's adventures on the planet of the Skrulls — with overtones of every gangster movie you've ever seen — are knocking fandom out of its collective tree! Take a bow, LEE and KIRBY!

In other words: "We all know that Jack was *paying homage* to and even gently lampooning ideas from *The Prisoner* and the gangster episodes of *Star Trek,* not just *copying* them because he doesn't want to give Marvel any new ideas. And we're especially glad that he actually has given us some new ideas for *Thor!* (Please don't go, Jack!)"

And there would be more Jack-flattering. In

404

the Bulletins in the January '70–dated comics, Lee wrote:

Speaking of JOLLY JACK, many longtime fans have been writing in to say that THE FANTASTIC FOUR is getting better with each issue — with the stories reading more like the memorable masterworks of the FF's early years!

And on that same page, he also wrote:

The votes have been counted, and a united Marveldom wants STAN and JACK to come up with an *Inhumans* mag for 1970 . . .

Then, in the April '70 Bulletins, he wrote:

JACK (KING) KIRBY has done both the script and the penciling for a dynamite thriller in the current ish of CHAMBER OF DARKNESS! For those of you who never knew that the Jolly One is as gifted a writer as he is an artist, this'll be a real serendipity.

Interestingly, that same month's Bulletins also notes:

Our own STAN LEE and his old friend CARMINE INFANTINO (our leader's counterpart at National Periodical Publications) shared

405

a lively lunch together recently. . . . In this dog-eat-dog world of ours, it's kind'a nice to know that a couple of all-out competitors can still retain their longtime respect and affection for each other.

Did Lee know of Infantino's ongoing negotiations with his other "old friend," Kirby?

In any case, three months later, in the July '70 Bullpen Bulletins, Lee cheerily announced:

We just had a visit from JACK (KING) KIRBY, who winged his way eastward . . . to rap it up with Stan about the new IN-HUMANS series the Jolly One will be producing in the forthcoming AMAZING AD-VENTURES. Sly ol' Stan . . . cajoled the King into doing the script as well as the penciling for this great new series!

Clearly aware of Kirby's desire to dialogue, as well as plot and draw, his own work, Lee gave him the *Inhumans* (demoted by Goodman for reasons of economy to half of a split title, not its own series) to do it on. Perhaps that would satisfy Kirby . . . ? After all, he and Lee and just finished a record-breaking hundred issues of *Fantastic Four,* more than any creative team had done on any comic book title. Maybe the idea of sticking around and extending his own record would keep

406

Kirby happy for a while?

Or not. The contract Kirby had been offered by Cadence proved, ultimately, to be unacceptable to him. And so, in the September-dated Bulletins, in comics on sale in May, Lee wrote, in Stan's Soapbox:

Who says lightning never strikes twice? Remember a few years back when Steve Ditko suddenly left the hallowed halls of Marvel to seek his fortunes elsewhere? Well, at the time of this writing (early in March), Jack Kirby has unexpectedly announced his resignation from our surprised but stalwart little staff.

He then assured readers that

your barnstormin' Bullpen is passionately preparing some of the wildest and wackiest surprises yet to electrify your eyeballs and stagger your senses!

And so, the worst had happened. With a short phone call to Lee, Kirby had resigned. Worse, he was going to DC to unleash his unbridled talents, writing, penciling, and even editing a line of comics of his own. What if Jack really *could* do it all — and do it *better* — without Stan?

While Marvel tried to process Kirby's depar-

407

ture — Marie Severin pinned an old cigar butt (supposedly Kirby's) onto a piece of art board and drew a word balloon coming from it that shouted, *"I quit!"* — there was a certain amount of panic. John Romita thought they might cancel *FF.* "I didn't think there was anybody else who could do it," he said. "I asked Stan who was going to draw it, and he said, 'You are!' I thought he was out of his mind."[4]

For his part, Kirby, who, like Lee, would change his reported recollections and feelings about events over the years, was saying things like:

> Well, I didn't exactly work with Stan Lee. . . . I'd tell Stan Lee what the next story was going to be and I'd go home and do it. . . .
>
> [At National] I can think things out, do them my way and know I get credit for the things I do. There were times at Marvel when I couldn't say anything because it would be taken from me . . . all my connection with it would be severed. . . . You get to feel like a ghost.[5]

Marvel sales, already softening, continued to do so — as did sales industrywide. New Marvel features, like the Roy Thomas / Barry Smith *Conan the Barbarian* comic, were suddenly the focus of much attention, and indeed, new artists were starting to enter the business at both Marvel and DC. Talented, young comics people were becoming less rare than they had been. Still, everyone was holding their breath until Kirby's DC work would hit the stands. In October's Bulletins (likely written in May), Lee wrote:

Let's face it — this is probably mighty Marvel's proudest and most crucial hour! Even here, at the world-famous House of Ideas, we've never made so many sudden, cataclysmic changes, or taken so many unexpected, unprecedented gambles!

He then went on to enumerate the personnel switches on a number of titles, including the "artistic genius" of John Romita on *FF,* "combined with biting satire and raw, rugged realism from the pen of STAN LEE," and to proclaim that, with the new team on *Thor,* "NEAL ADAMS will bring to life the saga of the mighty THOR — as only Stan can write it! . . . literature and legend may never be the same again!"

And in the same month's Soapbox, Lee confided that

as we face our second decade as the world's most popular purveyors of illustrated fiction, the challenges are greater than ever! . . . Sure, we're proud of the past, but like we always say — the best is just ahead!

409

At DC, Kirby's first comic for them — his revamp of *Jimmy Olsen* comics — came out in late 1970. The rest of his new work, an interconnected series of comics featuring his new superhuman characters, wouldn't be out until early 1971.

Meanwhile, as Martin Goodman was playing bait-and-switch with readers, retailers, and DC over what exactly the price and page count of his comics would be — and hurting sales at DC, which was caught flat-footed when Goodman ended up giving retailers a better deal on his comics than they were giving on theirs — Lee was dancing as fast as he could, on multiple fronts, both personal and professional.

Aside from working with Resnais, Lee was still writing three monthly comics, which, of course he was also editing, as well as editing — with help from Thomas and others — the entire Marvel line. And he was doing his best to fill the comics with attention-grabbing material.

For instance, responding to a request from the federal government, Lee had written the first part of a three-part *Amazing Spider-Man* story line (in issues #96–98, dated May–July '71) dealing with drugs, which the Comics Code forbade mention of. The story gave a very negative view of drug taking, with Harry Osborn — son of the Green Goblin, and Peter Parker's close friend — experimenting with unnamed drugs, as did a black teenager, whose drug usage was portrayed as a result of racism.

Lee sent the story to the Comics Code for approval by its head, Len Darvin — and the story was rejected. It seemed that Lee had sent the story in when Darvin was out, and the story was rejected by Code board member John Goldwater, president of Archie Comics. It's been speculated that Darvin would have let the story go, since it didn't explicitly break any Code regulation, but rather a general warning about not portraying certain types of negative behavior.[6]

In any case, the story was rejected. Lee relates, in *Excelsior!,* that he went to Goodman — who was still his boss although no longer owner of the company — with the rejection, and that Goodman courageously agreed to publish the issue — and the next two — without the Code seal.

Of course, Goodman, having already cashed the check he'd gotten for the sale of the company, had nothing to lose, and both he and Lee must have sensed that they could get some great publicity from the decision. And if Goldwater was indeed behind the decision to reject the issue, then perhaps tweaking their competitor might have given them some level of satisfaction as well.

The drug issues ended up sparking a liberalization of the Code, which enabled DC, a

411

few months later, to include a drug angle in its "relevant" *Green Lantern / Green Arrow* series, which pointedly addressed topical issues. The changes in the Code also allowed member publishers to produce series featuring "horrific" elements, such as zombies, werewolves, and vampires, which had been forbidden under the old Code. Marvel used the new freedom to release such series as *The Tomb of Dracula* and *The Monster of Frankenstein.*

While Kirby was brewing up his Fourth World saga for DC, and Marvel and DC were both testing the new Comics Code's boundaries, Stan Lee was making waves on his own on a National Cartoonists Society panel that included — among others — John Goldwater! The panel, held January 20, 1971, at the Lambs Club in New York, was about the state of the comics industry. Besides Lee and Goldwater, the panel included Will Eisner, Gil Kane, and Dennis O'Neil.

At the panel, Lee — perhaps smarting from the loss of Kirby and the conflict with the Code — let loose some startling "truth bombs." The most devastating was this:

I would say that the comic book market is the worst market that there is on the face of the Earth for creative talent, and the reasons are numberless and legion. . . . Even if you

412

reach . . . the pinnacle of success in comics, you will be less successful, less secure . . . than if you are just an average practitioner of your art in television, radio, movies. . . . The creator . . . owns nothing of his creation. The publisher owns it.[7]

In essence, Lee was here more or less advocating creators' ownership of their work, an enlightened point of view for a comics editor of the time. At one point, Goldwater was, for the third or fourth time, defending the ownership of all rights by the publishers:

I think [working for a publisher] is a wonderful apprenticeship. Why deny a young fellow the opportunity of . . . learning from the pros, and then going on from there to something else . . . ?

To which Lee replied:

But isn't it pathetic to be in a business where the most you can say for the creative person in the business is that he's serving an apprenticeship to enter a better field? Why not go to the other field directly?

Earlier, Lee had remarked — with a touch of irony:

I don't know how the publishers, some of them, become as wealthy as they seem to

413

be, because I have been told so often . . . that there have been so many years when the books lose money. . . . You have got to be a simpleton to stay in that field or else there is just something wrong somewhere.

Lee the idealist, the man thinking about what's right and what's not, was very much in evidence here, as he was in the *Spider-Man* drug stories, and as he was when, in the same period, introducing (with artist Gene Colan) the first African American superhero, the Falcon, in the pages of *Captain America.*

In the spring of 1971, Kirby's Fourth World titles — *Mister Miracle, New Gods,* and *Forever People* — were released by DC. At first glance, they resembled Kirby's recent Marvel output. But they were, just beneath the surface, very different from his collaborations with Lee. As Gerard Jones and Will Jacobs described the work:

The vision that had begun growing in Kirby's work at Marvel . . . came to full flower. Some of his Marvel ideas resurfaced, now distilled to pure Kirby terms, bereft of Lee's inclinations toward humanization and internal agony. The Marvel formula for characterization played no part in these new creations. The Fourth World was a theater for elemental drama, for the clash of absolutes.[8]

414

Kirby had actually shown, or at least described to, Lee what would become the Fourth World. "These were," according to Sean Howe, "the next-generation heroes which Kirby wanted to replace Thor and the other 'old gods'" after a story he and Lee had done about Ragnarok, the twilight of the gods. But this was a "direction that Lee had not allowed him to take." Lee had thought of its characters and story lines as just more material to be absorbed into one of Marvel's existing titles, not a separate line for Kirby to helm. Kirby decided, seemingly unnoticed by Lee, to hold that material back from the company.[9]

Along with the intensity of his visuals and concepts, Kirby also provided idiosyncratic scripting in a style seemingly designed to be the opposite of Lee's reader-friendly, narrative-clarifying, naturalistic word usage. For anyone who wanted to see unfiltered Kirby, without the influence of Joe Simon or of Stan Lee, this was the mother lode. The question was, was this what the larger reading public — as well as the powers that be at DC — wanted?

In a fascinating coming together of multiple viewpoints — those of Lee, Kirby, Goodman, Infantino, and Thomas — an article in the May 2, 1971, *New York Times,* entitled SHAZAM! HERE COMES CAPTAIN RELEVANT,

415

written by Saul Braun, presented the players at a pivotal time in the comics business.

The article portrays Goodman as an avuncular figure, a patriarch of some sort, and Lee and Kirby as perhaps his two most accomplished "children," now at odds with each other. In the piece, Goodman, a year away from being fully out the door, took a world-weary, big-picture point of view: " 'Industrywide,' says Goodman sorrowfully, 'the [sales] volume is not going up. . . . After a few years, an erosion sets in. You still maintain loyal readers, but you lose a lot more readers than you're picking up.' "

Of Lee, Goodman recalled:

> Stan started as a kid here; he's my wife's cousin. . . . He had a talent for writing. . . . I think when Stan developed the Marvel superheroes he did a very good job, and got a lot of college kids reading us . . . but when you play it to them you lose the very young kids. . . . Because I read some [of Stan's] stories sometimes and I can't even understand them.

After thirty years of professional association, and after ten years of Marvel success, Goodman was somehow unable to give his cousin-in-law much more credit than to say he had "a talent for writing" and that "he did a very good job." (Of course, just off hand-

416

edly mentioning in the article that they were related seems intended to diminish Lee as just a lucky beneficiary of nepotism.) Goodman seemed, even then, to in some way still be seeing Lee as the teenager who came walking through the offices one day in 1940, looking for an entry-level position. It's also possible that Goodman here already had some inkling of the coming power struggle between him and Lee that would eventually morph into a truly Shakespearean conflict.

Although Lee was featured prominently in the article, Braun seemed to describe him more as others saw him (as opposed to how he saw himself), starting with Resnais (described as a "Lee fan") and Goodman. Perhaps that was because, when asked about himself, Stan seemed to go into autopilot mode, rehashing tried-and-true chestnuts about the creation of Marvel's characters, his only off-script comment being:

For years the big things on campus have been McLuhan and Tolkien, and Stan Lee and Marvel, and everybody knew about McLuhan and Tolkien, but nobody knew about Marvel. Now our competitor [DC] is coming out with "relevant" comics and he has big public relations people, so he's been easing in on our publicity.

Unsurprisingly, while name-checking Mc-

417

Luhan, Lee made no mention of the professor's dismissal of him in his 1951 *The Mechanical Bride.*

Braun also spoke to Goldwater, who chimed in on the *Spider-Man* drug issues:

Goodman came before the publishers and promised not to do it again. So we're satisfied. Anybody with 15 solid years of high standards of publishing comic books with the [Comics Code] seal is entitled to one mistake.

Goodman, for his part, spoke of the whole drug issues controversy as "a tempest in a teapot."

Braun's main interest was clearly in Kirby. While Lee and Goodman, as portrayed in the article, seemed to be focused on past squabbles and triumphs, Braun spent hundreds of words describing Kirby's new comics.

Kirby told Braun:

I have no final answers. I have no end [for the Fourth World stories] in mind. This is like a continuing novel . . . and I'm feeling very good about this [his new comics]. My mail has been about 90 percent positive, and sales good.

The last quote of the article was given to

418

Infantino, who had been liberally quoted all through the piece. There seemed to have been some awareness on Braun's part that the people speaking to him on behalf of the pop culture tastes of the "youth culture" were — with the exception of Roy Thomas — all hovering on either side of fifty. Infantino seemed to be hoping that Kirby had brought some of Marvel's campus cred with him when he reflected:

> The kids at Yale think Kirby's new books are more tuned in to them than any other media. . . . We're tuning in to what [college students] are experiencing.[10]

Like Lee with Jeff Shero of *Rat Subterranean News* on the 1968 TV pilot, these responsible adults — Lee, Kirby, Goodman, and Infantino — seemed to have no real clue what it was "the kids" wanted or responded to, or what their roles as middle-aged comics creators were supposed to be. Were they supposed to glamorize psychedelic visions — provide them on paper, without drugs — or were they, as the Nixon people had requested of Lee, supposed to stigmatize drugs? Were college students *against* violence or *for* violence? What the heck did the audience *want*? Lee and Kirby, especially, had stumbled onto, and then rode, the zeitgeist for a decade. But what were comics creators

419

and companies supposed to do *now*?

In September 1971, future *Sopranos* writer and producer Robin Green's *Rolling Stone* article on Marvel appeared, complete with a specially-done Hulk cover by Herb Trimpe. (When another Hulk cover appeared on a 2015 issue, Lee remarked in an interview on the magazine's website: "What took ya so long to repeat it?") Green portrayed her former boss as a sympathetic character, but one who was a bit lost. She quoted Gil Kane's *Alter Ego* interview, where he'd said that "Jack and Stan had painted themselves into a corner by converting everything at Marvel into the same model, and now everybody's losing interest in that model."[11]

"Well," Green continued in the article, "Stan's alone in the corner, still Facing Front and smiling, but a little down sometimes." She described him as having sinus trouble, much as in the Braun article Lee complained about "always having a cold." (Problems with the East Coast climate, perhaps?)

Green allowed the deeper, caring Stan — the guy who emceed the talk show pilot — to shine through. For instance:

You know, I'm very square and preachy sometimes, but the more I realize that people are to some degree affected by what we write, the more I'm aware of the influ-

420

ence we have, the more I worry about what I write. . . . I never try to say to the reader, this is the way it should be, 'cause I feel, who am I to say it?

Green reported that he then philosophically added:

I think the only message I wanted to get across is, for Christsake, don't be bigoted. Don't be intolerant. . . . I think most people . . . want to live a happy family life, they want to be at peace. . . . But I think everyone sees us reaching that nirvana by a different path.

The publication of the *Times* and *Rolling Stone* articles might have seemed like some kind of coming of age for comics. This was, after all, coverage in major periodicals, with articles showcasing reflections on comics' past and future, and on where comics fit into the modern world, from key figures in the comics industry, and with casual bragging from one company about how popular their comics were at Yale. These were seasoned professionals talking, but they certainly weren't resting on their laurels. They seemed to be pushing the boundaries of the comics medium and the comics business in search of ways to keep their old audiences while finding new ones. But were the comics — as least

421

as presented by Marvel and DC — coming of age, or were they coming to the end of a momentary burst of popularity?

The early '70s were as tumultuous for comics as they were for the rest of the culture. Within the next few years, Infantino, Kirby, Goodman, and Lee would become more embroiled than ever in the upheavals engulfing their industry.

The Lieber family in 1932: Stan, Jack, Larry, and Celia.

Stanley Martin Lieber's
DeWitt Clinton High School
1939 Yearbook photo.

STAN LEE WAS CONSTANTLY STRESSING ACTION AND ACTING OUT WHAT HE WANTED...

WHAT I WANT IS ACTION, ACTION, ACTION!

Artist David Gantz's 2006 recollection of Stan Lee in action in 1941.

Courtesy of Rick Dee/Creative Juice Partners

Courtesy of Rick Dee/Creative Juice Partners

ABOVE: Timely/Marvel artist Ken Bald, Kaye Bald, Joan Lee, and Stan Lee at Leon & Eddie's nightclub in New York, late 1951.

LEFT: Stan Lee and Ken Bald at Mike Carbo's New York Comic Book Marketplace, March 2012.

Larry Lieber and Stan Lee, early 1950s.

Stan and Joan Lee at the 1961 wedding of
Stan and Pauline Mirsky Goldberg.

Photo by John Benson

ABOVE: Stan Lee receiving an award from SCARP (Society for Comic Art Research and Preservation) at the premier International Convention of Comic Book Art in July 1968. The award was presented by convention chairman and distribution pioneer, Phil Seuling, at the Statler Hilton Hotel in New York.

BELOW: Stan Lee and Jack Kirby at the 1975 MiamiCon.

Photo by James Van Hise

Stan Lee lecturing at
Virginia Commonwealth
University in 1976.

Scott Saternye

Robin Platzer/Twin Images

Robin Platzer/Twin Images

ABOVE: Stan Lee, mugging for the camera in 1978, at Marvel's 575 Madison Avenue offices. A bust of his wife, Joan, sits on the windowsill.

LEFT: Stan Lee in his Marvel Comics office in New York, 1978.

Photo by Jackie Estrada

LEFT: Stan Lee in the Green Room at the 1986 San Diego Comic-Con.

BELOW: Danny Fingeroth and Stan Lee on stage at the Wizard World Comic Convention in Nashville, Tennessee, October 2013.

Raymond Smotherman (wordpress.hegeekshegeek.com)

Featureflash Photo Agency/Shutterstock.com

Paul Rudd and Stan Lee at the world premiere of
the Rudd-starring movie *Ant-Man* at the Dolby Theatre
in Hollywood, June 29, 2015.

betto rodrigues/Shutterstock.com

Stan Lee and writer/artist Todd McFarlane at the
L.A. Convention Center, October 31, 2015.

15
POWER POLITICS

What's gotten into Parker?? He used to be a real little milk-toast! Who wised him up?
— J. Jonah Jameson in
Amazing Spider-Man #33,
February 1966, by Stan Lee and Steve Ditko

On September 9, 1971, the Attica Correctional Facility inmate takeover in upstate New York began. Prisoners had taken forty-two guards and other staff as hostages. By the thirteenth, failed negotiations between the inmates and the commissioner of prisons — and Governor Nelson Rockefeller — resulted in an attack on the prison by state troopers. Forty-three people died during the assault, including ten hostages. All those who died were killed by bullets fired by the attacking forces. The debate raged — and rages to this day — as to who was responsible for the chaos and deaths during those four days.

For some reason, Stan Lee decided that those events would be the lead-in to his

423

Soapbox for the April '72 cover–dated Marvel comics:

These brief random thoughts are being written just a short time after the Attica State Prison tragedy. Now I've no intention of imposing my own opinions upon you about which side, which party or parties might have been right or wrong. Instead, I'd like to discuss the theory of "right or wrong" itself.

And he proceeded to do just that, pondering, "I wonder what life would be like if we weren't so preoccupied with proving ourselves right and the other guy wrong." Perhaps not the most hard-hitting editorial of all time, it was notable that it was coming from someone who had produced countless stories that could be accused of being about proving oneself right — through the use of force! Even more interesting was the thought that Lee would start the conversation by bringing up a topical but controversial event. In the context of the '68 talk show pilot, the ecology-themed screenplay for Alain Resnais, and the attempts at social commentary in comics like *Silver Surfer,* this Attica-inspired piece can be seen as another step in Lee attempting to grow as a person, editor, and public figure.

The following month's Soapbox was short and to the point: a brief plug for the new *Luke Cage: Hero for Hire* comic. *Cage* was Marvel's

424

(if not anyone's) first comic book to feature a solo black superhero. Instead of ballyhooing that he *was* the first solo black superhero, Lee ran a picture of Cage and informed the readers that "he's really somethin' else!" The character's origin was set in a maximum-security prison, where Luke, who'd been framed for a murder he didn't commit, found himself given superhuman powers in an experiment sabotaged by a sadistic guard with a grudge against him.

The way comics timetables work, the character — credited to Archie Goodwin, George Tuska, Roy Thomas, and John Romita Sr. as creators — had to have been in the works for months before the Attica riots. (Lee had himself directed the quartet to come up with the comic book equivalent of hit action movies like *Shaft* as Marvel's answer to the blaxploitation fad.) As Thomas has said on Facebook:

> The success of that film [*Shaft*] . . . had led Stan to figure that, if we weren't going to do a solo Black Panther title, partly because of the controversial connotations of that name [the same as that of the radical political group], it was time to devise a new character. . . .
>
> Stan, Archie Goodwin, John Romita, and I brainstormed . . . all of us brought something to the table . . . but Stan was the ringmaster

425

through it all . . .[1]

Nonetheless, it's still hard to not somehow connect *Cage* to Lee's Soapbox from the previous month.

If nothing else, Lee's feel for the zeitgeist was still switched on, processing what was going on in the world, making it into fodder for comics. Perhaps the brevity of the plug for *Cage* was the result of conflicted feelings: pride that Marvel now had an African American superhero title, perhaps mixed with some embarrassment at realizing that a well-intentioned Soapbox attempt at "relevance" through invoking the Attica tragedy had preceded the promotion of *Hero for Hire* by only a single month.

While Lee was cultivating his role and image as a thoughtful, concerned conduit of recent events, trying to keep Marvel topical, there was still some old business going on that he'd have to contend with, like it or not.

Jack Kirby was as busy as ever, turning out breathtaking, if idiosyncratic, material at DC. Even so, he found the time to invent and include, in *Mister Miracle* #6, which would have been on sale in October '71, a character who was an obvious shot at Lee: Funky Flashman.

A self-involved hustler and promoter, Flashman — once his toupee and fake beard were

426

in place — looked exactly like Stan Lee of the era. Funky was a pathetic character, self-involved, leeching off a relative, willing to sell anyone out in service to himself and to the primary villain of Kirby's Fourth World, Darkseid. The intro copy to the story describes Flashman for us:

In the shadow world between success and failure, there lives the *driven* little man who dreams of *having it all!!!* — the opportunistic spoiler without character or values . . . !

Funky was served by a valet named House-roy, an equally unflattering version of Roy Thomas. In one instance, seeking to exploit Scott Free (a.k.a. Mister Miracle), Houseroy warns Funky of the dangers of Scott's risk-taking. Flashman responds, "So he breaks a leg or *dies*!! I'll just sip my martini by the ocean — and wait for the *next* fish to jump!!"

As the issue ends in disaster for Flashman, he watches his old "plantation" (a thinly veiled metaphor for Marvel, its owner, and its chief editor) burn down and muses:

There it goes! — everything — up in flames! The Mockingbird estate — and its *happy* memories! . . . *Happy* slaves singing for the *family*!

The issue's cover copy — presumably writ-

427

ten by Kirby — did offer a little ambiguity, posing the question: "Funky Flashman! Villain or *hero* — *you* decide!"

Funky's portrayal cuts deeper than just lampooning someone's vanity or speech patterns. It's a biting interpretation of Lee as a mean-spirited phony, free of any values, self-aggrandizing and greedy. The not-so-subtle portrayals of Funky and Houseroy may have gone past much of the readership, but to those who knew anything about the people behind the comics, this shouted out a last "Screw you!" from Kirby. It would be hard to imagine him and Lee ever making up or working together again.

Thomas recalled about the story:

The Funky Flashman stuff bothered [Stan] a little bit, because it seemed, to Stan at least, somewhat mean-spirited . . . even I was a little bothered the first time I saw the Houseroy thing, because it's a reading of me that's only partly true . . . and I hated to see what a lot of us felt . . . was a cheap shot at Stan, and I would've felt that whether Houseroy existed or not.

Jack of course said, "Well, y'know, I was just making stories" when I talked to him . . . but we all knew it was a little more than that. . . . Stan said he never let it bother him, but the relationship [between Lee and Kirby] was never quite the same.[2]

428

Kirby associate Mark Evanier remembered:

I know Roy was more upset about it than Stan was, and Jack was actually a little — I won't say *sorry* he did it, but he was sorry it came out the way it did, because what happened was that he started to do a story that was basically about [someone else] . . . but there was some interview that came out with Stan at the time that Jack took a lot of offense to. He thought it was really nasty. There were a bunch of those [kinds of hurt feelings on both sides] over the years, and the timing of them was never good. Jack got mad at Stan, Stan got mad at Jack.[3]

The real threat from Kirby, of course, was newsstand competition from the material he was producing. While the sales of his DC work weren't as great as the company had hoped, they were still more than respectable. And even if Kirby's scripting style was off-putting to some readers, the power of his drawing and visual storytelling, along with his novel characters and the sheer quantity of new ideas he was unleashing in every issue, were beyond impressive. He seemed to be fulfilling his aim to be an auteur, in charge of every aspect of his creations, so that, no matter what else, his DC work could be seen as a pure, personal vision, especially once he was able to pick the inker he wanted, Mike Royer.

Of course, there was the small matter of DC changing Superman's face to be more "on model" anytime Kirby drew the character, which was — especially in *Superman* spinoff *Jimmy Olsen* — quite a bit. Well, no situation is perfect.

Shortly after the appearance of Funky Flashman, Stan Lee took a major step to control and expand his brand. On January 5, 1972, *A Marvel-ous Evening with Stan Lee* was presented at, of all places, Carnegie Hall.

The brainchild of producer Steve Lemberg, who was also behind the album *The Amazing Spider-Man: From Beyond the Grave — A Rockomic,* it was a conscious effort by Lemberg — who had gotten the rights to many of Marvel's characters from Chip Goodman for bargain-basement prices — to try to make Lee a celebrity, using the Marvel characters as a steppingstone. The evening was a hodgepodge of eclectic elements and people, featuring dramatic readings of comics, on-the-spot drawing by John Romita and Herb Trimpe, and music by Chico Hamilton and his band (Hamilton had also signed on to do the score for Marvel radio programs that Lemberg was producing), as well as by Roy Thomas and Barry Smith. Alain Resnais, novelist Tom Wolfe, and actor René Auberjonois participated in readings from and about comics.

The event was also the public debut of Lee's epic poem, "God Woke." Recited by Joan and JC Lee, this was the come-to-life version of Lee's desire to, as he'd told Resnais, become a popular poet in the Rod McKuen mode. (Nearly forgotten today, McKuen was extraordinarily popular, appearing regularly on TV, selling millions of books of poetry.)

While the evening seems like it should have been a lot of fun, by most accounts, including Thomas's and Gerry Conway's, it fell quite flat. Perhaps the mistake was trying to make a multimedia extravaganza of Lee's college and comic convention appearances, to literally orchestrate his usual off-the-cuff talks into a showbiz spectacle, but one largely consisting of people who — with the exception of the Hamilton group — were not (including Lee) professional entertainers. The punch line to this version of the old joke setup "How do you get to Carnegie Hall?" was clearly *not* to have a bunch of writers, artists, and other amateur performers try to make a compelling evening of translating printed comic book characters into razzle-dazzle showmanship.

As critic Dean Latimer wrote of the evening in *The Monster Times:*

The audience left in stunned silence, after often yawning louder than the fabulously

431

fraught activities . . . all they got was lame sentimental drivel . . . you can understand why they were mystified. And bored.[4]

And, writing in *Women's Wear Daily,* critic Peter Ainslie reported:

[Lee] introduced a host of New York celebrities including Tom Wolfe, Alex Bennett, Brute Force, Rene Auberjonois and others, but the show never really got off the ground.[5]

Conway recalled for Raphael and Spurgeon:

The producer didn't know what he was doing. . . . Stan's strength and his weakness is his ability to improvise in the moment. Unfortunately, you can't improvise a two-hour show.[6]

Even producer Lemberg had negative memories:

It was really pretty much a terrible show. I feel very bad about the quality of the actual event.[7]

But at least one attendee, Scott Edelman — a future Marvel writer and editor, then a sixteen-year-old high school student from

432

Brooklyn — enjoyed the show immensely. "I loved the whole night," he recalled. Edelman believes many others also had a great time. "When people started writing [negatively] about it in the fanzines . . . I don't know what they were expecting. . . . Maybe it's not for them. . . . It was a glorious night for me."[8]

Lee's epic poem, "God Woke," which was recited that night, was — as pop poetry and, indeed, even as a meditation by a man in midlife trying to make sense of existence — not half-bad. The theme and subject seemed to be those that underlay Lee's *Silver Surfer* stories: Why do humans always have to create conflict when, if they just cooperated and appreciated what they had, life could be so much better?

Considering Lee's steadfast resolve to write a rhyming poem (he told philosophy professor Jeff McLaughlin that he didn't care for poems that didn't rhyme and that "I hated free verse") and to deliver some kind of message (he also told McLaughlin he hated poems where "you didn't know what they were saying"), "God Woke" sets up and delivers a long-form (around three hundred lines) poem that sets a mood and tells a story. And rhymes.[9]

The poem is clearly the product of an inquisitive, agile mind, written by someone who actually *is* concerned about human-

433

kind's purpose on Earth. Although Lee has claimed to not have ever given much thought to religious concerns, as Dr. Thomas Mick has remarked, someone who doesn't care at all about religion doesn't write an epic poem called "God Woke."[10]

As 1972 progressed, Martin Goodman's tenure was winding down. All was going according to plan, and Chip Goodman was on deck, waiting to ascend to his father's position as president and publisher of Magazine Management. As had his father before him, Chip was going to run the family empire, including Marvel Comics and Stan Lee.

There was, however, one person who had a significant issue with this anticipated turn of events.

While Lee was well paid by Cadence, Goodman's promise to him of great wealth resulting from the sale of the company never came to pass. Even if it had, Lee had put in more than three decades not merely working in the trenches for Goodman but reinventing the comics line — not to mention the entire comics business! Thirty years. Now he wanted to do things *his* way. He had all sorts of ideas he wanted to implement for new publishing initiatives. And, rumor had it, he had even been in discussions with DC about going over there. Maybe that friendly lunch with Carmine Infantino he'd mentioned in the Bullpen Bulletins wasn't held just to wax nostalgic over old times. (Kirby and Lee both working at DC at the same time is an alternate reality that would have been interesting, to say the least.)

And so, Lee was promoted, in the spring of 1972, to be the president and publisher of Marvel Comics.

Looking back in 2017, Lee reflected on the promotion:

> That was my one bit of revenge. Martin had his son working there, and he told Cadence that he wanted the son to be the publisher after he left. I said to Cadence, "If he's the publisher, I'm quitting." So I became the publisher.[11]

Or as Raphael and Spurgeon put it:

> Cadence had no shortage of business-minded individuals. They were less well-stocked with pop culture icons whose out-sized personalities could assemble a loyal fan following and headline at Carnegie Hall.[12]

But while Lee's status was elevated — and he simultaneously stepped away from writing and editing monthly comics — Chip Goodman was himself promoted to be president and publisher of Magazine Management,

435

which included Marvel. Lee had moved up but, at least on an org chart, still seemed to be reporting to a Goodman. Still, as late as March 27, 1974, Lee had sent a memo to Martin inviting him and Chip to a luncheon hosted by the Comics Magazine Association of America board of directors to honor someone named Bill Server for his years of service to the CMAA.[13] The existence of the memo indicates that relations between Lee and the Goodmans were at least cordial up to that point. They would not be for much longer.

Now Marvel's president and publisher, Lee took on what he thought should be the duties of his new role. After some infighting over job titles and responsibilities — a type of battle that would plague Marvel for the next several years — Thomas succeeded Lee as editor (the "editor in chief" title for the top editor at the company did not yet then exist), while Stan busied himself coming up with ideas for new types of comics — some different in format, others in content, some in both — from what the company had been putting out. He did this not just out of enthusiasm but because the old products were having trouble selling.[14]

It turned out that Goodman had indeed sold when the time was right. The comics business was then at the start of one of its

436

regular crisis periods. Increased suburbanization meant that there were fewer mom-and-pop corner newsstands and candy stores where kids could drop in on the way home from school for a malt and a few comics. There were a few dedicated comics shops, but they were just beginning to appear, the very beginning of what would come to be called the *direct market*. That market was just getting started, as pioneers like Phil Seuling started cutting deals with Marvel and DC to bypass traditional distributors to get comics they could sell for a deeper discount, but without return privileges.[15]

The momentum of the so-called Silver Age of comics — first the revived superhero wave at DC and then the inspired Marvel hero comics — was fading. While Marvel had an unmatched record of creative innovation and excitement from *Fantastic Four* #1 and on, by the early '70s, the company's characters, and its approach to them, had lost their novelty. The Marvel superheroes were, by then, well known and established. Spider-Man was almost as iconic as Superman. The more realistic approach that had made Marvel's characters new and startling no longer had that effect. The comics were now selling based on numerous factors, but novelty was no longer one of them — which was why Lee was so eager to try new genres and formats.

On one level, the question — as it would

437

be for the next forty years — was: Who were these things for? Who *was* reading comics? It was no longer as simple as in the '50s, when most kids — boys and girls — would read comics for a couple of years and then move on. Further, the very nature of what Marvel had ushered in — an interrelated fictional universe peopled with characters who behaved in a somewhat realistic manner — seemed to have become a cliché of its own. Even done well, by talented writers and artists, much of it seemed like it had been done before or, in some cases, was *so* idiosyncratic that it couldn't attract a large audience.

Add to that the changes shaking distribution and the loosening of the Comics Code — not to mention the entire alternate aesthetic of the undergrounds, which teen and college readers were buying — and it was obvious that the definition of *what* a comic book should be was in flux. And could comics really compete with TV for access to viewers' eyeballs, or with the movies for frank portrayals of sex and violence?

And while all parties — from creators to distributors to sales outlets to fans — were reevaluating comics' place in their cosmos, things were in turmoil in the comics business itself, as exemplified by the presence in executive positions of Carmine Infantino and Stan Lee. A decade before, they would not have had the opportunity to fill those chairs.

438

Lee would have been considered not serious enough, a lightweight compared to "real" publishing executives. Infantino would have been thought of as "just an artist," his head too much in the clouds for him to come down to earth and figure out a profit-and-loss sheet. But they were now in charge and were hiring all these intense, driven young people to make their comics, and now they were putting out some driven and intense comics. But those weren't selling especially well, either.

Martin Goodman had, it seemed, indeed timed everything perfectly. Soon he'd be gone, and, per his agreement with Cadence, Chip would be running the Magazine Management show.

So both Marvel and DC, as well as other companies, were inventing, publishing — and then canceling — dozens of titles in multiple genres. Marvel's number of titles doubled from 1972 to 1974, from around twenty to around forty. But the company's basic structure didn't change. Thomas had inherited an editorial and production system originally devised to function when one editor was overseeing eight or ten titles per month. That system proved highly unwieldy when that editor — Thomas — had to supervise more than forty monthly comics. Because of the overwhelming workload, a system had evolved whereby the writers of the comics served as

439

de facto editors of the titles they wrote, while Thomas and Lee tried to deal with more global issues of direction and philosophy. Lee or Thomas might decree that there should be a vampire series or a mystical motorcyclist series or a trio of comics featuring female superheroes. It was then up to Thomas (with Lee chiming in from the sidelines) to take those mandated or approved ideas and brainstorm them with writers and artists who would translate them into actual comic books that had to come out regularly and on time.

Bored by the minutiae of the business end of being publisher, Lee tried to focus on the creative end, trying new kinds of formats and subjects that Goodman had been hesitant about. At this point — four years after Goodman inked the sale papers — Marvel pretty much had nothing to lose through such experimentation.

Lee tried everything. A proposed series of comics to be written by literary heavyweights like Kurt Vonnegut and Václav Havel (who had a side job as president of Czechoslovakia) was discussed but never materialized. Stan invited *Mad* magazine inventor Harvey Kurtzman to do a new humor magazine, but Kurtzman wasn't interested in producing just another Marvel-branded product. Lee discussed with Will Eisner having Eisner either package a line of comics or publish *Spirit* reprints or new *Spirit* material through

440

Marvel, or even take over as Marvel's publisher, while Lee would retain the president title.

According to Eisner biographer Michael Schumacher, Eisner wanted no part of being a cog in Marvel's corporate structure. In addition, "Eisner informed Lee that if he was put in charge at Marvel, he'd want to initiate changes that gave writers and artists ownership of their work. Lee was in no position to negotiate such changes."[16]

By the same token, Jim Warren, the eponymous owner of Warren Publishing — producers of *Eerie, Creepy,* and *Vampirella* — wasn't too pleased when Lee, who had supposedly promised to never compete with him in the black-and-white comic magazine arena, did just that. But Warren could hardly have been surprised. Survival was the name of the game. Warren knew his frenemy well enough to know that Stan would do what he had to in order to survive.

Lee had said to *Rolling Stone* magazine in 1974, tongue firmly in cheek, "He [Warren] despises me. If I had any sense, I'd hire a bodyguard."

He continued, "I know he has often said to people we're out to destroy him. It's not that at all. . . . I figure if we do well, it has to help him. . . . I think he's a *nut,* the way he carries on. . . ."[17]

In interviews done in 1998 and '99, Warren

441

reflected:

I hate[d] anyone who is taking our concepts, our ideas, and because they have the big machinery of a big company like Marvel, flooding the market.

Do I really hate Stan Lee? Who can hate him? Stan is one of the most loveable guys in comics — but if Stan Lee is going to go head-to-head with me . . . I'm going to get a glass-bottom car so I can look over his face when I run over him.[18]

Lee declared in the Bullpen Bulletins in the September '72–dated comics (probably written in May), that this was the beginning of "Marvel, Phase Two." He wrote that, with Thomas now editor,

it means that I'll finally have the time . . . to devote myself exclusively to dreaming up new and exciting projects for the Bullpen, and new fields for Marvel to conquer in film, TV, books, and you-name-it-we'll-do it!

Tireless in his efforts to improve comics' image as well as trying to improve Marvel's sales, Lee also became active in the ACBA (Academy of Comic Book Arts). His vision of the organization — as a group that would function like the Motion Picture Academy, handing out awards and spreading goodwill

442

— was different from what some of the organization's writers and artists, such as Neal Adams and Archie Goodwin, eager for some kind of a guild or union to advocate on their behalf, were looking for.

After his promotions, Lee's celebrity status, unsurprisingly, continued to grow. For some examples:

In April 1972, he and Kirby appeared together at the Cartoon Symposium at Vanderbilt University in Nashville — along with Gahan Wilson, Garry Trudeau, Dave Berg, and others. No mention was made of Funky Flashman.

On May 3, 1974, he was awarded the Popular Culture Award of Excellence for Distinguished Achievements in the Popular Arts at the Popular Culture Association's Fourth National Convention in Milwaukee. His fellow award winners included Count Basie, James M. Cain, Agatha Christie, Howard Hawks, and Irving Wallace.

One speakers bureau promotional flyer of the period (which included him along with accomplished figures, including Richard Leakey, Norman Lear, Ramsey Lewis, and Art Linkletter), described him thus:

King of the Comic Books, publisher of Marvel Comics . . . writer, illustrator and guiding force behind the most popular com-

443

ics on campus today. Offers observations on how a man in his 50s, catering to a youth market, can "buck the system" to become the most published writer in America.

But celebrity or not, Lee still had that day job he needed to attend to.

At that day job, though Lee was president as well as publisher of Marvel Comics, Chip Goodman was president and publisher of Marvel's owner, Magazine Management. Technically, he was still Lee's boss.

But there was court intrigue going on around Lee and Chip. Onetime Goodman business associate Albert Einstein Landau — his namesake's godson — maneuvered himself into the position of president of Magazine Management and hence of Marvel, as well. Lee was made publisher of Marvel *and* of Magazine Management. Landau was both Stan and Chip's boss. In 1974, when Chip's contract was up, it was not renewed. Now, neither Chip nor Martin was employed by Cadence.

While it's hard to believe that a businessman as savvy as Martin Goodman would not have had the arrangement regarding Chip put into a contract, so that his son would be guaranteed some kind of executive position for more than just a few years, that was apparently what had happened. Martin, enraged

444

at how Chip had been treated, plotted revenge. He would hurt Cadence — and Lee — and he and Chip would triumph over them. The relationship between Stan Lee and Martin Goodman was coming to seem more and more like a Marvel superhero comic.

While this corporate and family infighting was going on, Marvel was experiencing growing pains, along with some pleasures. An entire generation of new artists and writers was entering the field, bringing the consciousness of the boomers to the creative side — as opposed to the consuming side — of the comics. Largely rising from fandom, names like Len Wein, Marv Wolfman, Steve Gerber, Mary Skrenes, Steve Englehart, Frank Brunner, Jim Starlin, Mike Friedrich, Linda Fite, Mimi Gold, and many others were adding their visions and broadening the idea of what a Marvel comic could be. While Marvel's superheroes would continue, horror, sword and sorcery, romance, science fiction, and other genres would be included under the Marvel umbrella. The nature of the business — including the shift in how comics were sold — meant that many of the experiments would fail. But the sense was there that Marvel was willing to try and that what Stan said in that Soapbox that he would do — devote himself to "dreaming up new and exciting projects for the Bullpen" — he would indeed do. The fact was, he really had no choice if the company were to survive. It was an exciting but scary time for Marvel and for comics as a whole.

While Marvel was busy trying out genres with imagery and story lines that they would not have dared to — or been allowed to by the Code — just a few years earlier, it was, as one would imagine, when they messed with their beloved superheroes that the most noses were put out of joint.

Looking for a way to boost sales on *Amazing Spider-Man,* someone — most recall it as art director John Romita Sr. — came up with the idea of killing a beloved supporting character as his artistic hero, Milton Caniff, had done years earlier by killing off Raven Sherman in his *Terry and the Pirates* syndicated strip. After discussions between Lee, Thomas, Romita, and series writer Gerry Conway, the decision was arrived at that it would be Peter Parker's girlfriend, Gwen Stacy, who would be murdered, which happened in issue #121, released in March 1973.

Fan reaction to her demise, especially as voiced at Lee's campus appearances, was largely negative. It didn't help that, the way the death was staged, it seemed as if it might have been Spider-Man who inadvertently killed her while trying to save her from the Green Goblin. Lee would tell audiences —

and perhaps truly believed — that the decision was made without his input while he was away on a business trip, although everyone else involved has denied this was possible — that even if he were away for a few days, he was enough on top of things that he had to have known about, and approved of, this crucial moment in the characters' lives.[19]

By the same token, and in many ways more significant to the company's core DNA, Lee *did* take responsibility and a strong stand regarding classified ads that had been running in the comics. In a letter found in Lee's archives at the University of Wyoming, dated July 3, 1974, a reader had written an alarmed letter to Roy Thomas, outraged that

> something has come to my attention that has caused me to seriously consider boycotting Marvel on *moral* grounds. Specifically I am referring to the neo-Nazi ads that you run in your classified ads section for a company called "Adolf's" that sells Nazi decals, ensignia [*sic*], etc.

Thomas had jotted a note to Lee on the letter that said: "Can we insist that [our ad people] refuse to accept such ads in the future?"

Lee sent a memo on July 11 to the company handling Marvel's classified ads that read:

447

Effective immediately, please accept no more ads of any type which may be considered Neo-Nazi. Such as the one referred to in the attached letter which takes umbrage with the ad run by a company called Adolf's.[20]

The ads stopped running.

Aside from his work in the office and on the lecture circuit, Lee was also working on *Origins of Marvel Comics* for Simon & Schuster. While largely composed of reprints of the origin stories and more recent adventures of Spider-Man, the Fantastic Four, the Hulk, and several others, the book also contained Lee's — and hence, Marvel's — official versions of how the characters were created, versions devised more to be entertaining than accurate and, seemingly, to make Lee as central and important to the characters' creation as possible — not surprising given that his two most important collaborators had abandoned him and the company.

In the book, as well as in several sequels, Lee was, to be sure, effusive in his compliments for Kirby and Ditko, but the narrative made it clear that it was Stan Lee who was the major creative force behind Marvel and its characters. One could imagine that, aside from enshrining Lee's own legend, Marvel would rather have an official history that

448

came from someone under contract to the company rather than from people who were working for other companies and who might even sue for ownership of the intellectual property at some point.

Whatever contractual obligations might have prevented Martin Goodman from competing with Marvel and Magazine Management must have run out by mid-1974. That summer, Martin and Chip started up a new publishing venture, housed literally around the corner from Marvel's Madison Avenue offices. The company would publish a variety of magazines, as well as color and black-and-white comics. The comics part of the company would go head-to-head with Marvel and DC and everyone else. The company was called Atlas Comics — also known as Atlas/Seaboard — appropriating the name of Martin's '50s distribution company.

Mid-1974, however, was not a good time to be starting a new comics enterprise. It was as if Martin Goodman, the shrewd businessman, who had sold out at just the right moment before the comics market had started to stumble, had lost his golden touch or was perhaps simply blinded by anger.

In the midst of a comic book circulation crisis, and a questionable national economy, the man who had played and won circulation and distribution wars since the 1930s, who

449

had ridden the zeitgeist along with Stan Lee (and before that with Funnies Inc. and Simon and Kirby), who seemed to always know when to zig and when to zag, who had known exactly the right time at which to sell Marvel . . .

It was then that *that* Martin Goodman decided to take a nap.

The Martin Goodman that chose to start an all-new comic book company seemed to have been instead the guy who had made one uncharacteristically poor decision in 1957 when he decided to stop doing his own distribution and signed on with the soon-to-be-bankrupt American News, which led to his nearly going out of business.

The Martin Goodman that was now starting a new comic book company for himself and Chip seemed to be carelessly running on spite and anger, looking for payback for something that he had failed to protect himself from in the first place.

The new Atlas offered significantly higher rates to writers and artists, as well as perks such as the return of artwork to its creators and participation in licensing revenues. This strategy did indeed make Atlas appealing to a number of prominent creators, but it couldn't increase the size of the comics-buying audience.

Multiple factors unrelated to the quality of the line's contents (many fans recall Atlas's

450

output fondly) seemed to almost guarantee Atlas Comics would not succeed. The question was not *whether* the Goodmans' new comics entity would fail. The question was, when it did, would it take the rest of the precariously perched comic book industry down with it?

451

16
THE CHAOS AND THE KING

It's like Nazi Germany and the Allies in World War Two.
— Letter from Stan Lee to Marvel's freelancers, 1974

Comics publishers' ownership of all rights to the stories and artwork produced by their creative staffs — including owning the actual art boards — was established early in the industry's history. Some creators maintained a degree of participation in their creations — most notably Bob Kane with Batman and William Moulton Marston with Wonder Woman — but it was never clear (since the contracts were kept confidential) what those deals were exactly, and they were the exceptions, not the rule.

Jerry Siegel and Joe Shuster, who had famously sold all rights to their brainchild, Superman, for $130, were at first well paid for producing stories featuring the character but, after not too long, were cut off from any part of their creation's massive revenues.

Their fate, especially, was seen as a cautionary tale by comics creators:

Don't let what happened to Jerry and Joe happen to you!

Nonetheless, the majority of comic book writers and artists of Jerry and Joe's era would indeed continue to sell the rights to their characters and stories to publishers without much attempt at negotiation. The creators were Depression-era young people, and the idea that someone would pay them *today* was what was important to them. Thoughts of possible big-time payouts for versions of their work in other media were some kind of pipe dream compared to the check they'd get *right now* for work they did the night before. But as Stan Lee had pointed out on that 1971 National Cartoonists Society panel, those conventions of company ownership, with no creator participation, were problematic, to say the least. *Onerous* might be a more appropriate term.

In the 1970s, younger writers and artists — baby boomers — were coming into the business. Though they, too, agreed to the conditions for receiving assignments, they were warier about them, many looking for ways around them. They had seen the fates of the elders in the business: if not early death, then a life of scrambling for assignments and being subject to editorial whims and demands. They saw the example of the underground

453

comix movement, where creators owned their material, as a model for an alternative approach. True, there wasn't as good a guaranteed page rate in the undergrounds as that offered by the mainstream — always useful when it came to paying for rent and food — but the potential upside was much greater. Underground cartoonists owned their creations and their artwork and made money on reprint editions of their work and licensed items based on their creations. No one owned Mr. Natural but his creator, Robert Crumb. Mister Miracle — who no one denied was created by Jack Kirby — was owned by DC Comics, even as they ballyhooed all over that *Kirby was there!*

One of the publishers the boomer creators were wary of, naturally, was Martin Goodman, who, while capable of generosity when he owned Marvel — loaning an artist money that he knew would never be repaid for a medical emergency, giving large holiday bonuses, allowing his staffers to moonlight as freelancers for his publications — nonetheless was also, before he sold the company, fiercely protective of his ownership of the Marvel characters. Even his cousin Stan Lee, cocreator of many of those characters, owned no rights to or interest in them.

So it was not without some irony that Goodman was now, through Atlas, offering various perks, including an interest in licensing revenues generated by any characters they created, to the freelancers he was seeking to poach from Marvel and DC. Goodman was now positioning himself as the freelancers' friend. And as long as his checks cleared, he was.

Stan Lee had been corresponding with underground writer/artist/publisher Denis Kitchen since 1969. He had tried to get Kitchen to edit some underground-style material for Marvel for a while, but it wasn't until 1974 when — battered by a weak economy, personal need for money, and a Supreme Court ruling that jeopardized underground distribution — Kitchen agreed to undertake a joint venture with Marvel: *Comix Book.*

An anthology title in magazine format — hence, not subject to the Comics Code — *Comix Book* would appear in late '74 and last for only three Marvel-published issues. (Kitchen himself published issues #4 and #5.) Lee, ambivalent about the content — not as extreme as the most cutting-edge undergrounds but more adventurous than the Code-approved Marvels — but eager to grab some underground "hipness," credited himself as "instigator." ("Call me 'instigator,' so if you get in trouble, I can say, 'I'm not responsible, all I did was instigate it.' But if it's a hit, then I can say, 'Hey, I *instigated* it!' ") While unable to get the underground's

455

biggest catch, Crumb, for the magazine, Kitchen *was* able to enlist numerous underground headliners — including Art Spiegelman, Justin Green, Trina Robbins, and Kim Deitch — eager for the exposure that publication by Marvel could bring, as well as the payment of a hundred dollars per page — 300 percent more than standard underground page rate. In addition, Kitchen had negotiated an arrangement for his artists whereby they would receive their artwork back (still not common in the mainstream) — so they could sell it in the emerging original-art market — and would retain ownership of the material they had published in the magazine.

The experiment was canceled after three issues by Lee. While sales weren't strong, another significant reason for axing it, according to Kitchen, was the jealousy the mere existence of *Comix Book* engendered among Marvel's regular artists, who didn't own any copyrights in *their* material and *didn't* get their original art back. Still, the idea was now planted that Marvel (and, by extension, other companies) could, if they chose, make arrangements outside the usual work-for-hire agreements.[1]

So when the Goodmans started the new Atlas/Seaboard in 1974, the idea of not just more money up front, but ownership of, or participation in, revenues generated by the material produced by the artist, was in the

456

air. Goodman took advantage of that. Numerous high-profile creators, including Howard Chaykin, Archie Goodwin, Neal Adams, and even Steve Ditko, decided to give the new line a try.

While Martin and Chip were the executives running Atlas, they enlisted a former Warren editor, Jeff Rovin, and, interestingly, Lee's brother, Larry (also, of course, the Goodmans' cousin) to edit their titles, which included color comics that would be approved by the Comics Code, as well as black-and-white, non-Code horror comics, a crossword puzzle magazine, and other publications. It would be a sort of mini Magazine Management.

At DC, Carmine Infantino's response to Atlas's challenge was to offer many of the same perks Atlas was offering — but only to creators who agreed to work *exclusively* for DC.

Stan Lee decided to address the Atlas challenge head-on. In a letter to Marvel's freelancers, he wrote:

Unfortunately, the fact that we're big, the fact that we're solidly financed, and the fact that we're ethically responsible actually acts against us. It's like Nazi Germany and the Allies in World War Two. Hitler, being a dictator and having no one to answer to,

457

could do as he wished whenever the mood struck him, and could make the most extravagant promises to his captive people, while being completely heedless to the consequences. . . . Marvel, like the Allies, simply cannot counterreact with impetuous pie-in-the-sky offers and promises.

After comparing his cousin's company to Nazi Germany, Lee then proceeded to remind the freelancers that Marvel provided health and life insurance for creators who did most of their work for the company, and that he was working on rate raises and bonus plans for them. He also noted that "years ago, when I wanted to return original artwork to the artists, one of the very people in the field who is now making such extravagant offers was the very one who refused to allow me to do so!"

He concluded by saying:

Marvel has never lied to you. Marvel never will. Stay with us. You won't regret it.[2]

Goodman had instructed his editors to imitate Marvel's look and feel in the Atlas comics, and indeed, there was a surface resemblance. But he couldn't catch the same lightning in another bottle. Despite the hard work of Lieber and Rovin and their creative teams, the Brute couldn't compete with the

458

Hulk, and Wulf the Barbarian was no match for Conan. By mid-1975, Atlas had closed its doors. All was forgiven by Lee as far as the staffers and freelancers who had gone to Atlas, including Lieber, who would soon have a staff editorial job at Marvel.

Martin Goodman retired to Florida. He and Lee would rarely, if ever, speak again. Chip Goodman acquired men's magazine *Swank* and, with that and a lineup of other magazines, became a successful publisher until his untimely death from pneumonia in 1996 at age fifty-five.[3] Former Marvel and Cadence executive Joseph Calamari observed that Chip had been lining up his roster of magazines even before Atlas came into being.[4] So it's likely that Atlas Comics was just a part of a larger, long-range plan by the Goodmans, a symbolic nose-thumbing at Lee and Cadence, but not the entirety of their plans to continue their publishing dynasty.

As if there hadn't been enough jolts to the industry in general and Marvel in particular, the small, incestuous nature of the comic book business again caused a serious problem. In mid-1974, just as the conflict with the Goodmans was beginning, Lee found out that a freelance artist had lied to him about his DC rate in order to negotiate a higher one at Marvel. Lee then had another lunch with Infantino, where the two agreed to share

459

information about what they were paying their freelancers.

Roy Thomas, having served as editor for two years, overstressed by his job — and annoyed that Lee had reneged on (or just forgotten about) a promise of a job to Roy's then wife — was appalled when he heard about the arrangement between Lee and Infantino, accusing Lee of engaging in collusion. Thomas resigned, and Marvel was now without an editor. Over the next three years, Marvel would have four editors.[5]

Paradoxically, while superhero comics sales were shrinking, the idea of the superhero as an American pop culture icon was something that had never ceased to be of some level of interest in Hollywood. The 1966–68 *Batman* TV series had shown that there was interest in such characters, as did the *Wonder Woman* 1974 TV movie and 1975 TV series, wherein Cathy Lee Crosby and Lynda Carter, respectively, embodied DC's Amazon heroine. Heroes whose bigger-than-life qualities intersected with superheroes — such as James Bond and the Six Million Dollar Man — had never gone out of fashion. A live-action *Shazam!* TV series — featuring the original Fawcett Captain Marvel — was a hit on Saturday morning kids' TV.

There was even a heroic space opera–style property called "The Star Wars" that *Ameri-*

460

can Graffiti director George Lucas was trying to convince Marvel to publish as a comic book prelude to the film — which was still in the planning stages — that bore a stylistic and thematic similarity to Marvel's and DC's comics, especially those that Jack Kirby worked on. But the common wisdom was that science-fiction comics didn't sell, and so Lee declined the offer. Nonetheless, Hollywood always seemed to have at least some interest in superheroes.

And in the first half of 1975, two former coworkers of Lee's were working on documents that would heighten that interest and would impact on his life and career.

To begin with, on behalf of producers Alexander and Ilya Salkind, Mario Puzo — after a few other writers had been tried — was writing a draft of a screenplay for a *Superman* live-action movie. Puzo had been a regular writer for Martin Goodman's men's "sweat" magazines, but when he'd tried his hand at writing comics for Lee, he found it too much work for too little money and decided it wasn't worth his time. Now, with his bestselling 1969 *Godfather* novel and two blockbuster *Godfather* movies on his résumé, Puzo had become a bankable name that, it was felt, could help get the film made.[6]

Meanwhile, former Marvel proofreader — and cocreator of Superman — Jerry Siegel was writing a lengthy press release that

461

started this way:

> I, Jerry Siegel, the co-originator of Superman, put a curse on the *Superman* movie! I hope it super-bombs. I hope loyal Superman fans stay away from it in droves. I hope the whole world, becoming aware of the stench that surrounds *Superman,* will avoid the movie like a plague.
>
> Why am I putting this curse on a movie based on my creation of Superman?
>
> Because cartoonist Joe Shuster and I, who co-originated Superman together, will not get one cent from the Superman super-movie deal. . . .
>
> Joe is partially blind. My health is not good. We are both 61 years old. Most of our lives, during Superman's great success, has been spent in want.

With support from popular artist Neal Adams and former Batman (and Timely) artist Jerry Robinson — both successful commercial artists, neither of whom depended on comic books to make a living — Siegel and Shuster were launching an offensive to try to get some justice — money of course, but also creator credit — from DC and parent company Warner Communications.[7]

Although independent of each other, Puzo's and Siegel's Superman-focused documents would end up extremely consequential

462

to the futures of comics creators, superheroes, and, indirectly, Stan Lee.

By 1974, Jack Kirby was more than a little dissatisfied.

The sales on his Fourth World titles, while reasonably good, were not as spectacular as DC had hoped. Infantino had decided to pull the plug on all of them after less than a year, except for *Mister Miracle.* Kirby's vision of a sprawling, years-long saga was dead. His dream had been to launch series after series, then hand them off to others to execute, while he supervised the titles and came up with new ones. Instead, he was now relegated to doing what he'd hoped to have moved beyond: piecework. True, he still edited his own titles, but the autonomy he'd imagined would be his at National — in effect, a Kirby-branded imprint that he would direct — was a dream that clearly wasn't going to come true.

Infantino instructed Kirby to come up with titles unrelated to the Fourth World to replace the ones that had been chopped and to keep him on target with his contractual obliga-tions. Kirby came up with *OMAC, The Demon,* and *Kamandi,* all interesting concepts, all done well, and even with some apparent enthusiasm. But it wasn't what he imagined he'd be doing. If all he'd wanted was to pump out work-for-hire comics, he could have stayed at Marvel, where Stan Lee was, near the end of Kirby's time there, pretty much giving him autonomy — and credit — anyway.

Jack Kirby was not happy, and his contract with DC was expiring soon. There seemed to be only one logical place for him to go — but he had pretty much burned that bridge. And yet, perhaps the bridge wasn't as charred as it seemed. "If only Jack wouldn't hang up on me," Stan Lee had been reported to say, "I'm sure something could be worked out."[8]

In the August 1975 Bullpen Bulletins, seemingly tagged on just before the end of the page, was a notice that read:

ITEM! This item is just a sneaky way of telling you that next month, JACK "King" KIRBY's newest earth-shaker will be hitting the stands! And we'll give you the full lowdown on our newest hit in our next Bulletin!

Apparently, something had indeed been worked out, or was in the process of being worked out. According to Kirby's colleague Mark Evanier, Kirby was very reluctant to return to Marvel, hoping things would improve at DC. Kirby might even have encouraged Lee to jump the gun on the announcement of his return. As Evanier recalled, "Marvel even leaked it [the news Kirby had

464

agreed to come back] . . . and Kirby was hoping that would pressure DC into giving him a better contract, and when it was apparent they wouldn't, he went back [to Marvel]."[9]

So it wasn't until the *December* Bulletins that Kirby's return was brought up again and explained. At that point, the announcement was given the attention it warranted as the sole subject of a lengthy Stan's Soapbox:

> This month's news is too big to hold off for another minute! Jack Kirby is back! Yep, that's right! Ol' King Kirby (and don't forget, it was at Marvel that he got that sobriquet) has returned to the bosom of the blushin' Bullpen!

After listing Kirby's first decided-on assignments — a one-shot adaptation of the movie *2001: A Space Odyssey* and taking over the *Captain America* series — Lee continued, speaking of the latter:

> Jack'll be writing and drawing the whole magilla by his lonesome. . . . But, as soon as Jack and I get a breather, and when you least expect it, watch for a gigantic special edition of — you guessed it — the SILVER SURFER!

The column then backtracked in time to the previous spring, when Marvel had held

465

its own branded convention at the Commodore Hotel in Manhattan. Lee related an event that took place on March 24, 1975, the last day of the three-day show:

> I mentioned that I had a special announcement. . . . As I started talking about Jack's return . . . everyone's head started to snap around as Kirby himself came waltzin' down the aisle to join us on the rostrum! You can imagine how it felt clownin' around with the co-creator of most of Marvel's greatest strips once more.

At that panel, after receiving a standing ovation, Kirby assured the audience that "whatever I do at Marvel, I can assure you that it'll electrocute you in the mind!"[10]

Apart from Kirby's ambivalence, perhaps Lee had been diverted from following up on the first "Kirby returns" announcement when he'd promised he would by new projects he was running, such as Magazine Management's *Nostalgia Illustrated* magazine and the sequel to *Origins of Marvel Comics* he was writing for Simon & Schuster. He could even have been distracted by two joint publications with Infantino's DC, the first the rival companies had ever undertaken. One was a comics adaptation of the classic 1939 *Wizard of Oz* film. The other was *Superman vs. the*

466

Amazing Spider-Man. Both were thick, tabloid-size comics and sold quite well.

Lee could even have been distracted by the fact that Len Wein had quit as editor after less than a year, as had his successor, Marv Wolfman. And Wolfman's successor, Gerry Conway — who was actually now writing the *Superman-Spider-Man* crossover — had resigned after only a month. Clearly, the job had become too much for one person. Consummate professional Archie Goodwin had taken on the job — now titled "editor in chief" — but some way had to be found to make the position less daunting.

Perhaps another big reason that Lee had delayed the Kirby announcement was that he was distracted by an internal event at Marvel that was not just challenging but that also had the potential to "electrocute you in the mind."

It turned out that Marvel and Magazine Management president Al Landau had been falsifying the companies' financial statements in order to make it appear that his regime was impressively profitable. In fact, his Cadence division had *lost* $2 million in the first half of 1975 alone. When this was discovered, Landau was fired. His replacement was publishing veteran Jim Galton, whose mandate was to turn things around within two years — or else there might be no more Marvel Comics.[11]

467

In addition to trying to increase sales on what they could and canceling weak-performing titles, Lee and Galton decided that Marvel needed to focus its attention on Hollywood and its potential to increase the company's revenues through licensing Marvel's properties for movies and TV *and* by acquiring licenses to make comics from popular media properties. In keeping with this new company emphasis, as well as with his own infatuation with show business, Lee was quite hands-on with two other new Magazine Management titles: *Film International* (which was a tad risqué) and *Celebrity,* the latter of which expended a fair number of pages on the celebrity known as Stan Lee.

This was not just a matter of ego. The comics business was in trouble again. Now was the time for Lee to go, once more, into survival mode, both for Marvel / Magazine Management *and* himself.

To add to the urgency, if Lee had imagined that Carmine Infantino might make room for him at National, as the two had at least once discussed, or that that possibility would be a useful bargaining chip if his position at Marvel was endangered, that pipe dream was abruptly ended.[12]

Carmine Infantino was terminated by DC in January 1976.

468

17
RETURNS AND DEPARTURES

I honestly think the reason I'm back is because I wanted to be back. I'm home. And being among the people of Marvel is good ground to be on. They're good people.

— Jack Kirby, "Kirby Speaks,"
FOOM #11, September 1975

Fortunately for Stan Lee, whatever Marvel was becoming in 1976, it seemed that the company still deemed it crucial that he remain a significant part of the picture.

And that picture included not just Jack Kirby — back at Marvel Comics, where he (twice) swore he'd never return. It now included the guy who'd seduced Kirby away in 1970. Yes, Carmine Infantino was back in the trenches as a freelance artist — not at DC, where, aside from being the boss, he'd also done his most well-known work — but at *Marvel,* where he'd last worked in the 1950s.

At the same time, a new set of laws called the Copyright Act of 1976 was working its

469

way through Congress. The act, which would be signed by President Gerald Ford on October 19, would potentially open the floodgates for comic book creators (and those in other fields, as well) to claim ownership of the freelance work they'd done for media corporations. But the act would not go into effect until 1978, so no one, at the time of the its signing, seemed to be giving it much thought.

As for Stan Lee, with the dependable Archie Goodwin installed as editor in chief, he was able to pay more attention to promoting Marvel (and Stan Lee), which included extending its reach in Hollywood, although he still showed up regularly at the company's Madison Avenue offices to make global decisions affecting editing and publishing.

Nonetheless, he and company president Jim Galton had embarked on their mission to save Marvel by licensing its characters as material for movies and TV shows. And indeed, there would be media successes, including, especially, the Lou Ferrigno-Bill Bixby–starring *Incredible Hulk* series, as well as the less successful Nicholas Hammond–starring *Spider-Man* series, and (in 1978) a *Fantastic Four* Saturday morning animated series, on which Lee would team with Roy Thomas to write scripts for which Jack Kirby would do storyboards.

Marvel's mid/late '70s comics lineup would

change in makeup — always with a core of superheroes — but with horror and monster titles, too, as well as martial arts–related titles, and a line of black-and-white magazines — not beholden, for a variety of reasons, to the Comics Code — indeed emulating the success of Warren Publishing's output. And there was always room for idiosyncratic comics, especially those with a Hollywood or show business angle, notably — harking back to the days when Timely/Atlas published TV and radio tie-ins — adaptations of other companies' movie and TV properties. The profusion of adaptations existed largely thanks to one decision that publisher Lee was convinced to go back on: *Star Wars.*

Lee had rejected "The Star Wars" as a property to adapt in 1975, going with his experience-born belief that science-fiction comics just didn't sell. But *Star Wars* creator George Lucas and the film's publicity director, Charles Lippincott, didn't give up. They felt that having a comic out before their movie was released would be great for building interest in the film. They approached Roy Thomas, by then a freelance writer and editor for Marvel, who at first — given Lee's initial declining of the project — said there was nothing he could do. But upon being shown stills and the script for the production-in-progress, Thomas realized that *Star Wars* wasn't hard science fiction but more of a "space opera" — a story that depended more on characterization, humor, and emotion than on real science. In other words, it was very similar to a Marvel comic. Thomas's enthusiasm — and the fact that Lucas would be giving the comics rights to Marvel for free; no upfront licensing fee was required — convinced Lee and Galton to green-light the comics adaptation, which debuted several months before the *Star Wars* movie opened.[1]

The *Star Wars* comic, by Roy Thomas and Howard Chaykin, which took six issues to adapt the movie, and then continued as an ongoing series with new, Lucasfilm-approved stories, was a massive hit. It's often credited with saving Marvel, if not from extinction, then from severe cutbacks. Its success led Marvel to take on many more licensed properties — *Shogun Warriors, Micronauts,* and so on.

A notable licensed property Lee was convinced to take on — by writer Steve Gerber — was the transformation of the then-new band KISS into superheroes with their own one-shot, magazine-format comic, which was promoted as having band members' *blood* mixed into the printer's ink, so everyone buying a copy would get at least a few molecules of authentic KISS blood. (This was, obviously, well before the AIDS epidemic.) Although their music was not, to say the least, his style, Lee attended a KISS concert

472

and even accompanied the band to the Buffalo, New York, printing plant where their blood was extracted and mixed into the ink used in printing the magazine. (Unconfirmed is a rumor that the blood-infused ink was accidentally used on an issue of *Sports Illustrated,* and not on the KISS comic.) The KISS comic was a huge seller.[2]

The *Star Wars* comic series was taken over with issue #11, which appeared in early 1978, by Archie Goodwin as writer and Infantino as penciler. The former DC publisher was now firmly ensconced as a regular Marvel artist, something he hadn't been for twenty years. He would continue drawing *Star Wars* — with some breaks — through 1982, as well as a number of other Marvel series.

In 1976, Lee and Romita Sr. started work on a *Spider-Man* syndicated strip, which debuted on January 3, 1977. While Lee's other '70s syndicated ventures, including 1976's soap opera spoof, *The Virtue of Vera Valiant* (when soap satire *Mary Hartman, Mary Hartman* was hot on TV) and the photo-funny-format *Says Who!,* hadn't been especially successful,[3] the *Spider-Man* strip proved popular and durable and was published into 2019. Larry Lieber would have the longest stint drawing it, penciling (and sometimes inking) the daily episodes from 1986 through late 2018.

Before getting that assignment, but after the Atlas/Seaboard imbroglio, Lieber had returned to Marvel, this time on staff, as the editor of the company's British division, which had offices in New York, as well as in London. Lieber was overseeing not just reprint material and new covers prepared in New York for publication in the UK, but also the development of a new character called, appropriately, Captain Britain. Interestingly, Lee himself took a great interest in the British Marvels — which were published on a weekly schedule — perhaps because he had a British wife, or perhaps because, unlike many other Marvel foreign editions, these were in *English*! (Neil Tennant, later to be a member of the popular band the Pet Shop Boys, worked as an assistant editor in Marvel's London office during this period. This author did the same in the New York office, having started out his comics career in the British department in July 1977.)

And then there was Kirby.

Jack Kirby, back at Marvel, was working on numerous projects, left — as a condition of his being there at all — on his own, writing, penciling, and editing his titles, choosing his own inkers, and not obligated to tie his stories into Marvel continuity, although they technically took place in the shared Marvel universe.[4]

In his *The Eternals* series, for instance — about alien space gods who have come to Earth (when Erich von Däniken's *Chariots of the Gods?*, about a similar topic, was popular) — this meant that there was minimal interaction between Kirby's new characters and his and Lee's old ones, who supposedly inhabited the same planet. Readers had to pretend that Kirby's characters — including a number of two-thousand-foot-tall armored entities — would not be noticed by any established characters aside from some newly-created S.H.I.E.L.D. agents. His *Captain America and the Falcon* series made no note of the previous run of issues, and his *Black Panther* likewise made no reference to the Panther series that had recently been running.

Whether Kirby's series would "electrocute you in the mind" was hard to say, but they did indeed have a good number of fans, especially in the growing direct-sales market. As at DC, Kirby did things more or less the way he wanted to, but neither Marvel's staff nor the buying public seemed to know what to make of these powerful but idiosyncratic works. There were rumors that staffers were deliberately printing a higher proportion of negative letters about Kirby's titles than were actually received and were making fun of his output with nasty annotated pages of his comics pinned up on the office walls. Whether this was somehow worse than the general level of in-house smart-aleck mockery at the offices is hard to assess. According to Evanier, Kirby was getting anonymous hate mail on Marvel office stationery and felt, overall, that he was being sabotaged from within. Significantly, Lee was an advocate for Kirby's autonomy. As Evanier recalled:

Stan backed Jack a lot when Jack was an editor [of his own comics] there. He was very supportive of Jack having editorial control of his comics, and he overruled [Marvel's staff] a few times.[5]

The thing that might have attracted a significant quantity of readers — Kirby teaming with Lee on *Fantastic Four* or *Thor* — was not something Kirby was interested in. And he certainly wasn't interested in anyone else, besides himself, scripting his stories. Roy Thomas offered to do so, but Kirby would only do it if Thomas wrote a traditional full script. Kirby had no intention of plotting stories for someone else to dialogue.[6] Lee promoted Kirby's books in the Bullpen Bulletins and Soapboxes, but the fan excitement over Kirby's return never seemed to materialize as much as had been hoped.[7]

Lee was, of course, continuing to build his personal brand. In 1976, he was well known

476

enough that he found himself a product spokesman, starring in a TV commercial for Personna Double II razor blades. Standing in the Marvel bullpen, he excitedly informed viewers that "the Personna is beautifully designed. . . . Like they told me, 'There's no finer shaving system made.' I may create a whole new character: Personna Man!"[8]

The same year, posing in front of posted proofs for the *Mighty Marvel Memory Album Calendar 1977,* Lee informed magazine readers that "when you create super-heros [*sic*], people expect you to look like one. I wear Hathaway shirts." The ad identifies him as: "Stan Lee, Originator of Marvel Comics."

Also that year, Lee would appear in photo-essays in the KISS comic and was continuing to write the Simon & Schuster *Marvel Origins* book series. But he was indeed still the publisher of the comics and paid a good deal of attention to them, coming into the office five days a week, giving up his long-time schedule of three days (and weekends, of course) working at home.[9]

According to Jim Shooter, Lee would, as he had been doing all along, go over the printed comics with Goodwin, and later with Shooter himself, who was associate editor under Goodwin, pointing out mistakes that had been made to ensure that they wouldn't be made again. And no cover could go out to the printer — if Lee was available to see it before it went — without him giving it final approval. Beyond critiquing individual stories and covers, though, Lee seemed to be doing his best to avoid the Sturm und Drang of day-to-day life in the Marvel editorial trenches. To interfere would be a no-win situation, risking either seeming to undermine his head editor or possibly alienating a valuable freelancer. Staying out of things seemed like the best strategy.[10]

And there was much Sturm und Drang in Marvel editorial. The process of comics being created with little editorial control was continuing apace, simply because there weren't enough editorial staffers with the authority to vet the comics at every creative stage. (Besides Shooter as Goodwin's associate editor, there were also several assistant editors on staff, but they had no real authority to compel changes.) And yet, no apparent move to reconfigure the system seemed to be in the works. Perhaps this reflected the attitude of Cadence management — and of Lee, as well — that the future of the company lay less with the comics than with possible success in Hollywood. From that perspective, the content of the comics was less important than the revenue that could be generated through media adaptations of the company's characters or through the company adapting media properties to comics form. Potential comics sales revenues would stay about the same or keep declining, unless there was a surprise breakout property like *Star Wars.* The way to save the company — to save everyone's *jobs* — would be to achieve success in Hollywood.

At the end of 1977, Goodwin, too, realized that the editor's job was not for him — and who could blame him? Certainly not Wolfman, Wein, or Conway, who had also been unable to manage the unmanageable job of supervising some forty titles, many of which were self-edited by writers who were not obligated to take any notes or suggestions the company's editor in chief or his assistants might give. On top of all that, the EIC was expected to deal with a plethora of business considerations, which none of those who'd succeeded Lee had training or interest in.

Goodwin, regarded as one of the top writers and editors in the business, was indeed overwhelmed by the details of the business aspect of his job, as well as by the reluctance of Cadence management to expand his staff and extend his authority or do anything that would make working at Marvel more appealing to artists and writers. This was the contradiction of the era. Young comics creators, who thought of themselves as unique talents, not just cogs in a machine, were insisting on better treatment — and more creative freedom — than their predecessors had received, despite the fact that comics sales were on the decline. And yet these younger creators were the ones whose work hard-core, dedicated fans — who were buying the comics regularly — were most interested in seeing. It seemed like a riddle that couldn't be solved.

Goodwin resigned at the end of 1977 — in a move that was reportedly handled somewhat clumsily by Lee, who impulsively, if well-meaningly, announced the move earlier than he'd promised Goodwin he would — to become a freelance writer/editor (though he'd be back on staff by 1979).[11] He was replaced by Shooter, who seemed to thrive on dealing with the minutiae of the business aspects of comic book editing, as well as with matters relating to story and character. Shooter hated that some writers were serving as their own editors. He saw the company, in its present state of disarray, as being in need of a strong, centralized editorial hand. Persuading Lee and Galton of the need for more structure, he set about replicating DC's system of multiple editorial offices with an editor in chief — him — over them.

Shooter would take drastic measures to ensure the survival of Marvel's comics. In doing so, he put a lot of noses out of joint. The chaotic, freewheeling atmosphere — which had proven unable to sell enough comics — would end (which is not to say that no fun was to be had), as Shooter instilled structure and regularity to the Marvel line. When he would come down harshly on Marvel veterans — for instance, Lee's old colleague and creative partner Gene Colan — Lee would try to smooth things over, but would not overrule his chief.[12]

And there was much conflict generated when young, hip writers felt suddenly persecuted. For instance, Steve Gerber, the writer of the KISS comic, was also the cocreator of the off beat Howard the Duck character, who was starring in his own popular series. But Gerber ended up in a dispute with Marvel over ownership of the duck and would soon be gone — ironically, to the animation business, where he would eventually work with Kirby on various features, as well as on *Destroyer Duck,* a comic created to finance Gerber's legal battle against Marvel.

Besides Kirby, two of Lee's other favorite and most reliable artists, John Romita Sr. and John Buscema, were still around and busy. Unlike Kirby and Ditko, they seemed to enjoy their association with Lee and to admire and respect him, even if they did grouse about some of his decisions from time to time. With Romita, who had helped increase *Spider-Man* comics sales when he took over the art and co-plotting from Ditko, Lee was doing the ongoing *Spider-Man* daily and

Sunday syndicated newspaper strip, which, at its height, was seen in around five hundred newspapers and which long outlasted such other Marvel strips as *Howard the Duck* and *Conan the Barbarian.*[13] In addition, Romita was on staff as art director, where he shared an office with his wife, Virginia, who served as his assistant and who would become traffic manager a few years later. Their son, John V. Romita — better known as John Romita Jr., or just JR — had started drawing for Marvel in 1976 and would become one of the company's top artists.

Buscema, ensconced in his studio on Long Island, was a prolific penciler who seemed to, like Romita, understand what Lee (and subsequent editors) wanted and to give it to him. The regular penciler on titles like *The Avengers* and especially the *Conan the Barbarian* comics, Buscema ran a comic art school where Lee guest lectured. Their rapport was so good that, together, they produced the 1978 book *How to Draw Comics the Marvel Way,* followed by a video of the same name in 1986. (While it's clear from their awkwardness on the video that neither Lee nor Buscema were professional actors, their stiff performances were somehow endearing.) The book version, still in print after forty years, is considered one of the standard texts on how to draw superheroes.

■ ■ ■

During this period, Lee was also consulting on the live-action *Spider-Man* and *Hulk* TV series, although frustrated that the producers didn't take many of his notes. While he felt the Bill Bixby/Lou Ferrigno *Hulk* series generally took an intelligent approach to the character, he was less fond of the *Spider-Man* series. As he said in a 1978 interview with *SunStorm* magazine:

> The people writing the *Spider-Man* show keep writing one bad script after another. So we're either going to have to drop the show or go with bad scripts — I don't know which is worse. The writers are all a bunch of hacks — the best of them — used to writing TV series with interchangeable plots. The problem is, our characters need specialized plots — they're unique.[14]

Still based in New York, Lee was spending more and more time in Los Angeles. As had been true from 1961 through the end of his life in 2018, the name *Stan Lee* could open doors and get meetings, and that is what he spent the second half of the '70s doing.

When Kirby's contract was approaching its end (it would expire in 1978), he was offered a renewal, but one that contained a clause saying he would never claim ownership of any of the characters he'd worked on.[15] That was unacceptable to Kirby, who elected to let the contract lapse — but not before one last hurrah with Lee.

Lee had signed a contract with Simon & Schuster to do a certain number of books. Kirby had signed a contract with Marvel to do a certain number of pages. To fulfill *both* obligations, it was decided that they would work together — as Lee had declared in the December 1975 Soapbox — on a "gigantic special edition of — you guessed it — THE SILVER SURFER!"

When asked, in Marvel's self-published fan magazine, *FOOM* #11 (dated September 1975), if he was working on the Surfer project, Kirby replied, "No. I haven't heard from Stan about it. . . . If SILVER SURFER comes up I'm sure Stan will discuss it with me and we'll work it out. I haven't heard a thing yet." Lee himself mentioned the project again in an interview with David Anthony Kraft (probably done in late 1976) printed in *FOOM* #17 (dated March 1977). And by January 1977, the duo was, indeed, working together — at Kirby's L.A. home — on the Silver Surfer project. This wasn't going to be just a single twenty-page story or even a forty-page story in a thicker-format annual. This was going to be a *hundred-page* Surfer saga, published in book format. It was called

The Silver Surfer: The Ultimate Cosmic Experience! on the cover, and simply *The Silver Surfer* in the book itself. But, especially since it was published in 1978, the same year as Will Eisner's groundbreaking *A Contract with God* graphic novel, it has come to be known as *The Silver Surfer Graphic Novel*.

In the book's preface, Lee wrote:

> After all these years, Jolly Jack and I actually managed to complete the one book we've always been threatening to foist upon a stunned and startled public . . . the Silver Surfer seems to have a special meaning to us both.
>
> Ever eager for a trip out west, I bravely journeyed to Jack's idyllic aerie high in the hills of southern California. There, during a fateful visit, we hammered out the main elements of the phantasmagoric parable soon to unfold before your bedazzled eyes.[16]

The story involved Galactus trying to convince — really *strong-arm* — the Silver Surfer to once again become his herald. Like the rest of the work Kirby did in this period at Marvel, the story stood outside regular Marvel continuity. In fact, part of it told of the initial arrival of Galactus on Earth, but without the presence of the Fantastic Four — so prominent in the original 1966 telling — anywhere in the story. Even more oddly, the copyright on the book is not to Marvel but to Stan Lee and Jack Kirby. Regarding these details, Evanier recalled:

The Silver Surfer had been optioned for a movie, but the option did not include the Fantastic Four, so it wasn't really possible to do the Galactus Trilogy. So they [the producers] tried to come up with a story line for a *Silver Surfer* movie . . . and they couldn't come up with a plot.

So at one point [producer Lee Kramer] went to Stan and said, "Why don't you and Jack come up with a plot?" Stan went to Jack and suggested the two of them work up a pitch for a story. But Jack thought, "Hey, Hollywood writers get paid well. Why don't they hire *us* to write the movie?"

Stan couldn't make that happen, though. So the compromise was — Stan came up with this idea — he was doing those Simon & Schuster books, and one of the publishers had said to him, "Hey, why don't we do an original story?" So he went to Jack and said, "Look, why don't we do a Silver Surfer graphic novel that could be the plot for the movie? I can arrange it so that we hold the copyright . . . so we get paid for doing the story as the graphic novel, and if they want it for the movie, they have to buy it from us at movie industry prices."

That sounded good to Jack, because he

wanted to get out of Marvel at that point, and he had to use up the [contractually obligated] pages anyway. . . . Jack wrote an outline, which he registered with the Writer's Guild. . . . Jack's the one who put it on paper . . . he wrote an outline of the plot and then wrote [on separate typed pages] what he would otherwise have put in the margin notes [of the art]. But nobody wanted to turn it into a movie, and that was the end of [Stan and Jack doing the movie].[17]

The correspondence, found at Lee's University of Wyoming archives, regarding the Silver Surfer graphic novel is probably the most complete view we have of the Lee-Kirby working process. In a personal letter to Kirby a few weeks after their January meeting, Lee wrote:

Just a line to tell you how much I enjoyed seeing you in Los Angeles. I am sorry we didn't have more time to spend together, but at least we did have a chance to talk awhile. I hope everything we discussed is clear and agreeable with you and that all will work out well. Keep rolling along on the SURFER — it is bound to be the "All the President's Men" of 1977![18]

The correspondence gives a sense of the nuts and bolts of how the story was constructed. Taking off from their California conference, Kirby proceeded to break the story down into pages and panels, which he submitted to Lee in batches, and he accompanied the art with typed-out notes — the equivalent of the margin notes he used to provide Lee with during their earlier collaborations. It was as if Kirby wanted to be sure that his thoughts on the pages literally could not be erased.

But even that documentation seems open to interpretation.

For instance, in a letter dated January 24, 1977, Kirby spent four typed pages describing for Lee an overview of the plot to the graphic novel. The letter opened:

Stanley,
Just in case a little reiteration is needed in view of our discussion, I believe that the over-riding points of the story lie in the Galactus-Surfer relationship and our own helter-skelter position in the universe. It's the Surfer's story, of course, and his experience should be dominant (his love story — his life among Earth people — his decisions). However, I believe the reader will clearly be intrigued by the larger question of his own vulnerability in the scheme of things.

The rest of the letter veers between discussing specific images and overall themes. But are these images and themes Kirby came up with and is unveiling for Lee, or are they "reiteration in view of our discussion"?

Kirby's cover letter for a batch of pages, dated March 14, 1977, read:

Stanley,
This is the second batch of continuity for the "Surfer" book. If you can overlook an occasional typing error, you'll find the pages explained in what I feel is the proper perspective in consideration of realistic rendering and dramatic value. Of course, it's all done within areas we discussed and I hope it comes across. I've also tried to cover all loose ends and set the stage for the Surfer's life among the humans.[19]

One can read whatever one wants into the correspondence and notes on file regarding the Surfer book. Clearly, both men agree that they did indeed talk out the story to some degree, certainly in more detail than they seemed to in the last couple of years of their previous collaborations. Yet, based on his notes (and on Evanier's recollections), Kirby seemed to again be doing the plotting details mostly on his own. He provided panel-by-panel art descriptions, along with some dialogue suggestions. But as in their '60s collaborations, there weren't dialogue suggestions for every panel, and the ones that are there were quite rough.

For instance, Kirby's notes for the three-panel page 6 read:

Page Six

Panel One — The Surfer glides in among the towering buildings. The noises from the streets below reach him.

Panel Two — As he swoops lower, the Surfer catches his first sight of humans. There are faces in the windows, all showing reaction to this stranger among them.

Panel Three — Then, at street level, the Surfer finds himself involved with the life and noise of the city.

For the same page, Lee's script accompanying the art was this:

PAGE 6

1. SS [Silver Surfer]: There are primitive structures, simple dwellings, and basic machines of every sort!

SS: It is an early culture, groping and stumbling its way towards a dimly-sensed

490

maturity!

2. SS: Yet, the very AIR seems to throb with a sense of LIFE! There is ENERGY here — there is SPIRIT — there is VITALITY such as I have never known!

SS: The sudden sight of me causes PANIC in the streets!

SS: They have yet to learn — only the SAVAGE fears what he does not understand![20]

Knowing he was on the way out the door, Kirby's attitude in the Surfer correspondence was friendly and collegial (although calling Lee "Stanley" can be seen as, simultaneously, a term of endearment as well as a way of reminding the publisher that he was once the *pisher* who was not then Kirby's boss, "Stan," but his flunky and the boss's relative, "Stanley").

Without too much of a stretch, the story can be looked at — whether the creators were aware of it or not — as a metaphor for Kirby's last go-round at Marvel. The company — and Lee? — could be seen as Galactus, devouring whatever it wants, including the embodiment of compromised innocence that is the Surfer (who can be seen as Kirby). And — as in the four-part *Fantastic Four*

491

"Worlds Within Worlds" story where the Surfer rejoined Galactus — here, too, after deluding himself into thinking he could be free of Galactus and still possess a clear conscience, the Surfer realizes that his fate is with Galactus, if only so that he might protect the universe from his master's depredations. And despite his saying in the *FOOM* interview that "the reason I'm back is that I wanted to be back," Kirby's return to Marvel was, in reality, made with great reluctance, as was the Surfer's return to Galactus.

The story seemed to say, essentially, that Galactus and the Surfer are fated to be together — like Kirby and Lee/Marvel? But was the message *Lee's,* ennobling the Surfer's decision to pragmatically ally with the predatory giant? Was the message Kirby's — a warning of a fate to be avoided, a fate he might have, at least temporarily, succumbed to?

Was it wishful thinking on Lee's part, maneuvering Kirby toward cocreating a story about idealism compromising with overwhelming power, power that is beyond good and evil? Was it Lee's way of trying to get Kirby to see that sticking around with him and Marvel was all for the greater good? *You tried DC, and that didn't work out so well, did it?*

One thing seems certain: both men saw the Silver Surfer as more than just a vehicle for making action-filled comic book stories with no message that they wanted to convey. So in this, their final combined statement on the character, which creator's message — whatever that message is — would dominate? While Lee would, as writer and publisher, have the literal final word, Kirby's visual storytelling had a power above and beyond words. Ultimately, each reader would have to determine for him- or herself what message the story contained.

On his way out the door the following year (1978), there would be one last chance for Kirby to both honor and tweak Lee. Roy Thomas was freelance-editing a series called *What If?,* whose concept was what it sounded like: depicting alternative outcomes to significant Marvel stories. The premise provided to Kirby by Thomas for issue #11 (dated October 1978) was "What If . . . the Original Marvel Bullpen Had Become the Fantastic Four?"

The story was to depict Lee, Kirby, Thomas, and Flo Steinberg as having become the FF at the time of the team's creation. When Kirby's pencils came in, though, Kirby had chosen to replace the Roy Thomas of the story — who in it becomes the Human Torch — with Sol Brodsky (who, by '78, was a Marvel VP).[21] Irked that Kirby had deleted him from the story, Thomas realized that it

493

actually did make more sense to have it be Brodsky, who was one of the original bullpen, whereas Thomas was not.[22] Nonetheless, Thomas gave the scripting of the story, which he originally intended to dialogue himself, to Kirby.

While Kirby was, in the story's dialogue and captions, reasonably complimentary toward Lee — who, in the story, became team leader Mr. Fantastic — Kirby would come to believe that Thomas — or someone — had altered the dialogue he'd written for Sol, Flo, and Stan, to make it seem more "natural," but had left the Thing — the avatar Kirby had assumed for himself in the story — speaking in a more uneducated vernacular, making him seem cruder than the others. Thomas has no recollection of changing Kirby's script, although he does recall Lee insisting that every reference to him as *Stanley* be changed to *Stan.*[23] Even this departing Kirby story, intended as a nostalgic memento, couldn't go out the door without conflict.

After the *What If?* story, and without the drama of 1970, Jack Kirby left Marvel Comics to go into animation, including working on storyboards for the DePatie-Freleng studio's *Fantastic Four* series (on which Lee was a producer).[24] Marvel was no longer the threadbare skeleton of a company Kirby had rejoined in the late '50s, and it wasn't even the chaotic free-for-all to which he had again returned in 1975. The company for which his presence and sensibilities had been so key had grown into something else. Kirby and Lee (and Ditko) had been the right people at the right place at the right time in 1961. Now, in 1978, they were two among dozens of Marvel creators and — though they had established the foundations of the company's present and future successes — were not perceived as creators with commercial heat. The entity they had birthed had in many ways outgrown them.

But the public taste for the types of stories they did seemed, if anything, stronger than ever. The *Star Wars* comics and the comics that Marvel was making from other licensed properties — *Rom: SpaceKnight, Battlestar Galactica, Micronauts, Godzilla,* and so on — were proving to be profit centers for the company. And at the end of 1978, the first *Superman* movie's great success proved that a comic book sensibility — played mostly straight — could be popular. (And there had even been something of a happy ending — if not an end to lawsuits — for Jerry Siegel and Joe Shuster. Neal Adams's, Jerry Robinson's, and others' efforts had resulted in DC granting the two aging creators modest pensions and "Superman created by" credits in the movie.) The future for people with skill sets and experience like Kirby's and Lee's seemed clearly to be in TV and movie properties, specifically in Hollywood. Kirby had already gone west. Lee would soon be there, too.

As he told reporter Ira Wolfman in a 1978 interview in *Circus* magazine: "I should have gotten out of the business [comic books] 20 years ago. I would have liked to make movies, to be a director or a screenwriter, to have a job like [TV producer] Norman Lear or [network programmer] Freddie Silverman. I'd like to be doing what I'm doing here, but in a bigger arena."[25]

According to Wolfman, the *Circus* interview had been initiated by Lee via a publicist.[26] So perhaps the Marvel publisher was using the journalist to help spread the word that Stan Lee was, more than ever, interested in, and available for, Hollywood opportunities, either for Marvel or — like his partnership with Alain Resnais — on his own behalf.

He was fifty-five years old. There was no time to waste.

496

18
GOODBYES AND HELLOS

"Jack, I love ya."

"Well, the same here, Stan."
— Conversation between Lee and Kirby
on WBAI-FM on August 28, 1987

It wasn't too long after Jack Kirby's unheralded goodbye that a somewhat more ballyhooed hello occurred at Marvel.

Steve Ditko returned.

Why? Who knows? Maybe he heard that Stan was spending most of his time on the West Coast.

In any case, Lee enthusiastically announced in the April 1979 Soapbox:

Ditko's back — and Marvel's got him! You'll be seeing his own brand of artistic magic in some of our greatest and most exciting mags, coming your way soon! . . . I feel incredibly sentimental about one of our original greats climbing aboard again, just as I felt when Jolly Jack Kirby returned to the scenes of his former glory!

(Technically, although he had not renewed his contract, Kirby was still working for Marvel, working off leftover obligations by doing storyboards for the *Fantastic Four* animated series — and he'd soon be done with that. It was all too conspicuous that he wasn't working on actual comics.)

And, indeed, Ditko *did* return with *Machine Man* #10, cover-dated August 1979. (The character was one created by Kirby in 1977.) Ditko would work for Marvel for a year — refusing to ever draw Spider-Man or Dr. Strange, even as guests in someone else's title — then disappear from the company for a while, then return again and do more or less continuous work there until 1996, along the way cocreating Squirrel Girl (who became an unlikely comic book star in the 2000s) and Speedball, a sort of Spider-Man for the 1980s. He would even come close to working with Lee again in the early '90s.

While Lee was no doubt genuinely glad to have Ditko back doing comics, his own interests were increasingly elsewhere, building Marvel's brand — and his own.

For instance, at about the same time that the "Ditko's back" announcement appeared in the Soapbox, *People* magazine ran a feature — written by Barbara Rowes — on

498

Lee and his family in its January 29, 1979, issue, entitled, "Stan Lee, Creator of Spider-Man and the Incredible Hulk, is America's Biggest Mythmaker."[1]

The article was a publicist's dream, a love letter to Lee as well as to a certain fantasy of life in a glamorous New York, one that in 1979 — during the depths of the city's '70s economic decline, just a few years after its near bankruptcy and the infamous *Daily News* headline FORD TO CITY: DROP DEAD — was an alternate reality in which Lee was perfectly cast to star.

After describing Lee dictating creative ideas into a mini-recorder at home at midnight, the article then joined him the next morning:

[Lee] proceeds along boutique-lined Third Avenue. His virile features are tawny and relatively unlined at age 56. His stomach is flat, "like iron," he brags.

As the media often did with Lee, the article misses the humorous tone accompanying his statements such as the one about his stomach being "like iron," portraying him to anyone who didn't know him as more of a braggart than a practitioner of self-deprecating comedy.

Having depicted Lee as a mythic figure of sorts (in the article, DC publisher Jenette Kahn referred to Lee as "the living superhero for the American comic industry"), author Rowes then established Marvel's bona fides:

> With upwards of $25 million a year in sales, [Marvel] is the largest and most successful business of its kind in the world . . .

She then noted that Lee spends much of his time "supervising the transition of his characters into other media."

In another common type of media shorthand that would bring out criticism of Lee, Rowes referred to Spider-Man and the Hulk (and, by implication, all of Marvel's characters) as "his characters," ignoring the existence of artist collaborators.

And then, as if the coolest guy in the world didn't already have the coolest job, the article continued:

> With so many pop groups fascinated by comic heroes these days, Stan has become the Werner Erhard of the rock world.

Erhard was the founder of the then-popular Erhard Seminars Training (EST) "self-realization" movement. In early 1979, he was well known, if controversial. Comparison to Erhard put Lee in lofty territory.

The article then did go into some of the harsh reality of the comic book business:

> One reason for Lee's 40-year loyalty to

Marvel may be that . . . Lee does not own the rights to any of his heroes. The company does. To leave would mean walking out on his creations.

In the article, as Lee, in his Marvel office, responded to the urgent need of John Romita (described, in the article, as the person "who draws the Spider-Man") for Lee to clarify a story point, Rowes added this endearing aside:

[Lee] pulls out a tissue and blows his nose. "I always have a cold," he cries. "Even when I don't have a cold, I sound like I do."

Of course, no one expected *People* magazine to do a searing exposé on Lee or comics. What the piece *did* do was continue the narrative that had so angered some of Lee's collaborators, the idea that Lee had created Marvel's characters completely on his own.

By mentioning Romita in several places, the article acknowledged that, in at least one instance, someone not Lee was drawing the comics. But a reader could be forgiven for coming away from the piece thinking that Lee had invented all the characters by himself.

Did Lee try to make clear to the reporter — who then failed to make note of it — that everything he did in comics was done with creative collaborators? Whether he did or not,

501

it's not hard to imagine some of his artistic partners — or even Marvel staffers — reading it and feeling to some degree miffed.

As editor in chief Jim Shooter consolidated power and attracted controversy, Marvel's comics started appearing on schedule and their overall quality improved, perhaps at the cost of some ecstatic highs, but also with fewer screaming lows. Shooter gained loyalists as well as detractors and, indeed, despite being firmly ensconced in management, campaigned vigorously for creators rights, including having Marvel institute an incentive (never called "royalty") program for creators. This, of course, continued the Marvel tradition of its editors having one foot in the world of management and the other in the world of freelance creating, trying to serve two masters. And why not? If superheroes could have dual identities, why not comics creators? The incentive program, though, would end up having momentous, if unintended, consequences.

One thing that Shooter was firm in was his belief that writers should not be their own editors. While he allowed and even encouraged his ever-growing roster of editors to do freelance writing after hours, no editor would be allowed to assign work to himself or herself. One writer-editor — Jack Kirby — had already departed for the animation business. That left Wolfman and Thomas as the only people still contractually allowed to oversee their own material. Their personalities and values clashed with Shooter's, and when they came into conflict with the editor in chief, publisher Lee backed Shooter.

Shooter was welcoming to, and helped cultivate and develop, new talent — people like Frank Miller and Bill Sienkiewicz — and gave freedom and opportunity to established talent, such as Tom DeFalco and J. M. DeMatteis. But people would fall in and out of favor with him, often without understanding why. The Marvel offices were a strange mix of rigid rule-following balanced by calculated risk-taking. The comics being produced were reading clearly if not always brilliantly, they were coming out when promised, and they were selling.

Shooter's reign coincided with the continued expansion of the direct-sales market and the evolution of the demographic profile of the comics-buying public that ensued from that expansion. In a nutshell, the dedicated comics shops serviced by the direct market received comics at a deeper discount than the traditional newsstands and drugstores. In exchange for this lower price, they gave up return privileges — which was fine, since they also did a business in back issues. At the same time, many comics buyers were older — many in their late teens, twenties, and thirties

— and were more interested than readers of previous decades in comics whose subjects and themes were relatively sophisticated. Publishers could be less hesitant to take risks on what they published because they knew that whatever they printed and shipped — based on specific advance orders — could not be returned.

Comics shops were, of course, eager to sell blockbusters. But now, they could also sell off beat material such as literary graphic novels from publishers of all sizes, or even individual self-publishers, who didn't need to make as much money as a multinational media corporation. More than ever, specific talents, as much as familiar characters, sold comics. This fact would have more and more significance over time for the comics industry in general and for Stan Lee in particular.

To add to the shifting marketplace's unknown factors, the provisions of the Copyright Act of 1976 had taken effect on January 1, 1978. Marvel sent around a one-page agreement, which it demanded freelancers sign, guaranteeing that all work they did for Marvel was work for hire that would be owned forever by the company. Neal Adams — in the midst of his advocacy on behalf of Jerry Siegel and Joe Shuster — annotated the contract with a warning to not sign it and circulated his version around the industry. He called a meeting of what he hoped would become a comics book creators guild. Writers and artists and a few editors showed up to the meeting on May 7, where things seemed to get off to a strong start. But the guild idea went nowhere. People signed the work-for-hire document — demanded by both Marvel and DC — or they didn't get assignments.

And on June 22, DC Comics underwent what would come to be recalled as "the DC Implosion." Many titles were canceled, many freelancers were suddenly out of work, and several staff editors were let go. People made a beeline to Marvel to sign the agreement.

Shooter used the fact that nearly all freelancers had signed the document to institute several successive incentive plans (although DC had forced Marvel's hand by doing it first), eventually settling on a plan where incentives were paid based on a set of sales benchmarks. For the first time ever, if a comic sold well enough, writer, penciler, and inker would make a significant amount of money above and beyond their page rates. *X-Men* writer Chris Claremont, for instance, used his incentive payments to purchase, among other things, a brownstone and, for his pilot mother, a private plane. This incentive system would end up changing things more than anyone had imagined possible.

While things were in flux in the New York offices, Lee spent much of 1978 and 1979 in California, working on projects like *The New Fantastic Four* animated series, as well as on a *Spider-Woman* cartoon (based on a comic character created by Archie Goodwin and Marie Severin in 1976). Both series were produced by DePatie-Freleng. During this period, Lee even found some time — and motivation — to bring the socially concerned Stan Lee out of mothballs.

In the October 1978 cover–dated comics, Lee announced in the Soapbox that a student at a recent speech he gave at "good ol' James Madison University in Harrisonburg, Virginia . . . reminded me of a promise I'd forgotten a decade ago! He said that I'd promised, in the late sixties, to do a column entitled 'What Is a Bigot?' " Lee then proceeded to present his definition:

From where I sit, bigotry is one of the many stains upon the human escutcheon which must be eradicated before we can truthfully call ourselves civilized . . . it's most easily recognized in the forms of cruel and mindless generalizations . . . [and] the turkeys that talk that way . . . are bigots, plain and simple!

And in the March 1980 Bulletins, after plugging the upcoming second season of the *Captain America* live-action TV series ("I've

506

already seen the script, and I can tell you it's gonna be one of the most exciting, adult, suspense-packed super-spectaculars you've ever marveled at!") and his new, non-Marvel-related book, *The Best of the Worst* (a potpourri of factoids), he then announced that "I've received lot of letters lately asking for my views on religion. While I don't feel I oughtta use this funky little forum to air my own opinions about such an extremely personal matter, there is one general, non-denominational view point I'd like to mention." He continued:

It's pretty hard for me to believe that the ever unfolding miracle of the universe . . . just happened to occur by chance! I believe that there is some entity far wiser and far mightier than we. I feel there must be some purpose . . . behind the mystic fabric of mortal existence.

With these notable exceptions, philosopher-Stan would be less and less in evidence as Lee's career and personal life came to focus more and more on Hollywood. Not only was he spending more time there, but in the January 1980 Bulletins, he announced that

mighty Marvel is getting so wrapped up in show biz that I've moved to Los Angeles for a while to set up our own West Coast film

507

production headquarters!

Lee's desire to leave New York behind was heightened when his Upper East Side apartment was burglarized while he and Joan were away on a trip to the West Coast. As he wrote to Alain Resnais in a letter dated May 23, 1979:

> We try not to think about it, but it's the most depressing and stressing thing imaginable. It's one of the reasons we'd like to pull up stakes and come out to Los Angeles permanently, if we can.[2]

And while he would soon move to L.A. for the rest of his life, working there would entail a long and frustrating learning curve for him as he went about meeting with Hollywood decision-makers and "introducing them to the wonderment of Marvel." And yet, while the world of theatrical motion pictures remained closed off to Marvel — despite the success of the *Hulk* series and, to a lesser degree, the *Spider-Man* series — the world of Saturday morning animation, always eager for new material, seemed welcoming to the characters and to Lee. Marvel did indeed set up its own animation studio.

The company bought out the DePatie-Freleng studio, which had been producing *The New Fantastic Four* and *Spider-Woman*, and proceeded to put together a number of animated series. Only a few of them, such as *Spider-Man and His Amazing Friends* and *The Incredible Hulk,* featured Marvel characters. (Lee would narrate the *Spider-Man* series episodes.) The main output of the studio was other companies' properties, including *G.I. Joe: A Real American Hero* and *The Transformers.* These were lucrative but did nothing to extend the Marvel brand.

Despite having settled into an apartment in Los Angeles, Lee shuttled back and forth between coasts, still serving as Marvel's publisher while trying to make further inroads for the company's characters on the West Coast. Lee was eager to delegate all he could regarding the comics to Shooter. But controversies engendered by the editor in chief's actions required Lee's attention, especially to issues regarding Roy Thomas and Marv Wolfman, who would both soon leave for DC, feeling that Shooter's requirements — backed by Lee and Jim Galton — gave them no choice.

By late 1979, internal strife at Marvel was so well known that it generated an article by N. R. Kleinfield in the October 13 *New York Times* entitled SUPERHEROES' CREATORS WRANGLE. After recounting Thomas's and Wolfman's dissatisfaction with the status quo, the article continued:

509

Two other Marvel staff members recently wrote to the chairman of Cadence Industries, Marvel's parent, venting distress that the comics were losing priority within the company. Stan Lee, Marvel's publisher, called a staff meeting recently and, among other things, stressed that the books were still the main event.[3]

The irony, of course, was that to Lee himself, the books were becoming less and less "the main event," although he would nonetheless end up writing a fair number of them.

In 1979, Lee would script the first issue of *The Savage She-Hulk* comic, a clumsily named Hulk spinoff, designed to both capitalize in the *Hulk* TV series's popularity as well as to head off the creation (and ownership) of a female Hulk character by the production company that was behind the *Hulk* series. During this time, Lee also wrote a short Silver Surfer story (drawn by John Buscema and Rudy Nebres) for the first issue of Marvel's answer to the artistically ambitious *Heavy Metal* magazine, *Epic Illustrated,* edited by the recently returned-to-staff Archie Goodwin.

In general, Lee would continue to periodically write comic book stories for Marvel, although his comics-style production was focused on the popular *Spider-Man* daily strip.

■ ■ ■ ■

Marvel Productions — the renamed DePatie-Freleng studio — successfully produced animated shows that were unrelated to Marvel's comics. But that didn't stop Lee from spending his time endlessly pitching ideas to networks. Producer Chuck Lorre — a creative force behind hit series such as the 2000s *The Big Bang Theory* and *Two and a Half Men* — recalled, just after Lee's 2018 death, working with Lee at Marvel Productions, in a short essay called "Remembrance." Lorre wrote of Stan:

> marching out of the office, day after day, lugging scripts . . . determined to convince a movie studio — any movie studio — to bring [Marvel's] comic book characters . . . to the big screen. And no one was interested. I mean no one. But Stan just kept plugging away. . . .
> You showed 'em, Stan.[4]

Marvel Productions, especially with the hiring of influential creative executive Margaret Loesch, would become one of the most successful animation studios in Hollywood, but Lee's involvement with their various series — mostly of non-Marvel properties — was limited. Despite that — or perhaps because of it — Lee seems to have been constantly

511

busy, pitching properties with, as Lorre recounts, little success.

As Lee's Marvel Productions colleague John Semper Jr. observed:

> [Stan] was a guy who had a tremendous amount of energy and wanted to be doing things, but there was nothing for him to do. . . . Nobody wanted to buy anything off of him because he was just old news. . . . No movie studio wanted to touch anything Marvel, because that was just stupid comic book stuff, and they were movie studios. They weren't going to make stupid comic book movies. . . . In the comic book world, Stan was still revered, but in the world of entertainment, Stan was nothing.[5]

With Loesch having moved to Marvel Productions, the company became a magnet for creative talent. Loesch was a big believer in Lee and Marvel, but even she couldn't get series starring the Marvel characters off the ground. This would change dramatically in 1991, but in the decade before that, Lee was still looking for his niche in Hollywood, since he certainly didn't want to go back to the day-to-day grind of putting out comic books. As Semper recalled of an '80s meeting with Lee:

> We had a private moment [during a meeting

with Marvel editorial in New York], and he said that he really didn't like coming back there and being at Marvel . . . that it really kind of depressed him. . . . It was not where he wanted to be. He did not want to be back in New York. . . . He did not want to be dealing with anything having to do with the comic books, period.[6]

And, indeed, by 1980, Lee was publisher in name only. Michael Z. Hobson had been hired as VP of publishing and was taking care of the business end of things, and Jim Shooter was ruling editorial. Lee's résumé for this period is filled with a wide variety of projects. For just a few examples:

He scripted a 1982 *Silver Surfer* one-shot comic that was plotted and penciled by John Byrne and inked by Tom Palmer. He scripted the 1984 *Amazing Spider-Man Annual* — plotted by DeFalco, with art by Ron Frenz, Bob Layton, and Butch Guice — in which J. Jonah Jameson got married. He consulted on and narrated the *Spider-Man and His Amazing Friends* animated series. He wrote at least one version of a *Spider-Man* movie treatment for producer Roger Corman and a *Silver Surfer* treatment for producer Lee Kramer that was to star Kramer's then girlfriend, Olivia Newton-John. And he, indeed, went to meeting after meeting, pitching projects.

But while Lee was occupied with his many projects, conflict was brewing between Jack Kirby and Marvel. Marvel had been returning recent artwork to the artists who created it and had started returning its warehoused artwork from the 1960s to the pencilers and inkers who had worked on that material. Most artists were required to sign a fairly simple document that essentially reiterated that Marvel owned the characters and all rights to the material. The document that Kirby was asked to sign, though, was much longer and more complex, designed to make doubly sure that he would never try to claim any ownership rights to the characters he and Lee had cocreated.

Aside from the fact that he had signed several such documents over the years, and so considered this one redundant, Kirby found the document insulting and punitive. The company had returned his recent '70s work without having him sign the special waiver, but wanted extra assurances for the comics that introduced and established the foundational Marvel characters. In addition, of the thousands of pages he'd penciled in the '60s for the company, fewer than a hundred were being promised to him. Even with a certain percentage of pages going to the inker of each story, this was still just a *fraction* of the work he'd done. Marvel claimed that the rest of the pages were lost, stolen, destroyed, or given away.

This conflict over the art became a cause célèbre in the fan and professional communities. Many wondered why Lee didn't just step in and make things right with Kirby. Lee's claim was that he had no control over such situations, that it was all about corporate decision-making and lawyers' requirements in order for the company to feel secure in their ownership and control of the characters. Negotiations with Kirby ground to a halt, with neither side willing to budge.[7]

In 1986, on a comics convention panel with Shooter in Chicago, Lee promised that Spider-Man in the newspaper strip would marry longtime love interest Mary Jane Watson. Shooter agreed to have the couple get married in the comic books, as well. The weddings would take place the following year in both media. To celebrate, Lee came to New York to officiate, on June 5, 1987, at the mock wedding of actors dressed as Spider-Man and Mary Jane, held before a sold-out crowd before a New York Mets home game at Shea Stadium in Queens — Peter Parker's home borough.

The year before, on August 1, 1986, the *Howard the Duck* movie opened. After years

515

of trying to get a Marvel movie onto screens nationwide, it seemed like the film — produced by George Lucas himself — could at last be the vehicle to get Marvel where it should be in Hollywood.

Unfortunately, the movie was a critical and commercial disaster, finding its way onto lists of the worst movies of all time. Lee wasn't very involved in the film, but it certainly didn't help his case as he went around trying to inspire belief in Marvel characters' commercial potential for feature films.

Also in 1986, Marvel celebrated the twenty-fifth anniversary of the debut of the *Fantastic Four* — and hence of modern Marvel — with special covers on the November-dated releases *(FF #1* was dated November 1961) that gave that month's comics a distinctive look. The other thing the company did to celebrate the anniversary was to come up with the New Universe, a line of comics set in an alternate reality outside of the one that contained the company's familiar characters. An ultimately failed experiment, the New Universe concept was viewed by many as a strange way to celebrate Marvel's milestone, given that it essentially ignored the fact that the mainstream universe was a quarter of a century old. In any case, Lee was hardly involved in any celebration, except for scripting a page of that month's *Fantastic Four.*

That summer, Shooter reported seeing Lee

and Kirby shaking hands and chatting amiably at the *Fantastic Four* twenty-fifth-anniversary party at the San Diego Comic-Con, despite the fact that Lee had, just before this meeting, cut his hand and was bleeding profusely under an improvised bandage. As Shooter described it:

> It was Stan Lee's finest hour. . . . He sticks out his hand, and Jack shakes his hand — and then Stan has to wipe the blood off of Jack's hand with his handkerchief. . . . Then Stan says, "Just once more — I don't care who owns it or gets credit — I'd like to do a story with you. . . ." And Jack said he'd like that — and [Kirby's wife] Roz said, "Bite your tongue."[8]

By the time Lee officiated at the Spider-Man wedding a year later, Marvel had been purchased by New World Entertainment, who, after a series of conflicts, had fired Shooter and replaced him with Tom DeFalco. DeFalco and Galton were able to work out a contract with Kirby — and to somehow find thousands more Kirby art pages — and the Kirby art crisis was over.[9]

August 28 that year was Jack Kirby's seventieth birthday. On that day, Kirby — on the phone from California — was being feted on WBAI's *Earth-watch* program, hosted by

Robert Knight, Max Schmid, and guest host — and former Marvel staffer — Warren Reece. Lee, in New York, was enlisted as a surprise phone-in guest. However, with Kirby apparently unaware of Lee's participation, he was asked by Knight what it was like working with Stan Lee at the Merry Marvel Marching Society. Kirby responded, "I didn't consider it merry. . . . You turned in your ideas and you got your wages and you took them home." Discussing how the stories were created, Kirby said, "I created the situation [in the stories] . . . all of it was mine besides the words in the balloons."

When Reece asked him to talk about the "legendary story conferences" he and Stan had, "jumping up on the desks and so forth," Kirby responded, "It wasn't like that at all. It may have been like that after I shut the door and went home." While Kirby was giving these dour responses, Lee was on the line, waiting to come on.

Knight then essayed, "And now we can announce the very special guest that we have for tonight's program, your colleague in arms, Stan Lee."

Attempting to be polite, Kirby said, "Well, Stanley, I want to thank you for calling, and I hope you're in good health and I hope you stay in good health."

After some strained repartee, Lee put forth the somewhat mixed compliment that "to me, nobody could convey emotion and drama the way you could. I didn't care if the drawing was all out of whack, because that wasn't important. You got your point across and nobody could ever draw a hero like you could."

Lee continued, "Whatever we did together and no matter who did what — and I guess that's something that'll be argued forever — I think there was some slight magic that came into effect when we worked together."

Kirby responded with his own set of qualified compliments, telling Lee, "It was a great experience for me and certainly if the product was good, that was my satisfaction. . . . And it's one of the reasons I respect you is the fact that, you know, you're certainly a good professional and you're certainly fond of a good product."

It wasn't a statement exactly overflowing with praise, but at least Kirby did his best to stay civil.

A few minutes later, however, when it seemed that the conversation would proceed reasonably pleasantly, Reece commented, "It would be interesting to know whether or not Galactus's exit speech in *FF* #50 was an example of Jack's dialogue or Stan's, but you —"

Lee here interjected, "Oh, I'll say this: Every word of dialogue in those scripts was mine."

The following heated exchange then ensued:

KIRBY: I wasn't allowed to write —

LEE: Did you ever read one of the stories after it was finished? I don't think you did. I don't think you ever read one of my stories. . . . You never read the book when it was finished.

KIRBY: I wrote my own dialogue. . . . So whatever was written in then was, well it . . . it, you know, it was the action I was interested in.

LEE: I don't think you ever felt that the dialogue was important. I think that you felt, "Well, it doesn't matter, anybody can put the dialogue in, it's what I'm drawing that matters." . . . I don't agree with it, but maybe you're right.

KIRBY: I'm only trying to say . . . if one man is writing and drawing and doing a strip . . . I believe that [he] should have the opportunity to do the entire thing.

Knight, Schmid, and Reece did their best to salvage the program, as Lee closed with:

LEE: I just want to say that Jack has, I think, made a tremendous mark on American culture if not on world culture, and I hope that ten years from now I'll be listening to a tribute to his eighti-

eth birthday, and I hope I'll have an opportunity to call . . . and wish him well
then, too. Jack, I love ya.

KIRBY: Well, the same here, Stan. But,
yeah, thank you very much, Stan.

[Here, Lee got off the call.]

KIRBY: Now, you can understand how
things really were.[10]

Despite the fact that Kirby's conflicts with
Marvel and Lee were hardly a secret, Knight
and Reece — and perhaps Lee himself —
seemed to have still been harboring fans'
hopes that the two would — like children
wish their divorced parents would — reconcile and perhaps get back together, or at least
behave nicely on a birthday. Instead, as in a
situation with an estranged couple where one
partner wants to reconcile but the other
doesn't, Lee's "Jack, I love ya" was met with
the less-than-passionate "Well, the same here,
Stan." By the same token, though, Lee's
profession of love was not only *not* rejected
by Kirby, it was — however hesitantly —
reciprocated. Once again, their relationship
showed itself to be complex indeed.

It was plain from the way the show had
gone that, no matter how much Lee tried to
immerse himself in Hollywood and leave the
past behind, the past would have a different
idea of how it should be treated.

The question that begged to be answered

was: Could Lee make use of the past to create a positive future — or would the past rise up to consume him?

19
CALIFORNIA DREAMIN'

> Loving Stan doesn't mean that they're going to give a green light automatically.
> — Don Kopaloff, Marvel's film agent during the mid-1980s[1]

In November 1987, a steamy novel called *The Pleasure Palace,* published by Dell, appeared in bookstores in the United States. It had the look and feel of books by bestselling authors like Harold Robbins or the Lees' friend Judith Krantz, producer Steve's wife. But this novel, which would go on to sell reasonably well, was written by a first-time author:

Joan Lee.

On what her husband recalled as more or less a whim, Joan wrote the novel that Lee showed to agent Jonathan Dolger. Dolger sold the book and it was published, with Joan being the first (and only) one of the Lees to have a prose novel published. The promotional cover copy for the book, published solely in paperback, read (with for some reason each word starting with a capital let-

523

ter): "Opulent, Sensual, Treacherously Seductive — Welcome Aboard the World's Most Luxurious Ocean Liner."

The book was dedicated, in part:

To my daughter, Joan, for giving me the first push, and to my husband, Stan, for supporting me all the way.

One of the novel's leading characters had the same name as Stan and Joan's deceased infant daughter, Jan.

Joan wrote two more novels but held them back from being published "because I wasn't hungry. . . . With Stan I was never hungry."[2]

At least one member of the family had published a novel.

As for Stan Lee himself, it seemed as if his life and career had segued into a steady, not uninteresting — and not, as we shall see, conflict-free — direction that could conceivably last the rest of his life. With Mike Hobson and Tom DeFalco keeping things at Marvel publishing running smoothly — without, for the most part, the drama of the Shooter years — Lee was free to participate in comics creation as much or little as he wanted. He was still promoting and consulting on Marvel's media projects as much as he was able, regularly traveled to conventions and other venues to promote Marvel, and, in general, served as a goodwill ambassador for the company.

New World seemed satisfied with this arrangement, even if they didn't take him all that seriously. "Stan's not in the loop because he's not a player," one New World exec said. "He's not a partner. He wasn't a vote. But he was like a pitbull. He just didn't want to walk away."[3]

Would Lee ever have another series of status quo–shattering innovations like that he was part of in the '60s and '70s? Maybe, maybe not. Either way, he'd had a pretty damn good run of creation, more than most people — even the most driven and talented — get. He was sixty-four years old in 1987, certainly with no thoughts of retiring. He was well paid for what he did, and enjoyed a pleasant lifestyle with interesting colleagues and good friends, and the possibility that the next pitch he made could be *the one* that would again change the world! Things could be worse — and they would be. But not just yet.

In 1988, Lee and French comics icon Moebius (the pen name of Jean Giraud) released a two-part Silver Surfer story, "Parable," which won an Eisner Award for Best Limited Series. Done Marvel-style from a six-page plot by Lee, it was indeed a parable, open to interpretation by readers.

In the story, loosely tied in to Marvel continuity, Galactus returns to Earth and, while hewing to his promise to not consume the planet, declares himself a deity and proceeds to cause havoc with his proclamation that all rules and laws are null and void, and that humans may act completely selfishly, without any restraints. As he had planned, the planet devolves into chaos. Sworn to not consume Earth, he acted out of pure *spite* to make the planet's inhabitants miserable.

(This was an interesting new thematic digression for Lee. His villains usually had a specific goal in mind — money, power, love, survival. The idea of Galactus acting out of pettiness was a more nihilistic approach than that of most of the "bad guys" Lee had written previously.)

The Surfer then enters the story and reveals Galactus to be far less than a god, thereby thwarting his former master's plans, only to have humans declare the Surfer *himself* a god they must worship. It seemed that here, Lee's conflicting feelings about religion were highly engaged. With the inclusion in the story of a corrupt — or possibly deluded — televangelist who seeks to exploit Galactus's nihilistic behavior, Lee seemed to be condemning religion as, at best, foolishness. Lauded as a deity himself, the Surfer laments:

It is madness. They thirst for leadership as a child thirsts for mother's milk. Surely this is why they so often fall prey to tyrants and despots.

Why cannot they realize that the truest faith is faith in oneself? What has made them so desperate to have others show them the way?

Rejecting this role that humans would thrust upon him, the Surfer takes to the skies — still trapped in Earth's atmosphere, per Galactus's long-ago decree — and, like the deity in Lee's poem "God Woke," bemoans the short-sightedness of humanity, then throws away his chance to be a god in order to give humankind the chance to work out its own problems, free from slavish fealty to any deity — even himself. The Surfer is last seen in the story standing sadly on his hovering board, lamenting:

I have known the heady exaltation of victory. I have known the gnawing pain of defeat. But I shall never cease searching for an oasis of sanity in the desert of madness that men call Earth. For the worst fate of all, amidst countless worlds and endless stars —
— is to be forever alone.

While Lee was not alone in Los Angeles,

"Parable" can be read as a lament of sorts over the fact that, after close to a decade in Los Angeles, he still had not scored the big hit for Marvel or himself that he was hoping for. He was still searching for an "oasis of sanity" in the "desert of madness" that men call Hollywood.

Accounts of Lee's time in the entertainment world of the 1980s do seem to portray a man on a lonely mission, unable to convince anyone to go all-in on Marvel's heroes or Stan Lee's ideas. It must have been doubly frustrating for him that Marvel was owned by a film and TV production company, and yet they were doing nothing meaningful with its characters. Indeed, as much as Lee enjoyed writing the Surfer and having the chance to work with the legendary Moebius, it's likely he would have been happy to have been working, in addition or instead, on a big-budget film, Marvel or otherwise.

In January 1989, shortly after *Silver Surfer: Parable* was released, financier Ronald Perelman's MacAndrews & Forbes group purchased Marvel from New World, which had hit rocky financial shores. Perelman declared he wanted to make Marvel "the next Disney." Lee's salary was — without him even asking — tripled. Here, at last, the company seemed to have ownership that was on the same page he was.[4]

On June 23, the first *Batman* movie opened, featuring Michael Keaton as the Dark Knight. More than even the *Superman* movie of 1978 (and its 1980 sequel) the movie's popularity boosted both Marvel's and DC's characters' credibility as story generators. It also catalyzed the licensed merchandise business for both companies. Comics-related merch was suddenly big![5]

One of the few Marvel properties to successfully navigate the Hollywood maze, the Incredible Hulk, was the focus of NBC's 1989 made-for-TV movie, *The Trial of the Incredible Hulk.* In this film, Lee made the first of his live-action Marvel cameos, a nonspeaking role as a juror in an imagined courtroom sequence. He would also appear, in 1990, in a small speaking role as a comic book editor in *The Ambulance,* a movie directed by his friend, cult director Larry Cohen.

That same year, an infamous interview with Jack Kirby was published in *The Comics Journal.* In it, Kirby essentially claimed that he single-handedly created Marvel's characters and that Lee was little more than a glorified office boy, carrying out errands for Martin Goodman. Even staunch supporters of Kirby thought the interview was over the top, Kirby reviling Lee to a degree that he had never before publicly done.

■ ■ ■

But while insiders' passions were inflamed by the perceived battle of words (and sometimes lawyers) going on behind the scenes between Kirby and Marvel, people who bought comics, whatever their sympathies or level of concern over who did what thirty years earlier, seemed largely unfazed by such inside baseball. Marvel's comics were starting on a historic climb in circulation. Fueled by popular young artists, including Todd Mc-Farlane, Jim Lee, and Rob Liefeld, as well as, in part, by a speculator-driven comics-as-collectibles market, Marvel's sales jumped by double-digit percentages from year to year. With editors now cut in for a small percentage of incentives from the titles they handled, they, too, were able to amass significant extra income based on the sales of their titles.[6] Contracts would tie them to the company, the result of DeFalco's insistence that talented editors were as valuable to the company as brand-name creators.

In the summer of 1991, Perelman's organization took Marvel public, and the stock skyrocketed. The announcement that Hollywood's hottest director, James Cameron, of *Terminator* fame, had signed on to direct a Spider-Man film — set to star equally hot Arnold Schwarzenegger as one of the villains

— helped light the fire under the stock and, at long last, under Marvel's properties that Lee had been trying to sell for such a high-profile project for so long.[7]

Also in 1991, McFarlane quit Marvel over an editorial dispute with DeFalco (and this author, who was editorial director of the *Spider-Man* line of comics), which would lead to an exodus of the then-top-selling creators at the company. They would soon start their own company — Image Comics — with the money that they had accumulated through incentive payments on their millions-selling comics. This was a phenomenon that would end up rocking Marvel and the entire comics industry.

That year, separate from Marvel, Lee had begun a film-production company with former New World executive and cartoonists' agent Peter Bierstedt.[8] Their first project, *The Comic Book Greats,* a Lee-hosted series of video interviews with industry notables past and present, which were sold for home video. Those interviewed included Lee's friends Will Eisner, with whom Lee seemed to have an easy rapport, Batman cocreator Bob Kane, and an ailing Harvey Kurtzman, who appeared along with fellow *Mad* magazine legend Jack Davis. Although gone from Marvel, McFarlane appeared on an episode with Liefeld. John Romita Sr. *and* Jr. also appeared in an episode.

The interviews were often revealing and insightful, and the artists would take part of each episode to draw, while Lee would engage in informative conversation with them, sometimes mocking his own reputation, joking that, as the interviewer, he should own part of the characters being drawn.

While Lee wasn't exactly slick as a moderator and interviewer, he had certainly improved by leaps and bounds since the production of his *How To* tape with John Buscema. His skills as editor, art director, and writer were on display as he asked insightful questions that stemmed from his knowledge and years of experience.

The year 1992 would bring the media phenomenon of the "Death of Superman" story line in DC's *Superman* titles, which was picked up by mainstream media and made the comics it appeared in astonishingly big sellers. Nonregular comics readers bought multiple copies of the issue featuring the Man of Steel's (eventually temporary) death, thinking he was actually going to be dead forever and — despite the law of supply and demand — believing that if they held on to their copies for a few years, they could send their kids to college on the proceeds of the comics' sales.

The same was true for other issues in the story line, and for "special" stories in the comics industry in general during this period. The public's misperceptions about the long-term value of certain "special event" comics would drive publishing decisions for the next several years until damage was done to the comics sales market from which it would never fully recover. Publishers and retailers would disappear; people would lose their livelihoods.

Unintentionally, Lee played a part in that investment cycle. Nineteen ninety-two was the thirtieth anniversary of Spider-Man's debut in 1962's *Amazing Fantasy #15. Amazing Spider-Man #365* (edited by this author) was the issue that would have an August cover date, as *AF #15* had had three decades earlier. The main story would involve the supposed return of Peter Parker's dead parents. The issue also contained several backup stories, including "I Remember Gwen," a story plotted by Tom DeFalco, scripted by Lee, with art by Romita Sr. Lee and Romita reuniting on a Spider-Man story was a selling point for the issue. It had been decided that, as a special anniversary issue, the comic would have a hologram cover, with a 3-D image of Spider-Man that was developed from a drawing by Romita. It was to be a special, celebratory item. In that spirit, "I Remember Gwen" was a touching, nostalgic, well-crafted story that helped the issue become something truly appropriate for a special anniversary.

But with the comics-as-collectibles mania that was then abroad in the industry, it was decided that, as a marketing strategy, all four of the main *Spider-Man* titles that month would have hologram covers. The ensuing sales success of these issues with special covers was proof enough for some marketing and sales executives that many of Marvel's covers for the next couple of years would take any flimsy excuse to add a gimmick — and jack the price of the comic up significantly. This was a tactic that became ubiquitous in the comics industry. Eventually, this kind of approach was a factor that would lead to multiple crises in the comics market that would directly affect Lee.

Another significant death — this one in the real world — occurred in 1992. On June 6, Martin Goodman passed away in Florida at age eighty-four. It had been twenty years since he'd left Marvel. In 2006, Lee would say of him, "I think Martin could have been one the great publishers of all time if he were a little more ambitious. . . . But he didn't want to be Bennett Cerf. Or Hugh Hefner."[9]

Earlier that year, the *X-Men* Fox Kids series — that had started in development during the New World era — was being readied to debut in the fall. The show had been greenlit by Margaret Loesch, president of Fox Kids, and a longtime friend to, and supporter of, Lee. Fox Kids was also home to the much-admired *Batman: The Animated Series.*

As *X-Men* showrunner Eric Lewald described in his 2017 book, *Previously on X-Men: The Making of an Animated Series,* he wanted to create a series that would equal or surpass the quality and sophistication of *B:TAS.*[10] In theory, Lee wanted the same thing. In *Excelsior!,* he described a 1981 meeting, early in his Hollywood tenure, with a studio executive to whom he was pitching animation ideas. She had asked him what he thought of the cartoons then appearing on network TV. As Lee recalled, he told her he thought that, overall, the shows' dialogue sounded unnatural and "cartoony." She replied, "We don't want our series to consist of talking heads."

Lee responded that he wasn't looking for talking heads, only "that whatever dialogue you use be better written."

Her response was to reiterate that she "wasn't looking for talking heads." After several go-rounds of this, Lee realized that the executive had hard-and-fast ideas about what a good cartoon was and wasn't interested in, or able to understand, what he had to say. Lee's pleas for a more sophisticated approach to animation had fallen on deaf ears.[11]

And yet, eleven years later, with Lee functioning as an executive producer on the *X-Men* show, some others working on it saw *him* as the roadblock to better cartoons. According to Lewald:

> What I didn't know was how driven Stan can be. From the beginning, he wanted to completely change the tone and storytelling of the show . . . Stan, who hadn't written for the X-Men since 1964 [in the comics], badly wanted to run the show.[12]

Lee had wanted to have himself introduce each episode and narrate it, like he'd done for the *Spider-Man and His Amazing Friends* show. But Lewald felt that the current series needed a different approach. He proceeded to ignore Lee's copious notes on the storyboards, causing Lee to erupt in anger at him. Eventually, Lee's friend and staff artist on the *X-Men* series, Will Meugniot, brokered a peace between the two. Lewald would describe the atmosphere afterward as "a love fest." Finally, Lewald related, "after the successful [series] premiere, I never heard a word from Stan about [any issues he might have had with the show]." He even said that "Stan and I would end up working happily together on a few other projects after *X-Men,* and I would always appreciate his storyteller's instincts — welcome at meetings that sometimes could be loaded with marketers and merchandisers."[13]

For his part, Lee told Tom DeFalco in *Comics Creators on X-Men:*

> I remember talking to Eric Lewald, the story editor. We discussed the first story he wrote. I didn't like some things about it. We argued about it and eventually reached a resolution. Eric and I later became good friends and even worked on some other projects together years later.[14]

That same year, a *Spider-Man* animated series (which would debut in 1994) was put into development at Fox Kids — with John Semper Jr. as producer / head writer / story editor — and Lee was again embroiled in a round-robin of clashing personalities with people, who, each in their own way, wanted to do justice to the character. As Lewald recalled in his book, he had observed, when working on a crossover between the *X-Men* and *Spider-Man* series:

> If *X-Men: TAS* had been a struggle to get focused and moving in the right direction, *Spider-Man: TAS* was a world war. . . . [John] Semper had established a method for dealing with the warring parties (Marvel's Avi Arad, Stan Lee, director Bob Richardson, Fox's Sidney Iwanter) who were trying to run the show. He would sit them down in

an office together, and then read out a line of the script's dialogue or action. The line would either have to be agreed to by all or modified until it could be agreed to by all.[15]

As Semper recalled, though, with the Cameron *Spider-Man* movie being a real possibility, Lee was losing interest in animation:

Stan was much more invested in Eric's show. By the time my show came on, there was a Jim Cameron movie, bigger things were happening. And Stan [who I'd successfully worked with before] trusted me a lot. . . .

I think part of the reason Stan thought of me [for Spider-Man] was because he knew [from our work together at Marvel Productions] that I could handle the job, he knew I understood the character. . . . I think Stan's involvement had more to do with Avi pulling him into it than Stan wanting to be involved, because now Stan was getting a little bit of attention in the movie world, with the whole Cameron association, and . . . I don't think the animation thing was as important to him as maybe it had been ten years earlier. . . . He said to me one day, "Look, I don't really want to be involved in this show. That's why I hired you. I hired somebody that I thought could get the show out the door" . . .

He was very heavily involved in the first

season [of the Spider-Man show]. He was very actively involved in plotting. His fingerprints are all over the first season. After the first season, he's done, he no longer wants to be involved.

Avi wanted Stan to be a part of [the *Spider-Man* show] because the feeling was that Stan's *the guy. . . .* and Stan's what's going to make it good. . . . So we would have these table readings of all the scripts. Stan had to be there. Someday I'm going to write a play that will just be one of our marathon table reads. . . . These were the greatest meetings ever![16]

And then, as if 1992 wasn't event-filled enough, there was significant activity for Lee on the comic book front beyond "I Remember Gwen."

At least since his screenplay written for Resnais for *The Monster Maker,* Lee had had an interest in issues surrounding pollution. Now, in 1992, he decided the issue was so timely that he wanted to do a comics story (and perhaps even an entire line) about a dystopic future where the Earth was overwhelmed by pollution, where trash collectors were figures who were crucial to society's survival. Lee was thinking of a kind of dark, *Judge Dredd*-style milieu. The project would be called *Ravage.* Marvel editor Jim Salicrup had agreed to help Lee find the right artist for the project. Tom DeFalco, then the editor in chief, who was committed (as Shooter had been before him) to keeping longtime Marvel artists busy, suggested Steve Ditko.

Surprisingly, Ditko agreed to come in to discuss the project during one of Lee's visits to Marvel's New York offices. As Salicrup remembered it:

> I had worked with Steve . . . so I called him up. We set up a meeting [with me, him, Tom, and Stan]. We met in then-Marvel-president Terry Stewart's office, and it was a lot of fun.
>
> The two men clearly still had great respect for each other, and I think if I wasn't planning to leave Marvel myself shortly, I could've gotten them to do a project together again. Steve explained to Stan why he didn't want to do *Ravage* — he didn't want to do a negative version of the future; he wanted to do something with a more positive view, like the original *Star Trek* TV series.
>
> Stan then made a pitch to do a Spider-Man graphic novel with Steve . . . and again got turned down, with Steve saying he could never care about the character as much as he did originally. Stan was truly disappointed, and Steve, I believe, would've been willing to do another project with Stan, but unfortunately, it was not to be.[17]

Of that meeting, DeFalco recalled that Lee and Ditko

were both so happy to see each other. When they saw each other, both their faces lit up . . . and Stan threw his arms around Steve, and Steve threw his arms around Stan. Stan explained to Steve what the concept was. Steve thought about it for a few minutes and decided that it was not something that really interested him, that said "hero" to him or whatever. They shook hands and said, "Maybe we can do something else again sometime in the future," and they both left the door wide open.

Then Steve walked away, and I had one of those surreal moments where, as I'm walking down the hall with Stan, Stan says to me, "You know, Tommy, I've always been curious about this. Do you know why Steve quit?"

I said to him, "Stan, I think I was in high school when that happened. I really have no idea."[18]

Mark Evanier, who had been visiting Marvel's offices that day, recalled hearing about the meeting right after it happened:

Ditko came in and said he was willing to consider working with Stan again. . . . Stan gave this outline to Ditko . . . and Ditko

541

thought it was a very ugly view of humanity, and he kept saying, "Let's change it like this. Let's change it like this." And apparently Stan, after enough of it, said, "No, no. I'm the writer of this. This is what I want to do. If you don't want to draw it, fine, but don't lecture me like I'm a beginner." And that was the end of it.[19]

(Stepping out of authorial voice here, I witnessed what turned out to have been the second part of the meeting, after a break for lunch, when Ditko entered the Marvel offices and walked into Salicrup's office, where Lee was seated, facing the door. Upon seeing Ditko — even though they had spent the morning together — Lee's face broke into a smile, as if he were seeing a long-lost, beloved friend.)

The *Ravage* series — which debuted in late '92 — ended up being called *Ravage 2099* and was incorporated into Marvel's *2099* line, set in that future year. The other series in the line were based around future versions of Spider-Man, the X-Men, and so on. Drawn by Paul Ryan and Danny Bulanadi, *Ravage 2099* would last close to two years, although Lee would only write the first eight issues.

Despite what seemed to have been a cordial reconciliation, Lee and Ditko would never work together again, and their relationship, as conducted through the media, would become painfully contentious.

Lee would continue with his numerous duties as a Marvel executive, as well as working on freelance projects. Thanks to high sales of Marvel's comics and the Cameron-sparked interest in the company, as well as the successful animated series, it seemed like things might be stable for a while.

But that stability would prove to be short-lived. Marvel was about to fall victim to its own success, and Stan Lee would be buffeted by the kinds of business-world machinations he had tried so diligently to insulate himself from.

20
FOLLOW THE MONEY

Do you feel that you're being screwed?
— *60 Minutes II* correspondent Bob Simon
to Stan Lee, October 2002

In 1993, things seemed reasonably stable in the world of comics and in seventy-year-old Stan Lee's niche at Marvel. The comics were selling. The stock was soaring. What was there to complain about?

After all, while Marvel seemed to not exactly be taking the world of Hollywood movies by storm, it was only a matter of time before James Cameron would be starting on his *Spider-Man* — just a few annoying contractual issues had to be worked out with some other rights holders. In addition, Marvel's characters were, or would be, appearing in a number of animated series which Lee was involved with to one degree or another.

Lee seemed to be able to do as much comics scripting as he could handle (not to mention writing the ongoing *Spider-Man* newspaper strip). Maybe the comics couldn't keep selling at the rate they were now, but even if sales dropped by half, they'd still be selling millions and millions each month, and the direct market was an efficient mechanism through which to sell them. No returns meant that the company couldn't lose on the wholesale end, and the comics shops would be able to sell any overages as back issues. Everyone was happy as long as the pipeline of comics from creators to publishers to retailers to consumers stayed healthy.

Ronald Perelman had certainly gotten his money's worth for the $82 million he'd paid for Marvel. In addition, Perelman was buying up other comics and comics-related companies, such as sticker and collectible-card enterprises. He was paying top dollar for them, but it was all part of a grand scheme. It ended up just not being the scheme people thought it would be.

Always restless — and always worried that disaster might strike comics no matter how good things looked — Lee was, as always, open to side deals.

Publisher and entrepreneur Byron Preiss had been friends with Lee for years. Born in 1953 (the same year as the Lees' deceased infant daughter, Jan), Preiss had been a fan turned book packager and publisher who had decided to not just *meet* his childhood comics and science-fiction idols but to *go into business* with some of them. Preiss had done projects with Will Eisner, Jim Steranko, Isaac Asimov, and many others.

In 1993, he worked with Lee on two projects. Preiss had licensed the rights to do — through publisher Berkley Books — a series of prose novels and short story collections based on the Marvel characters. He made Lee the titular editor of the short story collections — his "Ultimate" line (*Ultimate Spider-Man, Ultimate Silver Surfer,* etc.) — for which Lee would write forewords as well as some of the fiction.

Preiss had also brainstormed with Lee on a series of prose novels unconnected to Marvel that went under the overall title of *Stan Lee's Riftworld.* The first *Riftworld* novel came out in 1993, followed by two others. Written by veteran novelist Bill McCay, with spot illustrations by *Watchmen*'s Dave Gibbons, *Riftworld* was the story of comics publisher Harry Sturdley, who ran a comic book company, the Fantasy Factory, and how he dealt with events set into motion when he encountered actual superheroes — and villains — brought to Earth through an interdimensional rift.

Work was also begun at Preiss's on comics whose premise was that they were produced by writers and artists working for the Fantasy

Factory. And, eventually, a comics version of *Riftworld* was put into production, edited by this author (who moved from Marvel to Preiss in 1995), scripted by Lee, with pencil art by artists including Dan Jurgens, famous for his work on *Superman.*

With Avi Arad taking on more and more of Lee's film and TV producer duties, and with Lee's Marvel "futureverse" line of comics re-imagined as the Marvel *2099* comics — with Lee only working on one of its titles, *Ravage* — he embarked on a different line of comics for Marvel, this one called the *Excelsior* line. From his L.A. office, with trusted colleagues — including Roy Thomas and artist Sal Buscema (brother of John) — on board as creators, Lee was again editing a line of comics. According to Thomas, Lee was hands-on with all aspects of the line's titles.[1] For better or worse, it was kind of a reminder of the '60s.

But on February 6, 1994, another reminder of the '60s happened. Jack Kirby passed away.

According to Lee, he and Kirby had reconciled shortly before Kirby's death. As Lee recounted:

> I saw him at a comic book convention. And I walked up to him, and he said, "Stan, you have nothing to reproach yourself for." He smiled and we shook hands, and I walked my way and he walked his way.[2]

Regarding Kirby's funeral, according to Raphael and Spurgeon:

With Roz [Kirby]'s assent, Stan Lee attended Jack Kirby's funeral. "I stayed in the back," says Lee. "I didn't want anyone to see me . . . and start talking about Jack and me and our relationship."[3]

And according to Evanier:

Stan Lee was . . . sitting quietly in the back throughout the speeches, then departing without saying much of anything to anyone. Roz wanted to give him a big hug, right in front of everyone to show that . . . there was no bitterness left dangling. But Stan, quick as ever, was in the parking lot by then, gone before she could get near him.[4]

Raphael and Spurgeon noted:

A week or two after the funeral, Evanier arranged for a phone conversation between Stan and Roz. Lee was later instrumental in securing from Marvel a modest pension for Roz.[5]

As with many complicated relationships, Lee and Kirby's would prove to not be concluded simply because one of them had died. It would, in fact, become *more* compli-

548

cated as the years went by.

The year 1994 saw the syndicated debut of the animated *Marvel Action Hour,* on which Lee was executive producer and also doing writing and voice work. The *Hour* featured Iron Man and Fantastic Four cartoons. Later that year, Lee was voted into the Will Eisner Hall of Fame at that summer's San Diego Comic-Con.

In the meantime, some of the old contracts Marvel had signed off on over the years had come back to haunt its film plans. It would take another eight years to sort out the conflicting, overlapping rights to Spider-Man that were signed away. In fact, 1994 would see the release of an on-the-cheap, tacky *Fantastic Four* movie from Roger Corman's studio that was made simply to keep the rights in place and was never officially released.

Regarding the live-action area, Lee pointed out to reporter Frank Lovece, in 1994, that

> in the past, we [Marvel] were much more naïve about movies [and TV shows]. Somebody would come up to us and say, "Hey, we wanna make a movie of one of your characters," we'd say, "Wonderful! Oh, isn't that great!" We were flattered, and we'd license them the right to do it, and we had no control over it. But now we've grown up

and any movie that's made — I have a partner named Avi Arad . . . an incredibly creative guy . . . just a pleasure to work with — anyway, now any movies that are done, Avi and I are co-executive producers, which means that the movie company can't just do the movie any way they want to. We have to approve the story, the script, the casting, all of that. So it's a whole different thing now.[6]

Lee also told Lovece that Marvel had given him a lifetime contract. He'd certainly come a long way from his role as a "human pilot light" in the dark days of the post-Wertham 1950s.

By mid-1994, the enormous expansion of the comic book market of the past few years was rapidly losing steam. Marvel, especially, with the shaky status of the numerous companies it had recently purchased, and the financial machinations of the Perelman organization, was feeling unprecedented pressure to maximize profitability.[7]

Perhaps the company's most ill-advised move was the purchase of comics distributor Heroes World, with the intention of making it the sole supplier of Marvel's comics to comics shops. Overwhelmed by the sudden, massive increase of orders, Heroes World was unable to do the job adequately, and many retailers were unable to get the comics they had ordered, leaving consumers without their comics, and free to spend their money on other companies' comics — or on whatever else they might have wanted. In effect, this move destabilized a comics distribution system that was already suffering from over-expansion.

With the comics market in crisis, and with Marvel overextended from its purchase of overvalued companies, there came an urgent demand from upper corporate levels to cut costs. Marvel was restructured. Its staff was rearranged, shaken, and ultimately severely thinned by multiple waves of layoffs. As part of the cost cutting, Lee's *Excelsior* comics line was halted and, to this day, hasn't been seen in any way, shape, or form by the general public.

Indeed, by early 1995, it seemed to me, based on personal conversations at the time with Stan and Joan Lee, that Lee felt he was being marginalized by Marvel, and sensing that the company might look to renege on its generous treatment of him. Joan Lee commented how, periodically, if whoever owned Marvel would consider saving money by jettisoning or ill-treating her husband, that's when the Lees would call in aggressive lawyers to protect their interests, implying that this might turn out to be one of those times.

In May of that year, I had resigned from a chaotic Marvel — not an easy decision — to become head of Byron Preiss's Virtual Comics line, a roster of comics that were designed to be consumed initially on the fledging internet — in which Preiss was a pioneer — as well as, eventually, in print. At that summer's San Diego Comic-Con, Lee, aside from promoting Marvel, was also promoting the upcoming comics version of the *Riftworld* novels, which was part of the first group of Virtual titles.

Also in '95 — sporting a recently grown beard, as if in mourning for Marvel's fading glory — Lee appeared in Kevin Smith's film *Mallrats*. Playing a fictionalized version of himself, Lee had much more than a cameo. In the movie, wandering aimlessly — and somehow without attracting attention — in a New Jersey shopping mall, after a store-signing there, Lee crossed paths with the film's protagonist, Brodie, played by Jason Lee (no relation). Seeing that Brodie was in distress over a breakup with a woman, "Stan Lee" proceeded to deliver a soliloquy about a fictional long-lost love of his own, which ended with him advising the young man, "Do yourself a favor, Brodie. Don't wait. Because all the money, all the women, even all the comic books in the world, they can't substitute for that one person."

■ ■ ■ ■

Marvel would spend the next few years in financial turmoil, culminating in a 1998 battle of superhuman proportions between financiers Carl Icahn and Perelman. Before that, though, on February 23, 1996, Chip Goodman unexpectedly died of pneumonia at age fifty-five. Lee would later say that, "Chip was actually a good guy."[8] The younger Goodman had had a successful career as a magazine publisher of pretty much everything but comic books.

In late '96, Perelman took Marvel into bankruptcy, with the general belief he did so to protect the company from Icahn. A surreal period ensued where, depending on various court rulings, control of the company changed hands several times, with different teams of executives coming and going in a bizzaro-world version of musical chairs.[9]

Also that year, Marvel — which, in '94, had split its editorial department into character-related editorial divisions — restored the single editor-in-chief system, installing Bob Harras — who had led the X-Men editorial division — in that position. Harras did the best he could with a company that was recovering from financial chaos.

In 1997, after yet another restructuring and round of layoffs, Marvel decided that it did, indeed, want Lee to represent them to the world, and so the editorial department set about making every comic dated July of that year a part of "Flashback" month (featuring tales of the characters before their superhero careers began) in which each comic published would be introduced by a humorous, comic book version of Lee as imagined by the writers and artists of that comic. Lee actually scripted his own appearance in the *X-Men* "Flashback" issue.

After attempts to marginalize him, it was plain now that — at least in the comics division — when push came to shove, there was value in having the company's essence embodied by the most famous face and name in the medium. Whether either side liked it or not, Marvel and Stan Lee were as much as ever inextricably identified with each other.

Eventually, in September 1998, ownership of Marvel was, unexpectedly, awarded by the bankruptcy court to Avi Arad and Isaac Perlmutter's Toy Biz company, which had almost miraculously managed to outmaneuver both Perelman and Icahn. They set about rescuing the company from the wrecked state into which it had fallen. Perelman's company, nonetheless, walked away, by most accounts, with somewhere between $50 million and $250 million from his ownership of Marvel.

Part of the fallout of Marvel's bankruptcy

involved the fate of Lee's lifetime contract. The bankruptcy had the effect of voiding any contracts the company had entered into, including the one with Lee. When Perlmutter offered him a two-year contract at a severely reduced salary, Lee refused to sign, and his lawyer went into action. As Sean Howe observed:

> Without a contract, Lee might contest the ownership of some of the characters for which Marvel had, on innumerable occasions over three decades, credited him as the creator. And even if Lee didn't have much of a case, the damage to Marvel's public image would be devastating.[10]

Faced with this reality, the company negotiated another lifetime contract with Lee, guaranteeing him — in exchange for a small fraction of his weekly worktime — an increased annual salary, as well as pensions for his wife and daughter should he predecease them.

Significantly, the contract also guaranteed him a percentage of profits from any Marvel films or TV shows (at that point, a negligible amount), and also gave him the freedom to engage in any other work he chose, including laboring on projects that might directly compete with Marvel.[11]

So here was Lee, tied to Marvel, yet free to

do whatever else he liked. He was part of Marvel and yet not part of Marvel.

What was he going to do now?

Despite all this upheaval, and after decades of being unable to grab the brass ring on big-screen success, Marvel finally achieved a sizable hit with the screen adaptation of *Blade: The Vampire Slayer,* which debuted on August 21, 1998, focusing on a supporting character from Marvel's *Dracula* comic books. (The previous year's *Men in Black* was technically a Marvel hit, as well, since it was owned by Malibu Comics, which Marvel had purchased several years before. But the public didn't identify *MIB* with Marvel, and it did nothing to enhance the company's brand.)

So it was neither Spider-Man nor the X-Men that would put Marvel on the big-time Hollywood scoreboard, but Blade, a character — played by Wesley Snipes — that no one outside the circles of hard-core comics fans had ever heard of. It was *Blade*'s success that would lay the groundwork for the soon-to-come movie hits, *X-Men* and *Spider-Man.*

While Lee did film a cameo for *Blade,* it was not included in the released version of the film. But by that point, he had a vision for his future that didn't necessarily include Marvel as a major part of the picture, anyway.

He was taking advantage of the contractual clauses that allowed him to go into business against them. He was going into business for himself.

Well, sort of.

That year — even before Marvel was awarded to Toy Biz — Lee, with a sometime business associate named Peter Paul and a couple of other people, formed a company called, appropriately, Stan Lee Media. Lee's formal title was chairman. Paul had amassed an impressive roster of Hollywood names that he was associated with through the American Spirit Foundation (ASF), which he ran. The ASF had been established by actor Jimmy Stewart to improve public education. With Paul in charge, it had given annual Spirit of America awards to figures such as Ronald Reagan, Gene Roddenberry, Bob Hope . . . and Stan Lee.

Paul had enlisted Lee to become the ASF's chairman and to head up its Entertainers for Education committee. Paul would introduce him to such figures as Muhammad Ali, Bill and Hillary Clinton, and Tony Curtis. Paul proposed to Lee the idea of starting an intellectual property development company, which would focus on the internet, then a magnet for investment money.

Paul, though, had a checkered past, including having served time for a scheme involving an attempt to defraud the Cuban government out of more than $8 million. He claimed to Lee that this had all been a frame job on him (by whom kept changing) and that he was really part of a secret U.S. government plot to overthrow Fidel Castro. No proof has ever surfaced to confirm his claims.[12]

Lee chose to take Paul's explanations at face value, deciding to cast his lot with this guy with whom his direct experience was positive. More or less sidelined by Marvel — though still its public face — Lee, at seventy-five, remained energetic and ambitious. There would be something satisfying to be achieved in creating a successful new entertainment company, one on the cutting edge of new technologies.

While certainly not a techie, Lee was an early adopter of email — AOL had given him a special account as part of a venture with Marvel — and was made aware of the internet's possibilities by Byron Preiss. Stan Lee and Peter Paul had as good a chance as anybody else at being successful in a dot-com venture. When Stan Lee Media quickly went public, Lee and other executives became multimillionaires on paper, although he was forbidden to sell any stock for a lengthy period.

For Lee, SLM meant being back in the saddle, spending his days with teams of creative people — the staff would come to number 150 people — collaborating on new characters and stories. No one would tell him that starring in or narrating a cartoon series or comic book would be "corny" or "self-involved." Just the opposite. Lee's ideas were not merely tolerated — they were *necessary*. The company's main products were the ideas created or blessed by its famous chairman. As Evanier, who briefly worked for Stan Lee Media, put it, "Peter had thrown Stan a lifeline. Stan was not ready to retire quietly."[13]

Indeed, according to Evanier, Lee was terrified of ending up as purely a subject of nostalgia, the way some of his contemporaries had. When asked, during the Stan Lee Media period, to be on an old-timers panel that Evanier was slated to moderate at the San Diego Comic-Con, Lee responded, "Mark, I will do any panel you want me on as long as it's about current material. I will not do anything about history, no matter what. I am an active, current producer of material, and that's all I want to talk about."[14]

More than any internet forays by Byron Preiss or even by Marvel itself, Stan Lee Media gave Lee a chance to stay relevant in the hot medium of the present moment — and perhaps to even become incredibly wealthy. Veteran Marvel editor Jim Salicrup, who worked for a time at SLM, said about Lee's involvement with the company's products: "[Stan was] incredibly hands-on! It was his name on the company — which I don't think he was all that crazy about — and he wanted everything to be as good as possible."[15]

But for all Lee's enthusiasm and attention, the bottom would soon fall out from under the company. Evanier came to believe that, Stan aside, the other executives didn't really care much about the properties the company came up with, that "the purpose of the company was to be sold . . . to make [itself] look so damned successful that Yahoo! or Amazon or Sony or somebody would just acquire it for a huge sum of money."[16]

Whether a major investor would come along or not, Paul started surreptitiously committing various types of securities fraud with the publicly traded company. The fraud was discovered by the authorities, and Paul, after fleeing to Brazil, ended up in prison in the United States.[17]

Lee's paper multimillions disappeared. The company closed its doors in mid-December 2000, Lee avoiding any legal charges, but forced to see staff laid off en masse. It must have felt to him like the Timely Implosions of '49 and '57 all over again. It was reported that he collapsed when the layoffs were announced.[18]

Lee managed to emerge from the fiasco relatively unscathed, although he vowed, "I'll never be so stupidly trusting again."[19]

■ ■ ■ ■

On November 3, 1998, Lee's friend, Batman cocreator Bob Kane, passed away. Lee said of him, "He was fun. I got a big kick out of him."[20] Fond of each other, they also had a playful rivalry over the popularity of Batman versus Spider-Man. Lee also recalled:

We used to have a thing, he said to me, oh, a couple years before he died, he said, "Y'know, Stan, you and I ought to do a movie together. Can you imagine something by Bob Kane and Stan Lee?"

I said, "Yeah, it'd be great, something by *Stan Lee* and Bob Kane."

But I thought it was a good idea, and I said, "Well, let's do something." I said, "Here, I have an idea of a character we can use." He said, "No, no, don't tell me." I said, "Why not?" He said, "Well, it has to be a collaboration, it has to be something we both think of." I said, "Well, how can we both think of it at the same time?"

And we never got around to doing anything because he didn't want to use something *I* thought of, and he never really told me anything *he* thought of, and it was a very funny situation. But he kept saying, "We ought to do something together."[21]

Oddly, it was at Kane's funeral that Lee

561

found himself thinking about Ditko. As Evanier, who was also there, recalled, recounting a scenario worthy of its own movie:

Stan loved Ditko. We were at Bob Kane's funeral [where] the only people who showed up from comics were Stan, myself, Paul Smith, and Mike Barr. . . . Stan came up to me before the funeral and said, "I have to speak. What do I say?" And I told him some things he could say, and he went up and said them. I kind of wrote a speech for him.

So we're standing by the grave site, and they were having [mechanical] trouble lowering the coffin into the grave. . . . We were standing there waiting, and waiting, and waiting. Stan turns to me, and I swear this is true, he says, "You know, Steve Ditko was the best inker Jack [Kirby] ever had." And I did kind of a double take, like, "Why are we talking about that?" And I said, "Yes, he did a great job." And he said, "Of course, we couldn't use Ditko [to ink Kirby regularly]. He was too valuable as a penciler because he was a great artist." And he started telling me how much he loved working with Ditko. And he said, "Jack was more creative, Jack was a better artist, but I just loved working with Ditko. We had a lot of give and take."

Okay, fine. And he said, "I couldn't wait to write [the script for] a Ditko story when it came in." And I said, "Well . . . you gave the last couple of Dr. Strange stories that Ditko drew to Roy Thomas and Denny O'Neil to script." He said, "Oh, no, I didn't. I would never give them away to somebody else. Ditko's the last thing I would ever give away." I said, "The last couple of Dr. Strange stories Ditko did were dialogued by either Roy or Denny." And he goes, "Really?" And I go, "Yes, they were." "Oh, I'll check that, but I think you're wrong, because I loved working with Ditko so much. I was never happier than when I was dialoguing his stuff and writing his stuff." And then he talked a little more about Ditko. And it's like, why are we talking about Steve Ditko, for God's sake? Bob Kane is dead and in front of us.

Then, making conversation, I said, "Right around the other way here is where [comedian] Stan Laurel is buried." And Stan goes, "Really? Let's go look at it!" . . . . And he leads about eight people over to see Stan Laurel's grave site. . . . And he goes, "Wow, that's Stan Laurel. He was a great guy. He was the funniest man there ever was." And I said, "Shouldn't we get back to Bob for a minute? Shouldn't we wait until Bob is in the ground?" So we went back and waited that out.[22]

Though people at a burial may say or do odd things to avoid the reality of death, Lee clearly felt strongly about Ditko. And while

Ditko may, decades before, have felt some affection for Lee, by 1999, it seemed to be gone. *Time* magazine, in its November 16 issue, had covered Kane's funeral, including Lee's eulogy, and the magazine credited Lee as "the creator of Spider-Man." Ditko responded with a letter, which was printed in the December 7 issue:

> Re: the eulogy for Batman's Bob Kane by Stan Lee, whom you describe as "creator of Spider-Man": Spider-Man's existence needed a visual, concrete entity. It was a collaboration of writer-editor Stan Lee and artist Steve Ditko as co-creators.

This was the same year that Ditko's lengthy assaults on Lee started appearing in various magazines he put out through publisher Robin Snyder. In one, he noted *Time*'s omission, and commented that, "I was the only one with a printed clarification."[23]

Something had changed for Ditko. No longer was he the person who, seven years earlier, had exchanged hugs with Stan Lee and been willing to spend the better part of a day discussing doing possible new projects with him.

According to Lee's interview with Jonathan Ross in Ross's 2007 *In Search of Steve Ditko* documentary, Lee called Ditko after the *Time* letter appeared. Lee described the conversation to Ross:

> Steve said, "Having an idea is nothing, because until it becomes a physical thing, it's just an idea." And he said it took him to draw the strip, and to give it life, so to speak, or to make it something actually tangible. Otherwise, all *I* had was an idea. So I said to him, "Well, I think the person who has the idea is the person who creates it." And he said, "No, because I drew it." Anyway, Steve definitely felt that he was the cocreator of Spider-Man. And . . . after he said it. I saw it meant a lot to him. . . . So I said, "Fine, I'll tell everybody you're the cocreator." That didn't quite satisfy him. So I sent him a letter.

As we've seen, in an open letter, on Stan Lee Media stationery, dated August 18, 1999, Lee wrote a message that included the sentence:

> I have always considered Steve Ditko to be Spider-Man's cocreator.

As Lee recounted to Ross, "Ditko quickly pointed out that *considered* means 'to ponder, look at closely, examine,' et cetera, and does not admit, or claim, or state that Steve Ditko is Spider-Man's cocreator.

"At that point," Lee told Ross, "I gave up."

■ ■ ■ ■

From the ashes of Stan Lee Media, Lee, with his longtime lawyer, Arthur Lieberman, as well as colleague Gill Champion, formed a new intellectual property farm, which they called POW! (for Purveyors of Wonder) Entertainment. With no intention of expanding as quickly as, or on the scale of, SLM, POW! was designed to be the primary outlet through which Lee's ideas — often featuring Lee himself in some way — would be conveyed to the public and pitched to other media companies. These would include such concepts as *Who Wants to Be a Superhero?*, *Stan Lee's Superhumans,* and *Stan Lee's Mosaic.*

Lee would still do work for Marvel — the syndicated *Spider-Man* strip, of course (which Larry Lieber had been drawing since 1986) and, as always, serving as the company's friendly public face. But in theory and by contract, he was obligated to give no more than 10 percent of his time to the company.

As the 2000s began, new Marvel editor in chief Joe Quesada and his boss, publisher Bill Jemas — the latter of whom seemed to revel in coming out with controversial publishing initiatives and public statements (a great way for a cash-strapped company to get free publicity) — were hell-bent on getting headlines for Marvel's comics and reviving its battered public reputation. They were trying to reposition it — as Lee had decades before — as the little engine that could. This risk-taking led to conflicts with Arad, who was spearheading Marvel's media initiatives in Hollywood and wanted the company to project an air of no-nonsense stability.

All this, though, was not Stan Lee's battle.

The reality seemed to be that Lee's participation in Marvel's future would be largely from the sidelines, despite his lifetime contract with the company.

So Lee busied himself and POW! with developing numerous projects, many with prominent companies and celebrities — including Ringo Starr, Arnold Schwarzenegger, and Pamela Anderson — attached. Like SLM, POW! would also go public, although its shares would never reach the fantastic heights that SLM's briefly had.

And in 2001, thanks to an inspiration of Lee's friend and *Batman* movies producer Michael Uslan, Lee wrote a series of comics for DC called *Just Imagine Stan Lee Creating . . .* The simple but elegant premise was, what if DC's most famous characters were reimagined by Lee — who had only ever written comics for Marvel — and a who's who of top comics artists? Each issue's title was *Just Imagine Stan Lee with [artist] Creating [charac-*

ter]. So there were comics in the series such as:

- Just Imagine Stan Lee with Joe Kubert Creating Batman
- Just Imagine Stan Lee with Jim Lee Creating Wonder Woman
- Just Imagine Stan Lee with John Buscema Creating Superman

As Uslan recalled in a conversation with me:

> I said to Stan, "What if I brought you over to DC Comics and you re-imagined all of their superheroes the way you would have done them? Would that be of any interest to you? And what if I could team you up with the greatest artists who ever lived?"
>
> Stan was absolutely tickled by the idea, and I could see his creative juices flowing. He said, "Well, DC would never go for that." I said, "Leave that to me."[24]

Other artists involved in the project included such brand names as Gene Colan, John Byrne, Terry Austin, M. W. Kaluta, John Severin, Richard Corben, Dave Gibbons, Dick Giordano, Dan Jurgens, and Tom Palmer. Uslan wrote backup stories for the issues, and Mike Carlin was the series editor.

In the process of working on *Just Imagine,*

568

Uslan got to experience something that he had up until then indeed "just imagined." As he recounted:

I'll never forget being in Stan's office in L.A. when [John] Buscema's artwork [for *Just Imagine Superman*] came in. . . . Stan was raving about . . . what an amazing artist he is, [but] there were a page or two that he was not happy with how the plot was interpreted. He was trying to explain to John what he wanted, and he wasn't getting the point across.

After the conversation with Buscema ended, Lee put some tracing paper over the problematic art boards and handed Uslan a pencil. Uslan continued:

And he says, "Start drawing."
And he gets on a chair and starts striking a pose and explaining to me what the first panel should be. Then he goes into another pose and says, "Now draw this, from this perspective" . . . And I'm sitting there, and there he is, outstretched, showing a pose, telling me to draw it. I'm going, "Holy shit! I'm Jack Kirby! I can't believe I'm in this room with my idol, Stan Lee, and he's on the furniture, and he's telling me 'draw this.' " It was one of the most magical moments in my life . . . and I really felt like I

was experiencing firsthand the legendary creative process of Stan Lee as a writer, as an editor, as a visual genius in terms of his storytelling. And, boy, it doesn't get better than that.[25]

A highly publicized project, the *Just Imagine* series put Lee firmly in the comic-reading public's eye with a feel-good project that, rather than rehashing which artists were on poor terms with him, instead focused on what artists — from revered old pros to hot, young superstars — were quite pleased to attach their reputations to Lee's. It also served notice to Marvel that Lee was quite capable of not just competing with them on POW! projects that no one had ever heard of, but on prestige books featuring their biggest competition: *Superman, Batman, Wonder Woman,* and the rest.

Although still as determined as ever to not retire, Lee, in 2002, did finally take the time to — along with coauthor George Mair — write his memoir, entitled *Excelsior!* With a cover painting by Romita Sr. of Lee surrounded by his Marvel cocreations, the book's point of view was that of someone who'd been through a lot, both positive and negative, and had made peace with his life, his accomplishments, and even with his failures — and had now moved beyond comics into the wider storytelling world of Hollywood.

The book looked to the future not with a sense of ending but of beginning:

> So things are more exciting than ever. I'm doing just what I've always loved to do, creating characters and concepts with which to entertain the public, but now I'm doing it on the largest playing field of all.[26]

Indeed, Lee would end up living — and working — for another decade and a half, and he would, in that time, become more well known and admired than ever. As busy as he'd be with a wide variety of projects, this would largely be because of his cameos — his small but memorable parts in most Marvel movies and TV shows. The cameo sideline did, however, take a while to gather momentum.

After his debut cameo as a juror in the 1989 TV movie *The Trial of the Incredible Hulk,* there wasn't much Marvel live action for Lee to take part in. He was left on the cutting room floor in 1998's *Blade* and had a very short, nonspeaking role as a hotdog vendor in 2000's hit *X-Men* movie. Finally, in 2002's *Spider-Man,* which debuted on May 3, Lee got to be a *hero,* saving a little girl from falling debris during Spider-Man's battle with the Green Goblin. Those short bits were just the beginning of an idiosyncratic on-screen career which would bring Lee back to his original goal of being an actor.

But also in 2002, between the cameos, there would come to be — as had become standard for Lee and Marvel — a controversy over rights and payments that was about to take center stage. Lee would become embroiled again in real-world drama, thanks, strangely enough, to Marvel's growing success in the world of movies.

Both the *X-Men* and *Spider-Man* movies were huge moneymakers and established Marvel's properties as having incredible, never-before-realized potential. On deck for 2003 alone were movies including *Daredevil, The Hulk,* and a sequel to *X-Men.* Marvel had the potential to rake in revenues that would make its publishing money seem like the proverbial chicken feed.

There was one problem, however.

Lee's 1998 contract, negotiated from the ruins of the company's bankruptcy, guaranteed him 10 percent of Marvel's profits from the use of its characters in movies and TV shows. And, as Lee told a reporter for *The Times of London* the month after *Spider-Man* premiered, "I haven't made a penny from Spider-Man."

In late October of 2002, CBS's popular *60*

Minutes II program reported that Marvel, in violation of the 1998 contract — agreed to buy them when no one expected any of Marvel's movies to see the light of day, much less generate enormous revenues — had still not paid Lee anything beyond his admittedly generous salary, and that Lee was considering suing the company.

"Do you feel that you're being screwed?" asked correspondent Bob Simon.

"I don't want to say that," Lee replied. "After all, I'm still a part of the company. I love the people. I love the company."[27]

Nonetheless, on November 12, Lee initiated a lawsuit against Marvel, citing the provision in his contract that called for

> participation equal to 10% of the profits derived during your life by Marvel . . . from the profits of any live action or animation television or movie . . . productions utilizing Marvel characters.

The referenced portion of the contact further stated that

> Marvel will compute, account and pay to you your participation due, if any, on account of said profits, for the annual period ending each March 31 during your life, on an annual basis within a reasonable time after the end of each such period.[28]

Marvel had paid him none of the contractually promised profit participation.

Stan Lee, the ultimate company man, was suing the company he'd been employed by for over sixty years.

21
OF LOVE AND LAW

Is God talking to you? Did he say we have to stop?
— Stan Lee to the author at a 2014 convention panel

"The friendliest lawsuit on record."

That's what Stan Lee said he hoped his legal battle with Marvel to recover money owed him for his contractually promised percentage of movie and TV profits would be.[1]

Indeed, in 2003, while the suit was in progress, Lee, now eighty, kept working with Marvel, doing the *Spider-Man* newspaper strip and still making his cameo appearances in Marvel movies and TV series (in addition, of course, to his many projects with POW! and others).

The court found in Lee's favor in early 2005[2] and the suit was settled in April of 2005. The general belief is that Lee got a $10 million lump-sum payment for all current and future movie and TV profits, in addition to his $1 million annual salary, plus the $125,000 per year to do the syndicated strip. While $10 million isn't exactly small change, in light of Marvel's financial success in media in the years since, it wasn't really a great deal for Lee. But it did resolve the conflict between him and his longtime employer.[3]

The conflict with Marvel over royalties would not be the last lawsuit involving Lee. To the contrary, the final decade and a half of his life sometimes seemed like a surreal swirl of cameos, convention appearances, and depositions.

Similarly, two years earlier, in 2003, Marvel had settled a 1999 lawsuit over the rights to Captain America that had been brought, when another reclamation window opened, by the character's cocreator, Joe Simon. Like the 2005 settlement with Lee, it was achieved with little publicity, with details kept secret, but apparent satisfaction on both sides. Simon has implied that Kirby's estate was included in the settlement, but how is unknown.[4] *The New York Times* reported in a September 30, 2003, article that "the accord sets the stage for Marvel to transform Captain America into a star of movies, video games and theme park rides."[5]

Money aside, Lee's reward for all his work — and, as much as he enjoyed all his activity, it *was* work — was to come home to Joan. As his longtime chief executive assistant Michael Kelly wrote shortly after Lee's death:

> Stan was also a doting husband who called his wife from work at least once a day, if not more. No matter how important a meeting he was in, I was to connect him with his wife right away any time she called. Stan wrote heart-felt, private love poems to Joan every year for their anniversary and Valentine's Day. As much as he was a bit of a workaholic, sitting at his typewriter or computer for hours every day, he always looked forward to going home. At home he'd sit with his wife and talk about what had happened that day, no matter it be memorable or mundane.[6]

As he grew older, it seemed that as, or more, important to him as his work were the people that he cared about. Lee's 2002 memoir, *Excelsior!,* is a pretty short read, touching on what he felt it relevant for fans to know about him. The book is perhaps forty thousand words long, and a good 25 percent of them are cowriter George Mair's bridging narrative, leaving Lee free to add detail and commentary to the basic history of his life.

The better part of an entire chapter of the book, entitled "Friends Are Forever," consists of Lee and Mair talking about how great Stan and Joan's friends are. A couple of names — Bob (Batman) Kane and artist Ken Bald — are people that fans interested in comics history would know. But the majority are people who have no connection to entertainment or publishing and who are certainly not celebrities. And yet Lee decided that it was important to pay them tribute — not, as most authors might do, in a brief mention in an acknowledgments page but in substantial paragraphs that, really, weren't designed to do anything but make his friends feel good. (Space was devoted elsewhere in the book to his family, of course, including his wife, daughter, and brother, as well as his first cousin, Mel Stuart, director of *Willy Wonka and the Chocolate Factory.*)

One of the friends mentioned was Edith Finck, whose March 12, 2017, *New York Times* obituary stated, "For fifty years, her closest friends were Joan and Stan Lee, who used Edith as an inspiration for the Fantastic Four's Sue Richards."[7] This must have been news to any Fantastic Four fans who might have seen it.

A Google search of the names in that chapter finds that many of the Lees' closest friends predeceased them in the years since *Excelsior!*'s publication. Aside from losing "civilian" friends that he felt close enough to that he memorialized them even in his comic-fan-tailored memoir, Lee lived long enough to see most of the people he'd made his best-known comics with — many of whom he'd turned into household names, some of who were close friends — pass away. For some examples:

- Joe Maneely died tragically young in 1958, at age thirty-two.
- Bill Everett died in 1973, at age fifty-five.
- Sol Brodsky, sixty-one, and Carl Burgos, sixty-seven, died in 1984.
- Bullpen production stalwarts Morrie Kuramoto, sixty-three, and Danny Crespi, fifty-nine, both went in 1985.
- Frank Giacoia passed away in 1988 at age sixty-three.
- Vince Colletta went in 1991, at age sixty-seven.
- Harvey Kurtzman died in 1993 at age sixty-eight.
- Jack Kirby was seventy-six when he passed in 1994.
- Don Heck died the following year at age sixty-six.
- Bob Kane perished in 1998 at age eighty-three.
- Gil Kane's lantern went out in 2000, at age seventy-three; Dan DeCarlo's in 2001, at age eighty-two.

- John Buscema, seventy-four, died in 2002.
- Fellow DeWitt Clinton alum Will Eisner died in 2005, at age eighty-seven.

Lee's inclination, once he was elderly, had been to, by choice, surround himself at public events with younger people, not wanting to be solely an object of nostalgia. Now, as he moved into his eighties, that choice was starting to be taken from his hands. Even the few other remaining elders couldn't or wouldn't travel on a regular basis to make personal appearances.

In the meantime, like a zombie from *Menace* or *Fear,* the owners of the remains of Stan Lee Media would periodically rise from the dead to sue anyone within spitting distance, including Lee, over rights to characters (including Marvel's), as well as those created by Lee during the active years of SLM.

The basic rationale of these lawsuits was that there was a small window during Marvel's bankruptcy when ownership of Marvel's characters could conceivably have shifted to Lee (had he chosen to pursue it and won court battles over it — neither of which he did) and that during that window, Lee had, in effect, signed over the rights to those characters to Stan Lee Media.

By this reasoning, the people who ended

up with the remnants of SLM should therefore have the right to take ownership of the
characters from Marvel and Disney. At one
point, high-profile attorney Martin Garbus
— famous, among other things, for representing Lenny Bruce, Nelson Mandela, and Daniel Ellsberg — even got involved on the SLM
side, but he left after less than a year, complaining of "irreconcilable differences with
his clients."[8]

As of this writing, none of Stan Lee Media's
numerous lawsuits have proven successful.

On the creative front, Lee was as busy in the
2000s as ever with numerous projects for
POW! as well as with side projects, such as
convention appearances and signings. As Michael Kelly recalled, Lee

> just always liked to have things going. He al-
> ways liked to have something to do. He was
> very engaged [in his projects]. He always
> said — and I think he actually did believe it
> — if he's doing something he loves, he
> doesn't consider it work. He loved coming
> up with ideas and characters, and ways to
> make money from his ideas and charac-
> ters. . . . It kept him stimulated, it kept him
> going. It kept him happy.[9]

And journalist Abraham Riesman observed:

[T]here's a crucial thing you have to know about how Lee approaches these products [POW!'s projects]: He's not an absentee landlord. He's always substantially involved in the projects bearing his name, in part because he isn't happy just playing the role of showman — he wants the airtight creative credit that, in recent decades, has come into question, thanks to Ditko and Kirby. So while Lee's brand is slapped on so many products that you might imagine he's . . . letting any random product get the Stan Lee seal of approval for the right price, this is very much not the case.[10]

Some of Lee's many endeavors of the era included:

- *Who Wants to Be a Superhero?,* a Sci-Fi Channel reality series in which contestants presented themselves as some version of a superhero, with Lee choosing who were the best contestants.
- Stan Lee's Comikaze Convention (later called Stan Lee's L.A. Comic Con).
- *Stan Lee's World of Heroes,* a YouTube channel all about superhero pop culture.
- *Stan Lee's Superhumans,* a History Channel show that traversed the world looking for people with unique abilities.
- *Stan Lee's Lightspeed,* a movie for Sci-Fi.

- *Stan Lee's Mosaic,* a direct-to-DVD movie about a young woman who gains mystical powers.
- A line of Stan Lee–branded comics for BOOM! Studios (edited by prominent comics writer Mark Waid).
- *Stan Lee's Kids Universe* book series, done with 1821 Media.
- *Romeo & Juliet: The War,* a science-fiction graphic novel update (and possible eventual Lionsgate movie) of the Shakespeare play.
- A series of *Stan Lee's How To* books — instructions on various aspects of comic book creation — packaged by Dynamite Entertainment, published by Watson-Guptill.
- Stan Lee–branded apparel, jewelry, and, yes, cologne.
- *Stan Lee's Ultimo,* a manga comics series from Viz Media.
- *Stan Lee's Mighty 7,* a comic book co-venture with Archie Comics.
- A line of superheroes created for the National Hockey League's teams.

These were just some of the many Lee ventures that were announced. Some would come to exist; others would never get past the press release stage. Of the ones that were produced, several were moderately successful, but none would break out as any kind of blockbuster. Nonetheless, the sheer quantity of such projects made it clear that there was no shortage of people and companies who wanted to be associated with Stan Lee.

On November 17, 2008, Lee was presented with a National Medal of the Arts by President George W. Bush, with whom he exchanged witticisms at the presentation ceremony.

And in 2009, when President Barack Obama appeared in an issue of *Amazing Spider-Man,* Lee told reporter Michael Cavna of *The Washington Post:*

> I had read [recently] that the president-elect was a big fan of Spider-Man and Conan . . . maybe he still reads them, I hope! When I read that, I autographed a Spider-Man poster and sent it to him.[11]

Also in 2009, as if fulfilling Lee's long-ago stated goal to make Marvel "the next Disney," the Walt Disney Company purchased Marvel Entertainment for a reported $4 billion.[12]

That same year, Disney also purchased a 10 percent interest in POW![13]

And, also in 2009, the estate of Jack Kirby, through lawyer Marc Toberoff, filed suit against Disney (and other corporate entities associated with Marvel's movies) for ownership of the characters Kirby was involved in creating for Marvel. Many industry figures were subpoenaed to testify in the case, including Lee.

Most of Lee's May 2010 testimony is shielded from public disclosure, but some has been released. His testimony, at least as much of it as can be seen publicly, was, more or less, the history of the characters' creation as recounted by him in his 1974 book, *Origins of Marvel Comics.*

While giving Kirby great praise, the testimony depicted Lee himself as the source of all the ideas that made Marvel *Marvel,* with Kirby being portrayed as a gifted interpreter of those ideas, as opposed to their cocreator. For instance, Lee said of the creation of the Fantastic Four:

In the '60s, the ideas for the new characters originated with me because that was my responsibility. . . . [With the Fantastic Four] I tried to do everything I could to take these super-powered characters and in some way to make them realistic and human and have them react the way normal men might react if normal men happened to have super-hero powers. . . . I wrote up a very brief synopsis about that and naturally I called Jack [Kirby], because he was our best artist, and I asked him if he would do it. He seemed to like the idea. Took the synopsis, and he drew the story and put in his own touches, which were brilliant . . . that was the start of the Marvel success, you might say.[14]

Regarding the creation of Thor, Lee testified:

Now I was looking for something different and bigger than anything else [we had done] and I figured, what could be bigger than a god? . . . I thought the Norse gods might be good. I liked the sound of the name Thor and Asgard and the Twilight of the Gods' Ragnarok and all of that. Jack was very much into that, more so than me, so when I told Jack about that, he was really thrilled. We got together and we did Thor the same way [that we did the other characters].[15]

Lee's words were disappointing to some in the comics community. Mark Evanier, for instance, felt that Lee had a responsibility to at least reiterate what he'd said in the past regarding Kirby having been instrumental in creating the characters.[16] According to Evanier:

Cross-examined by Toberoff about the many times he'd hailed Jack as the co-creator, such as in his forewords for reprint collections, Lee responded, "I tried to write these, knowing Jack would read them. I tried to make it look as if he and I were just doing

586

everything together, to make him feel good."[17]

The Kirbys lost the case in the Federal Court for the Southern District of New York in 2011 and again in the Second Circuit Court of Appeals in 2013.

Even if Lee (who was called to testify on its behalf by Marvel) would have been more generous to Kirby in his testimony — the aim of which was to make clear that Lee had come up with the ideas for the characters while a Marvel employee — it's unlikely that the court of appeals would have ruled in the Kirby family's favor, anyway. As Judge Colleen McMahon had ruled in her original 2011 decision, it wasn't a matter of fairness but of whether Kirby had done the comics as work for hire — and the court was convinced that he had.[18]

The Kirbys tried to appeal the verdict all the way to the Supreme Court, which was deciding whether or not to hear the case, when Disney/Marvel, on September 26, 2014, decided to settle for an undisclosed amount. It seemed that keeping the present copyright laws intact, rather than risk a Supreme Court decision that could disrupt them, was more in Disney's self-interest than shelling out what, to them, was a relatively modest sum — estimates have ranged from $40 million to as much as $100 million — to the Kirby estate.[19] Significantly, it was also agreed that Kirby would be officially credited, along with Lee and, where appropriate, Lieber, as the cocreator of the characters he had helped originate.[20]

Disney had paid $4 billion for Marvel, and by 2014, its Marvel movies had raked in many billions, making the settlement seem small in retrospect. To pay even $100 million to make a threatening legal and public relations issue go away — while providing Kirby's heirs with what, by almost any "normal" standards, was a very nice chunk of change — must have seemed preferable by far to Disney.

Along the way to the settlement, though, Stan Lee's life was not without its significant events.

On January 4, 2011, Lee was awarded a star on the Hollywood Walk of Fame. Among the speakers that day was Todd McFarlane, who had always maintained good relations with Lee, even in the days when he and other Image founders were reviling Marvel.

In May 2012, Arthur Lieberman died of lung cancer. Losing Lieberman was not, for Lee, simply losing a friend and business partner. It was losing a key part of the team that had protected him from the unpleasantness of the world of business. Lieberman was an aggressive lawyer, one ready to go into battle to protect Lee's interests whenever necessary. He was someone Lee knew he could trust.

And in September 2012, Lee had a pacemaker successfully installed. It enabled him to do more and accomplish more. In his case, that meant keeping up regular appearances at POW!'s offices as well as being a guest at a dozen or more comic conventions each year, as well as at numerous local award shows and other entertainment business events in the Los Angeles area.

Among the conventions at which Lee made appearances were many of those put on by Wizard World, an outgrowth of the popular *Wizard* fan magazine of the '90s. Wizard was producing fifteen or so conventions each year all over the United States, and Lee was a regular guest at many of them.

This author, working for Wizard World as a programming consultant at the time, was Lee's regular moderator at his large public panels at their shows from 2014 to 2016. It was remarkable to see up close the rapport between Lee and convention audiences of thousands of people. For the most part, these crowds were unaware of — or didn't care about — the various controversies surrounding Lee. That he was a part-time employee of Marvel was also of little concern to them. Based on their questions for him and how they responded to his anecdotes and wisecracks, he might as well have stepped through a time warp in the 1965 Marvel offices — or from a movie screen showing one of his cameos — to come speak to them.

As Michael Kelly told me:

Stan pretty much took it in stride [that fans mainly wanted to hear about Marvel in its early years], and was so well-rehearsed in responses re: Marvel books he wrote in the '60s, that it was easy for him. One of his favorite lines was, "I've told this story so many times, it might actually be true!" He was genuinely proud of what Marvel did during that decade under his guidance.

His only frustration was when he really wanted to promote new POW! projects and no one wanted to talk about those, just about what he did at Marvel. But Stan usually was able to smoothly and interestingly promote his latest projects, as well, whenever he could.[21]

Among the more memorable of my convention appearances with Lee, there was one where he was delayed for a day by an adverse reaction to a flu shot from getting to a 2014 Wizard convention in Sacramento, California. Before our March 9 panel, Wizard's president announced that Lee would be doing only a twenty-minute interview (instead of the usual forty-five) because of his weakness from the reaction. And before he was introduced, he was indeed moving slowly.

But once he and I were seated onstage, he was clearly energized by the crowd's adulation. After he answered a few questions I asked him, we started taking questions from the audience. When twenty minutes had elapsed, I informed Lee that the promised time was up. I asked him if he had any final words for the audience before we ended the truncated panel. He responded, "Is God talking to you? Did he say we have to stop? I feel *great*! Let's keep going!"

Pandemonium erupted backstage as Lee's handlers and the Wizard staff were trying to figure out how to deal with this situation — and how to convey to me what they wanted me to do. We ended up doing an extra ten minutes, and even then, Lee only left the stage reluctantly.

Time and mortality continued to march on.

- Lee's close friend and colleague, Jim Mooney, passed away in 2008, at age eighty-eight.
- In 2011, Gene Colan, eighty-four, Jerry Robinson, eighty-nine, and the man who hired Lee at Timely, Joe Simon, ninety-eight, all departed this mortal coil.
- Dick Ayers died in 2014 at age ninety,

591

as did Stan Goldberg at eighty-two.

But Stan Lee kept going. Despite doctor's orders to not fly more than two hours at a time, he regularly flew cross-country and, indeed, all over the world.

On February 2, 2014, between convention appearances (one in Portland, Oregon, and one in New Orleans), at age ninety-one, Lee — who had never shown any particular interest in football — appeared, with superstar comics creator Todd McFarlane, at the Super Bowl in New Jersey. McFarlane was there to sign football-themed figures manufactured by his toy company. And Lee? He was there as part of a Doritos Super Bowl promotion, judging a commercial-making contest. (He also found time there to pose for a photo with Paul McCartney.)

For anyone, much less a nonagenarian, this would be a grueling travel schedule. Yet in New Orleans, on a panel he and I did at the Wizard convention, less than a week after the Super Bowl, he seemed as energetic as ever. On the panel, he filled me in on the Super Bowl promotion:

STAN LEE: Well, there's this little company called "Doritos" . . . and they're one of the sponsors of the Super Bowl, so they had a big contest . . . people could enter from every part of the world, and they were asked . . . to make up their own . . . thirty-second commercial [for Doritos] or maybe it was sixty, I don't remember.

The five winning commercials would be sent to the Super Bowl. And of those five, two of them would be shown at the Super Bowl. And of those two, one would be judged the winner and the person who did it would get a million dollars and a chance at [making] a real movie.

So, they received hundreds of thousands of entries and they boiled them down to a few dozen great ones that I had to look at, 'cause they wanted me to be one of the judges, because obviously my taste is so superb and I know so much about potato chips. . . .

I went [to the Super Bowl] and I met the people who submitted the five entries and I met the person that won and so forth and that's probably the dullest story I have ever told and why did you ask me about that?

DANNY FINGEROTH: Because it's the Super Bowl. The Super Bowl is something someone wouldn't normally associate with Stan Lee.

STAN LEE: I'm associated with *every-thing.*[22]

As had been shown multiple times over the years, and unlikely as it would seem, Lee and McFarlane were real friends. One would think McFarlane, the ultimate rebel, and Lee, the ultimate company man — and the living embodiment of the company McFarlane vowed to never work for again — would be anything but friends, that McFarlane, if anyone, would harbor eternal resentment against Lee on behalf of Jack Kirby and Steve Ditko. But obviously, none of that was the case.

Perhaps the explanation for McFarlane's goodwill toward Lee was based on something that occurred when McFarlane was an unknown sixteen-year-old who encountered Lee at a comic convention. As McFarlane recalled:

I was at a hotel that had a comics convention. He [Lee] was there and he let me sit next to him all day and ask him questions because I was thinking I may try to break in to comics. I'm 16 years old, I just started collecting. He let me sit there all day long. That day had a giant impact on my life. He, of course, had no recollection of that, but

594

he left an impact on me.[23]

As time went on, even the staunchest Marvel haters of years past were now suddenly eager to been seen in public with Lee. Perhaps it was because of something as simple as the realization that Lee — and they — would not live forever.

Whatever it was, Frank Miller, for another example, who had so vehemently trashed Marvel in 1986 over its treatment of Kirby, shared an L.A. Barnes & Noble conversation about Bob Kane with Lee in February 2016 and a quip-filled one-on-one panel with him at Chicago's C2E2 comic convention in April 2017.

In May of 2017, POW! Entertainment was bought by China's Camsing International Holding, which installed Camsing USA vice president Shane Duffy as CEO. Gill Champion stayed on as president and Lee as chief creative officer. Their main product was still Stan Lee's name and fame.

In his nineties, Lee's convention appearances took on something of a frantic pace, as if he were racing to do each one as quickly as possible — which he was. He'd arrive, get some sleep, do a couple of panels the next day, and then be on a plane back home. As much as he loved the appearances and the accolades, and to get paid the big money he got for doing them — the Depression kid never lost the worry about everything going away — he always felt a need to get home as soon as possible. He wanted to be with his wife, especially as her health began to seriously deteriorate.

As Michael Kelly recalled:

Losing his wife took over a year. She started being bedridden sometime in 2016, so that was a slow burden on him. . . . I knew from their interactions that that she was the light of his life. . . . They both had a great sense of humor, and there'd be a lot of laughter whenever they were talking or interacting with one another.[24]

Joan Lee died on July 6, 2017, of stroke-related complications, at age ninety-five. She and Stan Lee had been married for more than sixty-nine years.

Less than two weeks later, on July 15, Lee — and Kirby — were honored as "Disney Legends" by Disney chairman Robert Iger at Disney's D23 Expo (*D* for Disney, *23* for 1923, the year Walt Disney founded the company) at the Anaheim Convention Center.

Both awards were preceded by short video retrospectives on each man's career. Kirby's award was given first, received on the family's behalf by his son, Neal, who, before starting his acceptance speech, expressed condolences to Lee on the loss of Joan.

In accepting his own award, Lee was holding back tears, his voice cracking, as he said, "I was thrilled to see that testimonial to Jack Kirby. So well deserved."

Still deeply emotional, Lee spoke of himself as a boy:

One day in a bookstore, [I] saw . . . an expensive book . . . *The Art of Walt Disney*. . . . I couldn't afford the book and it drove me crazy, I wanted that book so badly. I saved my pennies, and after a few months, I bought *The Art of Walt Disney*. I loved that book so. I loved Walt Disney so. He was more than a man. He was an inspiration.

To think that, today, I'm standing here in the house that Disney built, and we've paid tribute to Jack . . . it is so thrilling, I can't tell you.[25]

Two days later, Neal Kirby's daughter (and Jack and Roz's granddaughter), Jillian, posted a message from her father on the Kirby4Heros Facebook page:

This past Friday I had the honor of accepting the Disney Legends Award on behalf of my father. . . . Stan Lee, also receiving an award, very graciously and emotionally paid tribute to my father . . .

I am mentioning this as, over the last two days, I have seen . . . mean-spirited remarks, about Stan Lee. . . . Regardless of how you may feel about events that occurred years ago, it's time to be done. . . . What's paramount is that my father is now getting the recognition he so truly deserves.[26]

Mourning the loss of his wife, Lee virtually doubled down on his convention appearances. He seemed to be everywhere.

But while that may have kept him busy and distracted, serious problems were soon to arise that would make Stan Lee's final act stranger than anyone could have imagined.

22
THE UNDISCOVER'D COUNTRY

They don't want you to die.
— Todd McFarlane, October 29, 2017

Neither do I!
— Stan Lee, October 29, 2017

The period leading up to and following his wife's death was a strange swirl of circumstances for Stan Lee. For fan and causal observer alike, the unfolding events of his life were an emotional roller coaster. If Stan Lee had been baby boomers' surrogate parent or uncle figure when they were kids, he now represented another archetype for them: the elderly parent. And his dilemma became a familiar challenge:

What do we do with Dad?

To some degree before, but certainly after Joan's passing, it's unclear who was calling the shots in Stan Lee's life. As with so many elderly adults in the United States — people who had survived the Great Depression, served in World War II, had lengthy careers,

599

and now were growing more and more help-less (but, if they were lucky, who still had a reasonable amount of their physical and mental faculties intact) — many questions arose about how Lee would spend his remaining time on Earth. His main emotional support had been his wife. But even while Joan was alive, certainly near her death, it was unclear who was running things in their lives.

While close with their daughter, it wasn't readily apparent what role, if any, she was taking in supervising their lives. Larry Lieber, living on the East Coast, though regularly in touch with his brother, wasn't involved in the couple's care or life decisions. Lee's partners and staff at POW! were responsible for helping them with some aspects of their lives, both at the office and at home. The same can be said for Max Anderson, his manager, who arranged travel for Lee. Memorabilia collector Keya Morgan's name popped up in the story of the Lees' last years, assuming various roles. Ditto for what seemed a constantly shifting roster of lawyers. But after Joan's death, questions arose whose answers were not readily evident. Who was deciding that Lee should continue on the convention circuit, even after his 2016 "farewell tour"? Who was hiring and firing staff at his home? Was anyone physically or psychologically abusing him? Stealing his money? Would he be better off in some kind of assisted-living or nursing situation? Should the State of California appoint some kind of guardian? Elderly Hollywood celebrities — famously Mickey Rooney and Groucho Marx — were often exploited by those ostensibly responsible for protecting them. Why would Stan Lee be immune from that danger?

Until very late in his life, Lee could be onstage at a convention and be highly entertaining to large crowds of fans. His memory seemed good, and his answers to questions were well thought out, spontaneous, and witty. He might have been a sometimes-confused old man who had trouble seeing and hearing before he got onstage and after he left it, but *onstage* he was dynamite. Even in the spring of 2017, when I did two phone interviews with him for this book, while he might have gotten some details of his past wrong, overall the conversation was spontaneous, insightful, and — of course — funny.

As someone who knew and worked with Lee for decades, and who was seen with him regularly in his later years on convention stages, I was asked if I thought there was elder abuse going on simply, if nothing else, from the endless schlepping (or being schlepped) from con to con that Lee did. Was it really enjoyable for him anymore? Or were other people just using him for financial or other reasons — maybe even well-intentioned ones? Since I wasn't socializing with him, all

I could do was reply with a question: "From what you know of Stan Lee, do you think he'd rather die at home, alone, in his sleep, or being adored by five thousand people in a convention auditorium?"

On July 23, 2017 — seventeen days after Joan Lee passed away (and the same weekend Lee was a guest at the San Diego Comic-Con) — Flo Steinberg, his 1960s gal Friday, died, at age seventy-eight, in New York.

While she and Lee weren't in regular contact, they were extremely fond of each other and were always happy to see each other when they did cross paths. "That Flo — what a gal!" he would say when asked about her. And in interviews over the years, Steinberg only had good things to say about Stan.[1]

Steinberg would go on to publish her own comics and to work in editorial and other capacities for *Arts Magazine* and for Warren Publishing. In the 1990s, and until a few years before she passed, she ended up back at Marvel as a proofreader and de facto den mother to a couple of generations of Marvel staffers.

While Lee would have numerous assistants over the years, Steinberg was the only one he regularly included in the imagined Marvel bullpen that he conjured up in the letter columns and Bullpen Bulletins. Fans lumped her in with Kirby, Ditko, Heck, Lieber, Brodsky, and Lee himself as one of Marvel's legendary staffers. And as the gatekeeper at Marvel, she was probably the one bullpen personality most kids trying to get into the offices would actually get to meet.

On his official Facebook page, Lee (or someone representing him), wrote, after Steinberg's passing:

> I dubbed her "Fabulous Flo" for good reason. Nobody cared more about her job or the people she worked with than Flo. She spoiled me for future secretaries. To most others it was just a job, to Flo it was her life's work. The whole comicbook industry knew and loved "Fabulous Flo" and her passing is truly a great loss.[2]

Her death so soon after Joan Lee's was symbolically significant, another piece of an era disappearing. But this departure of someone else who had once protected Lee was, unfortunately, a harbinger of things to come.

Lee continued doing convention appearances after Joan passed. At most of them, his panels would now be moderated by Max Anderson. While Stan's energy would vary, he usually perked up for the large-hall appearances that were open to all convention ticket holders. Though his voice might have become raspy, his replies to questions from his moderator or from the audience were clever, spontaneous, and appropriate. This was not a senile old man giving automatic responses to questions and comments. Which is not to say he couldn't go off on odd, if entertaining, tangents. As longtime Marvel staffer Jim Salicrup recalled of a September 2017 Lee panel at the Wizard World Madison convention, which both he and I attended:

Stan was brought onstage for an interview and a Q&A with the audience. He was at the top of his game — really funny and entertaining, the audience was loving him. . . .

[An audience member, for no apparent reason,] asked, "What's your favorite kind of wood?" Stan snapped, "I traveled hundreds of miles to get here so you can ask what's my favorite kind of wood?" But upon reflection, Stan offered, "Wait, wait! I just remembered my favorite wood! It's Biedermeier wood! We have some furniture that's made from Biedermeier wood, it's great! Very expensive. That's my favorite!". . . .

And most surprising of all, when asked what his favorite toothpaste is, Stan revealed that he doesn't use toothpaste! [Note: He used just a toothbrush and water.] Yes, ol' Smiling Stan confessed that when his dentist asked him to use a certain type of toothpaste, he didn't use it or any other. When he returned to the dentist, and was asked if he was using that toothpaste, he fibbed and said "Yes." The dentist said that he could tell, because Stan's teeth were in great shape.

After answering a few questions about the early days of Marvel and a few encounters with his old boss, publisher Martin Goodman, Stan suddenly grew wistful, and said something like, "Wow. Isn't this something." He explained he didn't have a punchline, he was just reflecting on how he never dreamed he'd one day be somewhere, in a big hall, and that so many people would come to see him. He just thought, "Wow. Isn't this something."[3]

And on Sunday, October 29, 2017, at Stan Lee's Los Angeles Comic Con (formerly the Comikaze Comic Con — Lee had lent his name to this annual gathering) in a public interview moderated by Todd McFarlane, he and Lee engaged in energetic banter peppered with information and recollections. When the subject of Lee's cameos came up, McFarlane imagined out loud a cameo where Lee's character would be watching an Alfred Hitchcock–directed film on TV when a superhero battle would burst through his apartment door. When the fighting superhumans had gone, McFarlane imagined Lee seeing

Hitchcock's cameo in the film (the director famously made brief appearances in his films) and derisively commenting, "What kind of an ego needs to be in all his movies, anyway?"

"We'll have an *anti-cameo* cameo by Stan Lee," quipped McFarlane.

Lee responded, "I don't want you to make fun of Alfred Hitchcock. Alfred Hitchcock was a great man."

Referring to McFarlane, Lee added, "Then he'll say 'I'm gonna make fun of Stan Lee.' This man is uncontrollable. Get him off the stage."

Taking up Lee's mock-combative attitude, McFarlane parried with the shocking (if illogical), "Stan, I'll do it [that scene] when you're dead. Don't worry about it. We'll do it once you're dead."

To this, the audience responded with spirited boos.

LEE: They don't want you to do it when I'm dead.

MCFARLANE: They don't want you to *die.*

LEE: Neither do I![4]

Lee and McFarlane would again share a stage, this time at the ACE Comic Con in Glendale, Arizona, on January 14, 2018, where Lee, though still quite alert, was exhibiting lower energy. During the interview, Lee praised POW!'s new owners, Camsing, and promised that, in eight months, he and they would be releasing comics with "new ideas for superhero books" that he was developing.[5]

McFarlane infused both events with a high energy level that was contagious, inspiring Lee, during the Arizona event, to effusively compliment his moderating and interviewing skills. (Indeed, while no one could duplicate Lee's unique career, it's certainly conceivable that McFarlane — a natural entertainer himself — could end up inheriting Lee's role as the friendly, enthusiastic face of comics.)

McFarlane later reflected:

> Especially as he got older, [Stan would] get on the phone and go, "I'm looking forward to this convention this weekend. It's gonna be a fun time, Todd." And it would just be almost like vitamins to him. When he went home, he felt like he was 10 years younger. Because he was pulling their [the fans'] energy and putting it into himself. I saw him. He'd have a bounce in his step for a couple days after conventions.[6]

In early 2018, not long after the Arizona appearance with McFarlane, Lee was stricken with pneumonia. By early February, he was recovered enough to be interviewed by me at the POW! offices for a video feature related to the *Marvel: Universe of Super Heroes* museum exhibition. Although frail and weak, his answers were, as with the McFarlane panels, appropriate, witty, and on target. Nonetheless, with his hearing and vision failing, Lee required help from POW! staffers to get from room to room.

In the months since Joan's death, numerous lawsuits had been filed by Lee and against him. Large sums of money were reported missing from various accounts of his, some the result of checks he had no memory of having signed. Numerous parties claimed to represent him, and he was recorded in videos posted on social media purporting to clear the air about who truly represented him and his interests, but then successive videos would contradict previous ones. A lawsuit against POW! for $1 billion — a nice, round figure — was filed in his name in May. The suit was dropped in July.

Sexual harassment accusations were leveled against Lee by nurses employed for his home care. In a statement, Lee vowed to fight the accusations, and they seem to have vanished. Anderson was banned from his circle, as was Morgan, who seemed to have been running Lee's life for an uncertain period of time. Some of Lee's blood was taken by a soon-banished advisor and mixed in with ink used by Lee to autograph comics that were then advertised as containing authentic Stan Lee DNA. Cringeworthy videos appeared online of Lee doing a signing at April's Silicon Valley Comic Con, where he was clearly exhausted and confused and seemed to have to be instructed about how to spell his own name.[7]

Lengthy articles about Lee's strange situation appeared in *The New York Times, The Hollywood Reporter,* the *Daily Beast,* and many other publications and websites. It was unclear who was in control of his life and assets. Although it didn't appear that he was being physically abused, it seemed clear that things were anything but stable for him. It also seemed that, as of early April, a coalition that included his daughter, JC, was taking care of him.[8]

While the battles over control of his life were being fought, pieces of Lee's past continued to drop away.

Wolverine cocreator and former Marvel editor in chief Len Wein passed away, at age sixty-nine, in September 2017. Although Wein had had serious health issues his entire life, his passing was an indication that the generation of fans who had entered comics in the 1960s was aging, too.

Two thousand eighteen would bring four deaths that struck at the heart of Marvel's, Lee's, and comics' very history.

On June 29, Steve Ditko was found dead in his Manhattan apartment by the New York

Police Department. He was ninety years old. Since he was living alone, it's unclear exactly when he died. Lee recorded a brief eulogy video for him, in which he rasped out a tribute:

> I really cannot let the week go by without commenting on Steve Ditko. Steve was certainly one of the most important creators in the comic book business. . . . He told a story like a fine movie director would. . . . [Steve,] you made a real impression here in the world.[9]

Lee's partner in humor and war stories, Russ Heath, died on August 23. He was ninety-one years old.

And then, in late August, two of the last members of the classic '60s Marvel bullpen — people who actually *did* work in the offices — were taken: Marie Severin on the 29th and Gary Friedrich on the 30th.

Severin had been indispensable to Lee as an artist, colorist, art director, and general all-around utility player. She was eighty-nine years old. A year earlier, she had fondly reminisced for me about how much she had enjoyed working with Lee. "He was fun to work with. He was crazy. He was delightful," she told me.[10]

Writer and editor Friedrich — who had been among the first hires when Marvel started expanding in the mid-1960s — was seventy-five at his passing. Friedrich was the one who'd brought Country Joe and the Fish to meet Stan Lee.

During this period, Larry Lieber decided to retire from penciling the *Spider-Man* newspaper strip, wanting to devote himself to his growing interest in writing prose fiction. The brothers spoke on the phone regularly, and Stan would frequently inquire how the work was progressing, encouraging Larry to keep going with it.

On October 8, Lee and his daughter, as well as her lawyer, Kirk Schenck, were interviewed — at Schenck's request — by Mark Ebner of the *Daily Beast* website. The site had previously written of how out of control things appeared to be in Lee's life, and the interview was an attempt to establish that JC was now — with her father's apparent willing support — running Lee's life, keeping away those who would do him harm.[11]

In the interview, conducted at Lee's home, Schenck said of JC that "she is the avenger; she is the person who protects that man [Lee]."

Of the relationship between himself and his daughter, Lee told Ebner:

We have a wonderful life. I'm pretty damn lucky. I love my daughter, I'm hoping that

611

she loves me. . . . We have occasional spats. But I have occasional spats with everyone. I'll probably have one with you, where I'll be saying, "I didn't say that!" But, that's life.

When asked if, per rumor, she yelled at her father, JC replied:

You know, he can't hear. We're not alone [in the house], and there's always other people and influences, and I find that, yes, I've been raising my voice for several years. And I've had these horrible people in my family's home. . . . And they turn my father so against me that he didn't know he had a daughter.

Asked by Ebner if, per rumor, she had ever "laid hands" on her parents, JC replied:

As long as I've lived, I have never touched my mother, my father, or a dog.

When the reporter asked Lee, "Are you okay with the way money is managed in the family?" he replied:

This money will be left to [my daughter], and instead of waiting until I die, I will give her as much as I can for her to enjoy now.

If the interview was intended to assure

anybody — fans, friends, local authorities — that everything was now fine in the Lee household, it's unlikely that goal was achieved. As many questions seemed to be raised as were answered, even if at least part of that impression could arguably be blamed on Ebner's provocative questions.

One important thing the interview *did* seem to achieve, though, was to establish that the person who would be the logical one to take care of a fading elderly person — that person's adult child — was indeed running his life.

On November 10, Roy Thomas and his manager, John Cimino, visited Lee. The visit, according to a November 15 article by Joshua Hartwig in the *Southeast Missourian* (a publication from Thomas's birthplace) was part of a birthday gift to Thomas from Cimino.[12]

In the article, Thomas said, "[Lee] didn't really want to see people much, but he found out that I wanted to come see him, and I was willing to fly across the country to see him for half an hour. He said, 'Yeah, I'd like to see Roy.' I was very flattered."

The article continued:

During the visit, Thomas said the first thing Lee said to him was, "You know, this living to be 100 isn't as much fun as I thought it'd be" . . . [Thomas added:] "I think I cheered him up for the half-hour I was there . . . I felt like I owed so much to him . . . both personal and professional."

Lee always talked about how much Thomas "saved his life," Thomas said, by coming along "to write the stuff when he was really getting tired of having to write everything."

Thomas then noted:

It really did more for me. He would've eventually found somebody else, but I never would've found another Stan Lee.

Discussing the meeting on Cimino's Facebook page, Thomas wrote of Lee that

he lacked much of the old Stan energy . . . but when I asked him about future cameos, he expressed a real interest in making them . . .

Thomas also noted in the Facebook entry that Lee

got fairly animated when talking about his battles with publisher Martin Goodman over doing Spider-Man. I opined as how maybe the one important creative decision Goodman ever made was when he commissioned Stan to create a super-hero group

614

back in 1961. Stan seemed to get a kick out of that.[13]

And Cimino told the SYFY website that:

I told [Stan] my feelings for Roy and that I'll always have his back no matter what. Stan took my hand and said, "God bless you. Take care of my boy Roy."[4]

Two days after Thomas and Cimino's visit, Lee was rushed by ambulance to the emergency room at Cedars-Sinai Medical Center in Los Angeles.

It was there, at 9:17 a.m., on November 12, 2018, that Stan Lee died, gone to the "undiscover'd country" of his favorite author, William Shakespeare.

Lee's death certificate listed heart failure and respiratory failure as the cause of death. It also notes that he suffered aspiration pneumonia, caused by inhaled food, stomach acid, or saliva.[15]

Lee's remains were cremated. POW! Entertainment announced that "Stan was always adamant that he did not want a large public funeral, and as such his family has conducted a private closed ceremony in accordance with his final wishes. Our thoughts and prayers continue to be with them."[16]

Lee's longtime executive assistant Michael

Kelly pointed out:

> Even though his passing was sad, espe-
> cially the year or two leading up to it . . .
> there wasn't a lot of unfinished business,
> not with me, and not with most of the people
> around him. His last couple of months, he
> was pretty much at peace. I could see it
> when he was sitting there looking out, and
> he would talk about being pretty much
> content, relaxed, at ease. He wasn't tor-
> mented.[17]

Stan Lee passed away after an almost unbelievable series of events, some surreally bizarre, others inspiring and endearing. In his last year, his life was turned on its head numerous times, as if the Fates themselves were conspiring to make sure his final days were anything but boring. To the very end, those watching the story of Stan Lee's life stayed engrossed. In fact, even after he passed, news relating to his tumultuous final months appeared regularly. For examples:

Keya Morgan, who for a time was directing Lee's affairs, was arrested in May 2019 on elder abuse charges related to Lee, including for "false imprisonment" for having, after Joan Lee's death the previous year, moved Lee for a time from his longtime home to a condominium where, as a 2018 complaint alleged, he had "more control over Lee."[18] In

June, Morgan pled not guilty to all charges.[19]

And in June, JC Lee, through her lawyer, Schenck, filed a lawsuit against Lee's former manager, Max Anderson, for "elder abuse, breach of contract and stealing."[20]

As of the date this book went to press, no trial date has been set for Morgan, and no response from Anderson has been publicly noted.

The Stan Lee era was officially over the day he died.

But the Marvel Age that Lee had proclaimed in 1963 was more vital than ever. Indeed, very soon after his passing, remarkable events would come to pass.

23
LEGACY

His legacy . . . is giant — we may need to come up with a new word to describe it. . . . What Stan Lee set in motion will not stop spinning, and will only continue to do so.
— Todd McFarlane

The characters that Stan Lee and his creative partners — especially Jack Kirby and Steve Ditko — invented are better known half a century after their creation than ever.

On January 21, 2019, it was announced that the *Black Panther* movie had been nominated for seven Academy Awards, including Best Picture — the first superhero film to ever be so nominated. Although it didn't take home Best Picture, it did win three other awards.

And on January 27, the film *won* the Screen Actors Guild top prize, the Best Ensemble in a Motion Picture award.

Stan Lee and Jack Kirby created the Black Panther in 1966, for *Fantastic Four #52* — not long after they came up with Galactus, the Silver Surfer, the Inhumans, and so much else that became the foundations of the Marvel Universe. The Panther — the first major black superhero — was just one of dozens of now-world-famous characters they invented. More than fifty years later, the Black Panther character in Marvel's movies is clearly recognizable as the figure that debuted in *FF #52.*

As of this writing, *Avengers: Endgame* — featuring numerous characters Lee and Kirby cocreated and/or worked on together — the finale to a decade-long Marvel movie story line, has passed the $2.6 billion mark in worldwide ticket sales and shows no sign of slowing down.

On a random night in 2019, you could go to a random movie in a random theater and — even if you weren't seeing a Marvel-based movie — you'd be likely to see more than one trailer for an upcoming Marvel film.

On television, there are current shows based on Marvel properties, and in our world of always-available-everything, you can spend hundreds of hours bingeing on Marvel-derived series.

Truth be told, even works that have nothing to do directly with Marvel or Stan Lee could nonetheless be recognized as following the template of the highly adaptable formula Lee and company put into practice: a tale of a person or a group of people, flawed in some profound way, trying to do the right thing, despite near-impossible odds, and in spite of his/her/their own worst, self-defeating tendencies — stories of "heroes with feet of clay."

Stan Lee didn't invent this template. It was there in great literature and drama and film from the beginning of such endeavours. But it wasn't in most popular culture largely aimed at kids. And it certainly wasn't in comic books.

A strong case can be made that it was thanks to Stan Lee's innovations that this is the world of genre culture that we live in. His was indeed the midlife crisis heard 'round the world.

Of course, he needed his creative collaborators to do what he did. Without Kirby and Ditko, there would be no Marvel Comics. But it was Lee who tied it all together, within each individual story, each individual series, and within the larger so-called Marvel Universe — just as it is in today's Marvel Cinematic Universe.

That this methodology for commercial storytelling has been scaled up from ten-cent, thirty-two-page pamphlets with thin profit margins to such a degree that multibillion-dollar entertainment franchises have spawned from it is beyond amazing. Stan Lee's bombastic 1963 claim that it was now the Marvel Age turned out to be true, today more than ever.

■ ■ ■ ■

Upon his death, countless tributes to Lee were paid. Some were heartfelt encomiums (a word I learned from his comics) from those associated with Marvel's media triumphs:

There will never be another Stan Lee. For decades he provided both young and old with adventure, escape, comfort, confidence, inspiration, strength, friendship and joy.
— Chris Evans (Captain America)[1]

Thank you @TheRealStanLee for the escape from this world & great joy inhabiting the ones you created!!
— Samuel L. Jackson (Nick Fury)[2]

Stan Lee and Dr. Seuss and Ray Bradbury. That's where it begins and ends with me. . . . Rest In Peace Dear Stan. You made our time here a better one.
— Josh Brolin (Thanos)[3]

Sad, sad day. Rest In Power, Uncle Stan. You have made the world a better place through the power of modern mythology and your love of this messy business of being

human . . .
— Mark Ruffalo (the Hulk)[4]

Onward and upward to greater glory! Excelsior! Good man, Excelsior!
— Angela Bassett (Ramonda)[5]

Icons of culture outside the Marvel media universe celebrated him, as well.

A fond farewell to Stan Lee, of Marvel Comics. He will be sadly missed. I was lucky enough to meet him . . . and we sat around for a while chatting about comic books and my admiration for his work. Actually he was suggesting making a superhero who would wield a Hofner bass guitar . . . and I must say the idea of becoming a guitar wielding superhero . . . was very appealing.

Sending love to his family and friends and always holding happy memories of this great man. Love ya, Stan!-Paul
— Paul McCartney (songwriter of "Magneto and Titanium Man")[6]

There were plays before Shakespeare, but the Bard's work revolutionized the theatre. . . . And Stan Lee did the same for comic books. . . . No, of course he did not do it all alone. The genius of Marvel's artists, especially Jack Kirby and Steve Ditko, should never be minimized. . . . But Lee

622

was at the center of it all. . . .
— George R. R. Martin (creator of *Game of Thrones* and kid letter-writer to Marvel)[7]

He lives forever through his work. What a giant. With great power comes immortality.
— Lin-Manuel Miranda (creator and star of *Hamilton* and fellow Washington Heights celebrity)[8]

His contribution to Pop Culture . . . cannot be overstated. . . . I loved this man & will never stop missing him. They say you should never meet a childhood idol. They are wrong. #RIPStanTheMan
— Mark Hamill (*Star Wars'* Luke Skywalker)[9]

A couple of moving tributes came from members of the Kirby family:

His passing brings great sadness, but I take solace in knowing that what my grandfather, Stan and so many others like them gave us, will continue to inspire both young and old across the globe! RIP Stan.
— Jeremy Kirby (Jack Kirby's grandson)[10]

My mother Connie, father Neal, and I, send our heartfelt condolences to the family of Stan Lee. . . . Stan's collaborations with my grandfather, and many other great creative talents, produced the Big Bang of the

623

Marvel Universe.

— Jillian Kirby (Jack Kirby's granddaughter)[11]

And, of course, members of the comics and animation industries chimed in with memorials:

Todd McFarlane noted that

I think Stan's legacy will only continue to grow. . . . His legacy to me is giant — we may need to come up with a new word to describe it. I think 20 years from now, you and I will have a conversation and we'll talk about how we sold him short.[12]

Screen and animation writer Tony Puryear, who'd worked with Lee in Hollywood, whimsically recalled on Facebook:

I loved this crazy old man. I loved every second of working with him. He was a bullshitter, a king bullshitter in a league of his own, a Mozart of bullshit, and I say this with utter admiration as someone who's made a decent living bullshitting over the years. His joy in his work was contagious.[13]

Writer/artist Frank Miller wrote:

Devastated by my pal Stan's passing. He was a childhood inspiration, an instructor to me when I was just getting started and a genuinely sweet man. Will miss him terribly.[14]

Neil Gaiman (writer of the *Sandman* series) recalled:

He was a powerhouse of energy and enthusiasm, and his death ends an era when giants walked the Earth and made up new kinds of stories.[15]

And a couple of prominent observers chose to address head-on the elephant in the room, the ever-present conflicts over Stan's relationship with his collaborators. Michael Chabon (author of *The Amazing Adventures of Kavalier and Clay*) opined:

One has only to look at #JackKirby's solo work to see what Stan brought to the partnership: an unshakable humanism, a faith in our human capacity for altruism and self-sacrifice and in the eventual triumph of the rational over the irrational, of love over hate, that was a perfect counterbalance to Kirby's dark, hard-earned quasi-nihilism. . . . It was Stan's vision that predominated and that continues to shape my way of seeing the world. . . . #olevhasholem[16]

And Paul Levitz, comics writer and editor

and former president and publisher of DC Comics, observed on his Facebook page that

> Stan has a complex legacy, with his own massive creativity clouded by unresolvable debates over the relative value of collaborators' contributions, actions he might have taken in a more perfect path to help them achieve more economic rewards, and his statements about their collaborative process. But as someone who knew and worked with pretty much all of them, I believe Stan was the irreplaceable catalyst, without whom the magic that was that first decade of Marvel Comics would never have happened, and perhaps neither would have the changes that spread through the comics field from there.[17]

It would be impossible to discuss Stan Lee's legacy without speaking about what, to many, was his most visible work: his famous cameos.

Lee appeared, usually with a short speaking role, in most of Marvel's movie and TV projects, and even in the company's video games. Looked at in the context of his life, this side gig makes perfect sense for a guy whose ambition as a teenager was to be an actor.

Technically, Lee's first live-action cameo was in the 1989 TV movie *The Trial of the Incredible Hulk,* when he played a juror in the courtroom drama. He had no dialogue.

You might also say his first cameo in a "real" movie was in the first *X-Men* movie, in 2000, when he played a hot dog vendor who is shocked by seeing a real, live mutant.

Of course, Lee also voiced his drawn appearance in the 1998 final episode of *Spider-Man: The Animated Series.* In this cameo, Spider-Man takes his cocreator out for a Spider-Man–style tour of New York, swinging on a web line from building to building. "You know, Spidey," Lee tells him, "I've always wanted to experience *real* web-slinging."

But, *technically,* Lee's first cameo would actually be in 1942's *All Winners Comics* #2, which contains a text story wherein one of the characters is referred to as "the editor of All Winners." The editor of *All Winners* was, of course, then-nineteen-year-old Stan Lee, only recently elevated to that position after the departure of Simon and Kirby. In the story, "the editor" interacts with the members of the All Winners team, including Captain America, the Sub-Mariner, the Human Torch, the Destroyer, and the Whizzer.

And in a similar vein, over the years, it's been a tradition for comics creators to insert themselves into stories with some regularity, and Stan Lee and his collaborators certainly did it. Whether in superhero stories, such as the one in 1962's *Fantastic Four* #10, where Lee and Kirby were forced to become pawns for Dr. Doom to use against the Fantastic Four, or in humor stories, such as 1969's *Chili* #3, when Stan Lee and artist Stan Goldberg were visited by Millie the Model and her frenemy Chili, who barged into Marvel's offices to discuss their problems with how the two Stans were portraying them in the comics.

But what most people think of as Stan Lee's cameos were, of course, those in Marvel's live-action movies and TV shows, starting with *X-Men*.

Lee clearly loved doing the cameos. Two days before he passed away, he told Roy Thomas that he'd love to do more, despite his fading energy. But, according to Tom De-Santo, who was a producer and screenwriter on the first two *X-Men* movies, the cameos were almost stopped before they got started in earnest. As DeSanto related it, *X-Men* was being filmed just after the Stan Lee Media fiasco, and some executives at Marvel were hesitant to have Lee in their movies because of all the negative publicity and legal jousting that situation was generating. On Kevin Smith's *Fatman Beyond* podcast (as reported by Joshua M. Patton on *Medium*), DeSanto discussed the event. It seems he

and the rest of the filmmakers were insistent that the film feature a cameo from Stan Lee . . .

. . . folks on the film were warned to not really talk to [Stan] because of the legal trouble. This was a directive precisely no one listened to. DeSanto said Stan's arrival on the set was like "Jesus" descending from the heavens . . . [and] that after the shoot, Stan talked with every extra, crew member, and anyone else who wanted to say hello or snap a photo.[18]

Sam Raimi, who directed the 2002 *Spider-Man* movie, as well as its two sequels, and who genuinely liked and admired Lee, recalled how Lee's cameo in that one, in which he rescued a little girl from falling debris created by the Green Goblin's attack, came about:

[Marvel film executive] Avi Arad said, "I want you to put Stan in the movie."
. . . [Raimi replied:] "No. I know Stan, and he can't act."
"I want him in the movie."
Now imagine you're a minor director in England doing *Macbeth* and you're told, "Put the writer in the play." It sounds absurd. "Fine, you want Shakespeare in the play, I'll put Shakespeare in the play." Now it's one of my favorite parts in the movie.[19]

Lee's longtime executive assistant Michael Kelly told me in an email about how the cameos worked:

As far as I know, no contract was ever drawn up.

The producers and directors of the various projects, starting with X-Men, of course, reached out to Stan to appear, and usually offered transportation, accommodations, etc.

However his fee was minimal. As a SAG/AFTRA member, Stan got the daily rate for appearances. Stan did them more because he loved to than for any monetary gain.

The directors would tell him what they had in mind for his appearance/one line and Stan would go along, with maybe a little collaboration if Stan felt he could make it more entertaining.

This was not considered part of Stan's Marvel responsibilities, though Kevin Feige started to make sure Stan appeared regularly in the slate of Marvel Studios Films he produces.

Stan's estate continues to collect residuals from his many cameos.[20]

As for 1995's *Mallrats* — the Kevin Smith movie, in which Lee had a fairly long speaking role — Kelly recalled:

That was a fully written "character" part for him, with him playing "Stan Lee." Stan

630

pretty much did the lines as written, with a few discussions with Kevin on the set to make any adjustments. He didn't offer any pre-written lines to Kevin Smith.[21]

In an especially meta moment — even by the standards of the generally tongue-in-cheek spirit of his cameos — in 2019's *Captain Marvel,* which is set in 1995, the same year Smith's film was released, Lee is seen on a train, de-aged for the movie, rehearsing lines from the screenplay for *Mallrats.* (Also of note is that in *Captain Marvel,* the first live-action Marvel film released after Lee's death, the usual Marvel opening character-image montage was replaced with a montage of Lee cameos, followed by a title card that read, "Thank you, Stan.")

In 2014, Lee said of his cameos:

The one I got the biggest kick out of was probably in the *Fantastic Four* movie when I wasn't invited to the wedding of Sue and Reed, and they wouldn't let me in. I said, "But I'm Stan Lee," and the security guy pushes me aside.[22]

But in other interviews, he's cited others as his favorites, so it doesn't seem he had any one consistent cameo he favored. It does seem that what many of them had in common was that they worked on multiple levels.

631

Lee's roles would convey plot points of varying degrees of importance, but they also acknowledged that the audience knew that this particular bit player wasn't just someone who auditioned for, and got, a part in movie after movie. Many viewers were well aware that this was Stan Lee — whoever they thought Stan Lee was.

So, like playing a version of himself who is barred from Reed and Sue's wedding (as he and Kirby were in the comic that portrayed that event, *Fantastic Four Annual #3*), Lee, in 2017's *Guardians of the Galaxy Vol. 2,* played a character who seemed to be "Stan Lee," who was recounting to a group of all-seeing cosmic beings called Watchers a long story that is, essentially, the plots of a number of Marvel movies (and comics). Lee's character so exhausts even their limitless patience that they walk away from him as he comically pleads with them to stick around to hear more and then berates himself for alienating them.

When I mentioned this role to Lee, it seemed even he (like the audience) wasn't 100 percent sure of the scene's meaning:

STAN LEE: It proves I'm really the Watcher.

DANNY FINGEROTH: Are you the Watcher, or are you giving the group of Watchers information?

STAN LEE: Well, I'm not sure, myself. I'll have to see the movie again.[23]

A rare *non*humorous Lee cameo was in 2016's *X-Men: Apocalypse,* in which Lee and his wife, Joan, play — no surprise — an elderly couple who are gripped with fear as numerous nuclear weapons are launched. Their acting for this short scene more than adequately conveyed the anguish the moment required without any words being spoken by either one.

One Lee friend and colleague, writer Jim McLauchlin, did voice some issues with the whole cameo concept:

> I "get" that the cameo appearances are fun and all, and a nice little wink to the audience, but in my mind . . . they were just the parsley on the edge of a massive plate of career achievements . . . and the fact that he felt he had to do these teeny movie shout-outs to validate the work felt incongruent to me.[24]

Still, there's no denying that Lee enjoyed being in the movies and that a significant percentage of people who know of Stan Lee *only* know him from his cameo roles. It was a strange, unexpected sideline career for Lee, one that brought him full circle from his days acting at the Hebrew Tabernacle of Washington Heights and the WPA Federal Theatre Project.

In 1957, there were three men who had nothing to lose.

Stan Lee had witnessed the company he'd worked for his entire adult life nearly disappear. He would never really recover from the insecurity this created.

Jack Kirby had recently experienced the dissolution of his longtime partnership with Joe Simon. Kirby's dreams of ongoing creative and financial success were replaced by a reality of doing bland stories drawn for crappy pay at a variety of companies. His visions of syndicated-strip glory were thwarted by DC editor Jack Schiff, who had the power to make his life miserable — and did.

Steve Ditko had come into the comics business at about the worst possible time — just as it was on the verge of disappearing — and then was slammed with tuberculosis, which disrupted his career for a year.

Lee, Kirby, and Ditko, in their ongoing collective autobiography known as "The Marvel Universe," were able to take elements of their personalities and backgrounds and graft them onto a fictional construct that was unlike anything that had come before it. They brought a sense of mission to their work in a way that few comics creators since Jerry Siegel and Joe Shuster had, with their creation of the New Deal warrior-hero, Superman, in 1938.

Right place, right time, right people.

There was one key insight, though, that Stan Lee had that Kirby and Ditko did not. Lee came to see that, in the early 1960s, there was an audience of adult fans who had read comics as children and were still interested in them. If the then-current *kid* audience for comics was being lost to TV, then maybe there was some way to reclaim some of those older readers, now in college or in the work world, to get them to help spread the idea that comics were cool or even relevant, while not losing the larger audience of children. To do that would require inventing comics that could operate on multiple levels.

Kirby and Ditko were perfect coconspirators for Lee in this endeavor. Ditko's Randian characters — the ultimate frontiersmen against the community — along with Kirby's view of a dog-eat-dog world where the only one you could trust was — maybe — your mother were key ingredients in a lumpy but tasty stew, undercooked in some spots, overdone in others. And Stan Lee's humanist point of view, simultaneously cynical and idealistic, and laced with humor, was the secret spice that blended it all together.

Having lived through his share of tragedy and melodrama, Lee seemed to share some of Kirby's and Ditko's bleak view of humanity, but was able to summon an overall upbeat attitude that pointed to the potential of individual humans (if not all humankind) to achieve some kind of happiness in a highly imperfect world.

This combination of contradictory impulses could have created confused comics with unappealing protagonists. But as editor, Lee had the final say in Marvel's messages, overt and subliminal, and allowed himself to follow his instincts. As he said:

I always wrote for myself. I figured I'm not that different from other people. If there's a story I like a lot, there's got to be others with similar tastes.[25]

As the Associated Press's Ted Anthony wrote of Marvel's characters:

Some moneyed, some working-class, all neurotic, they had powers thrust upon them by misfortune or questionable choices. . . . And sometimes it was hard to tell the heroes and the villains apart. Sort of like real life.
    This was in no small measure due to Lee . . . he breathed personality, ambiguity and a common narrative into soon-to-be-beloved characters.[26]

Somehow, catalyzed by his collaborators' work, Lee had a personal and professional breakthrough that enabled him to unleash something heretofore untapped in him or in them. He's claimed to never have engaged in psychotherapy ("Never had time," he told David Hochman in 2014), but it almost seems like the kind of breakthrough one might undergo after a period of psychoanalysis.[27]

Lee had the authority of an owner but the insecurity of a freelancer. He was still at the boss's mercy — even though most of his colleagues saw *him* as the boss. He could and did write stories where he could simultaneously inhabit the identities of oppressed and oppressor, king and subject, boss and flunky, leader and follower — and express eloquently what those positions felt like.

As editor, art director, co-plotter, and scripter — and relative of the owner — Lee was in a unique position among his peers, his employees, and the entire industry. In some ways, it enabled him to be an auteur, to be the one to really — with indispensable input from his boss and his cocreators — make the comics that fulfilled his vision. It might have been a vision that he partly stumbled onto, one that he achieved by sometimes mangling his partners' intentions. But in the end, it was *his* vision.

As the AP's Anthony noted:

Many felt Lee didn't share enough credit

637

with such comics pioneers as Jack Kirby and Steve Ditko. . . . Fair enough. But part of Lee's genius was his ability to be a master of collage.

Like a Bob Dylan or a Gene Roddenberry, Lee took cultural threads — elements already afoot in society — and constructed his own quilt.[28]

Lee often chose as his on-panel avatar the Silver Surfer. It was the Surfer he would use to channel his feelings about humankind's lack of appreciation for the beauty and bounty of Earth.

And yet, the solo adventures he wrote for the Surfer never sold all that well, despite beautiful art by John Buscema, Moebius, and others. The Surfer, to whom Lee gave voice, was a space-spawned messiah, bemoaning the lunacy of mankind. But heartfelt as it was, that voice — outside of the Galactus Trilogy — never sounded like the real Stan Lee. Perhaps aspiring novelist Stanley Martin Lieber was writing that dialogue. Ultimately, the Surfer, as written by Lee, was somehow *too serious* to be taken seriously.

On the other hand, with the words and thoughts Lee gave Peter Parker and Ben Grimm and Nick Fury — poor kids who, with talent and determination, improved their status in life — *this* was where Lee's gift for channeling the thoughts and emotions of regular people shone through.

In the first S.H.I.E.L.D. story in 1965's *Strange Tales* #135 (by Lee and Kirby), Nick Fury — around forty-five years old, more-or-less the same age as Lee — becomes the star of his own "modern" series (as opposed to his lead role in a WWII-era-set comic). While Fury is often rightly identified with Jack Kirby, there's an awful lot of Stan Lee in the character, too. In the story, Fury has just been chosen to be director of the superspy agency. His response to the offer: "Where do *I* come off leadin' a hot-shot outfit like this? I'd fall flat on my ugly pan!"

Suave, sophisticated Tony Stark, a member of S.H.I.E.L.D.'s inner circle (as well as secretly being Iron Man), reassures him: "You underestimate yourself, Fury! Your entire *life* qualifies you for this job!"

Stan Lee's entire life qualified him for the job of giving an authentic voice to Marvel's characters and comics.

His gift for knowing, in Marvel's formative years, what resonated with his readership made it possible for him to connect with them on an ongoing basis. His loyalty to his vision of the "regular guy" was one of the prime elements that made Marvel's comics magical.

That vision — along with countless tangible and intangible elements provided by Kirby and Ditko and others — is Stan Lee's legacy.

AFTERWORD

LAST THOUGHTS ON STAN LEE

Even when I made a good living, my dad didn't think of me as a success. He was pretty wrapped up in himself most of the time. Some of that rubbed off on me. I was always looking at people who were doing better than I was and wishing I could do what they were doing — Steven Spielberg or a writer like Harlan Ellison, or even Hugh Hefner. Part of me always felt I hadn't quite made it yet.

— Stan Lee, *Playboy,* April 2014

I'm going to tell you two secrets.

The first one is:

Although we're not supposed to say it, more than the colorful, cavorting characters, the in-your-face action, and the unified universe, what made Marvel comics different was that they were about unhappy, sometimes unpleasant people — and those were the *heroes!* These were people with problems.

Convenient shorthand could be to call them — as many reporters have — *neurotic,* suffering from neurosis, which is defined by dictionary.com as "a relatively mild personality disorder typified by excessive anxiety or indecision and a degree of social or interpersonal maladjustment." Yep, sounds like a Marvel superhero, all right.

As early as 1963's *Amazing Spider-Man* #4, Lee has a man on the street declaring that Spider-Man "must be a *neurotic* of some sort!" Even the theme song for the 1966 *Marvel Super-Heroes* animated series used the word *neurotic* to describe one of the heroes (the Sub-Mariner, if you were wondering, who was described as "exotically neurotic"). That's not a word you hear used a lot in kids' cartoon theme songs.

You could call the heroes' psychological state *neurosis* or *angst* or *soap opera* or *melancholy* or *depression*. Critic Greg Hunter called it *anguish*. As he wrote in *The Comics Journal*:

> If there's one thing Kirby and Ditko have in common, beyond some shared historical circumstances, it may be anguish — the gift for depicting it and an accord with characters hit by it.[1]

And advertising executive David Sable (as twelve-year-old schoolmates, he and I paid a visit to the Marvel bullpen; we got as far the reception area and Fabulous Flo Steinberg) observed that, as kids

we didn't know what *angst* meant, but
Marvel *had* it.[2]

Stan Lee shared a gift for portraying anguish, too. I won't venture to say if he was
"happy" or not. He did seem to get a kick
out of being Stan Lee, seemed to be someone
who, overall, enjoyed life. And he did tell
reporter David Hochman in 2014, "I haven't
had a lot of angst. . . . I've had a happy life."[3]
But I don't think you can write those ang-
sty — okay, *neurotic* — characters without
being at least a bit in touch with the sadder
side of life. At least for those moments when
he was creating, Lee needed to be in touch
with sadness and despair. I think he was
certainly able to access whatever part of him
resonated with the fear of failure that witness-
ing his father's troubled life instilled in him.
Lee was no stranger to *regret* and seemingly unafraid to voice it. In *Excelsior!,* he
expresses regret over all sorts of things,
among them: not leaving comics, not standing up to Martin Goodman, not being closer
to Larry. And he told interviewers, including
Ira Wolfman in *Circus,* that he wished he'd
gone to Hollywood twenty years earlier.
His experience with angst and sadness
could have come from any number of sources:
his troubled father; family anxiety over

money; the alternate boredom and terror of working in a fad-driven business; the alternate boredom and terror of working for Martin Goodman; the fear that his wife would agree with him that he really wasn't good enough for her; the fear that an atomic bomb — or even a *gamma* bomb — could destroy everything and everyone he loved.

And guess who *else* was in touch with that angst?

Me.

That's the second secret:

Stan Lee did all he did just for *me*.

Yes, I knew there were hundreds of thousands, indeed, millions, of other people reading the same comics. But the comics made me feel as if they were speaking directly to *me* and creating a world for *me* that a movie or a TV show couldn't. Reading a Marvel comic was simultaneously an individual, personal experience *and* a shared, communal experience.

Everyone reading — at least those who came back issue after issue — felt like Stan Lee was doing it *just for them.* With all the contributions to story and character that might have come from Kirby or Ditko, the voice that was bonding with us, for better or worse, was Stan Lee's. (This is perhaps why his movie cameos don't feel jarring to comics readers. We knew he was there all the time.)

There was something about the emotional baggage Marvel's characters dragged around that connected to us. For whatever reasons — and I'm sure we each had our own reasons, conscious or not — the neurotic superheroes and the world they inhabited, but didn't quite fit into, had great appeal.

Marvel and its voice weren't for everybody, of course. Some people preferred a different relationship with their comic book fiction — DC's voice or Dell's, for instance. Of the fifty kids in my elementary school class, maybe four of us were deeply into comics, or at least would admit it — so 8 percent were tuned in. I don't remember anyone ostracizing us for reading comics; we experienced apathy more than any noticeable derision — but for those 8 percent, Marvel created a *world,* a world we came to prefer to DC's. (I like to think that, even with the Marvel movies so popular, the characters still have more resonance for that 8 percent than for anyone else. But I could be kidding myself.)

Those comics created by Lee and his collaborators had a profound effect on my life. I had a family. I had friends. I had a variety of interests. But there was something special in these comics, something that felt like coming home — only better. Lee was able to take on some of the positive aspects of a relative or friend and not bother you with the less appealing parts. Certainly, he could talk about the comics with you — about both the stories and about what was happening behind the scenes — and there wasn't any other adult in your life who could do *that.* He embodied the company and really made his readers — me, in particular — feel special.

Although I got to know him to a certain degree as an adult comics professional and got occasional glimpses of the "real" person (who, overall, treated me very nicely), I really do think the truest and best Stan Lee came through — at least, for someone who wasn't in his close personal circle — in the comics stories, and especially in the text pages in the comics. *That* Stan Lee was someone who was endlessly fascinating to know. In the stories, he and his — and *your* — bullpen pals delivered exciting adventures filled with (angst-fueled) moments of insight. And the letters pages and Bullpen Bulletins pages drew you in, giving you the inside story on the characters *and* the creators, and gave you the feeling that you were right there, in that "Marvel Bullpen" that didn't actually exist.

He was *better* than a friend or a relative. He was *Stan Lee.*

Stan Lee in the Marvel comics of the '60s was a powerful imaginary companion to readers — so powerful that that version of Stan Lee would be passed down through generations from parent to child (helped along by his ubiquitous cameo presence). Ten-year-olds — brought to Lee's convention panels by nostalgic parents or grandparents — asking him questions in the 2000s might as well have been ten-year-olds time-platformed in from 1963. (Need I add that Lee invariably treated their questions with respect and thoughtfulness, and usually a wisecrack or two?) The idea of a perfect Stan Lee lived on — and lives on after his death.

Of course, Stan Lee *wasn't* perfect. He was a flesh-and-blood human who survived for more than seventy-five years as a sensitive, creative force *and* as a high-powered media executive. We didn't want to believe that, with all he did for us — for each of us individually, if you were attuned to that — that Stan Lee wasn't the idealized — the *superhero,* if you will — version of himself that we wanted him to be. We didn't want to know that Stan Lee was a real person, living in a real world, who had a real job and had real flaws. We didn't want to know that he had his own feet of clay.

I used to say that Stan Lee's "problem" was that people didn't compare him to other comics editors like Julius Schwartz or to other media executives like George Lucas. They compared him to Captain America — and there's no winning a contest like that.

But I've come to think that Stan Lee's actual problem, his biggest challenge, was that people invariably compared him to . . .

Stan Lee. That's an even harder contest to win.
'Nuff said?

ACKNOWLEDGMENTS

I hope that, in telling Stan Lee's story, I have given some sense of the context — the people and the times — in which he and his generation of comic book creators lived and worked. As part of telling his story, it was important for me to lay out, from Lee's perspective, how he and his colleagues responded as the times changed and the narrow niche of entertainment they started out in became a gateway to something much larger. If I have succeeded in some or all of this, it's because of the invaluable help I received from numerous people and institutions. I'm no doubt forgetting some, and my apologies for that. But here are at least some of those to whom this book is indebted:

First, thanks to Stan Lee for having a life worth writing about.

Many thanks to Larry Lieber, for being so frank in his interviews, and for hiring me to be his assistant about a million years ago.

649

Thanks to my superagent, Kevin Moran, who believed in this project.

Thanks to Peter Joseph, my original Thomas Dunne/St. Martin's Press editor who understood what I was going for, and to Peter Wolverton, who picked up where Peter J left off and kept the faith. Also thanks to assistants Hannah O'Grady and Jennifer Donovan. Thanks to Rafal Gibek and company at Macmillan for the invaluable copyediting.

Thanks to the incredible, thorough, and insightful scholarship of Dr. Michael J. Vassallo, Barry Pearl, and Nick Caputo, aka: The Yancy Street Gang. Thanks especially to Doc V, who guided me through his amazing archive of Magazine Management related materials. I'm also grateful for the meticulous research of Ger Apeldoorn, John Morrow, Peter Sanderson, Roy Thomas, Carol Tilley, and Ken Wong. Thanks also for the research of J. L. Mast, who is writing and drawing an upcoming graphic novel format biography of Stan Lee and Martin Goodman.

Thanks for the interviews, in person, via phone, and via email to:

Neal Adams, Dick Ayers, Ken Bald, Allen Bellman, Sal Buscema, Joseph Calamari, David Bennett Cohen, Gerry Conway, Judith Crist, Tom DeFalco, Victoria Dollon, Scott Edelman, Mike Esposito, Mark Evanier, Gary Friedrich, Linda Fite, Bruce Jay Friedman, Pauline Mirsky Goldberg, Stan Goldberg,

Robin Green, Michael Z. Hobson, Sidney Iwanter, Al Jaffee, Isabelle Kamishlian, Michael Kelly, Stan Lee, Paul Levitz, Larry Lieber, Todd McFarlane, Barry Melton, Jim Mooney, Dennis O'Neil, Tony Puryear, Jerry Robinson, John Romita Sr., John Romita Jr., David Sable, John Semper, Marie Severin, Joe Sinnott, Flo Steinberg, Roy Thomas, Michael Uslan, Irene Vartanoff, and Marv Wolfman.

Thanks for the photos to Ken Bald, John Benson, Victoria Dollon, Rick Dollon, Jackie Estrada, Pauline Mirsky Goldberg, Stephen Goldberg, Alex Grand, James Van Hise, Larry Lieber, Robin Platzer, and Scott Saternye.

Thanks for things too numerous to list to Fearless Face Fronter David Kasakove.

And thanks to:

- Jenny Robb, Caitlin McGurik, Susan Liberator, and the rest of the incredible staff at the Billy Ireland Cartoon Library and Museum at the Ohio State University in Columbus.
- Ginny Kilander, John R. Waggener, the late Mark A. Greene and the rest of the amazing folks at the University of Wyoming's American Heritage Center, where Stan Lee's archives are housed.
- the Freewheelin' Evander Lomke, who got all this started.
- the late Bob Silverstein, for important

651

advice and guidance.

- Jim Amash, Ger Apeldoorn, Bob Batchelor, Robert Beerbohm, Blake Bell, Al Bigley, Jon B. Cooke, Tom DeFalco, Mark Evanier, Jules Feiffer, David Hajdu, Sean Howe, Will Jacobs, Gerard Jones, Arie Kaplan, Tom Lammers, Jeff McLaughlin, Charlie Meyerson, Will Murray, John Morrow, Jordan Raphael, Bill Schelly, Tom Spurgeon, Roy Thomas, Steven Thompson, Maggie Thompson, and Craig Yoe, for scholarship and advice.
- Ryan Ball, Mike Bourne, Neal Conan, Ann Marie Cunningham, Rick Dollon, Gary Dunaier, Jackie Estrada, Roger Ebert, Barry Farber, Daniel Friedman, Drew Friedman, Carl Gropper, Nancy Gropper, Christopher Jansen, Michael Kelly, Frank Lovece, Joe Lovece, Mike Lynch, Russ Maheras, Country Joe McDonald, Patrick A. Reed, Christoph Scholtz, Lisa Arbisser Shapanka, Sam Shapanka, Mark Sinnott, Suzanne Soliman, Richard Weingroff, and Ira Wolfman, for various kinds of invaluable help.
- Steven Tice, for his championship transcribing. What a lifesaver!

And on the home front:
Thanks to Jim and Pat Fingeroth for their

commitment to this project. Thanks to the late Blanche S. Fingeroth for always believing.

Thanks to my son Ethan for his ongoing concern for "how the book is going" and for his inspiring love of superheroes, even if he does prefer them in the movies or on the basketball court.

Thanks to my son Jacob for his never-ending sense of wonder and for always sitting through the credits.

And thanks to Varda for creating a space in which I could research and write, and for her invaluable suggestions about the manuscript. I love you.

— D.F.

NOTES

Chapter 1: JFK, the Beatles . . . and Stan Lee

1 Migration User, "Appreciation: Stan Lee's Superheroes Changed Comic Book Industry," *Boston Herald,* November 13, 2018, https://www.bostonherald.com/2018/11/13/appreciation-stan-lees-superheroes-changed-comic-book-industry/.
2 Stan Lee and George Mair, *Excelsior!: The Amazing Life of Stan Lee* (New York: Fireside, 2002), 109–110.
3 Ibid.
4 Bill Schelly, " 'Fabulous Flo' & the First New York Comicons," *Alter Ego* #153, July 2018, 9–10.
5 Danny Fingeroth and Roy Thomas, eds., *The Stan Lee Universe* (Raleigh, NC: Two-Morrows, 2011), interview with the author, January 17, 2008, 52.
6 Marvel Bullpen Bulletins, August 1966.
7 *Fantastic Four* #28, letter column.

Chapter 2: The Dress Cutter's Son

1 Stan Lee, interview with the author, March 7, 2017.

2 Stan Lee and George Mair, *Excelsior!: The Amazing Life of Stan Lee* (New York: Fireside, 2002), 19.

3 Research of J. L. Mast; Bob Batchelor, *Stan Lee: The Man Behind Marvel* (London: Rowman & Littlefield, 2017).

4 Research of J. L. Mast.

5 Lee and Mair, *Excelsior!,* 10–11.

6 Lee, interview with the author, March 7, 2017.

7 Research of J. L. Mast.

8 Lee and Mair, *Excelsior!,* 7; Larry Lieber, interview with the author, December 28, 2018.

9 Lee, interview with the author, March 7, 2017.

10 Jordan Raphael and Tom Spurgeon, *Stan Lee and the Rise and Fall of the American Comic Book* (Chicago: Chicago Review Press, 2003), 4.

11 Lee, interview with the author, March 7, 2017.

12 Larry Lieber, interview with the author, December 16, 2016.

13 Stan Lee, interview on Yesterdayland.com (website discontinued).

14 Ibid.

15 Research of J. L. Mast.

16 Lee, interview with the author, March 7, 2017.

17 Ibid.

18 Ibid.

19 Lee, interview on Yesterdayland.

20 Lee and Mair, *Excelsior!,* 12.

21 Mike Bourne, "Stan Lee: The Marvel Bard," *Changes,* April 15, 1970.

22 Stan Lee, interview with Barbara Bogaev, *Fresh Air* on NPR, June 4, 2002.

23 Lee, interview on Yesterdayland.

24 Lee, interview with the author, March 7, 2017.

25 Lee and Mair, *Excelsior!,* 12.

26 Ibid., 13.

27 Ibid., 19.

28 Ibid.

29 Lieber, interview, December 28, 2018.

30 Lee, interview with the author, April 10, 2006.

31 Lee, interview with the author, March 7, 2017.

32 Lee and Mair, *Excelsior!,* 10.

33 Gerard J. Pellison and James A. Garvey III, *The Castle on the Parkway: The Story of New York City's DeWitt Clinton High School and Its Extraordinary Influence on American Life* (Scarsdale, NY: Hutch Press, 2009).

34 DeWitt Clinton High School 1939 yearbook.

35 Batchelor, *Stan Lee: The Man Behind Marvel,* 12.
36 *FOOM* #17, March 1977, interview with David Anthony Kraft, 7–8.
37 Lee, interview with the author, March 7, 2017.
38 Ibid.
39 Raphael and Spurgeon, *Stan Lee,* 6.
40 Lee and Mair, *Excelsior!,* 15.
41 *FOOM.*
42 Lee and Mair, *Excelsior!,* 18–19.
43 Lee, interview with the author, March 7, 2017.
44 *FOOM,* 8.
45 Research of J. L. Mast.
46 Lee, interview with the author, March 7, 2017.
47 Ibid.
48 *FOOM,* 8.
49 Sean Howe, *Marvel Comics: The Untold Story* (New York: Harper, 2013), 19.

Chapter 3: The Pied Piper of West Forty-Second Street

1 Jim Amash, "A Long Glance at Dave Gantz," *Alter Ego,* v3 #13, March 2002.
2 Jordan Raphael and Tom Spurgeon, *Stan Lee and the Rise and Fall of the American Comic Book* (Chicago: Chicago Review Press, 2003), 18–19.
3 Ibid.

4 Joe Simon, *My Life in Comics* (London: Titan Books, 2011), 108.

5 Stan Lee and George Mair, *Excelsior!: The Amazing Life of Stan Lee* (New York: Fireside, 2002), 25.

6 Simon, *My Life in Comics,* 108.

7 Joe Simon and Jim Simon, *The Comic Book Makers* (Lakewood, NJ: Vanguard, 2003), 54.

8 *FOOM* #17, March 1977, 9.

9 "Stan Lee (1922–2018) — The Timely Years," Timely-Atlas-Comics, December 8, 2018, http://timely-atlas-comics.blogspot.com/2018/12/stan-lee-1922-2018-timely-years.html.

10 Simon, *My Life in Comics,* 110.

11 Simon and Simon, *The Comic Book Makers,* 62–63.

12 Ibid, 63.

13 Simon, *My Life in Comics,* 113–114.

14 "Stan Lee (1922–2018) — The Timely Years," Timely-Atlas-Comics.

15 Lee and Mair, *Excelsior!,* 30.

16 Raphael and Spurgeon, *Stan Lee,* 24.

17 Al Jaffee, interview with the author, December 5, 2016.

18 *The Comics Journal* #181, October 1995.

19 Mary-Lou Weisman, *Al Jaffee's Mad Life* (New York: It Books, 2010), 148.

20 Danny Fingeroth and Roy Thomas, eds., *The Stan Lee Universe* (Raleigh, NC: Two-

Morrows, 2011), interview with the author, January 28, 2008, 28.

21 David Gantz, "Jews and the Graphic Novel," JBooks.com, http://jbooks.com/firstchapters/index/FC_Gantz.htm.

22 "Allen Bellman — The Interview," Timely-Atlas-Comics, March 25, 2012, http://timely-atlas-comics.blogspot.com/2012/03/allen-bellman-interview.html.

23 Fingeroth and Thomas, *The Stan Lee Universe,* interview with the author January 2008, 25.

24 Chris Knowles, "Jim Mooney Over Marvel," *Comic Book Artist* #7, March 2013.

25 Stan Lee, interview with the author, March 7, 2017.

26 "Stan Lee (1922–2018) — The Timely Years," Timely-Atlas-Comics.

27 Lee, interview, March 7, 2017.

28 *FOOM* #17, 10–11.

29 Lee, interview with the author, March 7, 2017.

30 Lee and Mair, *Excelsior!,* 46.

31 Knowles, "Jim Mooney Over Marvel."

32 Raphael and Spurgeon, *Stan Lee,* 32.

33 Jim Amash, "I Did Better on *Bulletman* Than I Did on *Millie the Model,*" *Alter Ego* #55, 2005.

34 Ibid.

35 Lee and Mair, *Excelsior!,* 50.

36 Gillian Telling, "Stan and Joan Lee's Amazing 69-Year Love Story: 'She Was the

Girl I Had Been Drawing All My Life,' "
People, November 12, 2018, https://people
.com/movies/stan-joan-lee-69-year-love
-story/.

37 "Joan Lee, Wife of Comics Legend Stan
Lee, Is Dead at 93," CBS News, July 6,
2017, https://www.cbsnews.com/news/joan
-lee-wife-of-marvel-comics-legend-stan-lee
-is-dead-at-93/.

38 Rowes, Barbara, "Stan Lee, Creator of
Spider-Man and the Incredible Hulk, Is
America's Biggest Mythmaker," *People,*
January 29, 1979, 52.

39 Ibid.

40 Lee and Mair, *Excelsior!,* 67–69.

41 "Stan Lee (1922–2018) — The Timely
Years," Timely-Atlas-Comics.

42 Larry Lieber, interview with the author,
December 16, 2016.

43 Lee and Mair, *Excelsior!,* 71.

44 Larry Lieber, interview with the author,
December 16, 2016.

45 Larry Lieber, interview with the author,
December 28, 2018.

46 Ibid.

47 Ibid.

48 Ibid.

49 Ibid.

50 Ibid.

51 Fingeroth and Thomas, *The Stan Lee Universe,* 129.

52 Raphael and Spurgeon, *Stan Lee,* 34.

53 Ibid, 38.

54 Lieber, interview, December 28, 2018.

55 Lee, interview with the author, May 2, 2017.

56 Victoria Dollon, interview with the author, February 4, 2019.

57 Knowles, "Jim Mooney Over Marvel."

58 Lee, interview, May 2, 2017.

59 Fingeroth and Thomas, *The Stan Lee Universe,* interview with the author, January 23, 2008, 23–24.

60 Denis Kitchen and Paul Buhle, *The Art of Harvey Kurtzman: The Mad Genius of Comics* (New York: Harry N. Abrams, 2009), 30.

Chapter 4: The Psychopathology of Comic Books

1 Jordan Raphael and Tom Spurgeon, *Stan Lee and the Rise and Fall of the American Comic Book* (Chicago: Chicago Review Press, 2003), 55.

2 "We Wish You a Fago Christmas and a Happy New Year!," Timely-Atlas-Comics, December 24, 2018, http://timely-atlas -comics.blogspot.com/2018/12/.

3 Raphael and Spurgeon, *Stan Lee,* 55.

4 Ibid., 57–58.

5 Carol L. Tilley, "Seducing the Innocent: Fredric Wertham and the Falsifications That Helped Condemn Comics," *Information &*

Culture: A Journal of History 47, no. 4 (2012): 383–413, doi: 10.1353/lac.2012 .0024.

6 Judith Crist, interview with the author, February 23, 2008.

7 "The People vs. Medea," Judith Crist, *Harper's Bazaar*'s January 1948 issue.

8 Stan Lee, interview with the author, May 2, 2017.

9 Crist, interview.

10 "The Comics . . . Very Funny," *Saturday Review of Literature,* May 29, 1948.

11 Crist, interview.

12 Judith Crist, "Horror in the Nursery," *Collier's,* March 27, 1948, http://www.lostsoti .org/ColliersArticleHorrorInTheNursery .htm.

13 Ibid.

14 Bradford C. Wright, *Comic Book Nation* (Baltimore: Johns Hopkins University Press, 2011), 98.

15 "Part 1: Fredric Wertham, Censorship & the Timely Anti-Wertham Editorials," Timely-Atlas-Comics, February 6, 2011, http://timely-atlas-comics.blogspot.com/ 2011/02/frederic-wertham-censorship-anti .html.

16 Danny Fingeroth and Roy Thomas, eds., *The Stan Lee Universe* (Raleigh, NC: Two-Morrows, 2011), interview with the author, December 25, 2008, 32.

17 Stan Lee and George Mair, *Excelsior!: The Amazing Life of Stan Lee* (New York: Fireside, 2002), 81.

18 Raphael and Spurgeon, *Stan Lee,* 60–61.

19 Fingeroth and Thomas, eds., *The Stan Lee Universe,* interview with the author, January 29, 2008, 31.

20 Pauline Goldberg, interview with the author, January 25, 2019.

21 Joe Sinnott, interview with the author, December 8, 2016.

22 Paul Gravett, "Bernie Krigstein: The Right to Silence," June 8, 2008, http://www.paulgravett.com/articles/article/bernie_krigstein.

23 Lee, interview with the author, May 2, 2017.

24 Blake Bell, *I Have to Live with This Guy!* (Raleigh, NC: TwoMorrows, 2002), 82.

25 Raphael and Spurgeon, *Stan Lee,* 37–38.

26 Stan and Joan Lee, personal conversation with the author, January 1995.

27 Bell, *I Have to Live with This Guy!,* 61.

28 Lee and Mair, *Excelsior!,* 74–75.

29 Joe Simon, *My Life in Comics* (London: Titan Books, 2011), 184–185.

30 "Testimony of Mr. Monroe Froehlich, Jr.," TheComicbooks.com, http://www.thecomicbooks.com/froehlich.html.

31 Sean Howe, *Marvel Comics: The Untold Story* (New York: Harper, 2013), 30.

32 Larry Lieber, interview with the author, December 16, 2016.

33 Raphael and Spurgeon, *Stan Lee,* 60–61.

34 Ibid.

35 Howe, *Marvel Comics,* page 32.

36 Raphael and Spurgeon, *Stan Lee,* 61.

37 "John Romita Interview: Spidey's Man," *Comic Book Artist* #6, fall 1999.

Chapter 5: Breaking Out and Staying In

1 Stan Lee and George Mair, *Excelsior!: The Amazing Life of Stan Lee* (New York: Fireside, 2002), 94.

2 Bruce Jay Friedman, interview with the author, January 20, 2017.

3 Stan Lee, interview with the author, March 7, 2017.

4 Letter from Edward Tabibian, Toni Mendez archives, Billy Ireland Cartoon Library and Museum, Ohio State University, Columbus, OH.

5 "Cub Scouts' Strip Rates Eagle Award," *Editor & Publisher,* December 1957.

6 Jay Maeder, "Stan Lee: 1974," Comics Feature, 1974.

7 Toni Mendez archives.

8 Lee, interview with the author, March 7, 2017.

9 Lee and Mair, *Excelsior!,* 86.

10 *FOOM* #17, March 1977, interview with David Anthony Kraft, 16–17.

Chapter 6: Gathering Forces

1 Jeff McLaughlin, ed., *Stan Lee: Conversations* (Jackson: University of Mississippi Press, 2007).
2 Sean Howe, *Marvel Comics: The Untold Story* (New York: Harper, 2013), 33.
3 *Comics Journal* #134, February 1990.
4 Larry Lieber, interview with the author, December 16, 2016.
5 Ibid.
6 "A Conversation with Artist-Writer Larry Lieber," *Alter Ego* v3, #2, October 1999.
7 Fingeroth and Thomas, eds., *The Stan Lee Universe,* interview with the author, January 28–29/2008, 22.
8 Larry Lieber, interview with the author, December 16, 2016.
9 John Coates, *Don Heck: A Work of Art* (Raleigh, NC: TwoMorrows, 2014).
10 Ibid.
11 Toni Mendez archives, Billy Ireland Museum, Ohio State University, Columbus, OH.
12 Ger Apeldoorn, "Get Me Out of Here!," *Alter Ego* #150, October 2017.
13 *FOOM* #17, March 1977, 15.
14 Mendez archives, Billy Ireland Museum.
15 Ibid.
16 *FOOM,* 15.
17 Stan Lee and George Mair, *Excelsior!: The Amazing Life of Stan Lee* (New York: Fire-

side, 2002), 104.

18 Steve Ditko, essay on Spider-Man, *Avenging World* (Robin Snyder and Steve Ditko, 2002), 57.

19 Mark Evanier, *Kirby: King of Comics* (New York: Abrams Comic Arts, 2017), 111.

20 Will Murray, "Stan Lee Looks Back," *Comics Scene,* vol. 3, #1, 2000.

Chapter 7: From the Ashes

1 "Stan the Man and Roy the Boy," *Comic Book Artist,* summer 1998.

2 Stan Lee and George Mair, *Excelsior!: The Amazing Life of Stan Lee* (New York: Fireside, 2002), 114–115.

3 Stan Lee, videotaped deposition, May 13, 2010, *Marvel Worldwide Inc., v. Kirby et al.*

4 Mark Seifert, "The Stan Lee Deposition on the Origins of the Marvel Universe for Kirby Family Vs Marvel Lawsuit," Bleeding Cool, March 9, 2011, https://www.bleedingcool.com/2011/03/09/the-stan-lee-deposition-on-the-origins-of-the-marvel-universe-for-kirby-family-vs-marvel-lawsuit/.

5 Will Eisner, *Will Eisner's Shop Talk* (Milwaukie, OR: Dark Horse, 2001), 217.

6 Mark Evanier, *Kirby: King of Comics* (New York: Abrams Comic Arts, 2017), 122.

7 Jordan Raphael and Tom Spurgeon, *Stan Lee and the Rise and Fall of the American*

Comic Book (Chicago: Chicago Review Press, 2003), 94.

8 Roy Thomas and Bill Schelly, *Best of Alter Ego,* vol. 1 (Ellettsville, IN: Hamster Press, 1997).

9 Ibid.

10 Raphael and Spurgeon, *Stan Lee,* 98.

11 Danny Fingeroth and Roy Thomas, eds., *The Stan Lee Universe* (Raleigh, NC: Two-Morrows, 2011), 35.

12 David Hajdu, unpublished interview with Stan Lee done for *The Ten-Cent Plague: The Great Comic-Book Scare and How It Changed America* (New York: Picador, 2009).

Chapter 8: Webs Tangled and Otherwise

1 Kurt Vonnegut, *Kurt Vonnegut: Letters,* ed. Dan Wakefield (New York: Delacorte, 2012).

2 Mark Alexander, *Lee and Kirby: The Wonder Years,* ed. John Morrow (Raleigh, NC: TwoMorrows, 2012).

3 Greg Rowland, "Steve Ditko," HiLobrow, November 2, 2009, http://www.hilobrow.com/2009/11/02/hilo-hero-steve-ditko/.

4 Stan Lee, interview with the author, October 24, 2006.

5 Blake Bell, *Strange and Stranger: The World of Steve Ditko* (Seattle: Fantagraphics, 2008), 15.

6 Craig Yoe, ed., *The Art of Ditko,* with an

introduction by Stan Lee (San Diego: IDW, 2013), 54.

7 Stan Lee, interview with the author, March 7, 2017.

8 Ibid.

9 Stan Lee and George Mair, *Excelsior!: The Amazing Life of Stan Lee* (New York: Fireside, 2002), 10, 17.

10 "Stan Lee on Realism in the World of Comic Heroes," NPR, *Morning Edition,* December 27, 2006, https://www.npr.org/ templates/story/story.php?storyId=668 4820.

11 Ibid.

12 Steve Chapman, "Who Is the Newest, Most Breath-Taking, Most Sensational Super-Hero of All . . . ?," *Harvard Crimson,* December 3, 1975, https://www.thecrimson .com/article/1975/12/3/who-is-the-newest -most-breath-taking/.

13 Larry Lieber, interview with the author, December 16, 2016.

14 Steve Ditko, "The Silent Self-Deceivers," *The Comics,* 2012.

15 Stan Lee, *Origins of Marvel Comics* (New York: Simon & Schuster, 1974), 133.

16 Ibid., 135.

17 Jordan Raphael and Tom Spurgeon, *Stan Lee and the Rise and Fall of the American Comic Book* (Chicago: Chicago Review Press, 2003), 100–101.

18 Ditko, "The Silent Self-Deceivers."

19 Steve Ditko, "Tsk! Tsk!," *The Comics!,* July 1999.

20 Steve Ditko, "A Mini-History Part 2 — Amazing Fantasy #15," *The Comics!,* vol 2, #10, 2001.

21 Lee and Mair, *Excelsior!*

22 Tom DeFalco, *Comic Creators on Spider-Man* (London: Titan Books, 2004), 13–14.

23 Mark Evanier, interview with the author, October 19, 2017.

24 Steve Ditko, "Roislecxe," in *The Avenging Mind* (Bellingham, WA: SD Publishing, 2008), 8–9.

25 Ditko, *Avenging Mind,* 8–27; Ditko's rebuttal to Lee's recollections and opinions in *Excelsior!* and elsewhere.

26 Raphael and Spurgeon, *Stan Lee,* 101.

27 Ira Wolfman, "Stan Lee's New Marvels," *Circus,* July 1978.

28 Tom DeFalco, personal conversations with the author.

Chapter 9: Creating Characters

1 Gerry Conway, interview with the author, May 2, 2017.

2 "Bob Dylan — Nobel Lecture," Nobel Prize, https://www.nobelprize.org/prizes/literature/2016/dylan/lecture/.

3 "Tripwire at 25: Will Eisner," *Tripwire Magazine,* February 26, 2017, http://www

.tripwiremagazine.co.uk/feature/tripwire-25 -will-eisner/.

4 https://themarvelageofcomics.tumblr.com/ post/16306907460/a-letter-written-by-stan -lee-to-super-fan-dr

5 Steve Ditko, "He Giveth and He Taketh Away," in *The Avenging Mind* (Bellingham, WA: SD Publishing, 2008), 18–19.

6 Mark Alexander, "Wah-hoo!! Sgt. Fury and His Howling Commandos," *The Jack Kirby Collector* #24, April 1999.

7 *Daily Californian,* March 29, 1966.

8 Neal Adams, interview with the author, May 3, 2017.

9 Ibid.

10 Norman Abbott, "The 'Spirit' of '41," *Philadelphia Record,* October 13, 1941.

11 Jordan Raphael and Tom Spurgeon, *Stan Lee and the Rise and Fall of the American Comic Book* (Chicago: Chicago Review Press, 2003), 104–105.

12 Ibid., 109.

13 Stan Lee, interview with the author, March 7, 2017.

Chapter 10: The Ties That Bind

1 Roy Thomas and Jim Amash, *John Romita, and All That Jazz* (Raleigh, NC: TwoMor-rows, 2007), 77–78.

2 Roslyn Davis, *South Shore Record,* Roslyn Reports column, July 4, 1963, Stan Lee

Collection, University of Wyoming, Laramie, WY.

3 Jim Amash, " 'I Wrote Over 800 Comic Book Stories,' " *Alter Ego* #90, December 2009.

4 Jordan Raphael and Tom Spurgeon, *Stan Lee and the Rise and Fall of the American Comic Book* (Chicago: Chicago Review Press, 2003), 125.

5 J. Ballman, "25 Facts That Made Flo 'Fabulous,' " *Alter Ego* #153, July 2018.

6 Cory Sedlmeier, ed., *Marvel Masterworks: Atlas Era Menace,* vol. 1, introduction by Michael Vassallo (New York: Marvel, 2009).

7 Geoffrey Magnus and Isabelle Kamishlian, letter to San Lee, March 24, 1964, Stan Lee Collection, American Heritage Center, University of Wyoming, Laramie, WY.

8 Isabelle Kamishlian, interview with the author.

9 "Stan Lee at Princeton, 1966: Steve Ditko's Departure Announced," YouTube video, 20:20, posted by Sean Howe, December 28, 2013, https://www.youtube.com/watch?v=A73KehrmpOU.

10 Stan Lee and George Mair, *Excelsior!: The Amazing Life of Stan Lee* (New York: Fireside, 2002).

11 Roy Thomas, interview with the author, February 8 and 22, 2017.

12 Jim Amash, "Roy Thomas Interview," *Jack*

Kirby Collector #18, January 1998.

13 Author interview with Bruce Jay Friedman, January 20, 2017.

14 Dwight Jon Zimmerman and Jim Salicrup, " 'It Was My First Job in the City' — An Interview with Flo Steinberg," *David Anthony Kraft's Comics Interview* #17, November 1984.

15 Jim Amash, " 'Roy the Boy' in the Marvel Age of Comics," *Alter Ego,* July 2005.

16 Roy Thomas, "Fifty Years On The 'A' List," *Alter Ego,* July 2001.

17 Zimmerman and Salicrup, " 'It Was My First Job.' "

18 *Esquire,* September 1966.

19 Ibid.

20 Danny Fingeroth and Roy Thomas, eds., *The Stan Lee Universe* (Raleigh, NC: TwoMorrows, 2011), 95.

21 Stan Lee, ed., *Ultimate Silver Surfer* (New York: Boulevard Books, 1995).

22 *Alter Ego* #148, September 2017, interview with Gil Kane, 45.

23 "Happy 100th Birthday to Carl Burgos," Timely-Atlas-Comics, April 8, 2016, http://timely-atlas-comics.blogspot.com/2016/04/happy-100th-birthday-to-carl-burgos.html.

24 Jim Amash, " 'The Privacy Act of Carl Burgos,' " *Alter Ego* #49, June 2005.

25 *Marvel Characters Inc. v. Simon 02-7221,* United States District Court for the Southern District of New York; Joe Simon, *My*

Life in Comics (London: Titan Books, 2011), 226–228.

26 Amash, " 'Roy the Boy,' " 23.

27 Blake Bell, *Fire and Water: Bill Everett, the Sub-Mariner, and the Birth of Marvel Comics* (Seattle: Fantagraphics, 2010).

Chapter 11: Boom Boom Boom

1 "Country Joe McDonald: The Aquarium Drunkard Interview," *Aquarium Drunkard,* August 16, 2018, https://aquariumdrunkard .com/2018/08/16/country-joe-mcdonald -the-aquarium-drunkard-interview/.

2 Correspondence between Stan Lee and Country Joe and the Fish, 1967, Stan Lee Collection, box #14, folder #8, American Heritage Center, University of Wyoming, Laramie, WY.

3 Ibid.

4 Danny Fingeroth and Roy Thomas, eds., *The Stan Lee Universe* (Raleigh, NC: Two-Morrows, 2011), author interview with David Bennett Cohen, 86.

5 Fingeroth and Thomas, *The Stan Lee Universe,* article by Gary Friedrich, 85.

6 Fingeroth and Thomas, *The Stan Lee Universe,* Cohen interview, 86.

7 Fingeroth and Thomas, *The Stan Lee Universe,* author interview with Barry Melton, 86–87.

8 Fingeroth and Thomas, *The Stan Lee Universe,* 46.

9 Jordan Raphael and Tom Spurgeon, *Stan Lee and the Rise and Fall of the American Comic Book* (Chicago: Chicago Review Press, 2003), 125.

Chapter 12: Revolution in the Air

1 Stan Lee, interview on Yesterdayland.com (website discontinued).

2 Danny Fingeroth and Roy Thomas, eds., *The Stan Lee Universe* (Raleigh, NC: Two-Morrows, 2011). Mike Hodel interview on WBAI-FM with Stan Lee and Jack Kirby, March 3, 1967, transcribed and edited from audiotape of the interview, Stan Lee Collection, box #69, American Heritage Center, University of Wyoming, Laramie, WY.

3 Interview on WRSU-FM with Stan Lee, April 1967, transcribed and edited from audiotape of the interview, Stan Lee Collection, American Heritage Center, University of Wyoming, Laramie, WY.

4 Fingeroth and Thomas, *The Stan Lee Universe, Barry Farber Show* interview on WOR-AM radio, with Stan Lee, Hilde Mosse, et al., November 12, 1968, transcribed and edited from audiotape of interview, Stan Lee Collection, box #71, American Heritage Center, University of Wyoming, Laramie, WY.

5 Leonard Rifas, "Especially Dr. Hilde L. Mosse: Wertham's Research Collaborator," *International Journal of Comic Art* 8, no. 1 (2006): 17–44.

6 Carol L. Tilley, "Seducing the Innocent: Fredric Wertham and the Falsifications That Helped Condemn Comics," *Information & Culture* 47, no. 7 (2012): 383–413, https://www.utexaspressjournals.org/doi/abs/10.7560/IC47401.

Chapter 13: Surfing the Waves

1 Stan Lee and George Mair, *Excelsior!: The Amazing Life of Stan Lee* (New York: Fireside, 2002), 175.

2 Danny Fingeroth and Roy Thomas, eds., *The Stan Lee Universe* (Raleigh, NC: Two-Morrows, 2011), 45.

3 Ibid., 41.

4 Mike Bourne, *Changes* magazine, April 15, 1970.

5 Ibid.

6 Ibid.

7 Jordan Raphael and Tom Spurgeon, *Stan Lee and the Rise and Fall of the American Comic Book* (Chicago: Chicago Review Press, 2003), 123.

8 Mark Evanier, interview with the author, August 2018.

9 Ibid.

10 Sean Howe, *Marvel Comics: The Untold*

Story (New York: Harper, 2013), 91.

11 Mark Evanier, *Kirby: King of Comics* (New York: Abrams Comic Arts, 2017), 145.

12 Lee and Mair, *Excelsior!,* 180.

13 Robin Green, " 'Face Front. Clap Your Hands! You're On The Winning Team!,' " *Rolling Stone,* September 16, 1971.

14 Roy Thomas, *The Marvel Age of Comics: 1961–1978* (Cologne: Taschen, 2017), 120–124.

15 "Stan Lee Talkshow 1968-Part 1," YouTube video, 16:48, posted by "misterX1964," September 7, 2015, https://www.youtube.com/watch?v=RV5NEU-l9bM.

16 Stan Lee, interview with the author, March 7, 2017.

Chapter 14: Tense Transitions

1 Stan Lee, from an audio recording transcription provided by author Sean Howe.

2 Stan Lee, interview with the author, May 2, 2017.

3 Jordan Raphael and Tom Spurgeon, *Stan Lee and the Rise and Fall of the American Comic Book* (Chicago: Chicago Review Press, 2003), 188–189.

4 Roy Thomas, "Fifty Years on the 'A' List," *Alter Ego,* v3, #9, July 2001.

5 *The Comics Journal Library, Volume 1: Jack Kirby* (Seattle: Fantagraphics, 2002), 15.

6 Joe Sergi, "Tales from the Code: Spidey

Fights Drugs and the Comics Code Authority," Comic Book Legal Defense Fund, July 18, 2012, http://cbldf.org/2012/07/tales -from-the-code-spidey-fights-drugs-and-the -comics-code-authority/.

7 Gary Groth, ed., *Sparring with Gil Kane: Colloquies on Comic Art and Aesthetics* (Seattle: Fantagraphics, 2018).

8 Gerard Jones and Will Jacobs, *The Comic Book Heroes* (Roseville, CA: Prima Lifestyle, 1996), 158.

9 Sean Howe, *Marvel Comics: The Untold Story* (New York: Harper, 2013), 118.

10 Saul Braun, "Shazam! Here Comes Captain Relevant," *New York Times,* May 2, 1971.

11 Robin Green, " 'Face Front. Clap Your Hands! You're On The Winning Team!,' " *Rolling Stone,* September 16, 1971.

Chapter 15: Power Politics

1 Roy Thomas Appreciation Board, Facebook, August 27, 2018. https://www .facebook.com/groups/664083247096026/ permalink/ 1003487153155632/?__tn __=K-R.

2 Jim Amash, "Roy Thomas Interview," *Jack Kirby Collector* #18, January 1998.

3 Mark Evanier, interview with the author, January 18, 2017.

4 Dean Latimer, "A Marvel-Lous Evening

with Stan Lee," *Monster Times,* #3, March 1, 1972.

5 Peter Ainslie, "57th Street's Answer to Disney World," *Women's Wear Daily,* January 1972.

6 Jordan Raphael and Tom Spurgeon, *Stan Lee and the Rise and Fall of the American Comic Book* (Chicago: Chicago Review Press, 2003), 132.

7 Ibid., 133.

8 Scott Edelman, interview with the author, February 6, 2019.

9 Jeff McLaughlin, ed., *Stan Lee: Conversations* (Jackson: University of Mississippi Press, 2007), 210.

10 Thomas Mick, personal conversation with the author.

11 Stan Lee, interview with the author, May 2, 2017.

12 Raphael and Spurgeon, *Stan Lee,* 140.

13 Stan Lee Collection, American Heritage Center, University of Wyoming, Laramie, WY.

14 Sean Howe, *Marvel Comics: The Untold Story* (New York: Harper, 2013), 121–122.

15 Ibid., 123–125.

16 Michael Schumacher, *Will Eisner: A Dreamer's Life in Comics* (New York: Bloomsbury, 2010), 182.

17 "Citizen Pain, the Publisher Who Built a

Vampire Empire," *Rolling Stone,* April 25, 1974.

18 Jon B. Cooke, "James Warren Interview," *Comic Book Artist,* spring 1999.

19 Howe, *Marvel Comics,* 136–137.

20 Stan Lee Collection, American Heritage Center.

Chapter 16: The Chaos and the King

1 John Lind, ed., *The Best of Comix Book,* foreword by Denis Kitchen (Milwaukie, OR: Kitchen Sink Books, 2013), 11.

2 Jordan Raphael and Tom Spurgeon, *Stan Lee and the Rise and Fall of the American Comic Book* (Chicago: Chicago Review Press, 2003), 148–149.

3 "Martin Goodman," Comic Vine, https://comicvine.gamespot.com/martin-goodman/4040-43801/.

4 Joseph Calamari, interview with the author, June 20, 2018.

5 Rob Gustavson, "Fifteen Years at Marvel: An Interview with Roy Thomas," *Comics Journal,* December 1980; Jim Amash, " 'Writing Comics Turned Out to Be What I Really Wanted to Do with My Life,' " *Alter Ego* #70, July 2007, 25.

6 Danny Fingeroth and Roy Thomas, eds., *The Stan Lee Universe* (Raleigh, NC: Two-Morrows, 2011), color insert section 2, i.

7 " 'A Curse on the Superman Movie!' — A

Look Back at Jerry Siegel's 1975 Press Release," *20th Century Danny Boy* (blog), July 8, 2012, https://ohdannyboy.blogspot.com/2012/07/curse-on-superman-movie-look-back-at.html.

8 Mike Gartland and John Morrow, "You Can't Go Home Again," *Jack Kirby Collector* #29, August 2000.

9 Mark Evanier, interview with the author, January, 18, 2017.

10 Nicholas Caputo, "A Shocking Story," *Jack Kirby Collector* #10, April 1996.

11 Sean Howe, *Marvel Comics: The Untold Story* (New York: Harper, 2013), 170.

12 Reed Tucker, *Slug fest: Inside the Epic 50-Year Battle Between Marvel and DC* (New York: Da Capo Press, 2017), 72.

Chapter 17: Returns and Departures

1 "*Star Wars:* The Comic Book That Saved Marvel!," *Alter Ego* #68, May 2007.

2 Sean Howe, *Marvel Comics: The Untold Story* (New York: Harper, 2013), 190–192.

3 "Vera Valiant, Vera Valiant," *Fabulous Fifties* (blog), October 19, 2014, http://allthingsger.blogspot.com/2014/10/vera-valiant-vera-valiant.html; Derf Backderf, "Stan Lee's failed comic strip 'Says Who!,' " *Derfblog* (blog), November 23, 2015, http://derfcity.blogspot.com/2015/11/stan-lees-failed-comic-strip-says-who.html.

4 Mark Evanier, *Kirby: King of Comics* (New York: Abrams Comic Arts, 2017), 195.

5 Mark Evanier, interview with the author, January 18, 2017.

6 Jim Amash, " 'Writing Comics Turned Out to Be What I Really Wanted to Do with My Life,' " *Alter Ego* #70, July 2007.

7 Evanier, *Kirby,* 199.

8 Stan Lee Collection, American Heritage Center, University of Wyoming, Laramie, WY.

9 Amash, " 'Writing Comics.' "

10 Jim Shooter, "The Secret Origin of Jim Shooter, Editor in Chief — Part 1," Jim Shooter.com, June 23, 2011, http://jimshooter.com/2011/06/secret-origin-of-jim-shooter-editor-in.html.

11 Howe, *Marvel Comics,* 200–202.

12 Ibid., 218, 238.

13 Jordan Raphael and Tom Spurgeon, *Stan Lee and the Rise and Fall of the American Comic Book* (Chicago: Chicago Review Press, 2003), 178.

14 Victor Forbes, "Presenting, the Man Behind Spider-Man, Stan Lee!," *SunStorm,* February 1978.

15 Evanier, interview with the author, January 18, 2017.

16 Stan Lee and Jack Kirby, *The Silver Surfer: The Ultimate Cosmic Experience!* (New York: Fireside, 1978).

17 Evanier, interview with the author, October 19, 2017.

18 Stan Lee Collection, University of Wyoming.

19 Stan Lee Collection, box #55, folder #4, University of Wyoming.

20 Stan Lee Collection, box #55, folders #1, 2, and 4, University of Wyoming.

21 Amash, " 'Writing Comics.' "

22 Ken Quattro, "Roy Thomas: More Corrections & Suggestions," *Comics Detective* (blog), December 15, 2012, http://thecomicsdetective.blogspot.com/2012/.

23 Amash, " 'Writing Comics.' "

24 Evanier, *Kirby,* 203.

25 Ira Wolfman, "Stan Lee's New Marvels," *Circus,* July 1978.

26 Ira Wolfman, personal conversation with the author.

Chapter 18: Goodbyes and Hellos

1 Barbara Rowes, "Stan Lee, Creator of Spider-Man and the Incredible Hulk, Is America's Biggest Mythmaker," *People,* January 29, 1979, https://people.com/archive/stan-lee-creator-of-spider-man-and-the-incredible-hulk-is-americas-biggest-mythmaker-vol-11-no-4/.

2 Stan Lee Collection, Box #14, American Heritage Center, University of Wyoming, Laramie, WY.

3 N. R. Kleinfield, "Superheroes' Creators Wrangle," *New York Times,* October 13, 1979.

4 "Remembrance," Chuck Lorre Productions, November 29, 2018, http://www.chucklorre.com/index-mom.php?p=603.

5 John Semper Jr., interview with the author, October 18, 2018.

6 Ibid.

7 Mark Evanier, *Kirby: King of Comics* (New York: Abrams Comic Arts, 2017), 213.

8 Jim Shooter, "Reminiscing About Jack Kirby," JimShooter.com, March 31, 2011, http://jimshooter.com/2011/03/reminiscing-about-jack-kirby.html.

9 Tom DeFalco, interview with the author, December 12, 2017.

10 Transcript of Lee-Kirby August 28, 1987 conversation on WBAI radio from Barry Pearl's *Comic Book Collectors Club* website: https://comicbookcollectorsclub.com/jack-kirby-and-stan-lee-radio-interview-earth-watch-wbai-1987/.

Chapter 19: California Dreamin'

1 Jordan Raphael and Tom Spurgeon, *Stan Lee and the Rise and Fall of the American Comic Book* (Chicago: Chicago Review Press, 2003), 193.

2 Blake Bell, *I Have to Live with This Guy!* (Raleigh, NC: TwoMorrows, 2002), 63.

3 Sean Howe, *Marvel Comics: The Untold Story* (New York: Harper, 2013), 311.

4 Stan Lee and George Mair, *Excelsior!: The Amazing Life of Stan Lee* (New York: Fireside, 2002), 215.

5 Joseph Calamari, interview with the author, June 20, 2018.

6 Howe, *Marvel Comics,* 307.

7 "James Cameron Spider-Man Treatment," Third Millennium Entertainment http://www.teako170.com/cameron.html.

8 Howe, *Marvel Comics,* 335.

9 Stan Lee, interview with the author, October 24, 2006.

10 Eric Lewald, *Previously on X-Men: The Making of an Animated Series* (San Diego: Jacobs Brown Press, 2017), 2.

11 Lee and Mair, *Excelsior!,* 207–208.

12 Lewald, *Previously on X-Men,* 70.

13 Ibid., 70, 74.

14 Tom DeFalco, *Comic Creators on X-Men* (London: Titan, 2006).

15 Lewald, *Previously on X-Men,* 115.

16 John Semper Jr., interview with the author, October 18, 2018.

17 Jim Salicrup, interview with the author, December 12, 2018.

18 Tom DeFalco, interview with the author, December 12, 2017.

19 Mark Evanier, interview with the author, October 19, 2017

Chapter 20: Follow the Money

1 Jim Amash, "Conan, Cthulhu, Cross Plains, Kryptonians, & Cadillacs," *Alter Ego,* May 2016, 31–32.

2 "#63-Stan Lee Interview | The Tomorrow Show," YouTube video, 49:28, posted by the Tomorrow Show, October 19, 2016, https://www.youtube.com/watch?time _continue=11&v=ftU8Ii2LjwI.

3 Jordan Raphael and Tom Spurgeon, *Stan Lee and the Rise and Fall of the American Comic Book* (Chicago: Chicago Review Press, 2003), 224.

4 Mark Evanier, *Kirby: King of Comics* (New York: Abrams Comic Arts, 2017), 211.

5 Raphael and Spurgeon, *Stan Lee,* 224–225.

6 Unpublished segment of interview with Frank Lovece, May 17, 1994.

7 Dan Raviv, *Comic Wars: Marvel's Battle For Survival* (New York: Marvel, 2004).

8 Stan Lee and George Mair, *Excelsior!: The Amazing Life of Stan Lee* (New York: Fireside, 2002), 182.

9 Raviv, *Comic Wars.*

10 Sean Howe, *Marvel Comics: The Untold Story* (New York: Harper, 2013), 398.

11 "Stan Lee Employment Agreement," U.S. Securities and Exchange Commission, https://www.sec.gov/Archives/edgar/data/ 933730/000093373002000013/ex10

-110q902.txt.

12 Raphael and Spurgeon, *Stan Lee,* 250.

13 Mark Evanier, interview with the author, October 19, 2017.

14 Ibid.

15 Jim Salicrup, interview with the author, September 22, 2017.

16 Evanier, interview, October 19, 2017.

17 https://www.politico.com/blogs/under-the -radar/2009/07/after-4-years-clintons -accuser-sentenced-to-10-020086.

18 Howe, *Marvel Comics,* 409.

19 Lee and Mair, *Excelsior!,* 233.

20 Stan Lee, interview with the author, October 24, 2006.

21 Ibid.

22 Evanier, interview, October 19, 2017.

23 Steve Ditko, *The Comics,* August 1999.

24 Danny Fingeroth and Roy Thomas, eds., *The Stan Lee Universe* (Raleigh, NC: Two-Morrows, 2011), author interview with Michael Uslan, 139.

25 Ibid.

26 Lee and Mair, *Excelsior!,* 233.

27 David Kohn, "Superhero Creator Fights Back," *60 Minutes,* October 30, 2002, https://www.cbsnews.com/news/superhero -creator-fights-back/.

28 "Stan Lee Employment Agreement," U.S. Securities and Exchange Commission.

Chapter 21: Of Love and Law

1 Robert Wilonsky, "Still Smilin'?," *SF Weekly,* July 9, 2003.

2 ICV2.com "Stan Lee, Gets, Spidey Cents" January 19, 2005, http://icv2.com/articles/news/view/6308/stan.lee-gets-spidey-cents.

3 Nat Ives, "Marvel Settles With a Spider-Man Creator," *New York Times,* April 29, 2005.

4 Joe Simon, *My Life in Comics* (London: Titan Books, 2011), 241–243.

5 Bloomberg News, "Dispute Over Captain America Is Settled," *New York Times,* September 30, 2003.

6 Mike Kelly, "The 'Adorable' Stan Lee," Real Stan Lee, November 26, 2018, https://therealstanlee.com/blogs/the-adorable-stan-lee/.

7 "Edith Finck Obituary," Legacy.com, March 12, 2017, https://www.legacy.com/obituaries/nytimes/obituary.aspx?n=edith-inck&pid=184461106.

8 Brian Baxter, "Chadbourne, Giuliani Lawyer Join Marvel Litigation," *Am Law Daily,* September 8, 2009.

9 Michael Kelly, interview with the author, January 7, 2019.

10 Abraham Reisman, "It's Stan Lee's Universe," *Vulture,* February 23, 2016, https://www.vulture.com/2016/02/stan-lees-universe-c-v-r.html.

11 Michael Cavna, "Obama the Comic Superstar: Stan Lee Explains All . . . ," *Washington Post,* January 14, 2009, http://voices.washingtonpost.com/comic-riffs/2009/01/obama_the_superhero_stan_lee_e.html.

12 Brooks Barnes and Michael Cieply, "Disney Swoops Into Action, Buying Marvel for $4 Billion," *New York Times,* August 31, 2009.

13 Jon Parkin, "Stan Lee's POW! Entertainment Expands Ties with Disney," CBR.com, December 31, 2009, https://www.cbr.com/stan-lees-pow-entertainment-expands-ties-with-disney/.

14 "Stan Lee, Jack Kirby et al . . . The Birth of the Marvel Universe," *20th Century Danny Boy* (blog), September 28, 2011, https://ohdannyboy.blogspot.com/2011/09/stan-lee-jack-kirby-et-althe-birth-of.html.

15 Ibid.

16 Mark Evanier, interview with the author, October 19, 2017.

17 Mark Evanier, *Kirby: King of Comics* (New York: Abrams Comic Arts, 2017), 228–231.

18 Dominic Patten, "Marvel Scores Another Win in Jack Kirby Copyright Case," *Deadline,* August 8, 2013, https://deadline.com/2013/08/marvel-scores-another-win-in-jack-kirby-copyright-case-560313/.

19 Rob Salkowitz, "Marvel Universe Co-

Creator Jack Kirby Is Having a Moment," *Forbes,* January 18, 2016, https://www.forbes.com/sites/robsalkowitz/2016/01/18/marvel-universe-co-creator-jack-kirby-is-having-a-moment/ #240775377f42.

20 Brooks Barnes, "Marvel Settles with Family of Comics Artist Jack Kirby," *New York Times,* September 27, 2014, https://www.nytimes.com/2014/09/27/business/media/marvel-settles-with-family-of-comic-book-artist-jack-kirby.html.

21 Michael Kelly, email to the author, January 14, 2019.

22 Robert Perkins, "NOCC: Stan the Man at Wizard World-Part I," Game Vortex, http://www.gamevortex.com/gamevortex/news.php/1673.

23 Mike Avila, "Todd McFarlane Remembers Stan Lee, His Friend and Mentor," SYFY, November 13, 2018, https://www.syfy.com/syfywire/todd-mcfarlane-remembers-stan-lee-his-friend-and-mentor.

24 Kelly, interview.

25 Jim Korkis, "Remembering Stan Lee and His Disney Connections," MousePlanet, November 16, 2018, https://www.mouseplanet.com/12235/Remembering_Stan_Lee_and_His_Disney_Connections.

26 Kirby4Heroes Campaign, Facebook, July 16, 2017, https://tinyurl.com/yxqf3ob2.

Chapter 22: The Undiscover'd Country

1 Danny Fingeroth and Roy Thomas, eds., *The Stan Lee Universe* (Raleigh, NC: Two-Morrows, 2011), author interview with Flo Steinberg, February 11, 2008, 34.

2 Stan Lee, Facebook, July 24, 2017, https://www.facebook.com/realstanlee/photos/flo-steinberg-was-my-first-secretary-at-marvel-which-was-then-called-timely-comics/10155599658141543/.

3 John Trumbull, "Memories of Stan Lee (1922–2018)," *Atomic Junk Shop* (blog), November 24, 2018, http://atomicjunkshop.com/memories-of-stan-lee-1922-2018/.

4 "Stan Lee's LA Comic Con 2017: Stan Lee Sunday Panel," YouTube video, 29:28, posted by "steven alvarez," October 31, 2017, https://www.youtube.com/watch?v=b2rCTLsUikE.

5 "Stan Lee in Conversation with Todd McFarlane at ACE Comic Con Arizona," YouTube video, 37:49, posted by ACE Universe, January 14, 2018, https://www.youtube.com/watch?v=b9Gz9KAPcHA.

6 Ed Masley, "Stan Lee Remembered: Todd McFarlane Shares His Favorite Memories," *Arizona Republic,* November 12, 2018, https://www.azcentral.com/story/entertainment/people/2018/11/12/stan-lee-todd-mcfarlane-shares-his-favorite-memories-legendary-marvel-comics-creator/1983943002/.

7 Mark Ebner, " 'Picked Apart by Vultures': The Last Days of Stan Lee," *Daily Beast,* March 10, 2018, https://www.thedailybeast.com/picked-apart-by-vultures-the-last-days-of-stan-lee.

8 Ben Widdicome, "Spidey's Creator in a Web of Strife," *New York Times,* April 15, 2018.

9 Stan Lee (@TheRealStanLee), Twitter, July 13, 2018, https://twitter.com/therealstanlee/status/1017862839623708672?lang=en.

10 Marie Severin, interview with the author, July 8, 2017.

11 Mark Ebner, "Stan Lee Breaks His Silence: Those I Trusted Betrayed Me," *Daily Beast,* October 8, 2018, https://www.thedailybeast.com/stan-lee-would-like-to-set-the-record-straight-will-anyone-let-him?ref=scroll.

12 Joshua Hartwig, "Comic Book Writer and Editor from Jackson Spent Time with Stan Lee 48 Hours Before His Death," *Southeast Missourian,* November 15, 2018, https://www.semissourian.com/story/2566769.html.

13 John Cimino, Facebook, November 12, 2018, https://www.facebook.com/john.cimino.73/posts/2385287848168040.

14 Dana Forsythe, "Marvel Legend Roy Thomas Visited Stan Lee Days Before His Death. Here's What Happened," SYFY, November 15, 2018, https://www.syfy.com/

syfywire/marvel-legend-roy-thomas-visited
-stan-lee-days-before-his-death-heres-what
-happened.

15 Gary Trock and Liz Walters, "Stan Lee's
Death Certificate Touts Marvel Co-
Creator's 80 Year Career," *Blast,* November
27, 2018, https://theblast.com/stan-lee
-cause-of-death-cardiac-arrest/.

16 Stan Lee (@TheRealStanLee), Twitter,
November 16, 2018, https://tinyurl.com/
y4glyj9b.

17 Michael Kelly, interview with the author,
January 7, 2019.

18 https://www.nbcnews.com/news/us-news/
marvel-comics-mogul-stan-lee-s-former
-manager-keya-morgan-n1010326.

19 https://www.apnews.com/b8930a7715ce
4f268399269d15d63cf2.

20 https://www.nydailynews.com/entertain
ment/ny-stan-lee-estate-sues-former-mana
ger-and-nurse-20190604-2upsauk6jzbrti
xnkeb636akby-story.html.

Chapter 23: Legacy

1 Chris Evans (@ChrisEvans), Twitter,
November 12, 2018, https://tinyurl.com/
y6pb47uu.

2 Samuel L. Jackson (@SamuelLJackson),
Twitter, November 12, 2018, https://tinyurl
.com/y5attj4h.

3 Josh Brolin (joshbrolin), Instagram, Novem-

ber 12, 2018, https://tinyurl.com/y45q4kou.

4 Mark Ruffalo (@MarkRuffalo), Twitter, November 12, 2018, https://tinyurl.com/y6bg3pg4.

5 Angela Bassett (@ImAngelaBassett), Twitter, November 12, 2018, https://tinyurl.com/y5jw6cu9.

6 "Paul Pays Tribute to Stan Lee," Paul McCartney's website, November 13, 2018, https:// tinyurl.com/y2rf bwl5.

7 George R. R. Martin, "Farewell to a Marvel," *Not a Blog* (blog), November 15, 2018, https://tinyurl.com/y7j6rrne.

8 Lin-Manuel Miranda (@Lin_Manuel), Twitter, November 12, 2018, https://tinyurl.com/yyh2duvj.

9 Mark Hamill (@HamillHimself), Twitter, November 12, 2018, https://tinyurl.com/y6q4whdf.

10 Jeremy Kirby (@JackKirbyComics), Twitter, November 12, 2018, https:// tinyurl.com/y3lv4zu6.

11 Kirby4Heroes Campaign, Facebook, November 12, 2018, https://tinyurl.com/yxe9s4vr.

12 Mike Avila, "Todd McFarlane Remembers Stan Lee, His Friend And Mentor," SYFY, November 13, 2018, https://tinyurl.com/yyeu5qu7.

13 Tony Puryear, Facebook, November 12, 2018, https://tinyurl.com/y4fao4bd.

14 Frank Miller (@FrankMillerInk), Twitter,

November 12, 2018, https://tinyurl.com/
yxngmggk.

15 Neil Gaiman (neilhimself), Instagram,
November 12, 2018, https://tinyurl.com/
y3ykc99r.

16 Michael Chabon (michael.chabon), Instagram, November 12, 2018, https://
tinyurl.com/y4qreaww.

17 Paul Levitz, Facebook, November 12,
2018, https://tinyurl.com/yyvuqe29.

18 Joshua M. Patton, "How We Almost
Didn't Have the 'Stan Lee Cameo' in
Modern Marvel Films," *Medium,* November
14, 2018, https://tinyurl.com/yxdvpnnm.

19 Sam Raimi, "Sam Raimi on Pitching a
'Thor' Movie with Stan Lee — and Getting
Rejected," *Hollywood Reporter,* November
14, 2018.

20 Michael Kelly, email to the author, January 10, 2019.

21 Ibid.

22 David Hochman, "The Playboy Interview:
Stan Lee on Superheroes, Marvel and Being Just Another Pretty Face," *Playboy,*
March 31, 2014, https://tinyurl.com/
y6hbwoon.

23 Stan Lee, interview with the author, May
2, 2017.

24 Jim McLauchlin, "12 Things You Learn
Over Two Decades of Lunches with Stan
Lee," *Wired,* November 12, 2018, https://
www.wired.com/story/stan-lee-rip-12

-things/.

25 Andy Lewis, "Stan Lee Reflects on His Successes and Regrets: 'I Should Have Been Greedier,' " *Hollywood Reporter,* July 21, 2016, https://tinyurl.com/yxvncq6f.

26 Ted Anthony, "A Universe of Flawed Heroes: Stan Lee Was Ahead of His Time," AP, November 13, 2018, https://tinyurl.com/y78g8c7y.

27 Hochman, "The Playboy Interview: Stan Lee on Superheroes."

28 Anthony, "Universe of Flawed Heroes."

Afterword

1 Greg Hunter, "Machine Man by Kirby & Ditko: The Complete Collection," *Comics Journal,* November 16, 2016, https://tinyurl.com/hx7azlz.

2 David Sable, interview with the author, July 26, 2017.

3 David Hochman, "The Playboy Interview: Stan Lee on Superheroes, Marvel and Being Just Another Pretty Face," *Playboy,* March 31, 2014, https://tinyurl.com/y6hbwoon.

ABOUT THE AUTHOR

Danny Fingeroth was an award-winning writer and editor at Marvel Comics. A highly regarded pop culture critic and historian, he is the author of acclaimed books including *Superman on the Couch: What Superheroes Really Tell Us About Ourselves and Our Society* and co-editor of *The Stan Lee Universe,* an annotated collection of rarities from Lee's personal archives. Fingeroth worked with Lee on numerous projects and conducted original, in-depth interviews with him (and many others) in the course of researching *A Marvelous Life.* Fingeroth has spoken and taught on comics-related topics at Columbia University, the Smithsonian Institution, and at Milan's Mimaster Institute, among many other venues.

The employees of Thorndike Press hope you have enjoyed this Large Print book. All our Thorndike, Wheeler, and Kennebec Large Print titles are designed for easy reading, and all our books are made to last. Other Thorndike Press Large Print books are available at your library, through selected bookstores, or directly from us.

For information about titles, please call:
(800) 223-1244

or visit our website at:
gale.com/thorndike

To share your comments, please write:
Publisher
Thorndike Press
10 Water St., Suite 310
Waterville, ME 04901